WAKARA'S AMERICA

WAKARA'S AMERICA

THE LIFE AND LEGACY OF A NATIVE FOUNDER OF THE AMERICAN WEST

MAX PERRY MUELLER

BASIC BOOKS
NEW YORK

Basic Books
Hachette Book Group
1290 Avenue of the Americas, New York, NY 10104
www.basicbooks.com

Printed in the United States of America

First Edition: November 2025

Published by Basic Books, an imprint of Hachette Book Group, Inc. The Basic Books name and logo is a registered trademark of the Hachette Book Group.

The Hachette Speakers Bureau provides a wide range of authors for speaking events. To find out more, go to hachettespeakersbureau.com or email HachetteSpeakers@hbgusa.com.

Basic books may be purchased in bulk for business, educational, or promotional use. For more information, please contact your local bookseller or the Hachette Book Group Special Markets Department at special.markets@hbgusa.com.

The publisher is not responsible for websites (or their content) that are not owned by the publisher.

Cover art: Painting "Sketch of Walker, War Chief of the Utahs" gift of the Estate of Belle J. Bushnell, 1941. Courtesy of the Peabody Museum of Archaeology and Ethnology, Harvard University, 41-72-10/427.

Acknowledgment of Cartographic Contribution and License:
Wenjie Wang created the maps in this book using geographic data from the U.S. Census Bureau, Utah's State Geographic Information Datasource (SGID), Utah Automated Geographic Reference Center (AGRC), U.S. Geological Survey (USGS), ESRI, National Oceanic and Atmospheric Administration (NOAA), U.S. Environmental Protection Agency (EPA), Food and Agriculture Organization (FAO), National Park Service, Bureau of Land Management, Babbitt Center for Land and Water Policy, and Colorado State University.

Library of Congress Control Number: 2025010578

ISBNs: 9781541602595 (hardcover), 9781541602601 (ebook)

LSC-C

Printing 1, 2025

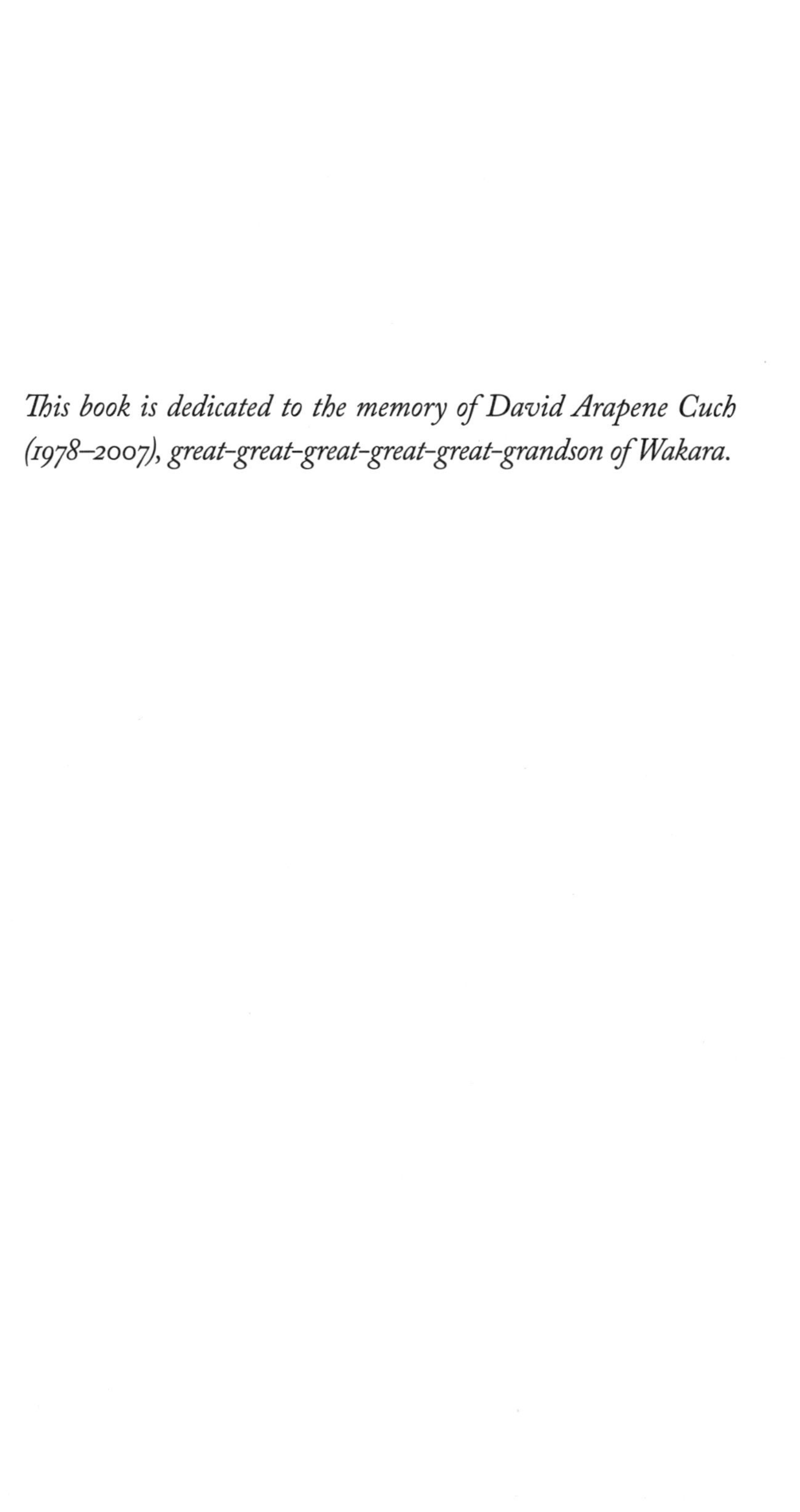

This book is dedicated to the memory of David Arapene Cuch (1978–2007), great-great-great-great-great-grandson of Wakara.

There's always someone looking out for the Utes.

—JOSEPHINE LA ROSE CUCH (1916–1970), GREAT-GREAT-GREAT-GRANDDAUGHTER OF WAKARA

Contents

List of Illustrations

A Note on Terms and Sources

The two most important terms in this book are "Native American" and "settler American." By Native American, I mean the peoples indigenous to the lands that are today known as the United States of America. Of course, there was no single Native American people in presettler history. And today, there is no single Native American identity. When possible, I name specific tribes by their federally recognized names (i.e., the Ute Indian Tribe of Utah) or their name in their Native languages (i.e., the *Nuche*). When possible, I also refer to specific bands (i.e., the Timpanogos). On occasion, I also use the term "Indian" to speak to a historical (and often) racist understanding of America's Native peoples. By "settler American," I mean the peoples and their descendants who mostly emigrated from European nations to the United States. These diverse peoples became settler Americans when they displaced Native Americans from their lands through war, disease, slavery, and environmental degradation. Wakara's life and legacy speak to the distinctions between and similarities among settler and Native American histories, experiences, and identities.

Wakara's unique place in the Native and settler histories of the American West leads us to consider another key term: "empire." Understandably, applying the concept of empire to Native nations has elicited controversy among scholars of Native American history because it risks imposing Eurocentric ideas on Native societies that functioned very differently from the European and American empires that vied for dominance in the early American West. Still, I describe Wakara as creating an empire because many of his actions fit standard understandings of that concept; that is, through violence, coercion, and indirect colonization, Wakara sought to expand his economic and political control over other sovereign peoples and nations, including sometimes over members of his own tribal nation and band. Still, Wakara's Native empire was not the same as the Euro-American empires with which he formed alliances, traded, raided, and warred. His relationships with other peoples were at times exploitative. At other times, they were based on reciprocity. He deployed violent raids as well as diplomacy to expand his influence. But, unlike the builders of Euro-American empires, he did so not to seek permanent and exclusive control over land and peoples. Instead, through a dynamic use of peacemaking and war making—which, as we will see, often took a particularly Native form of trade in Indian slaves—Wakara sought to further expand his network of commerce and kinship across racial, tribal, national, and even religious boundaries.

This book uses two other key terms. The first is "Mormon," the colloquial name for members of the Church of Jesus Christ of Latter-day Saints. I use "Mormons," "Latter-day Saints," and "Saints" interchangeably to refer to the largest branch of the religious movement established by Joseph Smith Jr. in 1830, whose headquarters are in Salt Lake City, Utah. I also use "Mormon" as an adjective. The other term is "Timpanogos," Wakara's band of origin. Part of the broader Shoshonean, Numic-speaking peoples of America's Great Basin, the Timpanogos were absorbed into the wider Northern Ute people starting in the 1860s. As I argue throughout the book, tribal boundaries among Numic-speaking Utes, Paiutes, and Shoshones were fluid before the arrival of settlers who sought to dominate, in part, by dividing Numic peoples into distinct tribes and pitting them against each other. The contemporary Timpanogos Nation is not recognized at the federal or state level. Some of its members are descendants of "mixed-blood" Northern Utes whose tribal memberships were terminated in the 1950s as part of governmental efforts to force Native Americans to abandon Native identities and land claims and to assimilate into the broader American culture. The chief executive of the Timpanogos Nation, Mary Meyer, claims that the Timpanogos' tribal origins were Shoshone, not Ute. Along with other members of the Timpanogos Nation, Meyer has sued for recognition and to win hunting and fishing rights on the Northern Utes' Uintah and Ouray Reservation.

Of course, the most frequent term that I use in this book is a name, "Wakara," whom Anglo settlers called "Walker." The exact pronunciation of Wakara's name has been lost to history. Based on my conversations with Numic-language experts and speakers, including Emeline Root (Ute Indian Tribe of Utah) and Koralene Tapoof (Ute Indian Tribe of Utah), and based on the work of linguist Thomas Givón, we have concluded that "Wakara" is the closest spelling for the sound of the Numic word for "yellow" or "brass," which is believed to be a translation of Wakara's name.

Readers will note that I avoid using the term "chief" when referring to Wakara and other Native American leaders. I do so for two reasons. First, as my Ute mentors Forrest Cuch (Ute Indian Tribe of Utah) and Larry Cesspooch (Ute Indian Tribe of Utah) have taught me, contemporary Utes object when non-Natives apply "chief" to Natives because in some uses "chief" has become a term of derision. Second, the Anglo-American understanding of chief as a permanent leadership position over all community decisions does not reflect the situational leadership model present in Ute culture. Through group consensus, certain leaders were assigned temporary and specific leadership roles; for example, Wakara assumed the role of "war chief" or "captain" when battling White settlers. During the Timpanogos' annual fish festivals, fish "captains" oversaw the fishing harvests. After the appointed service was complete, these leaders returned to their positions as members of the collective community.

Almost all contemporaneous written accounts about Wakara come from White settlers whom Wakara befriended and with whom he raided, traded, and warred. Following many others, in this book I write about the problems that such an archival imbalance poses for accurate historical narration. In citing historical sources (journals, letters, etc.), I have modernized and corrected spelling, unless the spelling choices convey meaning or tone.

In collaboration with Wakara family historians and genealogists, this book makes novel claims about who Wakara's children were and what happened to them before and after Wakara's death. These claims rely upon genealogical work that combines written records (e.g., federal and tribal census rolls, church records, military service documents), oral histories, and genetic testing, which together create a vast family tree. This tree begins with Wakara and his wives. Today, it spans more than eight generations, stretches out across the entire American nation (and beyond), includes citizens of at least five tribal nations, and counts thousands of members. This living testament to Wakara and his family's resilience, combined with the history of displacement and genocide that this book narrates, makes Native American genealogy particularly complex and sensitive. I am grateful to the many Wakara descendants who have contributed to filling out this multibranched family tree. At the request of some of these family members, I do not cite a public tree in this book. However, scholars and, most importantly, family members seeking to learn more about Wakara's family tree are welcome to contact me, and I will connect those interested with the appropriate family and tribal representatives.

Finally, the research on the topics covered in this book, from settler colonialism to rematriation, from Indigenous resource management to Indian slavery, fills literal libraries. To keep the notes from running as long as the book itself, I have limited citations to the scholarship most impactful on and/or most closely related to my own work.

The American Great Basin. As a prolific horse thief, slave trader, and sometime friend, sometime foe to explorers and settlers, Wakara (ca. 1815–1855) dominated the region during the 1840s and early 1850s. (Map by Wenjie Wang)

WAKARA'S AMERICA

Introduction

Wakara's Remains

KANOSH STARED DOWN INTO the emptied graves. Gone from the tombs, constructed out of huge sandstone slabs, were the bodies of Kanosh's son and brother. Gone too were the remains of Kanosh's fellow Ute leader, the most famous and feared Native American in the early American West: Wakara (often anglicized as "Walker").

The date was August 16, 1874, late summer in the Utah Territory and nearly twenty years since Wakara's death and burial. Anger and sorrow welled up in Kanosh's chest as he stood on a 7,000-foot-high ledge in the Pahvant Mountains. Sun beat down on Kanosh's crease-lined face. The head of the Pahvant Band of Utes, Kanosh untied the handkerchief wrapped around his neck. He wiped away tears and sweat that collected in his large, white mustache.

Earlier that day, Kanosh, along with two of his Pahvant lieutenants and two Mormon settlers, had saddled their horses. They rode up a zigzagging mountain path canopied by Gambel oaks. Their destination was the fifty-acre field of sandstone above Kanosh's farm and homestead. Today, White locals call the field "the Cow": From a distance the field resembles a mooing cow. Local Native Americans,

Ute Leader Kanosh (ca. 1821–1884). Carte de visite by Charles R. Savage (ca. 1877). (Courtesy of the Church Archives, the Church of Jesus Christ of Latter-day Saints)

however, have long called it "Walker's Mountain," home to a massive Ute burial ground of more than 100 graves.[1]

It was a Sunday morning, normally a time Kanosh and his fellow Mormons devoted to church. The Ute leader had been baptized into the faith years before. Still, Kanosh and his party spent the Sabbath making the arduous journey up Walker's Mountain to investigate reports that outsiders had recently been to the Ute cemetery—and with nefarious intentions.

What Kanosh found left the Ute leader livid. "The body of Shot, Kanosh's brother, and Stambo, Kanosh's son, are entirely gone. Stolen," reported Kanosh's longtime friend and local Mormon leader Reuben McBride in a letter to his superiors back in Salt Lake City, the capital of the Utah Territory and the central stake of the Mormon Kingdom. McBride, a seventy-one-year-old convert from upstate New York who helped establish the first Mormon settlement on Kanosh's ancestral homelands, had never seen the Ute leader so upset.[2]

Before that day, many thought Kanosh had done well for himself by throwing his lot in with the Mormons. Ever since the Mormons fled to the Intermountain West in 1847 to escape religious persecution, Kanosh had acted as a peacemaker between the settlers and Utah's Native peoples whose land they colonized. Kanosh cut his hair in the Mormon style. He became a private landowner and farmer. And Kanosh was married to several Native wives at a time. Still, most Utah Natives were wary of Mormons' colonization and way of life. This was especially true of Kanosh's fellow Utes, who, before the Mormons' arrival, had been the region's most formidable tribe.

To the Mormons, Kanosh appeared the rarest thing, a Native who had been civilized. But, according to another local Mormon, Thomas Callister, the grave robbing brought out the true Indian in him. "I am satisfied had we not held a controlling influence over Kanosh and his men," Callister wrote to the Mormon leader and prophet Brigham Young back in Salt Lake City, "the war whoop and the scalping-knife would have been heard and used in our defenseless towns, as the result of this dastardly act."[3]

Kanosh's losses on Walker's Mountain were painful. But the grave robbers had not been hunting Kanosh's relatives. They were after Wakara, the legendary horse thief, trader of enslaved Natives, cavalry leader, and defender of Native sovereignty, who had died suddenly in January 1855 and was buried in a massive tomb next to Kanosh's family plots.

The grave robbers had been successful. "The once sacred . . . burying ground of the great Chief Walker," wrote McBride, had been "desecrated." Before it was robbed, Wakara's grave had contained the bodies of the Ute leader and several other Natives who had been killed

"Sketch of Walker, War Chief of the Utahs. Taken from life by W. W. Major in Council Sept. 4, 1852." William Warner Major, the first settler artist to work in Mormon Utah, painted this portrait during a September 1852 peace meeting in Salt Lake City between the Wakara-led Utes and the Washakie-led Shoshones. (Courtesy of the Peabody Museum of Anthropology and Ethnology, Harvard University)

to join Wakara in the "happy hunting grounds" beyond the veil. But in August 1874, McBride reported that he and the visiting party "found but fragments remaining of the should be quiet sleepers."[4]

In the 1840s, Wakara became a living legend in the American West. Newspapers in small towns and big cities chronicled his horse-thieving exploits. Best-selling books authored by famed western explorers described Wakara as the "captain" of a feared and respected pan-tribal cavalry. For a time, Wakara also raided with the celebrated mountain men Thomas "Pegleg" Smith and Jim Beckwourth.

Starting in the early 1840s, Wakara and his cavalry dominated the 700-mile crescent of commerce known as the Old Spanish Trail. At the west end of the trail, they stole horses by the thousands from the California ranchos, then ran their bounties east, over high mountain passes and across expansive deserts, to markets in New Mexico. Wakara's raids earned him the title of "the greatest horse thief in history." By stretching thin the region's human and horse resources in an attempt to defend against his raids, Wakara also contributed to the fall of Mexico-era California to the United States.

Wakara also became the region's most merciless trader of enslaved Natives. On his way to and from California to raid horses, Wakara hunted and captured Paiutes—mostly women and children—in southern Utah. Wakara traded his captives for more horses, guns, and food along the trail. But he sold most of them in the New Mexican slave markets of Taos, Santa Fe, and Abiquiú. Each slave he sold earned Wakara a small fortune in cattle, trade goods, or cash worth tens of thousands of dollars in today's money. Young women and girls fetched the highest prices: They made the best house servants, field hands, and concubines.

Wakara's cavalry also exacted tribute from caravans moving goods and people along the Old Spanish Trail. Wakara even forced famed (and well-armed) western expeditions, including those led by "the Pathfinder," future presidential candidate John C. Frémont, to pay for the privilege of passing along the West's most vital overland route. Still, many of these expeditions, which were commissioned to map paths for wagon roads and rail lines, came out ahead in their encounters with Wakara. His familiarity with every inch of the Old Spanish Trail made him an invaluable, though rarely acknowledged, cartographer. Fluent in Spanish and several Native languages and conversant in English, Wakara knew the region better than anyone. Drawing in the air with sign language and on riverbanks with sticks, rocks, and sand, Wakara created maps of the best river crossings, mountain traverses, watering holes, and supply outposts. The explorers sketched these details into their journals, which were later printed in Washington, DC, as official government maps of the emerging West.

In this way, Wakara helped shape what became on paper the geographical and political boundaries of the American Southwest. And Wakara's empire of flesh provided the horse and human power that surveyors and colonists—many with the very maps Wakara helped create stuffed in their satchels—relied upon to further explore and settle what became Utah, as well as large sections of New Mexico, Arizona, Nevada, and California.

Wakara himself became one of the most influential forces in the colonization of the West. Soon after the Mormons arrived in the Great Basin in 1847, Wakara struck a bargain with Brigham Young. In exchange for Mormon cattle and guns and promises to buy his horses and enslaved Natives, Wakara approved of and personally oversaw the establishment of the first Mormon settlements outside the Salt Lake Valley. Like his fellow Ute leader Kanosh, Wakara was also baptized into the faith. He even became the first Native American in Utah ordained into the Mormon priesthood. Yet his participation in the colonization of Utah was not born out of religious fealty; Wakara used the Mormons' imperial systems of colonialism, commerce, and religious conversion to expand his own Native empire. He directed the Mormons to build settlements on lands of his rivals within his own Ute nation. The Mormons then displaced or massacred these rivals, allowing Wakara to consolidate power among the Utes. These settlements also lined his pockets. They became new nodes on Wakara's own network of markets for his Native captives and stolen horses.

In the early 1850s, Wakara's fame increased as Americans from coast to coast read in newspapers about his and Brigham Young's partnerships, violent fallouts, and reconciliations, as the two leaders vied for control over Utah's Great Basin. The Ute leader preferred diplomacy and trade over conflict. But Wakara also used violence—or the threat of violence—when necessary to defend his empire, his lands, and his Ute nation's sovereignty against the settlers. Starting in the summer of 1853, after the Mormons began to destroy the Utes' sacred fishing and hunting grounds and tried to take over Wakara's slave trade, war broke out between the settlers and Wakara's Utes. Wakara did not start the war; Brigham Young did. Still, sometimes with Wakara's blessing and sometimes acting on their own, Utes conducted a series of attacks against Mormon settlements, including those Wakara had helped found just a few years before. Hundreds of settlers abandoned their farms and ranches and took shelter in Mormon forts, leaving their crops to wither and die in the hot Utah sun. At the same time, Mormon militias massacred scores of Ute men and boys, many of whom were noncombatants. The Mormons also captured Ute women and children, forcing them to work as servants in their homes and fields. In 1854, Brigham Young sued for peace and conceded to Wakara's demands. The Mormon prophet promised to buy Wakara's Native slaves, agreed to supply Wakara with more Mormon cattle, and swore not to encroach further into Wakara's territory without his permission.[5]

On January 29, 1855, six months after the conclusion of this conflict, dubbed the "Walker War" by the Mormons and much of the rest of America, Wakara died suddenly. His burial ceremony reminded some settler observers of the funerals of the pharaohs of ancient Egypt. Befitting his stature as the "King of the Mountains," Wakara's followers killed a dozen of his favorite horses, which they then laid in a circle around his grave. They also slit the throats of two women (often described as Wakara's wives) and two children (often described as Paiute slaves) to join Wakara in the afterlife. Inside his massive stone crypt, these members of Wakara's death party were buried next to the departed leader, along with his favorite saddle, hunting and fishing gear, guns, ammunition, and a letter of friendship from Brigham Young. Outside the tomb, an enslaved Paiute boy was also buried up to his neck, so that scavenging animals would feast on him instead of Wakara. The boy died a few days later.

The local settlers who witnessed the burial firsthand in 1855 and the Americans who penned the most widely read narratives of the West's pioneering era professed shock at the high body count of Wakara's funeral. In truth, they were also relieved. By pointing to Wakara's "savagery" toward settlers and other Natives, settlers succeeded in misdirecting attention away from their own violence—in the form of disease, environmental degradation, their own trade in Native slaves, and wars of extermination—which put hundreds of thousands of Native Americans in the ground.

Wakara's infamy in life did not guarantee that in death he would rest in peace. When Kanosh's party visited Walker's Mountain nineteen years after his passing, they found that the grave robbers were in fact headhunters. They took the skulls and tossed aside most of the rest of the bones to become snacks for scavenging animals.

Following his 1874 visit with Kanosh, Reuben McBride wrote to his superiors in Salt Lake. He asked them if they had information about the grave robbing. For McBride, Kanosh, and the others who visited Walker's Mountain, the question of who stole these skulls "yet remain[ed] . . . a mystery."[6]

THIS BOOK IS ABOUT SOLVING THAT MYSTERY. IT'S not only about uncovering who stole Wakara's remains. It's also about how and why Wakara's remains were stolen and what happened to them afterward. More importantly, this book tells the story of how and for what Wakara died and how and for what Wakara lived. We will find that the answers to these questions appear straightforward. But these answers lead to more questions and mysteries, which will prove difficult to unravel; for these mysteries are woven into the fabric of the origin story of America.

At the center of this origin story is a massive cover-up. Wakara spent most of his life raiding and trading horses and humans in what would become the American Southwest. Yet this cover-up will prove much vaster than the territory that Wakara dominated in the 1840s and 1850s. In fact, it will prove as wide as the entire American continent and extend centuries before and after the forty years of Wakara's life. This cover-up implicates conquistadors and colonists; America's longtime pariah religious people, the Mormons, as well as Christian missionaries of every denominational stripe; famed western explorers, presidents, and Supreme Court justices; and archaeologists, anthropologists, and historians. This cover-up also implicates me, the author of this book. Most likely, it also implicates you, the reader.

This book challenges Manifest Destiny, the dominant origin story of the American West, which is an extension of America's central origin story as a wild wasteland that Euro-American Christians had a mandate from God to tame and civilize. Manifest Destiny holds that the West was won by fearless cavalries who conquered and killed Indians and by intrepid cowboys and pioneers who transformed a feral and unformed wilderness into an expansive American continent dotted by fecund farms, bustling cities, and thriving industries, all knitted together by networks of roads, train rails, and telegraph lines.

Yet Wakara's life and legacy show that Manifest Destiny is more myth than history. After all, this book argues that Wakara should be counted among the founding fathers of the American West. Wakara's influence should be compared to the influence of Junípero Serra, the founder of mission-era California, and Brigham Young, who led the Mormons to what they believed was their promised land in Utah's Great Basin. Like Serra and Young, Wakara built new trade routes and industries. He oversaw the establishment of new settlements. He helped create the geographical and political boundaries that would become the American West. And like Serra and Young, Wakara often did so through violent means, including the enslavement of Native Americans.

Just as important, as a defender of Native territory and certain Native lives, Wakara deserves to be counted among the greatest Native American leaders. Such leaders include Crazy Horse (Thašúŋke Witkó), the famed Lakota warrior; Black Hawk (Ma-ka-tai-me-she-kia-kiak), the celebrated Sauk war leader; and Ouray, Wakara's fellow Ute leader and one of Native America's most skilled diplomats. Like Black Hawk and Crazy Horse, Wakara's pan-tribal warriors stalled and, for a time, reversed settler colonial expansion. And like Ouray, Wakara negotiated peace and trade deals with American settlers in hopes of preventing further colonial growth and destruction of Ute homelands.

Wakara was a singular figure in the history of the American West. Still, the purpose of this book is not to romanticize Wakara. "He was a great man, but probably not a good one," Rena Pikyavit, an elder associated with the Kanosh Band of Paiutes, the multitribal band that Wakara's fellow Ute leader Kanosh first established in the 1860s, told me. Wakara was no innocent. He died with blood on his hands—the blood of the Navajos, Shoshones, and Paiutes he enslaved, sold, and killed; the blood of the fellow Utes he helped displace; and the blood of settlers whose killings he condoned. Yet Wakara was also a man of his time. As Rena has observed, Wakara was "a man doing what he believed was necessary to preserve his way of life, his land, his people." Or as Forrest Cuch, direct descendant of Wakara and my Ute mentor and friend, has put it, "Wakara was not some character in the White man's story. He was not some noble savage. He was not some evil Indian. He was a man. A human being."

Wakara's humanity has been forgotten, and it has been forgotten on purpose. Forgetting Wakara is not just a sin of omission. It's a case study in the cover-up of Native Americans' participation in the creation of America. It's also a case study in the cover-up of the continued Native American presence and resilience in America.

Wakara's America exposes this cover-up. It brings to light a history that the narrators of the origins of the American West have obscured, ignored, or failed to imagine in their full complexities. To prop up the myth of Manifest Destiny, Wakara had to be removed not just from the land—by displacing his people, destroying his way of life, and, ultimately, digging up his remains—but also from the history books. There is no place in the creation story of America for a figure like Wakara who played a central role in colonizing the American West *and* who fought as an anticolonial warrior.

In response, *Wakara's America* is a work of historical reimagination. It presents a new narrative of the origins the American West. It tells a history in which Wakara took advantage of the settler colonial system to expand his personal wealth and power and the wealth and power of his followers. It also tells a history in which Wakara fought with words of diplomacy and, on occasion, acts of violence against settler colonialists when they threatened Native lives, lands, and sovereignty. In doing so, Wakara made unparalleled contributions to what is today the American West.

STILL, *WAKARA'S AMERICA* AIMS TO DO MORE. REIMAGINING the history of the American West with Wakara at its center risks perpetuating Manifest Destiny's most dangerous myth: that it succeeded. Like other revisionist histories about Native-settler relations, this book centers Native Americans' participation in the creation of America. Yet, ironically, by studying Native America as a part of history—not as a part of today—some revisionist histories have perpetuated the myth that settler Americans succeeded in eliminating Native American lives and culture from the American landscape. Relegating Native Americans to the past has often meant that settler Americans do not believe that Native Americans exist in the present—or at least, that they do not exist in a meaningful way.[7]

This is not a new phenomenon. Since the earliest days of the colonization of what would become New England, Anglo-American authors depicted Native Americans as haunting the landscape and terrorizing settlers and their descendants. In the late seventeenth century, the Puritan theologian Cotton Mather described Indians as "Sooty Devils" who took bodily possession of innocent New Englanders. A little more than a century later, the American "renaissance" novelist James Fenimore Cooper's Chingachgook embodied settlers' greatest fear: that Indians would silently and without remorse strike them down when they least expected it. Yet Chingachgook also embodied the settlers' ultimate triumph over Indians. When this "last of the Mohicans" died, the Indian threat was also removed from the American landscape. In the late twentieth and early twenty-first centuries, Indian ghosts and burial grounds—in Stephen King's horror novel *Pet Sematary*, in films like *The Blair Witch Project* and the *Amityville Horror* franchise, and in TV shows including *Buffy the Vampire Slayer*—continued to haunt Americans' imaginations. In doing so, these pop culture Indian ghosts performed vital political and cultural work of embodying national guilt—as spectral manifestations by which settler Americans remember the nation's original sin of Native genocide and displacement. At the same time Indians as ghosts have allowed settler Americans to forget that many Native American communities have survived the centuries-long attempts to eradicate them.[8]

Thus, it's not surprising that when many settler Americans encounter living and breathing Natives, they often act as if they've seen a ghost. Or as Forrest Cuch has said, settlers view "us as if we are dinosaurs." "It's like Jurassic Park. They think we've been engineered out of some amber from the ancient past." Against the blinding and deafening gale-force winds—created by a cacophony of school lessons and mass media, natural history museums, roadside historical markers, patriotic holidays, political speeches, and ongoing Supreme Court rulings, which claim that Native Americans were at best passive actors in American history and have no meaningful presence in America today—Native Americans shout, "We are still here!"

Reimagining the history of the American West with Wakara at its center is more than an academic exercise. I hope that *Wakara's America* changes people's views about the present and the past, about the living and the dead. This book is not a history of erasure and extermination. It chronicles an ongoing story of resistance, survival, and resilience.

Accomplishing these goals requires a different kind of history writing. Native American mentors with whom I've worked to write this book, as well as Indigenous scholars whose works I've learned from, have taught me to approach Wakara's history as connected to—even in contact with—the present. That is, the past and the present touch and inform each other. Such an approach is fundamentally different from Settler America's understanding of history as unfolding in a straight line. As the great Native American historian and theologian Vine Deloria Jr. (Standing Rock Sioux) wrote in *God Is Red*, "The very essence of Western European identity involves the assumption that time proceeds in a linear fashion; further it assumes that at a particular point in the unraveling of this sequence, the peoples of Western Europe became the guardians of the world." But settler colonialism is an ongoing process, not a series of events. As such, how the story of settler invasion is told and understood has also changed over time. Its logic justified first the killing of Native peoples, then the digging up of the graves of dead Native ancestors and denying their place in the history books, then treating contemporary Native peoples like ghosts or long-extinct dinosaurs—all of which, we will see, happened to Wakara and his descendants. Still, Indigenous scholars, including J. Kēhaulani Kauanui (Kanako Maoli), have argued that settler colonialism went through these transformations because Native people refused to die off. In fact, history has shown that Native Americans relentlessly "exist, resist, and persist" against Settler America's ongoing efforts to destroy and replace them.[9]

In contrast, a Native American approach to history is not linear. Instead, it's spatial. Vine Deloria Jr. described moving from a settler history to a Native one as "a transition from thinking in terms of time to thinking in terms of space." Even more specifically, a Ute approach to history invites us to "stand in the center of the circle," as Larry Cesspooch, the Northern Utes' most prominent spiritual leader, has explained to me. This history is not a march through time and across space. Instead, this history is time spent in space, until that space becomes a specific place—a homeland.[10]

For example, a few years ago, when I first talked to Rena Pikyavit and her husband, Rick, about the robbing of Wakara's grave, they refused to acknowledge that it ever happened. "He's still there," they insisted, buried on Walker's Mountain. Rick and Rena are elders of the Kanosh Band of Paiutes, which includes some of Wakara's Ute descendants and whose ancestral homelands include the burial site. They told me that the stories of his grave robbing are made up. Just another set of lies in the long string of lies written down by Whites to justify stealing their homelands, Rick explained. For if Wakara's and the other Ute and Paiute ancestors' remains were removed, then their descendants' claims to the land would be broken. "We aren't traditional [Natives] if we aren't connected to our own land," Rick said.

Rick and Rena's insistence that Wakara "is still here" among the trees, rocks, and mountains that make up their peoples' homelands is another way of saying, "We are still here." They are watching over him and these lands, as their tribal founder Kanosh believed it was his duty to do. After all, Utes and Paiutes believe that at the beginning of time, God (*Sünawav* in Ute) made them caretakers of their lands and all that lives and dies upon these lands. So even if Wakara's physical remains were stolen, because the land is a part of Wakara, Wakara's spirit remains a part of the land.[11]

This spatial approach to history also invites us to reimagine America's past as relational—that is, "great men" like Wakara who shaped the lives of others were also shaped by their relationships to others. This means exploring Wakara's relationships with his family and with his own Timpanogos Band; his relationships to famed mountain men and other western explorers; his relationships to Mormon settlers and government officials; and his relationships to the Natives he enslaved. It also means exploring Wakara's relationships with nonhuman animals. This includes his relationship to the fish—specifically, as we will see, the June sucker—that were native to Wakara's home waters in and around Utah (Timpanogos) Lake and that sustained the bodies and defined the identities of the Timpanogos "Fish Eaters," as they were called by their fellow Utes. This also includes Wakara's relationship with horses—specifically the Spanish colonial horses—that he raided, traded, and rode and that made him a living legend.

History as relationships also means exploring Wakara's connections to the environment—the waterways, the mountains, the deserts—that make up the geography of the American Southwest. This geography shaped Wakara. It affected where, when, and how he traveled. In turn, Wakara helped shape the region's geography *literally* on the ground. Wakara helped shape and improve the Old Spanish Trail—clearing and expanding mountain passes, digging wells to create watering holes, burning fields to promote the growth of prairie grasses to feed his horses. Wakara also shaped the region's geography *literarily* on paper when he shared his unrivaled knowledge of the region with explorers who then created official government maps of the American Southwest.

Each member of what we might call these "ecosystems of relations"—from mountains to mountain lions, from fish to Fish Eaters, from ants to the arches and natural bridges in Arches National Park—is connected to and reliant upon the others. This is so because, as Ute elder and language scholar Emeline Root has told me, each of these relations is part of God's creation and is endowed with "the spirit of God," or *Puha* (power or life force) in Ute and Paiute and other Numic languages. Likewise, as Wakara descendant Forrest Cuch has written, such a belief in the omnipresence of *Puha* means that "when native people speak of 'all my relations,' the term refers to the entire living earth, not just blood relatives." Among the Utes, an "elder may mourn over a toxic waste dump as if a family member were critically ill, just as their heart will rejoice when a flock of birds flies north in the springtime."[12]

Finally, this reimagining of history as spatial and relational also means expanding the sources from which we draw to narrate Wakara's story. Written archives, mostly created and kept by Euro-American settlers and storytellers, have bound Wakara and other Native Americans *in history*, reducing them to what I call "paper Indians" of the settler historians' own invention. Settlers folded these paper Indians into puppets who did and said anything they wanted them to. Settlers then called these paper Indians' words and deeds "savage" and "heathen," while they named their own words and deeds "civilized" and "Christian." Settlers then justified their deployment of violence and other tools of displacement against actual bodies of Native Americans as righteous acts against Indian aggression. As such, written archives are insufficient and often inaccurate foundations upon which to reconstruct the Settler American West Wakara helped create and the Native American West Wakara defended. For that reason, here I explore archives of biology, geography, and archaeology, and I employ other methods, including ethnohistory, ethnozoology, and climatology, to name a few.[13]

These expanded resources and methods—along with a focus on space and place, on relationships among land, people, plants and animals, air, and water—contribute to a process of writing history not as a straight line. Instead, it's writing history as an ever-widening circle. For example, Larry Cesspooch has told me that Wakara is sending new people into the world to tell his story. These people include Wakara's own kin. Many of these descendants have been exiled by the legacy of anti-Indian policies to far-flung parts of America. But even on the Uintah and Ouray Reservation, due to arbitrary laws related to "blood quantum" and tribal disenrollment, some Wakara descendants have been denied tribal affiliation. Other descendants had long been oblivious of their ancestor Wakara's history but are now rediscovering his life and legacy. Such rediscoveries open the possibility that history moves in cycles, not in straight lines.[14]

SUCH A CYCLICAL VIEW OF HISTORY DEMONSTRATES, AS I argue in Part I, "Wakara's Burial," how Manifest Destiny not only removed Wakara and his people from the land. In the written histories of the founding era of the American West, Manifest Destiny also covered up Wakara's unparalleled role in creating the American West itself. Wakara's America is not gone. In many ways, it is the American West we see today. Such a cyclical retelling also shows that key elements of Wakara's Native—specifically Ute—ways of life also are not gone. They are in diaspora, sequestered in far-flung corners of Utah and across the country and boxed up on dusty shelves in governmental storage facilities from Salt Lake City to Washington, DC.

Part II, "Wakara's Fish," details how, for generations, Wakara's Timpanogos Band sustained themselves by eating the native fish that swam in what they called Timpanogos Lake, today named Utah Lake, the third-largest freshwater lake west of the Mississippi River. Wakara's fish-eating Utes also managed the native fish of this lake, home to the most abundant and diverse fishery of the Great Basin, including varieties of trout, chubs, and suckers. Within a generation of their arrival, Mormon settlers had killed off or displaced Wakara's fish-eating Utes and all but destroyed the Timpanogos' fisheries through overfishing, irrigation, and urban sprawl. This difference, in how Wakara's Timpanogos and Brigham Young's Mormons understood their relationship to the fish of Timpanogos (Utah) Lake, is the difference between Native and Settler America. Through trial and error, Natives learn to live in balance with the nonhuman animals, plants, and geology of a place until it becomes their homeland, while settlers move into another people's homeland and exploit its resources to maximize their settlements' short-term growth. And yet, today, through fits and starts, settler and Native Americans are partnering to return native fish—most importantly, the long-endangered June sucker, which was among the Timpanogos' favorite—to Utah Lake and to other native waterways. In doing so, they are beginning to end this long season of diaspora and to restore life-giving relationships among the land, water, people, and animals.

Fish made Wakara's ancestors into a people of a place: the *Nuche* ("the People" in Ute) of the Timpanogos ("Rocky" in Ute) River and Lake. Part III, "Wakara's Horse," shows how the acquisition of the horse remade the Timpanogos and other Numic speakers (namely the Shoshones and Comanches) into horse peoples and nations. Soon after the Spanish reintroduced the horse to the Americas in the sixteenth century, through raiding, trading, and warring with other Natives and settlers, Native horse nations reshaped the ecological and political borders of the Southwest and beyond. Imported European ideas of race and ethnicity also reshaped the region's ethnic borders, including the creation of distinct Ute, Paiute, Shoshone, and Comanche identities among Numic peoples, whereas before such identities were fluid. During the 1840s, Wakara emerged as the greatest horse raider in history. He made himself and his followers wealthy, powerful, and feared. His unrivaled raids and trades of horses and slaves with settlers also provided American settlers the enslaved humans and stolen horses that sped up the American conquest and colonization of the Southwest. Wakara's decade of dominance marked the high point of Ute horse culture. Since his death, settler Americans and the settler American state have tried to wipe out the remnants of this culture. Despite these efforts, the deep, even spiritual connection between the Utes and the horse has survived in and beyond their traditional homelands. And in one corner of the Great Basin, feral herds of Spanish mustangs—descendants of the horses that Wakara stole from California in the 1840s—continue to thrive despite governmental efforts to cull them.

Part IV, "Wakara's Slave," narrates the history of "Indian slavery" in the American Southwest, which was practiced by both Natives and settlers. Wakara's equestrian band bought and sold other Native peoples, especially their pedestrian Paiute neighbors, as if they were property. But Wakara also used slavery to build kin and trade networks. He even gave his own blood relations to settler families and expected the settlers to reciprocate. When they arrived in 1847, the Mormons introduced what they claimed was a new kind of Indian slavery to the Great Basin. In order to free them from slavers like Wakara and from their own Indian "heathen" families, Brigham Young commanded his followers to "buy up" the youngest Indian captives as fast as they could and raise them in Mormon homes as their own children. To the public, Young presented his new slave ideology as pure Christian benevolence in the face of pure savagery. But such grand proclamations covered up violence and abuse. Like antebellum Southern plantation owners, Mormons often bought, sold, and traded Indian slaves to work in the homes, fields, and bedrooms of their masters. This settler Indian slavery also destroyed Native families. Age and gender were key. Removing Native girls and women from their communities meant no more Native mothers to birth and raise future generations and carry on claims to Native lands and traditions. Yet, recently, using genealogical records and

DNA data, descendants of Wakara's daughters who were raised in Mormon homes, as well as descendants of Wakara's mostly female slaves purchased by Mormon settlers, who often became Mormon polygamous wives, are rediscovering their long-lost kin. They are also rediscovering in their family histories their Native matriarchs whom their White settler patriarchs worked to forget.

The written record of the "Walker War" has long portrayed the ten months from July 1853 to May 1854 as a Wakara-led campaign of guerrilla attacks against the bodies, buildings, and farms of Wakara's peace-loving Mormon brethren. Part V, "Brigham's War," argues that it was Young who wanted the conflict. Slavery removed Native women and children from the land. War killed off Native men. But because the settlers controlled the written narrative, they had the power to portray Wakara as the aggressor and themselves as innocent victims. Naming the war after Wakara was thus another cover-up, which continued the legacy of blaming Natives for wars that settlers started. This practice began at the beginning of American history itself. In the 1600s, Young's (and my own) Puritan ancestors blamed the Natives, whose land they settled on and stole, for starting "Indian wars," when the Puritans were the ones who instigated these conflicts.

Part VI, "Wakara's Skull," details how "science" became a final front in the settlers' campaign of Native American extermination. Following the Civil War, the US Army fanned out across the West to kill Natives who refused to relocate to reservations. Medical doctors embedded in army companies and in Indian agencies collected skulls from battlefields as well as from Native graves. They then shipped these remains back to Washington for "study." Settler scientists claimed that Natives had smaller crania than White settlers, which meant that Natives were incapable of participating in the American experiment of self-government. And thus, Natives were destined to go extinct as the White American republic continued to expand from sea to sea.

I conclude by narrating present-day efforts by Wakara's tribal, spiritual, and lineal descendants to complete the circle of history: to end this (long) season of diaspora of Wakara's fish, horses, and slaves and his own remains. Wakara's descendants are also beginning to restore to the historical narrative a more complete recounting of how together Native and settler Americans—through relationships forged in violence and cooperation—helped create the American West. Historically, such restoration projects have been described in terms of "repatriation." Yet repatriation is a legalistic process that empowers the very settler state that committed cultural extermination and genocide against Native peoples to oversee the process by which ancestors' skeletal remains and sacred objects are returned to the people and land from which they were stolen. Instead, Native activists and scholars call for "rematriation." As Steven Newcomb (Shawnee/Lenape), executive director of the Indigenous Law Institute, describes it, rematriation "restore[s] a people to a spiritual way of life, in sacred relationship with their ancestral lands, without external interference" by the settler state. Rematriation inverts the structures of settler colonialism that have systematically alienated Native peoples from their identities, cultures, lands, and bodies. Rematriation emphasizes ways of knowing and acting that are relational, spatial, and cyclical, not binary and linear, as settler religion, science, and law have long taught. Such efforts include reintroducing Native fish species to their ancestral waters, protecting feral herds of Spanish mustangs, and passing on Ute horse culture from generation to generation. Such efforts also include preserving Ute sacred histories about *Nuche* homelands. And finally, such efforts aim to bring the remains of Wakara and the other ancestors buried with him back to *Nuche* homelands.[15]

Almost as common as the proclamation "we are still here" among Native Americans and Indigenous peoples across the world is the refrain "Our ancestors are always with us." Ute spiritual leader Larry Cesspooch takes this relationship between contemporary Utes and their ancestors a step further. In fact, he collapses the distance between them altogether.

"We are our ancestors," Larry has told me. He means this in a very specific sense. "Wakara is out there among the Utes." So are all Ute ancestors embodied in the Utes of today. For example, Larry points to his cousin, Forrest Cuch, who has spent forty years defending Indigenous sovereignty around the world. Larry declares that Forrest is the spiritual, perhaps even physical, embodiment of Antonga. Known to the settlers as Black Hawk, Antonga, one of Wakara's kin, led the last of the "Indian Wars" in Utah in the 1860s.

Larry's idea that "we are our ancestors," along with Rick and Rena's notion that Wakara "is still here," means that I, the author of this book, also have a relationship to my own ancestors. It also means that I have a relationship to Wakara and the places and people that he shaped and that shaped him. They shaped me too.

Indigenous historians—and, increasingly, non-Indigenous historians—reject the idea that historians are objective observers, set apart from the events they narrate. Instead, historians cannot help but write from their own point of view. Often when they speak or write, Indigenous scholars name their tribes, clans, and bands of origin. Following their example, an increasing number of settler scholars name their own family history on the American continent and before. Doing so makes it clear from *whom* and from *where* they come and how those identities inform their relationship to history. In this book, I include my own personal narration, conscious not to further colonize Wakara's history by once again displacing Native history with settler history. My intention is to implicate myself and my family, so that I recognize, as I hope my non-Native readers do, how our lives might also be implicated in Wakara's life and legacy.[16]

I was born in what is today Casper, Wyoming, to parents with English, German, Polish, and Swedish ancestry. Casper is built on the ancestral lands of the Lakota, Arapaho, Cheyenne, and Crow tribes. Most summers, the Shoshones and Wakara's Utes also hunted bison on these lands. After my parents' divorce, my mother and I left Wyoming. We eventually settled in Oneonta, New York, on the lands of the Oneida peoples of the Haudenosaunee (Iroquois) Confederacy. Still, many summers, I returned to the West to visit my father and stepmother. We spent much of this time hiking and camping throughout the West, including in Utah's national parks, which occupy some of Wakara's ancestral lands as well as the lands that Wakara's Old Spanish Trail passed through. Yet the Native American history of, and continued presence in, these national parks has been at best ignored—and at worst covered up.

My familial connection to the erasure of Native American lives and history goes back further. In my search for Wakara's ancestors using genealogical records, I discovered my relationship to Edward Converse, a founding father of colonial New England. Converse, my eleventh-great-grandfather, was a member of John Winthrop's Puritan fleet that first came to Massachusetts in 1630 seeking refuge from religious persecution in England. Like the Mormons in Utah, Edward Converse established colonies that were, in part, missionary outposts to Native Americans, which also became Indian killing fields. My family's claims—and those of many other American families like my own—to American identities and American lands were made possible by the displacement and genocide of Native Americans.

The point of implicating our own histories in the history that we write is not to shame settler Americans like me and like many of you. To the contrary, the point is to liberate us from shame. It's to show us that, as I argue about Wakara, we are not bound by history. If Larry Cesspooch is right that Wakara is present today, embodied in contemporary Utes, then our ancestors are here in us too.[17]

We, settler Americans like me and like many of you, have the ability—and the responsibility—to do better than our ancestors. As my colleague Margaret Huettl (Anishinaabe) has told me, "The way settler colonialism unfolded was not inevitable. There were alternatives for settlers and Natives to live together on this land that we now call America." My hope is that a historical reimagining of the Settler America that Wakara helped build and the Native America he defended leads to a moral reimagining. My hope is that with this knowledge, we are empowered—I, the author of this book, and you, the reader—to reimagine relationships between settler and Native Americans. My hope is that we are also empowered to reimagine our collective relationships with the American land that we all call home.[18]

Part I

Wakara's Burial

Chapter 1

Wakara's Last Days

WAKARA DID NOT SEE the end coming. In the final months of 1854, Wakara, the famed Ute leader, horse raider, and slave trader, was at full strength. At about forty years old, Wakara wasn't a young man by the standards of the early American West. Still, despite his advancing age and average size—he stood five feet, seven inches tall—Wakara's stamina and speed were legendary. Admirers and enemies alike agreed that his physicality was surpassed only by his intelligence and audacity.

Wakara was especially formidable from his perch on a colonial Spanish horse, descendants from the breed that the Spanish brought to the Americas in the early 1500s. From California to Kansas, on the backs of these compact, clever, and nimble horses, Spanish and Mexican vaqueros and Comanches, Apaches, and other master horse people like Wakara's Utes traversed snowy mountain passes, raced across dry, open deserts, and crisscrossed seas of grasses to expand their competing empires.

In the 1840s, astride his mounts—which he decked out in his signature brass-colored caparisons, embroidered saddles, and clanging metal cones that announced his arrival from miles away—Wakara and his cavalry dominated the 700-mile Old Spanish Trail that since the 1820s connected New Mexico, the Ute and Paiute homelands, and the California ranchos. From the New Mexican outposts of Santa Fe, Taos, and Abiquiú, the trail curved northwest around impassible canyons of the Colorado River toward Wakara's homelands in central Utah. It then sloped southwest, traversing Paiute territory in southwestern Utah, cut across the Nevada desert, and ended at the missions-turned-ranchos near the California coast.

History and legend record Wakara participating in horse and slave raids on the same day at distant points on the Old Spanish Trail. In 1840, in one single raid, Wakara and his cavalry allegedly stole 3,000 horses from the California ranchos at San Luis Obispo and San Miguel. Yet competing claims from traders and raiders of wrangling alongside Wakara reflect more the Ute leader's reputation as the most merciless trader of Indian slaves and "the greatest horse thief in history" than some magical ability to transport himself across space and time. Western mountain men and horse thieves tried to bolster their own reputations by borrowing from Wakara's. Who could blame them? After all, though today few people even know his name, Wakara was a founding father of the American Southwest.[1]

In December 1854, at his winter home at Summit Creek, seven miles southwest of the picturesque Mormon settlement of Parowan, Wakara laid plans for a springtime trading blitz. He planned to visit the Mormons in the north, then New Mexican settlements in the south. He also hoped to move further into Navajo territory, though he recognized he would need more men and horses to fulfill that ambition. While he envisioned expanding his own Native empire, Wakara also kept a lookout for further Mormon incursions into Ute territory. A few days before Christmas, Wakara dispatched his brother Sanpitch to have a talk with the Mormons who were building another mission among the Paiutes in southwestern Utah. That

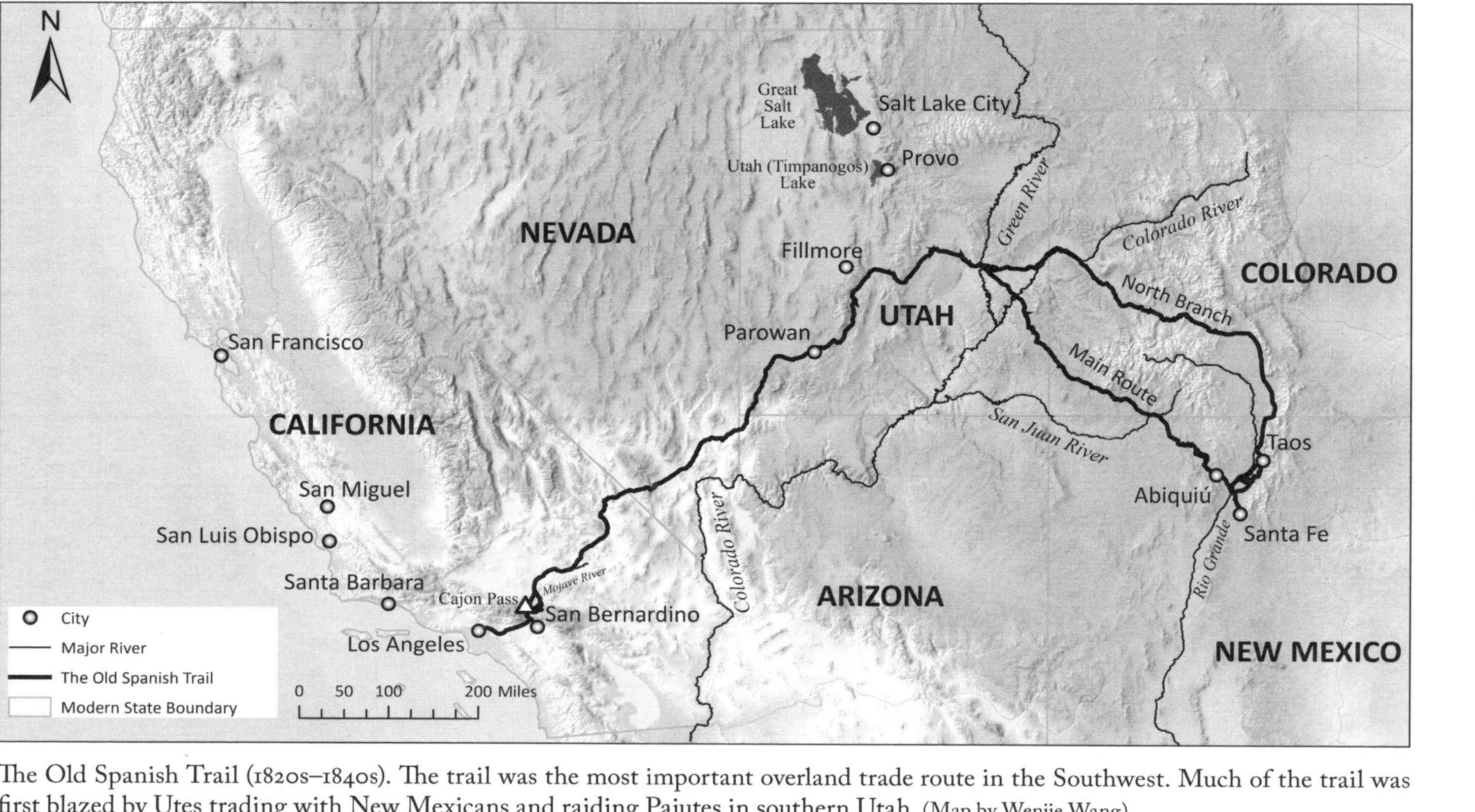

The Old Spanish Trail (1820s–1840s). The trail was the most important overland trade route in the Southwest. Much of the trail was first blazed by Utes trading with New Mexicans and raiding Paiutes in southern Utah. (Map by Wenjie Wang)

land, Sanpitch warned the missionaries, belonged to Wakara. They should not erect any permanent houses on it, lest those houses be taken down.[2]

In early January 1855, Wakara and his main lodges started their trek north. The lodges comprised fifty men, women, and children, along with a caravan of dozens of horses, several oxen, sheep, goats, cows, and a handful of Paiute slaves. By mid-January, Wakara began to feel ill. Each day he grew weaker. His coughing fits grew more intense.

In hopes that Wakara would regain his strength with a bit of rest, the lodges set up camp near Wakara's farm just south of Fillmore, then the political capital of the Utah Territory. Within a week, Wakara could no longer walk. He struggled to remain conscious. Wrapped in buffalo robes and huddled in his tent, Wakara told his men that he was going blind. To alleviate his suffering, Wakara ordered his followers to kill two Paiute children and a few horses as an offering to the Great Spirit.

The offerings did not work. But the business of Wakara's Native empire had to continue. On the morning of January 28, Wakara crawled out of his tent. Though the weather was unseasonably warm, Wakara pulled his woolen bonnet over his ears and wrapped his favorite blanket over his shoulders. One of Wakara's most prized possessions, the blanket was a toll that he collected from John C. Frémont when Wakara and his cavalry intercepted the famed "Pathfinder" in May 1844, as they patrolled the Old Spanish Trail to collect tribute from caravans journeying between New Mexico and California. Wakara's men then hoisted him upon his horse. So that he would not tumble off his mount, they held him by the shoulders as they rode north toward Fillmore for what would be Wakara's last business meeting.[3]

A few years before, the Mormons had chosen the town of Fillmore as Utah's territorial capital because it lay along one of the proposed routes of the transcontinental railroad. But in the 1850s, two conflicts—a "war" between the Mormon settlers and the Utes that came to bear Wakara's name and a "war" between the Mormons and the US government that came to bear the Mormons' name—forced the Latter-day Saints to abandon Fillmore's partially finished capitol building and relocate their legislative sessions to Salt Lake.

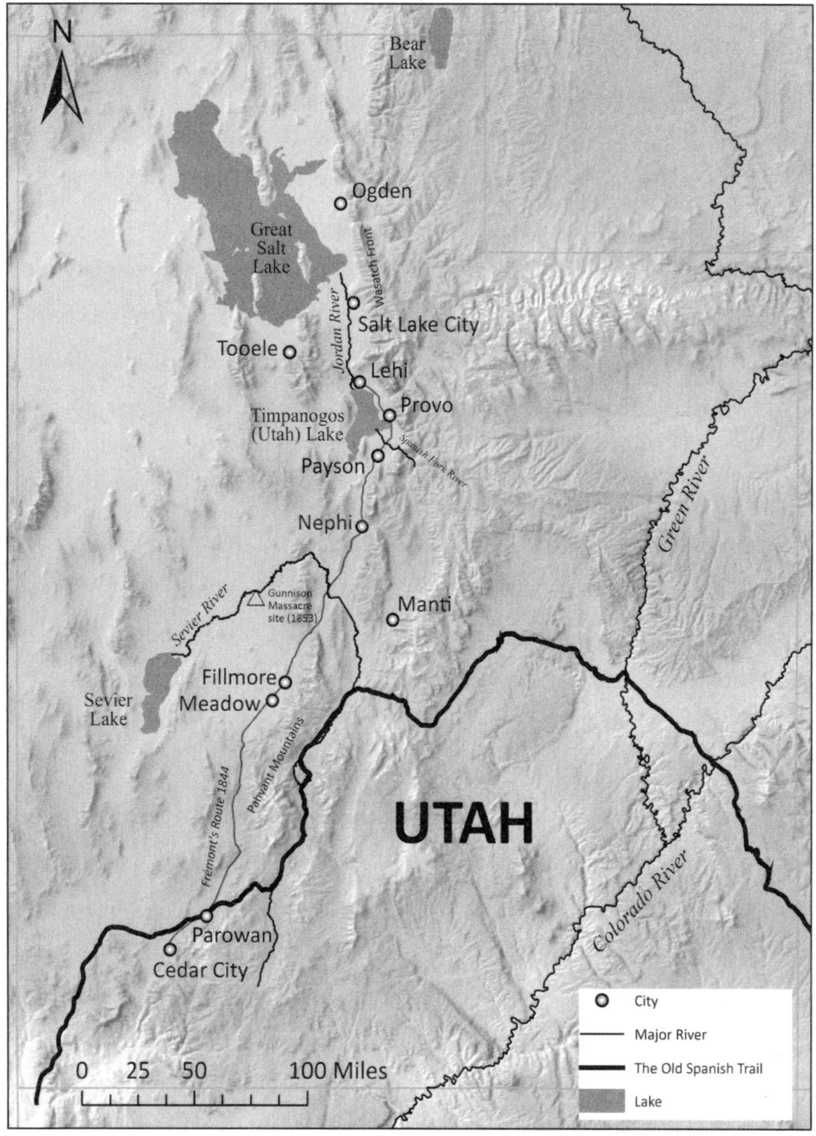

Utah, 1855. Utah as it was on the eve of Wakara's death. (Map by Wenjie Wang)

On the road between Meadow and Fillmore, Wakara and his men met an expected Mormon delegation led by David Lewis. The summer before, Brigham Young, the president and prophet of the Latter-day Saints, the territorial governor, and the ex officio superintendent of Indian affairs in Utah, sent Lewis south as a missionary to the Indians. Young's brief to Lewis, a hard-charging forty-something Southerner and a veteran of the Mormon wars in Missouri, was to firm up the uneasy peace between the Mormons and the Utes that Young had recently established with Wakara. The peace put an end to the bloody and costly "Walker War."

Wakara offered Lewis a feeble handshake when they met on the road. Wakara hoped to make Lewis an ally. The two men were already brothers in the gospel of the Church of Jesus Christ of Latter-day Saints. Lewis had joined the church in his native Kentucky twenty years earlier. Wakara was a more recent convert. In March 1850, he was baptized in the cool spring waters of City Creek in Manti, a Mormon settlement on the eastern side of Utah's Wasatch Front that Wakara had helped the Mormons establish the year before. Soon after his own baptism, more than 100 of Wakara's followers were also dipped in the creek—an event that thrilled the Mormons, who believed they were divinely mandated to bring their Christian faith to America's Native peoples. Wakara ultimately became the first Utah Native to be ordained in the Mormon priesthood.

Beyond their shared religious affiliation, Lewis and Wakara had another thing in common: They were both slavers. Lewis brought at least two enslaved Black girls, whose names have been lost to history, and an enslaved Black man named Jerry with him when he came to Utah in 1851. Over the next decade, the Mormon leadership sent Lewis and other Southern slaveholding converts to southwestern Utah near present-day St. George, where they hoped to build a plantation culture in the image of the antebellum South they had left behind.[4]

Because of Wakara, slavery was well established in the region that would soon be dubbed Utah's "Dixie." The Indian slavery that Wakara practiced was different in its form, though often not in its inhumanity, from "African" chattel slavery. Wakara may have been famous for his horse raiding. But he became feared and made his sizable fortune as the greatest trafficker of Indian slaves in the Old West. Wakara enslaved Navajos, Shoshones, and even other Utes. But his favorite targets were the Paiutes whose women and children he captured in southwestern Utah during his seasonal horse-raiding trips back and forth along the Old Spanish Trail. He then sold his captives to Mexicans at the annual slave auctions in Taos, Santa Fe, and Abiquiú, to the proprietors of the ranchos in California, and to the Mormons after they settled in Utah in 1847.

Lewis and Wakara had met earlier that winter when Lewis traveled to Wakara's camp near Parowan. During that visit, the Ute leader gave the missionary "a papoose," a boy about three years old, and told Lewis to bring him to Brigham Young in Salt Lake. The papoose was an expensive gift. At the New Mexico slave markets, Wakara could sell such a child for between $150 and $200, a small fortune in today's dollars. Such a sale would have likely committed the boy to a lifetime of "labor as Negroes do in the states," as another slaveholding Mormon convert described the plight of Indian slaves in the Old West. This gift came with strings attached. In return for the Indian boy, Wakara hoped Young would send him "a good gun, a coat, and a white blanket." Wakara also requested cattle, rifles, flints, some powder, lead, caps, and a "stud colt." If the papoose wasn't enough, however, Wakara said he'd pay for these requests with Spanish colonial horses from his prized herd.[5]

SLAVERY WAS STILL ON WAKARA'S MIND WHEN HE met with David Lewis on the morning of January 28, 1855. Wakara was too weak to dismount, so the two men talked astride their horses. Wakara asked Lewis if he would accompany him to Navajo country in the springtime. The Ute leader was looking for new supplies of Indian captives and new markets in which to sell them.[6]

Since their first days in Utah, the Mormons professed disgust for Wakara's slaving. And they had told Wakara as much soon after his baptism and ordination. He was wrong to value enslaved Indians by how much gold or cash they could fetch him at the auctions in Abiquiú or by how many blankets and guns they could fetch him at a rancho in San Bernardino. Learn to read the Book of Mormon, the Saints implored Wakara. In that newly restored gospel, Wakara would discover that Indians weren't truly Indians at all, members of distinct tribes with distinct cultures and histories. Instead, the Mormons told Wakara that his equestrian Utes and the pedestrian Paiutes upon whom he preyed were in fact descendants of the same ancient Israelite family. According to the Book of Mormon, millennia before, a small group of people who belonged to the oldest of Abraham's covenant with God fled to the New World and, in the process, forgot their true identities. The forgetfulness of these people, whom the Book of Mormon called "Lamanites" and whom early Mormons claimed were the ancestors of America's Native peoples, led to the savagery and tribal division that the Mormons said were the hallmarks of American Indians' way of life. The Mormons believed themselves to be charged with saving the Indians from their savage natures by civilizing them and by restoring them to the knowledge of their true Lamanite identities. Once the Indians had been restored to the faith of their forefathers, the Lamanites and White Mormons would create covenants of faith and marriage and together build a new Zion in America fit for the return of Christ.

Hoping to fulfill this mandate, from their earliest days in Utah, the Mormons coupled colonizing Native lands with missionizing Native people. When Wakara, the most powerful man—Native or

White—in the Great Basin, offered to help them with their settlement efforts and asked to be baptized and ordained a Mormon elder, the Mormons took it as a sign that the fulfillment of their divine mandate was at hand. Wakara was also thrilled with this new partnership; yet his excitement focused on more immediate and earthbound reasons: the opportunity to add to his constellation of trading posts across the Southwest. He was also more than willing to assist the Latter-day Saints in settling Native lands when they belonged not to him but to his rival Native leaders whose territory he coveted for himself.

Despite protestations over the immorality of Wakara's slaving, within three years of their arrival in Utah Wakara's Mormon brethren moved to take over the trade in Indian slaves themselves as part of their mission to redeem and civilize Native Americans. But instead of buying enslaved Natives from Wakara, they started to go directly to the source. With payments of cash and cattle, threats of violence, and promises that they'd be cared for in Mormon homes, the Saints coerced Paiute parents to hand over their own children. The all-Mormon Legislative Assembly of the Territory of Utah also passed laws making it legal to hold these children in indenture until they worked off the cost of their own purchase price. And they passed laws making it illegal for non-Mormon slavers like Wakara to transport captured Indians to New Mexico and California and illegal for Mexicans to come to Utah and purchase slaves from Wakara.

Wakara did not like that the settlers had moved to cut him off from his slave supply chain. Nor did he like that they dictated how he traveled and traded on the Old Spanish Trail. Nor did he like that the Mormons expanded settlements without his blessing, especially on his band's sacred hunting and fishing grounds around Timpanogos (Utah) Lake, among the largest freshwater lakes in the Great Basin, home to one of the basin's greatest fisheries, and the source of Wakara's band name.

So Wakara fought back. Starting in July 1853, Ute warriors sporadically attacked Mormon settlements throughout central and southern Utah—including settlements like Manti and Parowan that Wakara had helped to establish. For the next ten months, Wakara's Utes pilfered Mormon cattle, crops, and horses. They also destroyed settler homes, fences, and farms. The settlers' losses were so severe that in Parowan the Mormons posted a reward of $15,000—equivalent to $500,000 today—for Wakara's head.[7]

Brigham Young was thrilled. Finally, the Mormon prophet had a reason to unleash war on Wakara, his greatest rival for control of the Great Basin. The Mormons' own militia, the Nauvoo Legion, went on the offensive, attacking Ute villages often with indiscriminate violence. When a group of Ute or Goshute noncombatants sought shelter in the Mormon fort at Nephi, they were "shot down like so many dogs," recalled one Mormon witness. Their bodies were "picked up with pitchforks [put] on a sleigh and hauled away," then dumped in a mass grave. As for Wakara, Young didn't collect his head. But he did send him a peace letter and a gift of tobacco. Young suggested that the tobacco might be laced with poison.[8]

This series of conflicts, which the Mormons called the "Walker War," led to the deaths of an untold number of Utes, Paiutes, and Goshutes, along with a dozen White Mormon settlers. Hundreds more settlers abandoned their homes and farms for the safety of Mormon forts. But Wakara and Young both knew that war was bad for business. War disrupted Wakara's horse and human trading and curtailed Mormon settlement expansion, even forcing farmers to abandon precious crops in their fields before they were ready for harvest. In May 1854, Wakara agreed to a peace parley. But believing that Young had failed to show him the respect he deserved as a fellow "great chief" and as a fellow holy man who also talked with the "Great Spirit," Wakara demanded that the Mormon prophet travel south to meet him at the center stake of his own Native empire. Young accepted.[9]

On May 11, 1854, Young and a train of more than 100 wagons, sixteen oxen, fifty mounted militiamen, and a coterie of church apostles, rolled into one of Wakara's summer camps at Chicken Creek, near the Mormon settlement of Nephi. Wakara met the Mormons' show of force with his own. Mounted warriors and a dozen Ute leaders stood guard over eighty Ute lodges throughout the camp.

Young pulled back the heavy flap of Wakara's tent, ducking his head as he entered. Not sure if he was ready to make peace, Wakara refused to rise to greet the prophet. Still, at Wakara's request, Mormon leaders laid hands upon the Ute leader in prayer. Feeling better, Wakara, Young, and their councils passed a peace pipe. The details could be worked out later, Wakara explained as he puffed on the calumet. Young agreed, taking his turn with the pipe. As a sign of goodwill, Young gave Wakara a peace letter that guaranteed that the Ute leader could trade horses and humans with the settlers without fear of reprisal. In return, Wakara pledged to let the Saints sow their crops in peace. Together, Mormons and Utes would make sure that the road between Salt Lake and the settlements to the south, as well as Wakara's road, the Old Spanish Trail, would be free of any more bloodletting.[10]

During the meeting, Young also supplied Wakara with gifts of guns, clothing, cattle, medicine, and foodstuffs upon which Wakara's Utes increasingly relied. Every year, Mormon settlements grew by thousands. Colonization brought diseases, especially smallpox and measles, which killed thousands of Utah Natives, including many of Wakara's kin. Colonization also crowded out Utah's native flora and fauna. Most worrisome, as the settlers cleared land to make way for forts and cabins, dug irrigation ditches, and hoed row crops, they muddied the clear, sweet waters of the Great Basin in which Utah's native fish had swum for millennia. Declining fish populations—due to overfishing by the Saints and environmental degradation—forced the fish-eating Utes to eat more Mormon wheat and beef. And to fund the acquisition of these calories, Wakara's Utes increasingly depended on earnings from trading Indian slaves. At the May 1854 peace meeting, in exchange for a few pounds of flour, Wakara gave Brigham Young two Native toddlers whom the Ute leader had recently captured.[11]

SEVEN MONTHS LATER, IN LATE JANUARY WAKARA ENVISIONED a more hopeful future than the genocide that would come to pass. Wakara expected that the Native empire he had built—an empire that intersected with and crossed over parts of the Mexican, Mormon, and American empires—would remain after him. Yet Wakara believed that he needed his brother in the gospel and fellow "big chief" Brigham Young to help him shore up that future.

So, when Wakara and Lewis met on the Mormon Road between Meadow and Fillmore, he asked the missionary if Young "talked good" about him—that is, if Young saw Wakara as a partner in these empire-building projects. Rest assured, Lewis told Wakara: Young "talked very good [about you]." In fact, as Wakara had requested, Young had given Lewis permission to go with him to the Navajos. Lewis told Wakara that he carried with him another letter from Young to that effect. Wakara was relieved. But he was too weak to hear any more specifics. Wakara told Lewis to come to his camp tomorrow and they'd make their plans. Wakara and his men then turned their horses around and rode back to camp at Corn Creek, while Lewis rode north to Fillmore.[12]

But Lewis and Wakara never met again. Wakara died the next day, January 29, 1855. Soon after the medicine man stepped out of Wakara's tent, Ute riders were dispatched to the Mormons at Fillmore. Wakara was dead, the riders told Lewis. Lewis penned a letter to Young to share the news, then sent his own rider to Salt Lake. Lewis wrote that the cause of death was "a cold settled on his lungs," what today we might call pneumonia.[13]

Riders were also sent to the Utes spread throughout their homelands. Since it was winter, they were scattered in what they called Lower Earth—the warmer and lower-lying valleys and canyon bottoms of central and southern Utah. But before the end of the day, scores of mourners, including Kanosh, as well as non-Indian onlookers, descended on Wakara's camp in the shadows of the snowcapped Pahvant Mountains.[14]

As they congregated, Wakara's Utes prepared an extravagant send-off for their fallen leader. Before assisting Wakara on his final horseback ride up the mountain to a large stone sepulcher—the "Hawk of the Mountain" would be buried in the rocky ridges and peaks of Upper Earth—they gathered his possessions that would join him in his tomb. Some were symbols of his Ute life: bows and arrows, hunting and fishing traps. Others were symbols of his career as one of the West's most proficient horsemen, traders, and statesmen: ornate horse tack, metal cutlery, copper bracelets, Spanish beads, and a pocket pistol.

WAKARA'S FUNERAL WAS ELABORATE. IT WAS ALSO DEADLY. Ute customs mandated company for a legendary leader as he passed into the spirit land. Arapeen, Wakara's brother and heir to the leadership of the Utes, slashed the throats of two of Wakara's child slaves (no more than four years old) and two of Wakara's women, one of whom, it was reported soon after, "was in a delicate condition." Other women wrapped Wakara in his favorite blanket and wrapped the sacrificed women and children in robes. The bodies were then carried by horseback up a canyon to what Natives would soon call "Walker's Mountain," the women singing the death dirge that echoed in the canyon below.[15]

After climbing through switchbacks that weaved through mountain forests, they reached Wakara's crypt. To construct it, Wakara's followers had unearthed sandstone slabs ranging in size from watermelons to bison calves and buttressed the walls with pine logs. The result was a tomb eleven feet wide and eight feet long—big enough, remarked one visitor to the grave, to be "the last resting place of an elephant." The Utes laid Wakara and his death party on animal skins, covered them with saplings, and provisioned them with dried fish—the defining food staple of Wakara's Timpanogos Band—and hunting weapons. A dozen of the leader's horses were also slaughtered, then placed in a circle around the tomb. Other gifts, including a peace letter from Brigham Young, were laid on top of Wakara's body. The final step was to select a living slave whose task would be to distract scavenging animals. This unhappy duty fell to a teenager who was buried alive up to his neck. During the day, crows and insects picked at his face. At night, dogs, foxes, and wolves snacked on him. The boy died of thirst and exposure a few days later.[16]

In early February 1855, Wakara's death made headlines in Utah's lone newspaper, the *Deseret News*. The next month, in Los Angeles, *The Star* and *The Southern Californian* printed detailed reports of Wakara's demise. At the same time, telegraph operators on the West Coast tapped out "Walker, the famous Utah chief, died near Fillmore city on the 29th January." The message then sped east along copper wires, so that by May papers from Pittsburgh to Baltimore, from Yorkville, South Carolina, to Swanton, Vermont, had printed Wakara's death announcement. Newspaper readers around the country understood the significance of the message. For the previous decade, press coverage of Wakara's exploits had made the Ute leader a national fixture in the drama of mapping and colonizing the West. As more details reached cities across the country, other reports speculated that Wakara's end was so abrupt that perhaps it had been hastened by poison.[17]

During his life, Native and settler Americans alike viewed Wakara as a living legend to be feared and admired. But how they remembered Wakara after his death could not be more different.

For Wakara's Utes, their leader's elaborate death ceremony marked passage to the spirit world where he would live on as an ancestor for eternity. And his burial on Walker's Mountain helped stake his people's claim to their homeland. Settler Americans, however, were titillated by the ceremony's brutality. To them—especially those who would write the story of the creation of the American West—Wakara's burial marked the beginning of a time when his legendary life would be remembered too little and his scandalous death and burial would be remembered too much.

Chapter 2

A Pilgrimage into the Wilderness

In 1990, I was ten years old when I first crossed the American West that Wakara helped create. It was the middle of a hot Utah summer. I sat in the backseat of an ancient Ford Bronco, squished between my cousin Ben, who was two years older, and an overstuffed box of camping supplies. My stepmother drove while my father navigated. He also handed out carrots—green stems and all—when the passengers grew hungry and bored. We had no air-conditioning. My father occasionally lowered the hand-cranked windows to let in dry desert air. A few minutes later, he raised the windows when the whip of the wind or the smell of burning brakes from a passing eighteen-wheeler became unbearable.

It was the start of a two-week pilgrimage to some of America's most sacred spaces, the national parks in southern Utah. We sped along the region's main highway, Interstate 15, and joined the long line of adventure-seeking pilgrims packed into similarly overstuffed cars. We also merged with an even older history of seasonal migration. I-15 is built atop an ancient north-south thoroughfare traveled by ancient wild horses and long-extinct Ice Age mammals like mammoths; by the longtime Indigenous stewards of these lands, the Shoshones, Paiutes, Goshutes, and Utes; and by the Spanish, French, Mexicans, and Americans who attempted to map empires of trade in furs, horses, cattle, and captive Indians onto this hotly contested territory.

As our modern caravans made their way south, cars crammed onto smaller highways, often leading to mile-long traffic jams. In recent years, some residents of Moab, Utah, have come to call this late-spring arrival of tourists "ant season." The vehicles backed up bumper to bumper at the entrance to Arches National Park—with waits as long as two hours to get in—resemble ants lined up, antennae to abdomen, marching to a food source.

Once in the parks, as is the case for all pilgrims, our time was marked by rituals. Ours were set by the course of the sun across the sky. We began the day in the cool, predawn hours. We wiggled out of our sleeping bags and shivered as we pulled scratchy sweaters over our heads. Ben and I whined about our growling stomachs.

"When we get back, first pancake for the camper who puts on their boots the fastest," my father whispered so as not to disturb still-sleeping campers nearby.

Breakfast could wait, but daylight would not. The day's first ritual was a forced march. My father insisted that we witness the sun break over the horizon to expose the gravity-defying Hoodoos in Bryce Canyon, the awe-inspiring arches in Moab, the majestic domes of Cathedral Valley in Capitol Reef. In the heat of the day, when the temperature soared above 100 degrees Fahrenheit, we retreated to our campsite, where we hid from the sun underneath a blue tarp strung between spindly Utah junipers. When we grew bored of card games, my cousin and I scampered over nearby sandstone cliffs. The lizards, our unwilling playmates, dropped their tails to avoid our grasp.

Dusk brought relief from the heat as the setting sun turned the sky from orange to blue-black. At supper time, we clutched our dinner bowls and lined up, like communicants, before a pot of steaming beef Stroganoff cooked over a tiny camping stove. The tents remained unpitched. At bedtime, blankets of stars served as our ceiling as we dozed off in our sleeping bags. More than once, the day's final ritual was our screaming with pain. Ants, attracted to our bodies' warmth, lined up to make feasts of our skin.

MY FAMILY REENACTED AMERICA'S FOUNDING MYTH IN OUR journeys to Utah's national parks. We imitated America's first pilgrims, who, in their own caravans of tall ships instead of SUVs, sought sanctuary in nature from the fallen world of men. According to the early-seventeenth-century Puritans, the Fall then manifested in an England "filled with the fury of malignant adversaries" against Christ's true followers, explained Edward Johnson in *Wonder-Working Providence of Sions Saviour in New England* (1654), the first published history of New England.[1]

In the 1630s, my eleventh-great maternal grandfather, Deacon Edward Converse (Convers), joined Johnson and other members of John Winthrop's vanguard fleet of Puritans in founding a series of towns along and near the coast. On the lands of the Massachusett, Pawtucket, and Agawam peoples, Converse built the first house and the first mill in Woburn, today a leafy suburb ten miles north of Boston. A half century later, his grandson and my ninth-great-grandfather, Captain James Converse, led search-and-destroy missions against the Penobscots during New England's Second Indian War. The Converse family's substantial landholdings and wealth in early America came from the stolen lands and the spilt blood of Native Americans.

In 1630, my Puritan ancestors' pilgrimage into the "wild-woody" New World—an unmapped territory of "lions, wolves, bears, foxes," wrote Johnson, "a place that never afforded the Natives better than the flesh of a few wild creatures and parch't Indian corn"—was supposed to be temporary. The Puritans' divine mandate was to build a new

Jerusalem in which the body of Christ and the body politic would be joined together. Once built, the Puritans would bring this model society home to England, which would lead to the "downfall of the Antichrist, and restauration of that ancient people of the Lord."[2]

Yet, within a generation, Old England proved too fallen to be redeemed. Still, through God's providence, the "barren desert" had "become a second England." This New England even surpassed Old England in "fertileness" and in English tidiness. "The Lord hath been pleased to turn all the wigwams, huts, and hovels the English dwelt in at their first coming" to the New World, Johnson wrote, "into orderly, fair, and well-built houses . . . with orchards filled with goodly fruit trees, and gardens with variety of flowers."[3]

Three hundred and fifty years later, according to the weekly sermons at my childhood family's nondenominational Bible church, the Fall then manifested as an America filled with godless feminists, Democrats, divorce lawyers, and abortionists. Cribbing from Hal Lindsay's *The Late Great Planet Earth* (1970), our pastors assured us that the truly faithful would be raptured up at any moment. In the waning days of the Cold War, the apocalypse that followed the Rapture might announce itself as a nuclear mushroom cloud rather than trumpet blasts from heaven.

The national parks served as our sacred canopies. God's favorite (geological) creations in God's favored but fallen nation shielded the godly from the profanity of modern America—a country, my parents taught us, that had become hell-bent on persecuting Christians out of existence. After a few weeks of hiking, playing, and praying, we would reemerge: our bodies sunburnt and dust-covered, our souls cleansed and fortified to fight the Antichrist and his minions. Camping doubled as survival training. I learned how to pack a "bugout bag," pitch a tent, find water, and forage for food in the most desolate of environs. If, God forbid, I was left behind, these survival skills would come in handy when the Rapture or nuclear war arrived.

We saw our summer retreats in America's national parks as sacred time, during which we strengthened ourselves for the battles we would face during ordinary time spent in anti-Christian places. And we were taught that few places were more anti-Christian than public schools, especially since the early 1960s, when school-sponsored prayer had been removed by Supreme Court mandate. And yet, public school curricula and calendars—then as now—mandate that students learn how God's blessings shined on America's past.

In public schools most Americans are taught that Manifest Destiny is the first article of faith of the American gospel. The "doctrine of discovery"—a theology made canon law by Catholic popes in Rome in the 1500s and instantiated into American jurisprudence by the Supreme Court in Washington, DC, in the 1800s—gave Europeans, and later Americans, the rights of ownership over lands that Native Americans merely occupied. The doctrine holds that God had blessed settlers, like my ancestors, with superior tools of civilization—namely, guns and grains, Christianity and capitalism, and the printing press. In public schools, a liturgy of holidays venerate Columbus as the founding father of American explorers and the Pilgrims as latter-day Israelites fleeing the pharaohs in England. The Wampanoag, if they are remembered at all, were the friendly Indian guests at America's first Thanksgiving feast. Social studies lessons teach students to celebrate explorers like Meriwether Lewis and William Clark for bravely mapping the wilds west of the Mississippi River and to explain away the 1830s Cherokee Trail of Tears and the 1890 slaughter of 300 Lakota men, women, and children at Wounded Knee as tragic but inevitable events in westward expansion.[4]

These lessons about the inevitable demise of Native Americans during the school year continue in the national parks to which Americans and visitors from around the world flock during the summer. National parks further the belief that American lands in their natural, pristine state were free from human occupation. The forethought to preserve the most beautiful of these American spaces was a uniquely American phenomenon, a manifestation of John Muir's nature-based spiritual poetry and Theodore Roosevelt's nature-based democratic populism. The first national parks also served to erase Native American history, and even Natives' very presence, from American lands, especially in the American West. President Ulysses S. Grant signed into law the Yellowstone Act of 1872, which established the nation's first land area to be "reserved and withdrawn from settlement occupancy and sale . . . and dedicated and set apart as a public park or pleasure-ground for the benefit and enjoyment of the people." By "the people," David Treuer (Ojibwe) has noted, Grant meant settler Americans. "Grant's declaration made trespassers of the Shoshone, Bannock, and other peoples who called the parkland home for centuries."[5]

As the nineteenth century ended, it seemed that westward expansion would mean both the West's wild landscape and its original human inhabitants were destined to vanish. American politicians like Grant and Roosevelt established America's national parks to save the American wild they loved and to corral and kill the Indians they loathed. In a speech in New York City in 1886, Roosevelt, then a cattle rancher in the Badlands of the Dakota Territory, declared, "I don't go so far as to think that the only good Indians are the dead Indians, but I believe nine out of every ten are, and I shouldn't like to inquire too closely into the case of the tenth." As president between 1901 and 1909, Roosevelt signed legislation to establish five new national parks and created tens of millions of acres of national forest reserves. In 1916, with the Mormon Reed Smoot serving as the bill's sponsor in the Senate, President Woodrow Wilson signed a law that formally established the US National Park Service, with a mandate to control and eventually remove Native Americans living within and around the boundaries of these parks. The result is that the vast majority of the "natural" parks—the parks that are not battlefields, presidential homes, and famous buildings and monuments in Washington, DC—have deep ties to Native Americans' ancestral lands or the lands set aside for their occupancy as part of the reservation movement.[6]

IN UTAH, THE FIVE NATIONAL PARKS—ARCHES, ZION, Capitol Reef, Canyon Lands, and Bryce Canyon—were carved out of Ute, Paiute, Navajo, and Pueblo homelands. For at least half a millennium, the lands in and around what would become my family's favorite park, Arches, were home to the Seuvarits Band of Utes. The Seuvarits were known as the Water People due to the Colorado River, which passes through their homelands in present-day Moab, Utah. That area was also a vital stop along what was the "Ute Trail" before it was renamed the Old Spanish Trail. Ute kin, including Wakara, as well as Navajos, watered and fed their horses as they made their seasonal treks along what was the Southwest's most important trade route, long before the settlers arrived.

At our campground in Arches in 1990, my family fell asleep watching the stars make their nighttime journey across the sky. In the last few decades, Ute delegations have made their own pilgrimage to the park—an act of rematriation of Ute people and Ute histories to this sacred land from which they had been exiled by US law and culture. During one recent visit home, a Ute elder explained that centuries before, while most of the Utes' slept, specially trained "observers" stayed awake to watch the night sky. These observers traced the moon, stars, and planets to gather seasonal information about where and when the people should make their plans to harvest rice grass, hunt game, and catch fish. That the arches and natural bridges rose high off the desert floor also made them a preferred final resting place for the Utes' deceased. "When our people passed away they just put them where the wild animals could not get them," one Ute elder said. Another Ute elder explained that the region was not only a gateway to the Southwest. The arches served as "portals" through which "time travelers" passed to journey to other times. When they came back, they brought with them visions of what they had seen, including "predictions of the white man coming."[7]

White settlers did come, replacing Native presence and histories on the land. First, they arrived as a trickle in the 1830s in the form of fur trappers and mountain men. Starting in the 1840s, they came as a steady stream of Mormons seeking refuge from religious persecution. In the last decades of the nineteenth century, they came as a torrent in the form of miners, ranchers, and eventually tourists. Throughout Utah, northern Arizona, and New Mexico, these floods of settlers forced the Utes, Paiutes, and Diné onto the reservations established in the 1860s. Because of its relatively isolated location, the Seuvarits' homeland in and around what would become Arches became a refuge for Utah Natives who resisted removal. Between 1865 and 1872, the Seuvarits joined Wakara's Timpanogos kin Antonga (Black Hawk, as the settlers called him), as well as Diné, Apache, and Paiute fighters, in the so-called Black Hawk War. For five years, Antonga attacked Utah settlements that had sprawled into Native homelands, forcing the Mormons to seek shelter in strongholds. Antonga died in 1870 from a gunshot wound received years earlier that never healed. Two years later, federal troops slaughtered dozens of Utes, forcing the survivors onto reservations in Utah and Colorado. A half century later, Paiute leader William Posey (Sagwageri) led another group of Utes and Paiutes who resisted further settler incursion into their homelands. Posey and his "Bronco Indians," who practiced traditional seasonal hunting methods, were in constant conflict with local stockmen and their herds. In March 1923, when Posey tried to negotiate with a posse that had chased down some of his followers for allegedly stealing sheep, the posse shot Posey dead. They then rounded up more than eighty Utes and Paiutes and interned them in an open-air stockade where local settlers came to gawk at the captives. They were freed only after a US marshal found Posey's body, buried it, and proclaimed the "war" over. Like Wakara, Posey did not stay buried long. Local settlers dug his body up, then posed for pictures with Posey's remains.[8]

Hunting for the graves of dead Native leaders was already a settler pastime in Utah. Just a few years before, a Mormon miner, William Croff, had dug up the remains of Antonga (Black Hawk). To memorialize his find, Croff stood over the grave, smiling for a camera as he cradled Antonga's skull in his hands. On its front page, the September 20, 1919, evening edition of the *Deseret News* reprinted Croff's trophy picture as part of a report announcing that the History Museum of the Church of Jesus Christ of Latter-day Saints, located just outside Temple Square, had opened an exhibit displaying "the Bones of Black Hawk" and sundry funerary items that had also been buried with him.[9]

Forcing Utah Natives off their lands and onto reservations, killing those who refused, and digging up the remains of Native resistance leaders for sport were all means of removing Native Americans' presence and history from the West. So was the expansion of national parks and monuments. In 1929, almost exactly three centuries after my Puritan ancestors declared the New World ripe for colonization, Herbert Hoover issued a presidential proclamation that established Arches as a national monument. The purpose was to protect the area's unique array of arches, natural bridges, and spires of rocks in order to ensure that Americans could visit these natural, national treasures for centuries to come. And yet, these places were not naturally free of human presence. Native Americans—like the Seuvarits Band of Utes and Posey's band of "Bronco Indians," who had called Arches home for generations—had to be removed before the West's national parks could become "natural."[10]

Apparently, building roads, campsites, and museums to make parks more accessible doesn't detract from their naturalness. Arches receives more than 1.5 million annual visitors. A conservative estimate would suggest that at least a million of them drive the graded, paved park roads, then walk along a carefully sloped trail to Delicate Arch, the crown jewel of the arches—so synonymous with Utah that it is embossed on the state's license plates. Not unlike the scrum in the Louvre to get a peek at the *Mona Lisa*, thousands of nighttime visitors to Delicate Arch jockey for position to get their Instagram shot. Far fewer follow the small trail just off the arch's parking lot to visit the "Ute Panel."

Delicate Arch, Arches National Park, Moab, Utah. Summer crowds at sunset await their turn to take photos under the iconic arch. For Utes, the arches were sacred burial grounds and portals to other worlds and times. As such, contemporary Utes discourage climbing on and around the arches. (Courtesy of NPS/Marty Tow)

The immaculately preserved wall of petroglyphs depicts Utes on horseback hunting bighorn sheep. Archaeologists date the petroglyphs to between 1650 and 1850; the main clue for this date is the presence of horses. The Utes were among the first Native Americans

The Ute Panel, Arches National Park, Moab, Utah. (Courtesy of NPS/Marty Tow)

to adopt the horse after the Spanish reintroduced horses to the Americas in the 1500s. The Park Service funnels visitors to Arches' natural wonders. Arches' Native human presence, embodied by the Ute petroglyphs, is a footnote.

Likewise, when my family visited the park in 1990, rangers warned us to stay on the well-manicured paths (the rangers paid particular attention to me and my cousin; preteen boys are prone to wander off-trail). Even one misstep, we were told, could destroy the natural history embodied in the "cryptobiotic crust," the black, lumpy soil that covers much of the park's desert floor, which takes decades to form. Made up of an ecosystem of mosses, fungi, and blue-green algae, the crust stores vital moisture and serves as a seedbed for larger plants. Today, signs throughout the park explain to visitors the importance of the crust to the natural life cycle of the land.

There are far fewer signs informing visitors of the human history of the region, almost nothing that describes how the Utes and other Utah Native peoples once farmed the lands in and around Arches, irrigating it with water from the Colorado River, to raise corn, squash, and beans. There are no signs explaining that walking in and around the arch does damage to the Utes' sacred portals and their ancestors' burial grounds. "That is why we do not just rush out there and start climbing all over [the arches]," explained a Ute elder during a recent visit to the park, "because we do not want to disturb them [the ancestors] and upset their spirit."[11]

WHEN WE FIRST VISITED THE AREA, ARCHES NATIONAL Park wasn't isolated enough for my parents. My father had heard about a more secluded arch outside the park. One morning, we packed ourselves into the Bronco and followed US 191 south from Moab.

A half hour later, we turned onto a dirt road. After a short, bumpy ride, we parked in the shade of another spindly juniper. The four of us scrambled up steep sandstone to reach Looking Glass Arch. I don't recall if my father took the picture using a timer or if Ben or I snapped the photo. Nevertheless, in the photo my father stands in the main arch, soaring thirty feet above his head. My stepmother scampers up to sit inside the smaller arch to the left.

I know now that, as we climbed hand over foot to get ourselves ready for the photograph, we did not know we were trespassing. Perhaps not in a legal sense. The arch sits on land controlled by the Bureau of Land Management and thus is open to the public. But we were certainly trespassing in a spiritual and historical sense. Like its more famous cousins in the park, Delicate Arch likely served as a Ute burial ground. Since it sits a few hundred feet west of the Old Spanish Trail, Wakara himself certainly passed by the arch on his way to the Ute Crossing twenty-five miles north in present-day Moab. There he rested and watered his horses. And there he visited and traded with his Seuvarits Ute kin.

Looking Glass Arch, South of Moab, Utah (1990). In the 1830s and 1840s, Wakara regularly passed a few hundred yards to the east of the arch during his seasonal raiding and trading journeys on the Old Spanish Trail. (Photo courtesy of Charles Mueller)

We got what we came for. A photograph for our scrapbook. Today, the memento sparks memories of that first time I visited Arches—a period I recall with wonder at the natural beauty (and unbearable heat) and fear about the impending apocalypse.

We did not know it then, but for Wakara's Ute kin who had long called what is today Arches home—and for Wakara, who had long viewed the place as an oasis on his long journeys across the desert—the apocalypse had already come. That apocalypse was us.

Chapter 3

Pioneer Days

Just before dawn on July 24, 1849, nine cannon blasts roused the Latter-day Saints from their beds and called them to gather in what is today Salt Lake City's Temple Square, the religious center of their new kingdom in the Intermountain West. Some rode in wagons, others on horseback. But most walked to the thatched-roof Bowery in Temple Square.[1]

Exactly two years before, Brigham Young's Vanguard Company had first entered the Salt Lake Valley. Rising from his sickbed in the back of a wagon on that day, Young famously (and likely apocryphally) declared that Utah "is a good place" that the Lord had set aside "to make Saints."[2]

The Mormons' flight west occurred 200 years after the Puritans' Great Migration to the New World and 150 years before my family reenacted that flight into the wilderness with our visit to Utah's national parks. To celebrate the first of what would become Utah's annual Pioneer Day, on July 24, 1849, the latter-day pilgrims sang hymns and offered prayers of thanksgiving. They recited poems. And they gave lots of speeches. "We had to leave the United States,"

Brigham Young (1801–1877). Daguerreotype (ca. 1852–1853). (Courtesy of the Church Archives, the Church of Jesus Christ of Latter-day Saints)

Brigham Young proclaimed during his address to several thousand fellow Mormons. Young explained that their fellow Americans had forced the Mormons into exile because they dared to do the most American thing possible: confess their faith. They believed "that Joseph Smith was a prophet," declared Young, Smith's successor, "and that the Book of Mormon was true." Yet, with Young serving as the Mormon Moses, the Latter-day Saints turned exile into exodus. Young told his followers that it was providence that had led them out of the land of "pure mobocracy" to the "howling wilderness" of the Salt Lake Valley.

According to Young and other church leaders who spoke that day, just as the Puritans had done in New England, the Mormons quickly made "the barren waste" that they first encountered into a homeland fit for Heavenly Father's chosen people and Christ's imminent return. With God's grace shining upon them, the Saints worked like bees in a hive. As the First Presidency, the church's highest governing body, declared in its 1849 Pioneer Day announcement, the Saints left "the mark of their industry, enterprise, their perseverance and indomitable courage" on the land that they named "Deseret," which means "honeybee" according to the Book of Mormon. "Now the 'desert blossoms like the rose.'"[3]

The time frame of this transformation—two years, not twenty—signified that the Saints had outdone their Puritan predecessors. The fruits of these labors meant that the thousands assembled at the Bowery could feast on "an abundance, and plenty." So big was the bounty that the Saints offered "gracious hospitality to hundreds of strangers."[4]

"THE NOBLE WALKER" WAS ONE OF THESE STRANGERS, recalled one chronicler of Early Mormon Utah. Wakara attended that first Pioneer Day, accompanied by "two hundred of his best dressed and mounted cavaliers, who stacked their guns, and took their places at the ceremonies." The Saints hoped to turn these Indian strangers into kin.[5]

The Book of Mormon taught that American Indians descended from an ancient Israelite family who had fled six centuries before Christ's birth to the wilds of America to escape religious persecution before Jerusalem fell to the Babylonians. But over the centuries, these Israelites had warred with each other. The victors of these interfamily wars became the "Lamanites," a "dark, filthy, and loathsome people," the ancestors of American Indians. Their dark skin served as a divine reminder that they had rejected the faith of their forefathers and embraced Indian bloodlust savagery. Yet all hope was not lost; the Book of Mormon prophesied that, in the last days of history, Christ's true servants would bring forth a long-lost gospel. An unspoiled, pure Christian church, led by a new prophet, would restore this gospel to America's Indians, who would then remember their true, Israelite identities. Their change of heart would lead to a change in skin color;

they would become, as the Book of Mormon declares, "a white and delightsome people" like their White Mormon brethren.[6]

In the first years of Mormon Utah, the Latter-day Saints believed that they had met the Indians whom they would make White and delightsome. These few but promising Natives showed their potential for redemption by supporting Mormon settlements and thus the prophesied Mormon version of Manifest Destiny, which foresaw the creation of a New World Jerusalem in the heart of America.

Chief among these supporters was Wakara. "[I] never killed a white man," the Ute leader told Brigham Young when they first met on June 14, 1849, at the Council House at Temple Square. Young and the other Mormon leaders in attendance might have raised an eyebrow at this claim. Long before they reached Utah, in newspapers and published journals of western explorers, the Mormons had read about Wakara's violent trade in humans and horses and his armed control of the Old Spanish Trail. But when they met him in the flesh, Wakara disarmed the Saints with words of friendship. While they passed the peace pipe, the Ute leader explained that he and the Mormons were a lot alike. Both wanted to expand their empires, ambitions that placed the Utes and the Mormons at odds with other Native nations and belligerent non-Mormon settlers seeking to stake their claim to lands of the American West. To demonstrate his goodwill, Wakara invited the Saints to build settlements in what Wakara claimed were his lands in what would soon be called the Sanpete Valley. This thrilled the Saints. In exchange, Young promised Wakara that the new settlers would help him and his men learn White ways of farming and ranching, and Mormon women would teach Ute women how to cook in a civilized fashion. Young also promised Wakara that they'd teach Ute youths how to read the Book of Mormon so Wakara and his Utes would know about their Lamanite and Israelite forefathers. Wakara seemed to agree to these changes that the Mormons brought to him and his people.[7]

Young hated killing Indians. Or at least he claimed to. When he did kill them, Young told Wakara at their first meeting in June 1849, it was because "they dared us to do it." Wakara understood. In fact, just a few months later, following the Fort Utah Massacre in February 1850 when Mormon militias killed several dozen Timpanogos Utes, Wakara told the Saints that he approved. They didn't know that Wakara viewed Old Elk, the leader of the massacred Utes, as a personal enemy, who had killed Wakara's father in a succession dispute. With Wakara's friendship in mind, but also with Mormon minutemen at the ready to "exterminate" those who might threaten their settlements, Young developed the policy: cheaper to feed the Indians than fight them.[8]

Just ten days after he first met Wakara, Young put into practice this philosophy of meals first, minutemen second. At that first Pioneer Day celebration, the Saints fed Wakara and his followers, hoping that breaking bread with the Mormons might convince Wakara to join the Mormons in faith. Thomas Bullock, Young's clerk who recorded the minutes for that day's events, drew parallels between this inaugural Pioneer Day in Salt Lake City and the first Thanksgiving meal at Plymouth in 1621. Such a "feast of the body, coupled with a feast of the soul, has not been experienced on this continent for a length of time."[9]

The first Pioneer Day feted not just the fact that the Latter-day Saints in Utah had finally found the religious freedom they had long sought. Coming days after Wakara and Young had agreed that in the fall Wakara would himself pilot settlers to the choicest lands in the Sanpete Valley, it was also a meal to commemorate that the long-prophesied covenant between Mormons and Lamanites was coming to pass. The Mormons could assimilate rather than exterminate some of Utah's Natives. In the case of Wakara, they saw a Book of Mormon prophecy of the Lamanites' racial redemption come to pass before their eyes, with a literal change of skin color. James Case, an early Sanpete Valley settler, reported that, following Wakara's baptism in Manti's City Creek in 1850, "bro[ther] Walker . . . was as White as me."[10]

Young publicly celebrated Wakara's baptism. The hour of the Lamanite was finally at hand. Privately, however, Young behaved as though he believed that Wakara's whitening was only skin deep and that Wakara would soon return to his "Indian" ways. But it was Young who proved two-faced. After Wakara and 126 other Utes were baptized at Manti, Young told his faithful to keep the converts at arm's length. He forbade them from selling guns and ammunition to the Utes, fearing that Wakara would take up arms against his new brethren once he learned that the Mormons planned on taking over more Ute territory and taking over Wakara's slave trade. While he promised Wakara that he'd never seize his lands, Young began petitioning the federal government for the authority, funds, and military support to remove the Utes from the Utah Territory, even though it was territory upon which the Mormons were the squatters. After Washington refused to send assistance, Young realized that the Mormons would have to do the removing themselves. To that end, he foresaw that Wakara would be the most formidable obstacle. The prophet would prove to be right.

Wakara and hundreds of his followers might have been present at the first Pioneer Day in 1849. But since Wakara's death in 1855, July 24 stands as an annual ritual of forgetting Wakara's influence on the American West, especially the colonization of the Great Basin. It is also a ritual of forgetting that land's fecundity—the fish, fowl, roots, and berries of Native Utah—that sustained Wakara's Utes for centuries and saved early Mormon settlers from starvation and death.

At a Pioneer Day celebration in 1890 at Cottonwood, just a few miles south of Temple Square, lawyer and advocate for Utah statehood Franklin S. Richards declared that before the Mormons' arrival, Utah was a lifeless, formless tabula rasa. "Forty-three years ago today, this beautiful valley, which now teems with fertility and life, was a scene of utter desolation," Richards explained before a crowd of several hundred. "No sign of human life, except the Indian savage, was to be found in all the dreary waste extending hundreds of miles in every direction."[11]

Richards's 1890 description of pre-Mormon Utah as empty of meaningful life was false. The Mormons were drawn to Utah because of the abundance of fresh water, grasslands, and game. They were also pulled west by the large populations of Paiutes, Navajos, Goshutes, and Utes whom they hoped to convert. What's more, in July 1847, when the Mormons first arrived in Utah, they were at their weakest. The murder of their founding prophet and the first revelations of the practice of polygamy had caused a nasty succession crisis. The Latter-day Saints were fractured and eventually homeless, forced to flee from persecutors, some of whom declared that the Mormons themselves should be exterminated. In contrast, in the summer of 1847, Wakara was perhaps at his strongest. His horse-raiding and slave-trading exploits and his cavalry's dominance over the Old Spanish Trail had made him a living legend.

As such, when they first set eyes upon the Great Salt Lake Valley, the Mormons knew more about Wakara than Wakara knew about them. In fact, Wakara's reputation likely affected the location of the Mormons' first settlement in the Great Basin. When they met Jim Bridger in late June 1847 at the Sandy River Crossing in southwestern Wyoming, the famed mountain man dissuaded Young from his plans to make the resource-rich Utah Valley (see map on page 104) the center of their mountain kingdom. The area around Timpanogos (Utah) Lake was the homeland of Wakara's powerful and well-armed Utes. Bridger warned, "If they catch a man alone they are sure to rob and abuse him, if they don't kill him."[12]

Young heeded Bridger's advice. He decided against settling on the Utes' land until the settlers could get to know them better. Instead, the Saints settled in the less-populated Salt Lake Valley, a region between the Ute and Shoshone homelands. Wakara, it seems, just as much as God, had influenced Young's decision about where to drive the center stake of Zion into the ground.[13]

Franklin Richards's 1890 description of pre-Mormon Utah as free of meaningful human life was also ironic. Richards's own family knew Wakara well. In June 1849, Franklin's great-uncle, longtime apostle Willard Richards, joined Young in his first meeting with Wakara when the Ute leader agreed to support Mormon settlement on Ute lands, pledges for which the Mormons paid in promises of trade in horses, beef, bullets, and broadcloth suits. On June 20, 1849, Franklin S. Richards was born in Salt Lake City to Mormon apostle Franklin D. Richards and the first of his eleven wives, Jane. A month later, the newborn Franklin almost certainly attended the first Pioneer Day. Under the thatched brush canopy of the Bowery, baby Franklin fussed and slept in his mother's arms as his father joined other leading members of the church to fete Wakara as a partner in the building of Zion. By Pioneer Day 1855, the bountiful fish at Timpanogos (Utah) Lake, which had sustained Wakara's Timpanogos for generations, saved the exploding number of settlers from starvation, when an unprecedented drought decimated Mormon crops. The crop failure was so severe that farmers became fishermen. They squatted along what had been the Timpanogos River but was rechristened the Provo River, dragging nets to catch fish by the barrelful. The fish were then preserved in salt and distributed to feed the settlements up and down the Wasatch Front. Were it not for Wakara's fisheries, which his band had carefully managed for hundreds of years and which the Mormons would decimate within two generations, Zion would have starved to death.[14]

By Pioneer Day 1890, Franklin S. Richards claimed to know none of this. In particular, he knew nothing of Wakara, who, like his father and great-uncle, was a founding father of Utah. He did not even know that he had shared a meal as an infant with Wakara in the Bowery on July 24, 1849. By the time Franklin S. Richards gave his 1890 Pioneer Day speech, Wakara had been all but erased not only from the memory of the first Pioneer Day but from most of Utah history.[15]

CHAPTER 4

Fillmore

IN THE 1840S AND 1850s, Wakara's horse-raiding and slave-trading empire, his encounters with famed expedition leaders, and his partnerships and battles with the Mormons for control over the Great Basin made him among the most powerful and feared men in the Southwest.

But what happened to Wakara's empire after he died? Did it really crumble as soon as the last boulder was rolled over his mountainside tomb? Even if it did, why hasn't history remembered Wakara as the legendary figure that newspapers from coast to coast described him as while he was alive?

Finding answers to these questions, I believed, would more than just help Americans better understand the vital role that Wakara played in the formation of the American Southwest. Unearthing what remains of Wakara's America would also, I hoped, trouble the long-standing line between Native and settler American, colonized and colonizer in American history writ large.

To excavate this history, in the summer of 2022 I returned to Utah with my own children and spouse for another pilgrimage to

Utah's national parks. I wanted to share with them the grandeur of my childhood experiences of hot days and cold nights in the deserts, of chasing lizards around our campsites (our two school-aged girls were not permitted to catch them), and of chasing ants away from our sleeping bags.

The 2022 visit was not my first return to Utah. During the previous decade, I had made dozens of trips, retracing the path that Wakara blazed across the Southwest. Working with Ute, Paiute, and Shoshone mentors and friends who are themselves keepers of sacred histories, I found evidence that, in fact, much of the American West that Wakara helped build remained present after his death. Wakara's America includes the fish and fishing waters that his Timpanogos Band relied on to fill their bodies and souls. It includes the horses that Wakara's cavalry used to dominate vast territories. And it encompasses the enslaved people whom Wakara captured and those people's living descendants (some of whom were also Wakara's kin). To this day, Wakara's America remains shaped by the battlefields and massacre sites where the Mormons waged war against Wakara and other Utah Natives and where Wakara's Utes defended their lands and way of life. Wakara's America also extends to Washington, DC, where his physical remains, and those of the six other people who were killed to be buried alongside him, have been stored for the last 150 years. Though the fish, horses, and people, as well as the histories of Wakara's America, have been in diaspora, separated from their homelands, in fits and starts, they are also coming home.

In 2022, I wanted to see what remains of Wakara are visible in Fillmore. After all, Fillmore was a place that, along with other Mormon settlements, Wakara helped shape into being in its earliest days. And Fillmore is where, at least superficially, Wakara's Native empire seemed to end, and end abruptly, with his death in January 1855.

ON AN UNSEASONABLY CHILLY MORNING IN JUNE, WE piled our girls into our well-worn Mazda for the 145-mile drive south on I-15 from Salt Lake City, where my family was based for the summer while I conducted research. As we began the journey to Fillmore, out of the driver's side window, we watched the towering Wasatch Front rise from the Salt Lake Valley floor. In their height and cragginess, the Wasatch Mountains compare favorably to my native Casper Mountain in eastern Wyoming.

Deep canyons cut into the Wasatch massifs. Around the mountain bends, we tried to catch glimpses of Utah's famed ski areas. During the summer, the runs shed their winter white and turn bright green. But the ski areas were too far up the canyons to see them from the highway. Still, in early June, many of the summits of the mountains that we passed—Lone Peak, Pfeifferhorn, and, a few miles north of Provo, Mount Timpanogos and "Squaw Peak," as it was still named then—remained snowcapped.

Over the last decade, even more than the mountains, what increasingly catches the eyes of voyagers on this stretch of I-15 are massive glass-and-steel edifices. Affixed with the logos of household names like Adobe and Oracle, these enormous buildings cast their own shadows over the highway as it passes through Utah Valley. The orogeny of tech companies began with the arrival of personal-computing pioneers like WordPerfect and Novell in the late 1970s. But it really took off with the post–Great Recession tech boom in the early 2010s. With promises of tax incentives, Utah politicians lured eBay and Intel to build customer service and research centers in what became known as the "Silicon Slopes." The result is that Utah Valley looks more like the West Coast than the Wild West, a suburbanite's utopia of corporate campuses, tract homes, box stores, and chain restaurants. But clear markers on the land indicate to drivers that they are passing through the center of the Mormon empire, not Northern California. The most prominent of these markers are the spires of the Mormon temples in South Jordan and Provo that stretch into the mountain skies.

After Provo, where the Western Utes from all over the Ute homelands once gathered annually for their spring fish festival and Mormons from around the world today gather to attend Brigham Young University, we passed the city of Spanish Fork. A bedroom community for Utah Valley's larger cities, Spanish Fork is named after the location where two Spanish explorers, Franciscan friars Silvestre Vélez de Escalante and Francisco Atanasio Domínguez, made their first *entrada* into the Wasatch Front. During their famed 1776 expedition, the padres described what is today called the Spanish Fork River as *Aguas Calientes*, or "Warm Waters," due to the geothermal hot springs that run into the river. On the banks of this river—the Utes called it *Pequi-nary-no-quint*, or "Stinking Creek," due to its high sulfur content—Wakara was born around 1815.

After a few hours' drive we reached Fillmore, a windswept desert town of some 2,000 souls. Our exit seemed foreordained. Nature was calling, and we needed to eat lunch.

The town was named after President Millard Fillmore, who helped secure the initial $20,000 for the settlement and appointed Brigham Young the territory's ex officio governor. Mormon leaders chose Fillmore in 1851 as Utah's territorial capital because of its location halfway between Salt Lake and Utah's breadbasket, mines, and Indian missionary outpost in the south. Fillmore's position near the thirty-eighth parallel, one of the proposed routes for the transcontinental railroad, also emboldened the town fathers to dream big. They envisioned an inland port city on the 3,000-mile rail network moving people and goods east and west, day and night. They also envisioned Fillmore as the political metropole of a vast State of Deseret.

If the Mormons' 1849 petition for statehood had been approved, Deseret would have outstripped Texas, which had joined the Union four years before, as America's largest state. Deseret would have

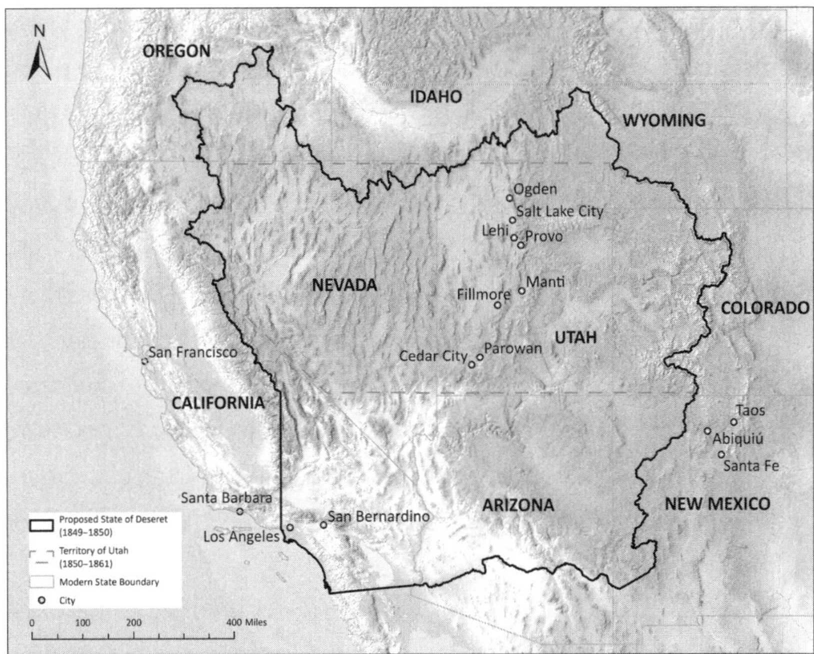

The State of Deseret, 1849–1850. The Mormons' proposed Deseret would have been the largest state in the nation, covering some 400,000 square miles. The much smaller Utah, named after Wakara's Utes, became the forty-fifth state in 1896. (Map by Wenjie Wang)

stretched north from the Mexican border to the Oregon coast and west from the Rockies to California's Sierra Nevada and Santa Monica Mountains. The original design for the Deseret statehouse building called for the construction of four massive wings joined together to hold up a towering Moorish dome, dominating Fillmore's future skyline.

Deseret never came to be. Only after the Mormons officially abandoned polygamy did the much smaller area of Utah, named after Wakara's Utes, win statehood in 1896. And only the southern wing of the statehouse was completed. Utah's territorial government held just a handful of sessions in the three-story building—constructed from local timbers and red sandstone quarried from the nearby Pahvant Mountains, the same sandstone out of which the architects of

Wakara's tomb constructed their leader's intended last resting place. In the mid-1850s, the Mormons engaged in a pair of "wars"—the first with Wakara and his Utes, the second with the federal government—that forced them to consolidate church and state in Salt Lake City. After the territorial assembly moved north, the former statehouse became home to law offices, a jail, a library, and a photo studio. But the building's main use was for social gatherings: dances, fairs, church conferences, meetings of the American Legion, and schools of various stripes. After the statehouse fell into disrepair, in the 1920s the Daughters of Utah Pioneers converted it into a history museum, then passed control to the state, which turned it into Utah's first state park. In the 1970s, the building was added to the National Register of Historic Places.[1]

In 2022, my family and I came to Fillmore to hunt for visible remnants or remembrances of Wakara. Inside the Territorial Statehouse State Park Museum, we found ample evidence of Wakara's influence on the West. We found no mention of Wakara himself.

A sandy-haired park ranger greeted us as we entered the museum. "Start your tour in the basement and work your way up," he suggested. "But watch your step!" More than a few guests have tripped on the uneven sandstone floor while caught in the gaze of the 100 portraits of Mormon pioneers that line the basement's hallway. These pioneers have long passed into what the Mormons call the Celestial Kingdom. Still, from beyond the veil and from inside their gold frames, scores of eyes keep watch.

The South has Confederates in the attic, the late Tony Horwitz famously wrote. Utah has polygamists in the basement. The Statehouse Museum's hall of pioneers contains portraits of husbands placed near portraits of their plural wives. One such former resident of Fillmore is longtime Mormon apostle Amasa Lyman, one of the earliest practitioners of Mormon polygamy.

Hall of Pioneers, Utah Territorial Statehouse State Park Museum, Fillmore, Utah. (Courtesy of Utah Division of State Parks—Territorial Statehouse State Park Museum)

Lyman was a member of Brigham Young's 1847 famed Vanguard Company. A few years later, Lyman cofounded the Mormons' colony in California when they purchased the massive Rancho San Bernardino from the Lugos, one of the largest landowning families in early California. The Lugos were happy to part with the land, which had become a yearly target of Wakara's horse and cattle raiding. After settling in Fillmore, Lyman was excommunicated from the church for daring to criticize Brigham Young's leadership. After both Young and Lyman died in 1877, the Lyman family erected a monument in Fillmore to restore Amasa's good name as a pioneer and patriarch of a large Mormon family; a roll of the names of the thirty-seven children whom he sired with his eight wives was etched into the monument. The effort paid off. Amasa Lyman was reinstated to the church posthumously in 1909. In 2003, a Lyman family reunion gathered more than 1,000 descendants at the Statehouse Museum. The Lymans are representative of many of the museum's visitors who come to take selfies with their pioneer ancestors' portraits in the basement hall—a portrait of Eliza Maria Partridge Smith Lyman hangs near the portrait of her husband—or to locate other artifacts that tie the Mormon settler past to the Mormon present.

Because of its fixation with pioneer history, when we visited in 2022 the Statehouse Museum made little room for Utah's Native Americans. While the museum provided customized "living history" tours for descendants of Mormon pioneers to roam the halls and commune with their dead ancestors, because all the Indians were dead, or so the museum's displays seemed to assume, for Native visitors such transmortal family reunions were impossible. Instead, remnants of Native history were stationary, literally boxed up.

The one display dedicated to local Native history was a glass case stuffed with "Indian" corn, bows, arrows, moccasins, baskets, arrowheads, and the butt of a rifle. A museum placard atop the display case left visitors to assume that these relics belonged to Kanosh, the Pahvant Ute leader who "befriended the Mormon Pioneers" near Fillmore. The rangers I spoke to said that the museum has no record of the items' actual provenance. Some even had stamps on their backsides that read, "Made in China."[2]

These artifacts were displayed not for the sake of living descendants of Kanosh. Instead, the items were meant to remind settler Americans, who can find their ancestors' actual personal items in the museum, of the Indians that their ancestors displaced and killed to bring forth the Settler America of which they have long been taught they are the rightful and righteous heirs.

Still, the museum did draw parallels between Natives and Mormons. Like Lyman—his fellow Latter-day Saint and cofounder of Fillmore—Kanosh also practiced plural marriage. According to the museum placard, his first three wives met violent ends. His first wife, Julia, went insane because she couldn't bear children, and a tribal council condemned her to death by horse dragging. Kanosh's second wife, Betsykin, murdered Mary, Kanosh's third wife, out of fear that Mary would give birth to a child first. A tribal council also condemned Betsykin to die. She chose death by starvation instead of horse dragging.[3]

In the display, Sally, Kanosh's fourth wife, was separated from the rest—figuratively and literally. A carte de visite of Sally, taken by Charles Savage (see photograph on page 205), who took portraits of Utah's most prominent men and women, was propped up inside the Indian display case. Next to the photograph of Sally appeared a painting based on Savage's 1870 photograph of Kanosh (see photograph on page 2).

In the 1870s and in 2022, Kanosh and Sally served as the exemplars of the power of Mormonism to turn Indians into Lamanites. Before marrying Kanosh, Sally had been a servant of Brigham Young for thirty years. In her carte de visite, Sally wears her Sunday best, presenting herself to Savage's camera in a way that matches other female members of Young's household whose likeness the famed photographer took. The image of Kanosh mirrors that of his Mormon mentor, Brigham Young. Kanosh wears a tan suit with a silk handkerchief. His graying hair is cut to fall just over his ears. His face sports a pioneer-era handlebar mustache.

The description of Sally at the Statehouse Museum did not include the fact that she was likely the first enslaved Native American whom the Mormons purchased from Wakara's Utes in 1847. Nor did it mention that it was not Sally's choice to marry Kanosh. After she had cooked countless meals and emptied countless bedpans in Young's various homes in Temple Square, in June 1877 Sally was traded to Kanosh as a token of thanks for Kanosh's support of the Mormon settlers. The marriage was performed at the Salt Lake City home of Clarissa Young, Brigham Young's sixth wife. (Clarissa's brother Charles Decker had purchased Sally from Baptiste, a Ute slave trader who was also one of Wakara's lieutenants and brothers.) Within days after their marriage, Sally and Kanosh departed Salt Lake on the Utah Southern Railroad, which ran parallel to the wagon road that would become I-15. A wagon team was sent north from Fillmore to greet Kanosh and Sally at the railroad's southern terminus. But Sally refused to continue until a more dignified mode of travel—namely, a stagecoach—could be arranged to bring her the rest of the way to the farm.[4]

Sally and Kanosh's marriage was short-lived. On December 9, 1878, less than a year and a half after she wed Kanosh, Sally died, likely from one of the diseases that the settlers brought to Utah, diseases that would also kill all of Kanosh's children and most of his closest relatives. The Fillmore display notes that both Kanosh, who died in 1884, and Sally were buried in the Kanosh Cemetery, and thus not in the stone crypts of Walker's Mountain where Wakara and dozens of other Utes, including Kanosh's son, had been interred until their bodies were stolen in 1872. However, members of the Kanosh Band of Paiutes have told me that Kanosh's body is buried in a secret location in the Pahvant Mountains to prevent his grave from being robbed.

The Kanosh placards at the Territorial Statehouse State Park Museum made no mention of how Sally died. But they were sure to highlight that all the rest of Kanosh's wives either killed themselves or killed each other. The implicit message was that their innate savagery had led to the termination of Kanosh's family line. But in truth, it was the settlers who brought the apocalypse to the Natives of Utah in the form of disease, but also by taking their land, their resources, and their children. For all his efforts to bind himself to the settlers, none of Kanosh's offspring lived long enough to birth the next generation.

Kanosh's fellow founding father of Fillmore, Amasa Lyman, likely has several thousand living direct descendants. Kanosh has none. Ironically, the only descendant of Kanosh to have children of his own was John Kanosh, an enslaved Native American boy of unknown tribal origin whom Wakara gave to Kanosh around 1850.[5]

American museums like Utah's Territorial Statehouse State Park Museum have long presented "Indian" items in display cases as relics of conquest. Settler American visitors to the museum, like Amasa Lyman's descendants, can peer into these cannibalized boxes of Indian relics. They can remember the disappearance of Native Americans while they celebrate their ongoing fecundity.[6]

In contrast, Kanosh Band elders have told me that when they visited the museum, the "Indian" display, rather than producing feelings of triumph, reproduced feelings of trauma and loss. In their eyes, these glass boxes are trophy cases of what Maria Yellow Horse Brave Heart (Hunkpapa/Oglala) and Lemyra DeBruyn, among others, have described as the "American Indian Holocaust." Or, to put it another way, the Statehouse Museum is a museum of holocaust. But instead of honoring and remembering the victims of this holocaust—as other holocaust museums do—the museum made heroes of the perpetrators and blamed the victims for their own communal death.[7]

JUST SOUTH OF FILLMORE IS THE LOCATION OF another historic site, although it's not found on any register of historic places. The federal government has long ignored its mere existence: the location of Kanosh's farm and homestead.

According to his closest Mormon friend, Thomas Callister, after Kanosh signed the Spanish Fork Treaty in 1865, which relinquished his land claims in central Utah, Kanosh and his people acted as if they were resigned to joining other Utes on the newly formed Uintah Reservation in northeastern Utah. Kanosh's Pahvants took down their camp at Corn Creek, burning the corrals and fences that had enclosed their farm's fields. By the summer of 1867, Callister wrote to Brigham Young that Mormon settlers had moved swiftly to take over the land now free of Pahvant presence, laying out the plat of a new Mormon town. Though they named the new settlement "Kanosh

City," in which they allocated lots to settler families, no lots were allocated to Kanosh. Still, while Kanosh moved camps, he did not, in fact, move away. Despite receiving no assistance from the federal government and minimal help from the Mormons, Kanosh established another successful farm just a few miles away, where he cultivated wheat, corn, and potatoes to feed his people.[8]

Kanosh stayed to care for the present and future generations of Utah Natives. He also remained on his ancestral lands to care for his dead kin. Over the next two decades, as the number of living Utes dwindled, graves of Ute ancestors and kin on Walker's Mountain proliferated. During a series of interviews in the home of Thomas R. King, a longtime resident of Fillmore who had defended the settlement during the "Walker War," in December 1872 Kanosh explained that in the last decade his band had been decimated by disease, cut down from several hundred to just fifty-eight. Of his ten children, only one, a little boy named Steptoe, had yet to succumb to illness. Despite all the losses wrought by living in close proximity to White settlers, Kanosh insisted on staying put. He would rather die than move to the Uintah Reservation, he insisted.[9]

There would be more losses. Sometime in the next four years, Steptoe died. So did another brother. Still Kanosh worked to protect them in death. He traveled the 160 miles north to the Endowment House in Temple Square, where he performed baptisms by proxy for his dead sons Steptoe and Stambo, his brother Hang-a-tah, and at least ten other Pahvant men and boys. Sally, Brigham Young's "adopted" daughter, who would be forced to marry Kanosh the next year, performed baptisms for seven dead Pahvant women or girls. Important as these Mormon ceremonies were, Kanosh also refused to relocate because he believed he could protect his people by living, dying, and being buried "around the graves" of his kin—including his son Stambo, his brother Shot, and his fellow Ute leader Wakara—on Walker's Mountain.[10]

In December 1872, as he sat around the warm fire in the Kings' house in Fillmore explaining the fate of his band, Kanosh didn't know that the remains of Shot, Stambo, and Wakara had already been stolen from their graves just months before.

WHEN WE VISITED FILLMORE IN 2022, WE DID so not primarily to tour the Statehouse Museum. As I've noted, Wakara is nowhere to be found in the museum's narrative on the history of Fillmore, a conspicuous absence that reveals a great deal. Instead, we came to see a series of placards found at the southwest corner of the museum's grounds, in which Wakara is the main character.

In the mid-1980s, archaeologists from the US Forest Service erected the placards, titled "Land of the Yuta," the fruits of a survey that the archaeologists conducted of Wakara's gravesite in 1984. Walker's Mountain (the Cow) is located in the nearby Fishlake National Forest and thus falls under the jurisdiction of the Forest Service.

The placards are unique in Utah. They are the only public history lesson that attempts to encapsulate the geographical scale and economic power of the "greatest warrior and chief during the early pioneering era," as one placard describes Wakara. The source of the power was Wakara's "skill and prowess as a 'procurer'" of both horses and humans as well as his control of the flow of other goods along the Old Spanish Trail. The placards do not label this vast, pre–American Western region that Wakara controlled an "empire." But they do include a map of what would become the American West—including the states of Idaho, Wyoming, Colorado, Nevada, California, Utah, New Mexico, and Arizona—that speaks to the scope of Wakara's dominance over the region. Just above the map appears a drawing of Wakara astride one of his prized horses. "The Hawk of the Mountains" surveys his vast territory.

And yet, this history lesson also points to an inescapable conclusion: that American continental dominance was destined to remove Wakara's Native empire from this map and replace it with a map drawn by American settlers (the map of Wakara's territory closely mirrors the Mormons' proposed State of Deseret [see map on page 71]). As such, these placards—like the displays of Kanosh and Sally inside the Statehouse Museum—serve myth, not history.

The myth of Manifest Destiny—the story that settlers and pioneers conquered the American West—has no place for Wakara, the American entrepreneur, the American cartographer, the American colonist, the American defender of Native sovereignty. The "Land of the Yuta" placards make no mention of the fact that the settler economies were intricately connected with Wakara's Utes, especially their participation in trade in humans and horses. Nor do they reveal that to expand his own empire, Wakara used the Mormon settlers to drive his Native rivals off their lands. Instead, to make way for America, the removal of Wakara's Utes from "the Land of the Yuta" became "inevitable," wrote the authors of the placards.

The archaeologists who erected these placards presented themselves as protectors of dead Indians. They did not rob Indian burial sites, as did the original raiders of Wakara's tomb, or as did the settlers who stole Antonga's and Posey's bodies from their graves. They worked to protect Native history, not erase it. Or at least, so the archaeologists claimed.

Still, when my family and I visited the Statehouse Museum in 2022, one of the placards, titled "Death of a Chief," allowed us—scions of the American empire—to participate vicariously in relic hunting. We studied the Forest Service archaeologists' drawings of Wakara's funeral procession and burial. And doing so, we understood what had attracted looters to Wakara's grave. Our mouths agape at the spectacle, we gawked at the dozen dead horses around the gravesite. We peered into Wakara's large crypt formed from neatly stacked boulders. We stared at the deceased Wakara lying in state, covered with a blanket, with his dead women at his sides. At his feet lay a dead enslaved Indian, Wakara's would-be future servant in the world to come.

Yet, contemporary Utes and Paiutes, most notably descendants of Wakara who have become mentors and friends, have different reactions to these placards. They view the 1870s "relic hunters" who stole Wakara's remains and the 1980s archaeologists who erected the placards as different in degree, not kind. On another recent visit to Fillmore, I stood before the "Land of the Yuta" display with Forrest Cuch, Wakara's fifth-great-grandson. "This thing turns my stomach," Forrest remarked. The source of Forrest's disgust was not the "savagery" of Wakara's death but the savagery of a set of photographs—also on the placard—that capture the archaeologists climbing in and out of Wakara's tomb.

OVER THE LAST FEW YEARS, I'VE RETURNED TO Utah again and again to seek out the remains of the American West Wakara helped build. In some ways, I found that Wakara's America has been erased by settler Americans who covered up his story with their own. Wakara is a founding father of the American Southwest. But Wakara's paternity has long gone unrecognized because parts, though not all, of Wakara's Native empire—the territories he settled, the routes he carved into the plains, mountains, and deserts, his exploitative practices that extracted wealth from land, animals, and humans—became hallmarks of the American empire. As I began to narrate Wakara's history, I found that the carefully maintained line between Native and settler began to dissolve.

Recently, I have also learned more about the history of the grave robbing of Wakara's tomb. The grave robbers in 1872 were not the last to plunder Walker's Mountain. In fact, the very archaeologist responsible for erecting the "Land of the Yuta" placards in Fillmore—an act intended, he claimed, to help protect Wakara's legacy—allegedly stole from Wakara's grave. For a time, the fruits of this theft were placed in another display case in another nearby state museum. But these grave-robbing actions also proved poisonous—"bad medicine," as Rena Pikyavit, an elder associated with the Kanosh Band of Paiutes, put it. The archaeologist died suddenly. Several who knew him said that his untimely death resulted, in part, from his actions at Walker's Mountain—a death that added to the body count associated with Wakara's grave.

Most importantly, I have also learned that Walker's Mountain was far from the final resting place of Wakara's America. Neither the grave robbers in the 1870s and the 1980s, nor the narrators of the creation myths of the American West that covered up Wakara's influence in their histories, nor government agents, schools, missionaries, or museums could erase Wakara's legacy and continued presence in the Native and Settler America he helped create.

But what remains of Wakara's America is the end of this story. The beginning of Wakara's story starts, as many good stories do, with a fish story.

Part II

Wakara's Fish

Chapter 5

The Name of a Lake

WAKARA WAS IN HIGH spirits when he stepped out of his lodge and into the warm sunlight in late spring of 1847. His belly was full. His signature bespoke suit of rich broadcloth, cut in the European fashion, stretched tight over his frame.

Wakara was attending the Timpanogos fish festival held each spawning season at his band's hunting and fishing grounds on the eastern shores of Timpanogos (Utah) Lake. Dozens of other lodges dotted the rich, grassy plains. Wakara watched as fellow Utes waded in the Timpanogos (Provo) River, pulling fish from the cool, clear waters. And he watched as others prepared the daily catch, slicing them from belly to throat, ready to be eaten immediately or dried for leaner times later in the year.

Fish flesh had replenished Wakara's body, which had grown gaunt during the previous season raiding horses from the California ranchos on the western end of what the settlers called the Old Spanish Trail. These raids, which began in the fall, lasted two or three months. By late January or early February, Wakara and his cavalry would begin the return trek to his band's homelands in central Utah. He often brought back 1,000 horses, dozens of cattle, and more than a few Paiute children whom he had captured or traded for along the way.[1]

Wakara timed his return to Timpanogos Lake with the spawning runs of what the Utes called *pagü* (fish). As the days grew longer in mid-March, the lake's icy seal began to thin. The warming waters drew trout, mullet, chubs, whitefish, and suckers out of the lake's dark depths. Over the next few months, distinct species in distinct waves, guided by internal compasses attuned to the slightest variations in temperature and mineral concentrations, swam up the snow-fed streams and rivers around Timpanogos Lake to find the waters of their own births and spawn their own young.

For about the first 6,000 years of the existence of Timpanogos Lake—a vestige of an inland, freshwater sea—countless generations of fish returned to their birth waters without human interference. Then, starting 12,000 years ago, when the first humans established temporary communities around the lake, through to the last five centuries, when Utes gathered at the lake for their annual festival, enough fish populated their spawning waters not only to sustain Timpanogos Lake's fisheries but to make living easy for the Utes during the spawning season.

Some of the fish were caught in the Utes' nets, weirs, and baited traps. Others were shot by Ute arrows or yanked from the water by Ute hands.[2]

The fields and waters around Timpanogos Lake were the Utes' springtime Eden, where the fish refilled the Utes' bodies and spirits. When Wakara and his fellow Utes were not feasting on suckers, chub, and trout, they watched youngsters participate in races on foot and horseback. They danced the *mamakönühkay* (Bear Dance), which signaled the start of spring—the season of pairing off Utes into couples or, in Wakara's case, perhaps adding to the ranks of his wives. Wakara and other horse raiders also regaled festivalgoers with tales of the cavalry's latest horse-raiding exploits from the season in California.

The festival involved more than feasting, games, and courting. There was also business to attend to. Wakara exchanged the profits of his horse and slave raids for other valued commodities with fellow Utes and with visitors from near and far. From the south, hoping to barter for Wakara's Paiute captives, New Mexican traders brought guns and ammunition and Navajos brought their well-crafted blankets. From the west, caravans returning from California along the Old Spanish Trail also came to trade for Wakara's new crop of captives and horses.[3]

There was also band politics to conduct. Ute kin, who had spent the winter months in smaller family units, came together at the festival. Heads of families gathered in the head bandsman's lodge. They reaffirmed their fealty to the leaders and appointed new lieutenants. They also redrew territorial boundaries of band control. Once the business was completed, the peace pipe was passed, the smoke that enveloped the participants signaling agreement and kinship.

For Wakara, such meetings were sometimes difficult affairs. Wakara was a blood member of the Timpanogos ruling family, but his fellow Utes did not always recognize him as a band leader. Years earlier, rivals had assassinated his father—an act that Wakara did not forgive or forget. Still, Wakara commanded respect and fear. After all, in 1847, the "Napoleon of the Desert," as some settlers would come to call him, oversaw a vast empire of flesh. Wakara built this empire by trading horse and human bodies with empire-building explorers and settlers. These horses and humans provided essential labor, commerce, transportation, and war making with and against other empires that competed for control of the American Southwest.[4]

A FEW WEEKS LATER, WAKARA RODE HIS HORSE north at the start of buffalo hunting season, when he and his Utes chased bison across what is today southern Wyoming and western Nebraska. Wakara followed the well-worn path—a two-day horse ride between Timpanogos Lake and the Great Salt Lake. Wakara could have ridden this path blindfolded; he knew every twist and turn, every rock and root. Still, Wakara kept his eyes up and his ears perked. A hundred or so newcomers, whom the Utes called "Mormonees," had entered the valley a few weeks before.

Wakara tapped his legs against the sides of his horse. She slowed, then stopped in the shade of a thicket of trees and bowed her head to snack on a tuft of grass. Her rider stayed mounted. He surveyed the newcomers, busy as bees, erecting their embryonic settlement a few miles south of the foothills of the northern Wasatch Front. After months on the trail, followed by weeks of backbreaking labor, the bodies of the newcomers had been reduced to skin and bone. Corn mush, salt-rising bread, and the occasional bacon strip could not keep pace with the caloric expenditures of pioneer life.

Wakara was curious about these newcomers. He watched one group shove hoes into the red-clay earth to form irrigation ditches for a thirty-five-acre farm. He also listened to a rhythmic thump, thump, thump as another group swung axes into trees that grew along a river that the newcomers would soon name Jordan. Wakara heard the whine of a whipsaw slicing felled trees into eight-foot poles, which the newcomers raised to form a palisade around their ten-acre fort. The palisade doubled as the back wall for twenty-nine log houses. Narrow gunports, through which the newcomers could aim their long guns at unfriendly Natives, were the houses' only openings to the outside.

After watching the newcomers chop down trees, Wakara and his horse rode north, stopping again to survey more newcomers laying out what would become Temple Square. Two years later, under the shade of the Bowery, Wakara would feast at the newcomers' first annual Pioneer Day celebration.

These newcomers did not warrant concern, Wakara concluded that summer day in 1847. Their numbers were small, their bodies weak and fragile, and their building skills laughable. The Bowery was unimpressive, constructed haphazardly with rough-hewn logs and branches, not cloth and animal-skin tents like his own lodges. Instead, Wakara saw potential to turn these newcomers into buyers of his horses and humans and even into targets of raiding to supply himself with more horses, cattle, and trade goods. If they began to pose a danger, Wakara believed he could root them out with little effort. After all, Wakara had bested far better foes in California. And he had brought to heel any number of explorers along the Old Spanish Trail.

Later Wakara would have regrets. Over the next few years, he would watch as caravans of Mormon settlers, stuffed into endless wagon trains, swarmed into the Utes' ancestral homelands. To build their forts and settlements, like insatiable ants, they would gobble up forests, grasslands, game, and, most worrisome for Wakara's fish-eating Timpanogos, fish.

The 1847 fish festival would be among the last. In less than a decade, Mormon settlers would massacre many Timpanogos and displace the rest from their sacred festival grounds, where they had gathered for half a millennium. Within fifty years, through year-round fishing and the introduction of invasive species like the common carp, the settlers would all but destroy the 12,000-year-old Timpanogos Lake waterway, leading to what ecologists have called a "stage change" to the lake's ecosystem. The settlers' unwelcome interventions converted a clear lake that supported a wide diversity of plant and animal species into a turbid, eutrophic lake in which the levels of dissolved oxygen in the water were so limited that most aquatic animals could no longer catch their breath. Before the settlers arrived, there were thirteen fish species native to Timpanogos Lake. Today, only the June sucker and two other native species swim in the lake. And they do so in tiny numbers compared to the carp, which until recently outnumbered native fish 100 to 1 and made up 90 percent of the lake's biomass.[5]

Soon after the arrival of these newcomers, in more than name, Timpanogos Lake became Utah Lake.

THE STORY OF HOW TIMPANOGOS LAKE—ONCE THE geographical and cultural heart of the Utah Valley—became Utah Lake is the story of the difference between Native and settler Americans.

Traditionally, Native Americans have seen themselves as part of, not separate from, the landscapes they inhabit. Through trial and error, Wakara's Timpanogos learned what worked and what did not in their reciprocal relationship with the fields of woods, plains of grasses, and rocky waterways, as well as in their relationship to the nonhuman animals who also called Utah Valley home. Wakara's Timpanogos defined themselves through their connection to the fisheries that they learned to care for, so that both the fish and the Fish Eaters could thrive. Over the course of a year, the Timpanogos moved through the different "earths" of their homeland in rhythm with the seasons, with the fish festival on the shores of the lake at the sacred center of their calendar. And yet, over the course of generations, the Timpanogos mostly stayed put within the boundaries of their homelands.[6]

In contrast, settler Americans moved onto the land with the purpose of extracting from the land and from the land's people and nonhuman animals. Starting in the late 1840s, through disease, violence, slavery, and environmental degradation, Mormon settlers displaced the Fish Eaters from the fisheries that they had managed for centuries. Because they did not know how to care for the land and water, settlers also ate up almost all the native fish. And their farms drank up much of the water and poisoned the rest with runoff from their fields and, later, their factories. Once they extracted what they could from the lake, they turned their back on what they renamed Utah Lake and reoriented themselves and the rest of the Utah Valley toward the mountains.[7]

Despite all these challenges, the lake, though sick, remained healthy enough to sustain an underappreciated but invaluable native inhabitant: the June sucker.

"'THE LAKE KILLED THE FAMILY DOG.' THAT'S WHAT those who want to 'pave over Utah Lake' want you to believe!" So exclaimed Captain Todd Frye of the Bonneville School of Sailing as we motored the *Bella Vie*, a twenty-seven-foot Catalina, toward the open water of Utah Lake in the summer of 2022 to see firsthand the June sucker's imperiled, but not irredeemable, home waters.

Sporting a floppy hat over thick, white hair, Frye moved around his sailboat with confidence developed over forty years of sailing oceans around the world. But he's spent the last two decades sailing Utah Lake, the third-largest body of fresh water west of the Mississippi River—approximately the size of New York City's Manhattan, Brooklyn, and Bronx boroughs combined.

Not ten minutes before Captain Todd made this declaration about the dead dog—a story I often heard from some Utahns who say that the lake is sick and polluted beyond saving without drastic human intervention—I boarded the *Bella Vie* docked at the Utah Lake State Park marina in Provo. Some even proposed "paving over" Utah Lake with a massive network of human-made islands, a plan that echoed in its human-centered arrogance the attitude of Mormon settlers toward the lake and nature in general a century and a half before.

Isabella Errigo, then a Brigham Young University (BYU) graduate student and conservationist, had invited me to join this sunset sail. I squeezed into the narrow cockpit, taking my seat among local scientists from BYU and Utah Valley University in Orem, along with a cadre of city council members from the booming bedroom communities that surround the lake. Errigo made a quick study of my fair complexion and passed me a bottle of coconut-scented sunblock.

"Let's send you back home the same shade as when you got here," Errigo teased.

Errigo was happy to have me along. But her target audience was the politicians. She and her BYU mentor, Ben Abbott, a professor of aquatic ecology, wanted to show off the lake at its most splendid, when the orange, setting sun glimmered on the water's rippling tide. Sunset was also when the evening easterly winds would most likely fill the sails and blow away biting bugs that swarm on the lake's surface.

Abbott, Errigo, and Captain Todd hoped the politicians would take in the lake's beauty while absorbing lessons from the scientists about the lake's natural history, its abundant wildlife, and, most importantly, its ability to heal itself—if humans would only get out of the way.

The most exciting lesson that the scientists and sailors wanted to share was about the June sucker. For the past twenty years, inspired in part by Wakara's Timpanogos descendants, a multiagency effort called the June Sucker Recovery Implementation Program (JSRIP) has improved the health of the entire Utah Lake ecosystem by restoring the habitat and population of the June sucker and removing literal dump truck loads of invasive carp.

"The June sucker can only be found in Utah Lake," explained Errigo as we sailed toward the former mouth of the Provo River, where Wakara's Utes had their festival grounds and where the June sucker and other native fish started their spawning journeys. Today, a massive project is underway there to recreate the braided river channels and wetlands of presettler times, so that the suckers can once again spawn as they did for millennia. "The sucker is an indicator species," Errigo explained. This means that "as goes the June sucker, so goes the lake." As a result of the success of the JSRIP, the June sucker has recently been removed from the endangered species list.

By highlighting the recovery of the June sucker, the sailing junket challenged the dominant narrative about the lake that has emerged over the last two decades: that it is so sick and polluted that, as Captain Todd alluded, in 2014, after swimming in the lake for less than an hour, a family dog died from ingesting toxic algae blooms.

The narrative that the lake is not only beyond saving but also a danger to humans and hounds alike motivated a Utah-based company, Lake Restoration Solutions (LRS), to propose "killing" the lake in order to save it. In 2018, LRS released a plan to dump the pesticide rotenone into the lake to kill off all plant and animal life. Then, to deepen the naturally shallow lake, LRS proposed to unleash sixty dredgers to scoop one billion cubic yards of sediment. LRS would then sculpt the dredged mud into 18,000 acres of islands, linked together, and to the shore, by bridges and causeways. These islands would become new areas for wildlife and recreation as well as residential and commercial properties for some half a million people. If implemented, LRS's plan would be the most expansive and expensive (costing some $6.4 billion) environmental "restoration" project in American history.[8]

LRS believed its plan would bring about two miracles at once: raise the lake from the dead and create more land for Utah Valley's booming population. Utah Lake would become akin to Dubai, with its infamous artificial islands off the Persian Gulf coast, which LRS-associated designers had helped develop.

Errigo and Abbott's crew of scientists on the sunset sail did not strongly push their opinion that LRS's plan was a very bad idea. They did not mention that the Dubai project had gone tens of billions of dollars over budget or that only one of the four proposed archipelagos was completed. They did not mention that the project degraded the water quality of the Persian Gulf, leading to more harmful algae blooms, erosion of the coastline, and massive sea life die-offs. Instead, as we tacked back and forth, they told stories from the beginning of the twentieth century when the lake was a major site of recreation for citizens of the Utah Valley, as it had been for Wakara's Timpanogos for centuries before that. Resorts had dotted the shoreline, where visitors fished and bathed during the day and danced under half-shell bandstands at night. The scientists invited the politicians, whose support LRS would need to move forward, to imagine what could be again. The hope was that the politicians would see for themselves that the scheme to "pave over Utah Lake," as some of the plan's opponents described it, was a financial boondoggle and an ecological apocalypse in the making.[9]

Yes, the dead dog was bad PR, BYU fish scientist Ben Abbott explained to me. "The lake has been sick, but not 'terminally sick,' as LRS says." Still, what Abbott describes as LRS's "engineering-focused" approach—to mold the environment to fit humans' notions of what the lake should look like—is what led to the lake's poor health in the first place. And not just in recent decades, but over the last century and a half, starting when the Mormons cut down trees that lined the lake's tributaries, dug irrigation ditches, and waged war against the region's long-standing stewards, Wakara's Timpanogos. Later, these settlers introduced commercial fishing operations that decimated most of the native fish species in the lake. By the mid-twentieth century, they even treated the lake as Utah Valley's toilet, dumping human waste directly into it. One longtime local described water-skiing on the lake in the 1980s as "skiing the scum." "We did slalom between the islands of floating shit."

Human waste isn't the only fertilizer in the lake. Phosphorus and nitrogen run off from farmlands and lawns, which feed the algae blooms. The lake's tributaries are choked by huge stands of phragmites, tall, invasive perennial reeds that have crowded out native grasses along the lake's shore. The lake's natural shallowness, combined with the unnatural decrease in mountain runoff from its tributaries and the warming of the lake's temperature due to climate change, has created such massive blooms that, in the last decade, the Utah County Health Department has issued occasional warnings to keep dogs and humans from spending time in any part of the lake. The blooms have also become the dominant image in the public's psyche about the lake. In 2010, 300,000 people visited Utah Lake. In 2017, that number was down to 100,000.[10]

"People remember the dead dog and the algae blooms, as if it's the lake's fault, and not the people who came here and changed the entire landscape," Isabella Errigo explained toward the end of the sail. Abbott agreed. "The settlers and their descendants have taken a human-centered approach to how they view the lake . . . that the lake exists to serve our needs. Instead, we need to think of ourselves like the Timpanogos did, as part of the ecosystem, in relationship with the water, the land, the fish." Utah Valley's residents have forgotten that the lake is what drew their Mormon ancestors here in the first place, Abbott continued. And they've forgotten that the fish saved the settlers from starvation when their crops failed in the 1840s and 1850s.

Perhaps remembering the lake will help restore the lake to what it once was—the ecological and cultural heart of the Utah Valley. By centering the health of fish, in particular the June sucker as the Timpanogos did, and by restoring its habitat to something close to its presettler state, June sucker advocates hope that fish and humans can together save the lake and once again draw people to it, as the fish did for the settlers 170 years ago. And as the fish did for Wakara's Timpanogos for hundreds of years before that.

Chapter 6

Spawning Season

THE FISH GASPED. HER oval-shaped mouth opened and shut, desperate to pull water across her gills. Seconds before, muscled hands had scooped the June sucker (*Chasmistes liorus*) out of what was still known that late-spring day in 1849 as *Timpanoquint*, or "water running over rocks." (It would be soon rechristened the Provo River, after French-Canadian fur trapper Étienne Provost).[1]

Fingers touched her white-green belly. Then whole hands lifted her from her watery home and thrust her into the warm spring air.

In shock, the sucker flailed. But the grip held fast. As the fisherman gently squeezed her three-pound body, he detected that she was swollen with eggs. And so, he bent down and gently released her back into the clear water, just above fifty-five degrees Fahrenheit. The fisherman apologized for disturbing her swim and prayed that she would have a healthy hatch and return for many more spawning seasons to come.

The sucker raced upstream as the fisherman plunged his hands back into the water. This time he grabbed a male sucker with a red stripe on his side. The fisherman offered a quick word of thanks to

June sucker (*Chasmistes liorus*), Utah Lake, Provo, Utah. (Courtesy of Utah Division of Wildlife Resources)

the fish, whose body would soon feed the fisherman's band of Fish Eaters. He tossed the fish onto the river's bank. Soon other Timpanogos sliced the fish into pieces, then tossed them into boiling water in clay pots. Or they split the fish from mouth to anus, pulled out the spine with one motion, and laid it across two elevated wooden poles, so that dogs would not help themselves to a snack as the fish dried in the mountain air.

Back in the water after her near capture, the female June sucker regained her breath and restarted her journey to her birth waters. Five spawning seasons before, in the shade of trees that kept the waters cool and the soil in place, she hatched, then spent her first few weeks of life. No bigger than a fingernail, she and thousands of her siblings sucked in zooplankton until they doubled in size. Most became food themselves, sating the hungry Bonneville trout (*Oncorhynchus virginalis utah*), the largest species in the fishery. But this June sucker was part of the fortunate few who had survived long enough to swim downstream into the depths of Lake Timpanogos, where she spent the next four years eating and avoiding being eaten. A few weeks before her fifth birthday, the lake's warming waters set off some ancient timer in her body. Her ovaries produced eggs, and she felt an urge to swim back up the river and find the rocky place where she had been born.

Less than an hour's swim farther upstream, she stopped over a riverbed of gravel and cobblestones. As she swam in sync with the current, two males maneuvered alongside her, gently rubbing their bodies against hers. The sucker lowered herself above the riverbed and dumped her yellow eggs, no bigger than pinheads. The eggs stuck to the gravel. The males then released semen over the eggs in a milky cloud.

When she was empty of eggs and exhausted from the ordeal, the sucker let the current pull her back downriver toward the lake. As she swam, she weaved between other returning suckers and between the legs of Timpanogos still working to snatch fish from the water. If her luck continued, or the prayer of the Timpanogos was answered, the June sucker could live up to forty years and make this spawning journey dozens more times.

But that year, the arrival of a new kind of fishermen to her home waters, with little knowledge or appreciation of the value of the June sucker and her belly full of eggs, meant her luck would soon run dry.

IN THE SPRING AND EARLY SUMMER OF 1849, George Washington Bean gazed with amazement at what seemed like an endless sea of fish spawning in the Timpanogos River. "So great was the number of suckers and mullets passing continuously upstream," wrote Bean in his autobiography, "that often the river would be full bank to bank as thick as they could swim for hours and sometimes for days together." Bean, who at the age of eighteen was already a seasoned pioneer, having trekked across the Mormon Trail in 1847, was equally impressed with the Timpanogos' skill at removing fish from the river with bows and arrows, weirs, and baited traps—or as if by magic, with bare hands. Earlier that spring, Brigham Young had sent Bean, his father James, and twenty other Mormon men, including Young's brother-in-law and the Mormons' chief Indian interpreter, Dimick Huntington, sixty miles south from Salt Lake City's "Old Fort"—the Mormons' original stronghold in Utah—to establish a fishing colony and a future mission to the Natives along the banks of the Timpanogos River.[2]

The year before, the Saints had experienced the first of several major crop failures. Late-spring frosts killed most of the early buds on their row crops. And "Mormon crickets" (*Anabrus simplex*) gorged themselves on what the frost did not kill. As a result, the main company of Saints at the Old Fort—already thousands and growing—were forced to ration their dwindling supplies of grain and beef. To stave off starvation, the settlers needed a new source of calories. So in 1849, Young sent the Beans and the rest of Provo's first settlers to fish the fecund waters of the Timpanogos Lake and River.

But before they could reach these fish-filled waters, they had to contend with the water's human protectors. The Timpanogos were wary of the newcomers. On April 1, a party of Timpanogos, possibly led by their war leader Old Elk, stopped Bean's caravan just shy of the band's sacred river. Huntington explained the Saints' purpose: to fish and to be, as Bean recorded, *Too-ege tik-a-boo*, or "good friends." Another chronicler of early Mormon Utah recalled that Huntington "was made to raise his right hand and swear by the sun that they would not drive the Indians from their lands, nor take away their rights." Their fears allayed, the Timpanogos allowed the Saints to proceed. That night, the settlers feasted on fish they had caught in the river. The next morning, they broke ground on the Mormons' first settlement in the Utah Valley located on the south side of the

Engraving of Fort Utah (1850). Note the cannon on the platform, which, during an accidental firing in summer 1849, killed Nauvoo Legion Lieutenant William Dayton and left George Bean badly injured. In February 1850, legionnaires fired the cannon on purpose as part of the Fort Utah Massacre, which resulted in the deaths of dozens of Timpanogos Utes. (From Howard Stansbury's *Exploration and Survey of the Valley of the Great Salt Lake of Utah* [1852])

Timpanogos River, two miles east of its mouth at the lake. There, they felled cottonwoods to build their houses. Twelve-foot-long pickets filled in the gaps between the houses, forming a fort in case of Indian attack. They also started farming outside the fort.[3]

The settlers' arrival in April 1849 coincided with the start of the Timpanogos' annual fish festival. George Bean, who had spent much of the previous two years husbanding every calorie, watched with envy as the Timpanogos feasted morning to night on what Bean learned the Timpanogos called "'Pah-gar' (suckers), 'At-um-Pah-gar' (speckled trout)—good fish." Soon after their arrival, the stomach of the barrel-chested Bean, still growing into his six-foot, four-inch frame, was also full of fish. Seeking adventure, Bean joined his new neighbors in fishing, in games on foot and horseback, and in gambling. He quickly grew proficient in the *Nuche* language. In June, during the height of the sucker run, apostle Parley P. Pratt, the most beloved Saint alive after the assassination of Joseph Smith, visited the Provo settlers. Pratt watched settlers and Timpanogos pull fish with ease from the greatest fishery he'd ever seen. Pratt estimated that the settlers could harvest 5,000 barrels of fish each year.[4]

Pratt assumed that God had made this unrivaled fishery for the settlers. But in fact, through Ute resource practices that balanced bounty for the Fish Eaters and births for the fish, it was the Timpanogos who created—or at least managed—the fisheries and derived their identity from them.

Yet, long before the fisheries and the Fish Eaters made each other, the waters of the Great Basin made the fish.

THE GREAT BASIN IS A LAND OF EXTREMES (see map on page xvii). At one extreme, it is dry, flat, low, and hot. Most of the basin's 200,000 square miles—spread across what is today Utah, Nevada, California, Idaho, and Oregon—receive on average five inches of precipitation each year. At 282 feet below sea level, Nevada's Death Valley is the lowest point in North America. It's also the hottest place on earth, reaching temperatures north of 130 degrees Fahrenheit in the summer. At the other extreme, the Great Basin is steep, wet, and cold. Just eighty-five miles southeast of Death Valley is Mount Whitney, which at 14,505 feet is the highest point in the contiguous United States. In the spring, mountain waters drain to the center of the basin, making it the largest endorheic watershed—a watershed without an outlet to the sea—in North America. In other words, every drop of water that falls into the Great Basin flows not out to an ocean but inward to the Great Salt Lake.

Over the last several million years, plate tectonics have stretched the region east and west, thrusting rock up and down to form mountain ranges and the basin in between. California's Sierra Nevada forms the region's western boundary. Its eastern edge is Utah's craggy

Wasatch Front, which runs from the Utah-Idaho border south for 160 miles, passing to the right of the Great Salt and Utah Lakes and terminating in the deserts of central Utah. The deep canyons that cut across the front served as thoroughfares for human and nonhuman populations who traveled between the Great Basin to the west and the Uintah Basin and Colorado Plateau to the east. It is through these canyons that Padres Silvestre Vélez de Escalante and Francisco Atanasio Domínguez, and later the Latter-day Saints, first entered the basin, bringing with them dreams of settler colonial dominion over the resource-rich lands and waters they saw.

Long before the arrival of the settlers, the Utes described these canyons as one of three interconnected "earths," which were created by the Great Spirit and are distinguished by their relative elevation and the animals who reside within them. Ute historian Clifford Duncan, Wakara's direct descendant, described "Lower Earth" as valley floors, home to fish, beavers, and waterfowl. "Middle Earth" is made up of foothills and alluvial fans around rivers, home to elk, bear, and antelope. "Upper Earth" contains mountain tops and ridges, home to nimble-footed sheep and high-soaring hawks.[5]

It is as if the Great Spirit pressed its thumb down in the center of what is now Utah to create the Utah Valley.

The result is a crescent-shaped indent, about forty-five miles long, northeast to southwest, and twelve miles wide, west to east, ringed by the Wasatch Front to the east and the Lake Mountains to the southwest. To the north, the Traverse Mountains form the cap of the crescent and separate the Salt Lake and Utah Valleys. In the center is the twenty-mile-long and seven-mile-wide lake. Though it's shallow, averaging about eight feet deep, the lake is also the deepest part of Utah Valley's Lower Earth.

The lake's waters are ancient. In part, they are a remnant of Lake Bonneville. Starting some 30,000 years ago, this great inland sea expanded to become larger and deeper than present-day Lake

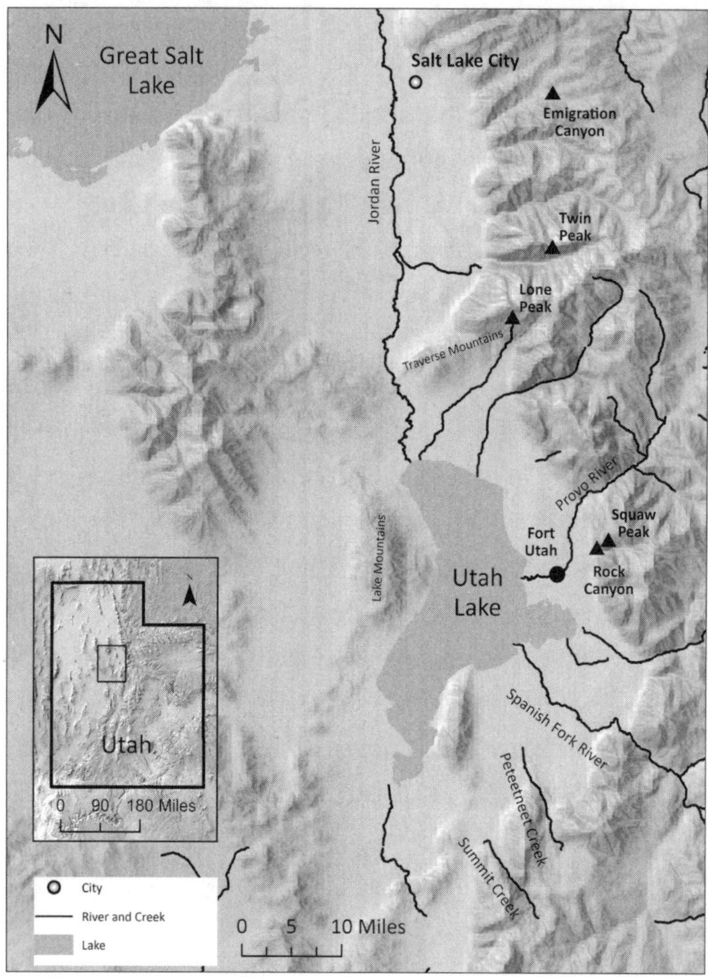

Utah Valley, 1849–1850. (Map by Wenjie Wang)

Michigan. During much of this era, the Wasatch Front was a water world. At its highest, about 5,000 feet above sea level, the waters of Lake Bonneville would have submerged all of Salt Lake City's skyscrapers. Only the 1,215-foot smokestack of the Kennecott Copper Mine—the tallest human-made structure in Utah—and a few spires of the dozens of Mormon temples with the golden angel Moroni atop would have been visible above the surface. Along its 2,000 miles of shoreline, mammoths, American camels, and native horses fed on marsh and plains grasses. Bears fished in stream inlets, and saber-toothed cats hunted herds of herbivores.

A warming planet and accompanying lava flows some 18,000 years ago caused a sudden and dramatic rise in the Bonneville Lake's water level. The rise created a massive breach at the Red Rock Pass in present-day southeastern Idaho, which had served as a natural dam for the lake's northern shore.

The flood that came next was biblical in scope. A wall of water, 300 feet deep and more than a mile wide and reaching speeds of sixteen miles per hour, rushed north. The tsunami-like wave overwhelmed the channel of the Snake River, stripping the tops from the river's plateaus for miles on each side, cutting new channels into the river's walls, and gouging out sand and rocks on the river's floor beds. The four-legged animals in the region heard the roar and felt the earth shake minutes before they saw the mountain-high wave on the horizon. When the wave arrived, many were knocked off their hooves and feet and drowned. Fossilized bones of muskox, mammoths, bears, foxes, and wolves bear witness to the diverse fauna that lived around Lake Bonneville.[6]

The waters of Utah Lake are also always new. The lake is fed from below by springs and from above by streams and rivers draining mountain snow runoff, which, before the arrival of settlers who altered the landscape, poured down through channels on the lake's east side. These channels created fertile alluvial flatlands ringing the lake—a water system that the June sucker restoration project hopes to recreate. Deer, mountain sheep, antelope, elk, marmots, squirrels, and porcupines roamed the upland valleys and the mountains above the lake. Eighty-five bird species, from ducks and geese to swans and herons, made their homes for all or some of the year in the Utah Valley. Fishing birds swam with muskrats, beavers, and otters who dove for freshwater shellfish, which grew in dense beds on the lake's muddy bottom. Pondweeds and other native vegetation flourished in the lake's coves and bays, keeping the waters free of soot and allowing the fish to see and smell as they swam the lake and spawned in its feeder streams and rivers. The Utah Valley fish developed their own spawning rhythms, allowing each species time and space to produce new generations, with Bonneville trout among the first to spawn each year, starting in March when the sun began to warm frozen waters. Suckers and chubs spawned in spring and early summer.[7]

These vast resources drew humans to settle the valley starting some 12,000 years ago. The compactness of the area especially around Timpanogos Lake—an island of water surrounded by seas of desert—meant that human residents could fish in streams and rivers in the morning, pick berries on the lower slopes at midday, hunt for deer and antelope in the foothills in the afternoon, and still be home for an evening meal at lakeside camps.

The archaeological consensus has long held that about 1,000 years ago, speakers of Numic languages—a branch of Uto-Aztecan languages that, before European settlement, were spoken by Indigenous peoples from contemporary central Mexico to the southern United States—migrated north and east into the Great Basin. Most scholars believe that when these Numic speakers arrived in the Utah Valley, they acted like the settlers who would come 600 years later, displacing then replacing the "Fremont Indians" already present in the area. Yet this so-called ethnic replacement of peoples theory has come under scrutiny due to new archaeological studies, which show both continuity and change in the basketry, ceramics, and rock art between the Fremont and the Numic cultures from which Wakara's Timpanogos emerged. Many contemporary Native Americans also object to the replacement theory. "If you talk to an archaeologist, they say that the Fremont just disappeared," Rena Pikyavit, an elder associated with the Kanosh Band of Paiutes, explained to me when I visited her at Utah's Fremont Indian State Park and Museum, where she worked for more than a decade. But it's clear to her that the Fremont didn't disappear.

"The Fremont are our ancestors. We are Fremont, too." Rena and other Native scholars believe that archaeologists have drawn marks on timelines to signify distinct cultural and ethnic differences between the Fremont and the Numic—just like they have among Numic peoples—when in reality the lines were much blurrier.[8]

For example, when they gathered for seasonal celebrations, Numic families and bands who spent most of the year living apart distinguished themselves by where they lived and what food they ate. The Timpanogos were called "Lake People" (*Pawanuch*) and "Fish Eaters" (*Tumpanawach*); Numic speakers from what is today Idaho were known as the *Guchundeka*, or "Buffalo Eaters." So were the buffalo hunting Shoshones from southern Wyoming. Yet these names changed when the people changed what they ate and where they lived. When Buffalo Eaters moved to the Snake and Salmon Rivers during spawning season, they became the *Agai'-deka*, or "Salmon Eaters." During their lifetimes, families, groups, and individuals also changed their names and their community affiliations. Or such changes were imposed upon them if, during inter-Numic conflicts, Fish Eaters captured Buffalo Eaters, and vice versa.[9]

These Indigenous geographic and food-name identities are not the same as modern tribal identities. In Wakara's time and after, with the introduction of new technologies and ideologies—the written word, the horse, and European concepts of land ownership, slavery, race, and religion—the differences among Utes, Paiutes, Goshutes, Shoshones, and Comanches became increasingly rigid. But before settlers introduced ideas about racial and ethnic fixity by writing them into treaties and drawing them onto maps, the different names that Numic people used for each other often implied kinship. The *Nuche* Fish Eaters called the *Numunu*, who lived to their north, *Kumansti*, or "Left-Handed Ones." Before the name *Kumansti* became "Comanche" in the settler archive and changed its meaning in the Ute language to mean "enemy" or "foreigner"—the Utes and Comanches became on-again, off-again allies and foes in the eighteenth century—the name implied kinship between *Nuche* and *Numunu*, people who were related but different. The *Numunu* might have been left-handed, while the *Nuche* were right-handed, but since they both used their hands, they were all "the People."[10]

THE NUMIC SPEAKERS AT TIMPANOGOS LAKE BECAME THE Fish Eaters not just because they ate fish. In the 1850s early Mormon settlers also ate fish by the tons, often caught by massive trolling nets. These fish kept the settlers alive when their seeds failed to take root in the Great Basin soils to which they were not native and where the Mormons' farming methods, developed in New England, did not translate. The Mormons, who saw themselves as farmers, not fishermen, viewed the fish and the waters in which they swam wholly differently than the Fish Eaters did.

For Wakara's Timpanogos, the grassy plains where the Timpanogos River flowed into Timpanogos Lake were the center of their world, the place where, in concert with their plant and animal neighbors and kin, they marked the rhythms of the seasons. On these lakeshores where they gathered for their annual fish festivals, the Timpanogos established what historian Joshua L. Reid (Snohomish) has called a "bioregion," in which natural boundaries—mountain ranges, riverbanks, coastlines—carry more import in the formation of communities than human-made borders. The Timpanogos' relationship to and knowledge of their bioregion—where the fish lounged around submerged rocks, where the beavers made their dams, what time of day the antelope fed on spring grasses, what time of year the piñon nuts were the ripest—made the Timpanogos Lake and River their homelands and home waters.

Timpanogos elders, including Wakara's grandchildren John Duncan (Ungatowinorokant) and Stella Kurump Longhair, described various methods of harvesting these waters and lands. In the daytime, some waded into river shallows to shoot arrows at spawning fish. From willow trees, they weaved funnel-shaped traps, which they staked into the riverbeds. A member of George Bean's settlement party in the summer of 1849 watched in awe at how easily the Timpanogos caught spawning fish barehanded, as if their fingers were magnetized. Yet it wasn't magnets or magic but hand muscles developed over seasons and fish-wrangling techniques developed over generations that made fishing appear easy. The Timpanogos ate their catches raw or roasted. Once their bellies were full, the Timpanogos dried the fish, then stuffed them into rawhide sacks and buried them in holes in the sides of hills to be retrieved after the spawning season.[11]

The Fish Eaters did not just fish. Archaeologists estimate that 70 percent of the calories in their diet came from other sources, including waterfowl and water-dwelling mammals such as beavers and mink. The Timpanogos also trapped rabbits with nets. In the mountains, they hunted deer, bighorn sheep, elk, and pronghorn antelope.[12]

While the Timpanogos ate other things, the fish made the Fish Eaters. But the Fish Eaters also made—or at least managed—the fisheries, keeping them healthy and plentiful for at least a century, and likely much longer. Eyewitness accounts, from Escalante and Domínguez in 1776 to early Mormon settlers in 1849, describe the same fisheries and very similar fishing practices. In this bioregion, Wakara's Timpanogos established an ecological equilibrium with the Timpanogos Lake fisheries and the region's other resources, allowing the ecosystems to thrive. The Timpanogos did so intentionally through resource-management practices that they honed over generations of living in this one bioregion, learning through trial and error what worked and what didn't.

The Timpanogos likely saw the management of the fisheries as an ecosystem of relations—one whole project based on interdependence among humans, fish, and other nonhuman animals, as well as plant life, waters, and the geography of Timpanogos Lake. Still, we can understand their management of the fisheries as having three interrelated parts.

The first part is fishery governance based on multigenerational, place-based knowledge. The Timpanogos had specifically trained fish "captains" who oversaw fish harvesting during spawning seasons. These leaders managed when, how, and how much fish would be caught. The second part of sustainable management was the kind of fishing technologies the Timpanogos employed. During upstream migration, the Timpanogos built weirs across the rivers and streams below waterfalls. The fish got caught in weirs and traps when they attempted to jump the falls. A few weeks later, the Timpanogos used fish traps to catch fish moving downstream once they had completed spawning.[13]

Catching the most fish was not the goal. Just as important was making sure that enough fish, and the right kind of fish, made it past the weirs and traps to produce the fisheries' next generation. As such, selective harvesting was the third part of the sustainable management of the Timpanogos Lake fisheries. As members of the Haíłzaqv Nation and Lake Babine Nation did for centuries in the waterways of the Pacific Northwest, Timpanogos fish captains likely oversaw when and how weirs and traps were deployed to guarantee sustainable catches. Standing at the weirs and watching fish jump the falls—or, later in the season, standing in the shallows and watching fish caught in the traps—they monitored the size and strength of the season's trout, suckers, and chubs, keeping older fish past their spawning prime and releasing the younger fish. If they practiced fishery management like Coast Salish peoples, then Timpanogos fish captains selected for sex as well as age, harvesting males and releasing females to complete their spawning cycle as one male could mate with several females.[14]

From Utah to British Columbia, Indigenous peoples throughout the West employed multigenerational governance, sustainable technologies, and selective harvesting for hundreds if not thousands of years. Such systems were based on the premise that the needs of the people and the fish were interconnected. The systems were also adaptable to seasonal changes and to the addition of new technologies and methods through trade with other Indigenous peoples as well as Euro-American explorers and settlers. The systems were also adapted to the specific resources available within the bioregions that Indigenous peoples helped create. For example, while Coast Salish were primarily salmon eaters, archaeological findings suggest that the Fish Eaters at Timpanogos Lake selected the lake's chubs and suckers, including the June sucker, over the salmonoid trout because they were less oily and were easier to dry for storage.[15]

BEFORE THE ARRIVAL OF SETTLERS, IT'S HARD TO gauge how many fish-eating Timpanogos and other Ute bands lived in the Utah Valley, as the size of the bands fluctuated with the seasons. But the steady supply of fish from Timpanogos Lake meant that the valley was a seasonal home to more people than any other place in the eastern Great Basin. Attendance at the fish festivals likely numbered in the thousands.

In September 1776, the Spanish explorers and Franciscan padres Domínguez and Escalante first entered the valley on an expedition to establish an overland route between Santa Fe and the Spanish missions in California. Climbing the Timpanogos (Provo) River's old lake bench at the mouth of Spanish Fork Canyon, they got their first view of the valley of the "Timpanogotzis," wrote Escalante in the expedition's journal. Soon after, the padres met Wakara's Timpanogos ancestors and bought dried fish from them.[16]

When the padres looked at the lake, they saw something different than did Wakara's Timpanogos. The explorers saw not a carefully managed bioregion but a virgin valley, full of wood, water, and rich land

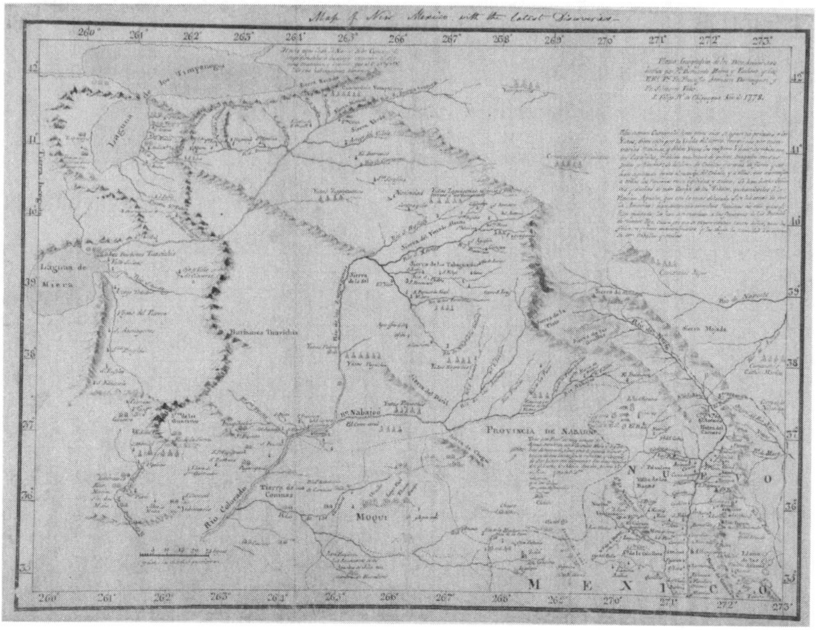

Pacheco's Map of North-Western *Nuevo México* (Spanish New Mexico, 1776). Miera was the cartographer for the Domínguez-Escalante expedition. Note "Laguna de los Timpanogos" in the upper-left corner, which comprises modern-day Utah Lake and the Great Salt Lake. (Courtesy of Yale's Collection of Western Americana, Beinecke Rare Book and Manuscript Library, Yale University)

ready to be exploited. Inside this wilderness, Escalante laid out in his mind cities and farms that would rival any settlement in New Spain. Escalante's cartographer, Bernardo de Miera y Pacheco, who sketched what became the first Euro-American map of the region, envisioned on the shores of Timpanogos Lake a settlement as large as Mexico City. This new 100,000-person city could become the long-awaited hub for a network of settlements across New Spain's northern frontier.[17]

Miera's and Escalante's plans would not come to fruition. Still, many other Europeans and Americans who visited Timpanogos Lake in the next decades also documented the valley's yet-to-be-exploited natural riches. In July 1827, trapper Daniel T. Potts described the valley as among the most beautiful places he'd ever seen, crisscrossed by clear streams and covered by thick grass, with, at its center, a massive lake that the "Utaw Tribe" fished for their principal food supply. Almost two decades later, in late May 1844, a few days after Wakara forced him to pay a toll for traveling on the Old Spanish Trail, John C. Frémont surveyed the valley during the Timpanogos fish festival. In the care of more cultured hands, the Pathfinder foresaw that the lake, the river, and the fertile plains could be transformed from seasonal meeting grounds for Indians into a yearlong home for settlers and stockyards like those he grew up around in his native Georgia.[18]

In early December 1847, almost certainly with Frémont's map of the Utah Valley in hand, Parley P. Pratt led the first Mormon party to survey the lake, catch fish, and scout for future settlements. In a flat-bottom skiff that the settlers had constructed out of pine logs, Pratt and a handful of Saints spent a few days exploring the lake's western shore. The fishing was of limited success; the nets that the Saints tossed into the lake brought back just a handful of trout. The settlers did not know what the Timpanogos had understood for generations: In the fall and winter, the fish migrated into warmer waters deeper in the lake. The next summer, Pratt returned to Utah Valley and had better luck catching trout and suckers. Pratt believed that the valley's rich soil and fisheries meant it could support settlements, farms, and ranches for millions of people.[19]

What Escalante, Domínguez, Miera, Potts, Frémont, and Pratt had in common when they looked at the fish, fowl, and fertile plains of Timpanogos Lake, was that they saw before them a blank canvas, an untouched wilderness waiting for them to civilize and exploit for their own benefit. They failed to see that, in fact, the tableau was already painted—it was a space that humans had been cultivating for countless seasons. Through trial and error, the Timpanogos learned to live with the water, fish, game, grasses, and mountains of the valley. They became partners with the nonhuman natural world, in sync with its rhythms rather than imposing their human-centered will upon it, as the explorers and settlers hoped to do.

When the settlers arrived in the late 1840s, they dug up the grasses, cut down the trees, and dammed up the rivers and streams to water their wheat fields and cattle. Yet their way of farming, which they had learned over generations working the land in New and Old England, did not take well to the soils of the Great Basin. So, out of necessity, these Beef and Grain Eaters became fish eaters too. The problem for the Mormons, for Wakara's Timpanogos Fish Eaters, and for the fish of Timpanogos Lake was that these newcomers fished too much.

CHAPTER 7

Too Much Fishing

WAKARA ARRIVED FOR SPAWNING season at the mouth of the Timpanogos River on May 10, 1849. He was not surprised to see a small batch of Saints toiling in the warming spring air to raise a fort and log houses. Wakara's brother Arapeen had visited the Mormons' camp the week before to suss out the settlers' strength and learn their intentions.[1]

Among the Mormons, rumors had spread that Wakara objected to their decision to establish a foothold in the Utah Valley. Word was that Wakara would not tolerate the Mormons' choice to locate Fort Utah, plant their crops, and corral their cattle right next to the Timpanogos festival grounds. Some even claimed that Wakara was uniting Ute bands to drive the Mormons off their lands.[2]

In response, Brigham Young urged the Utah Valley settlers to prepare for attack. Complete the fort, Young commanded. Raise the cannon and guard the horses and cattle. Don't give the Indians any presents, especially guns and powder, "but, if they will be friendly, . . . teach them to raise grain and . . . order them to quit stealing [ours]."[3]

Indian interpreter Dimick Huntington, who was at Fort Utah to serve as an intermediary between the newcomers and the Utes, wrote to the Mormon prophet that the settlers were ready for Wakara's arrival. Many of the fort's settlers were from border states and had experience trading and warring with Indians. They marshaled their arms. Huntington reported that they had about twenty muskets but needed cartridges. While they awaited Wakara, they worked to sort out friend from foe among the Timpanogos already at the lake. To help any fence-sitting Timpanogos make up their minds, "we fired the cannon once and it had a good effect," Huntington wrote to Young.[4]

Wakara and his horse trotted into the fish festival grounds a few days later, flanked by a dozen mounted warriors and with more than twenty lodges following close behind. At the entrance of the Mormons' fort, Wakara dismounted. Standing in the mud, Wakara and a cadre of his men shook hands with Huntington and a few other settlers, including young George Bean. Despite Wakara's show of force, he had not come to fight, Wakara explained to Huntington. He didn't need to. He had seen many newcomers visit the valley during previous spawning seasons. Like the Mormons, the eyes of those previous visitors grew big at the sight of the rich valley, which would-be settlers dreamed of remaking in the image of their own homelands. But these visitors never ended up staying. The valley was too far away from their metropoles. And the area was firmly in the control of Wakara's Utes, who were well armed and large in number. Instead, Wakara saw the Mormons' arrival as an occasion to further enrich himself and his followers at the Mormons' expense. He left the raising of his tents to his wives, children, and slaves and set out to trade with these newcomers.[5]

After offering his greeting to the Mormons, Wakara and his men followed Huntington and the settlers inside the interpreter's log home. Before they conducted business, the Utes and Mormons sat down on rough benches and passed a pipe, a ceremony that, according to Ute tradition, bound them together as kin and required fair trade and honest speech. The smoke exhaled from the new family's lungs rose to the ceiling, mixing with the tangy smell of sap from the freshly milled logs. Despite the Mormon prophet's prohibition on arms sales, Wakara traded a horse for one of Huntington's flintlock guns, perhaps among the guns Wakara would be buried with a few years later.

With covenants of friendship and trade established, the party moved outside the fort and toward the mouth of the river. The late-spring sun's rays danced on the waves of Timpanogos Lake, whose surface had been stirred by the evening breeze. Light, fading from above, roared up from the ground as the Utes lit bonfires to keep the evening's cool air at bay. Huntington sat with Wakara by the fire. Wakara smiled with the satisfaction of a proud patriarch as he watched his people dance and sing on their ancestral festival grounds. When the singers and dancers grew tired, they slept around the fire. Wakara also reclined. He lay in Huntington's arms as the two talked.[6]

In a mixture of English, *Nuche*, and sign language, Wakara explained to the interpreter that the Saints should expect more Utes to gather at Timpanogos Lake over the next few days. But Huntington should not fear them. Yes, there were some bad Indians among the "Timpenny Utes," Wakara admitted, including renegade youngsters who earlier that year had stolen cattle from the Mormons' small herds without their leaders' permission. But the Mormons had already learned that they could dispatch such marauders easily enough. In early March 1849, thirty-five Mormon settlers marched south from Salt Lake City. In a creek canyon a few miles northeast of the lake, the militiamen cornered a Timpanogos family, then killed at least four of the young men and boys whom the settlers had accused of cattle theft. (The militiamen eventually let close to twenty women and children escape the slaughter, remembered today as the Battle Creek Massacre, and they ran back to the main Timpanogos village to report the horrors they had endured). Still, Wakara told Huntington that he thought it was "good" that the Mormons had killed those boys who failed to abide their elders, and if necessary, they "ought to kill some more." But most Utes would be friendly, Wakara explained, if the Mormons were friendly to them.[7]

Yes, Huntington replied to Wakara. We want to be friends. The Book of Mormon tells the Mormons that Utes and Whites are destined to build together a new Zion to await Christ's return. Wakara explained to Huntington that he understood this prophecy; he had prophecies of his own. Wakara told Huntington that he wished his son would learn English so he could better understand what the Mormons' book said. Then Wakara asked Huntington to write a letter to Brigham Young, inviting Mormons to settle on his land 200 miles south of Timpanogos Lake. There, Wakara explained, the wood, water, and soil were good, and there was a mountain spring and a deposit of salt, essential for drying fish and meat.[8]

WHILE HE LAY IN HUNTINGTON'S ARMS, WAKARA TOLD the interpreter of his life—a life that, by that spawning season, had already made him one of the most famous Natives in the world, recognized from coast to coast as the head of a horse-raiding and slave-trading empire. This unrivaled life also put him outside the structures of his own Ute nation and Timpanogos Band, sometimes even at violent odds with its leadership. And yet it was a life that always brought him back to Timpanogos Lake each spring.[9]

Wakara told Huntington that in 1815, or thirty-four spawning seasons before, he had been born at *Pequi-nary-no-quint*, or "Stinking Creek," which would later be called Spanish Fork River. He came of age during a time of great change for his people. Wakara remembered that when he was about twelve, herds of deer and buffalo in the valley were thicker than the Mormons' cattle were then. But the arrival of the Spanish and other explorers had changed how the Utes hunted. His father, whose name might have been Uintah, bought the band's first horse from the Spanish. But Uintah did not know how to care for it, so he left it tied to a corner of his hut until it starved to death.[10]

Wakara told Huntington that he had been raised to seek peace and prosperity, not war. But when others took Ute lands, broke bonds of trust or kinship, or unjustly spilled the blood of his family, vengeance would be his. While he was growing up, his band had no problems with the White traders who visited their valley. Instead, their quarrel had been with the "Snakes," or Shoshones, to their north who tried to encroach on Ute lands. As far back as he could remember, Wakara told Huntington, he had joined his father and other Ute warriors in battling the Snakes.

But a decade or so before the Mormons arrived, a portion of the Timpanogos broke off and joined the Shoshones. Soon the breakaway band warred against the Timpanogos at the lake. Wakara's father and forty others wanted no part of this inter-Numic fight, so they took their families and went to Stinking Creek (Spanish Fork). Some of Uintah's fellow Timpanogos leaders took offense. They attacked their village and shot Wakara's father in the back while he was smoking his peace pipe—an unforgivable offense. After burying their father in a canyon close to Stinking Creek, Wakara and his brother Arapeen took their revenge. They stole into the Timpanogos village and killed four of their former bandsmen.

Wakara told Huntington that after satisfying this blood debt, he took over the leadership of his father's breakaway lodges. And over the next decade, he put his people on a path of greater wealth and territorial reach by becoming the greatest slaver on the Old Spanish Trail. Wakara explained how he and his men stole Paiute children from southern Utah, then traded these captives in lower California for cattle. Wakara also regaled Huntington with stories about how he became the West's greatest horse thief by outsmarting the *Californios* (Californians of Spanish or Mexican descent). In the dark of night, Wakara dispatched his cavalry to different ranchos to steal horses by the dozens. Wakara acknowledged that the posses the *Californios* sent after him and his men recovered many horses. But Wakara's strategy of horse thieving in bulk meant that they still often got away with 1,000 head. To get home, he and his cavalry ran the horses over the mountains and deserts of California and Nevada. On their return trip, they lost more than a few. Some died of exertion, while others escaped to become feral in the deserts of Utah and Nevada. Still, a typical raiding season saw Wakara bring 600 or 700 California horses back to Utah by early spring.

Huntington rose from his seat to throw another log on the fire. He told Wakara that the Saints would buy some of those horses, for they needed a supply of their own. He also told Wakara that the Latter-day Saints had something to give Wakara: the true faith of the Indians' forefathers. In fact, God mandated that the Mormons come to Utah, Huntington said, in order to share with the Indians this faith. Again, Wakara responded with his own prophecy, telling Huntington that God had also sent him on a mission to secure peace between his people and the Whites who would soon settle in his lands.

Wakara explained to Huntington that a few years after his father's murder and two years before the arrival of the Latter-day Saints, Wakara was trading with some White men when he suddenly took sick and died. Miraculously, his body remained warm, though his spirit ascended to the heavens, where he saw *Shinaub* (*Sünawav*, God) sitting on his throne with a great multitude of angels dressed in white. During this visit, God gave Wakara, whose name translated to "yellow," or brass, to match his famous raiding outfit, a new name: Pan-a-karry Quinker, which according to Huntington's translation meant "Iron Twister." God told Wakara that he was to return to his earthly body and that soon "there would come to him a race of white people that would be his friends, and that he must treat them kindly."[11]

YOUNG WAS NOT HAPPY WHEN HE READ HUNTINGTON'S report about the intimate night that he and Wakara had spent together. Despite the Book of Mormon mandates and Young's own professed desires to create bonds of kinship and commerce with the "Lamanites," such familiarity between the Mormons and the Utes bothered the Mormon prophet. Young chastised Huntington. Finish the fort, keep the Indians out of the settlement, and, for God's sake, don't give them weapons. To Young's eyes, Wakara's displays of affection were careful calculations to soften the settlers for a coming bloodletting.[12]

The settlers did not follow the prophet's admonitions. George Bean and other settlers continued to play, dance, and gamble with the Utes during the rest of the fish festival. In early July, Parley P. Pratt returned to what the settlers began to call "Utah Lake," where he purchased fish on the cheap. "I could buy a hundred, which each weigh a pound, for a piece of tobacco as large as my finger," Pratt exclaimed.[13]

Soon, just as Young foresaw, the era of good feelings ended. One August morning, three settlers, Jerome Zabriskie, Richard A. Ivie, and Rufus Stoddard, headed toward the lake to hunt. On their way, they crossed paths with a Ute called Old Bishop. The Ute was wearing a hickory shirt that Ivie claimed was his. Old Bishop said he had bought the shirt fair and square. What's more, Old Bishop accused the settlers of hunting deer without the Utes' permission. A shouting match turned into a scuffle. Old Bishop drew his bow, and Ivie shot Old Bishop in the head, killing him instantly. To hide the murder, the settlers ripped open Old Bishop's corpse and stuffed it full of rocks, then tossed it into the Timpanogos (Provo) River.

The murder of Old Bishop did not stay covered up. Back at the fort, Zabriskie, Ivie, and Stoddard bragged about their bloody deed. Within days, the Timpanogos found Old Bishop's body floating in the river. The Timpanogos rushed to the fort, demanding that the Mormons hand over Old Bishop's murderers. The settlers said no. The Timpanogos then demanded that the settlers compensate them for the murder with blankets and food. The settlers said no. The settlers' refusal to repair this breach in the bond between the two peoples enraged the Utes, who, just as Wakara had prophesied they should, had shared their lands and fish with their new neighbors.[14]

In late summer, Provo men and boys conducted militia drills, readying themselves to fight if the Utes became "saucy." Yet these war preparations also brought some Mormons into even more contact with Wakara's "friendly" Utes. One evening, when militia Lieutenant William Dayton and George Bean were setting off practice rounds of the cannon that the settlers had placed on an elevated platform at the center of the fort, the cannon exploded. Dayton was killed instantly. Bean's left arm was almost torn from its socket. Celia Hunt found Bean's left hand, which she identified from the ring on his little finger, at her doorstep. A rider was sent north to Salt Lake to fetch a doctor. Dr. James Blake, who was in Utah as part of Howard Stansbury's expedition of the US Topographical Engineers surveying potential paths for the transcontinental railroad, rushed to the fort. Blake removed 200 pieces of shrapnel lodged in Bean's body. During his weeks-long recuperation, Bean received visits from leading settlers, including Brigham Young, who anointed Bean with consecrated oil. Utes also checked in on Bean, including Sanpitch, Wakara's brother, as well as Washear (the settlers called him Squash Head due to his misshapen skull). Washear spent hours at Bean's bedside, during which Bean became fluent in Ute, a skill that would serve him well when he became one of the Mormons' most important interpreters during the so-called Walker War.[15]

In the first week of January 1850, brutal cold and heavy snows left the Utes starving. Worse, a measles outbreak hit the valley. It began among the Mormons at Fort Utah, then spread to the Timpanogos village after a handful of infected Utes who had lodged at the fort following the Battle Creek Massacre were sent home. Dozens of Utes died. Freezing, sick, angry, and hungry, the Timpanogos began taking Mormon cattle corralled near the fort. Before the Mormons could recover them, the cattle were butchered and eaten.

On January 7, it was the Mormons who rushed to the Timpanogos' village for restitution. And this time, it was the Utes who refused. They even raised "war whoops," reported Utah Valley settlers, signaling their willingness to engage in violence if the Mormons pushed the matter. While the settlers considered the taking of Mormon animals to be acts of "depredation," the Utes viewed them as reparations for Old Bishop's murder and reciprocity for the Mormons' use of their lands and fisheries. Outnumbered and wanting more direction from Salt Lake before they started a war they might not win, the settlers returned to the fort. The next day, Young sent a letter south urging the settlers to double their efforts to protect their cattle and horses. Post guards day and night, the prophet ordered. Secure the fort, and don't let any Indians come inside. But later in January, sick with measles, the Timpanogos leader Old Elk entered the fort looking for help for himself and other sick Utes. Provo settler Alexander Williams saw him at Celia Hunt's house, where the Ute leader begged for medicine. Instead of treating him, Williams grabbed him around the neck and kicked him out. Though they couldn't get Celia Hunt's medicine, the Utes did take some of her and other settlers' cows.[16]

The Fort Utah settlers feared that the angry and well-armed Timpanogos would soon start targeting more than cattle. Young hoped to avoid open conflict. In early January, when the Utah Valley settlers asked Young's permission to kill Utes who stole Mormon property "on the spot," Young encouraged his faithful to practice patience and empathy steeped in racial hierarchy. Young reminded the settlers that the Utes lacked White men's moral character and thus should not be faulted for failing to abide by White men's notions of property and decorum. Instead, the Utes were "wild, uneducated, naked, destitute and mostly [stole] out of necessity."[17]

In late January, a leader of the Utah Valley settlement, Isaac Higbee, traveled north to Salt Lake with proof that patience wasn't working. Higbee explained to Young and other church leaders that the Timpanogos continued to hunt settlers' cattle and had threatened to gather more Indians and attack the settlers themselves. Parley P. Pratt backed Higbee's appeal to deploy violence. Young agreed. "Go kill them," he commanded. Better the Mormons take the fight to the "Indians" than wait for them to strike first. When Pratt and Young said "Indians," they meant Indian men. "I would take the women & children," Pratt added, "& make them do what we want"—that is, turn them into servants and perhaps even wives in Mormon households. Young called for the formation of two companies totaling 100 minutemen drawn from the ranks of the Nauvoo Legion, which the church's first prophet, the martyred Joseph Smith Jr., had formed to defend the often-persecuted faithful years before. When possible, the legionnaires were to "sue for peace." But when they confronted those Utes who did "not separate themselves from their hostile clans," the legion's Major General Daniel H. Wells instructed that "exterminating" those Indian fighters would be his men's standing orders.[18]

In the first week of February 1850, whiteout snowstorms slowed the gathering of the minutemen at Fort Utah. But by the morning of February 8, the Mormon forces began a siege of the Timpanogos village at the mouth of the Timpanogos River—a siege that, when he heard about it, Wakara would not only approve of but say hadn't gone far enough to root out "bad" Indians among his Timpanogos kin. The plan called for mounted legionnaires and infantrymen to surround the village and prevent anyone from escaping. Then artillerymen would bombard the village with shrapnel shot from the cannon.

The siege did not go as planned. The minutemen underestimated the Timpanogos' knowledge about how to defend their homeland. As Aroet Hale, a convert from New Hampshire, wrote in his journal, "[We] found the Indians fortified in an old bed of the Provo River. They had felled Cottonwood trees along the bank and piled up snow, with port holes through the snow which completely hid them from our view." With their targets invisible, the Mormons' rifle shots hit wood and earth, not Timpanogos bodies. The cannon shots were even less effective. Many splashed into the river or thudded into the riverbank. William Walker, who served in the artillery division, recalled hearing the Utes "laugh heartily at the 'harmless gun.'" Bullets fired from the rifles of the Ute warriors—many of which Mormons had traded to them the year before—weren't much more accurate than those of their Mormon neighbors turned adversaries. Walker recalled the effect of the frigid air mixed with the Timpanogos' hot bullets. "It was so cold and clear that I could see the blue streaks of the balls as they passed over."[19]

The next day, February 9, went better for the settlers. The Mormons restarted their offensive, shooting as they moved forward behind A-shaped batteries they constructed from logs and brush. By evening, they were within 100 feet of the Timpanogos village. From there, they rained down sheets of bullets. When their hands grew exhausted from reloading and their gun barrels overheated, the minutemen stopped shooting and returned to the fort. They had likely killed more than a few Timpanogos and had advanced a great distance, wrote one militia member to the leadership brass in Salt Lake City, but failed to fulfill their mandate of "routing" out all the Indians from the lake.[20]

Back in Salt Lake, Young grew angry with the slow pace of Indian death and displacement. During an emergency meeting of the church's senior leadership, Young once again blamed those Saints who had traded guns and ammunition to the Timpanogos the summer before for placing weapons of war in enemy hands. Young framed the fight against the Timpanogos as an existential battle for the survival of Zion. "If we yield in this instance, we have to yield this land," he exclaimed. Don't just take my word on the righteousness of killing Indians, Young said. Citing an uncanonized prophecy from the founder of the faith, Young continued,

"Joseph [Smith] prophesied many of the Lamanites will have to be slain, many of them by us." To further buttress the rationale for slaughter, Young said that Wakara also advised the Mormons to kill the Timpanogos at the lake.[21]

Young dispatched General Wells to gallop south all night through a raging blizzard with orders to declare martial law and conscript all the Provo men into an expanded militia. Their orders were to clean out the remaining hostile Timpanogos wherever they were hiding. Soon after dawn on February 10, the militiamen moved closer to the strangely quiet Timpanogos village. When they entered it, they found it deserted save for scores of dead bodies. The surviving Utes had fled through heavy snows to take shelter in nearby canyons. Over the next several days, the militiamen killed dozens of Timpanogos warriors and noncombatants, often without discriminating between friend or foe. During one campaign, the militia cornered a family of Utes on the southeastern shore of the lake near Table Point, captured the women and children, and shot the men en masse. A few who tried to escape across the frozen lake were hunted down and killed. The soldiers brought the women and children to the fort, where they were housed under the cannon platform before being divvied up to live as domestics with Mormon families.[22]

For many of the massacred Timpanogos, even death did not provide rest. The surgeon James Blake, who had cared for George Bean after his cannon accident, hired two Mormon settlers to help him locate the remains of the victims at Table Point and scattered throughout the rest of the valley. The doctor and the Mormons sawed off forty to fifty heads from the Timpanogos' bodies, boxed them up, and brought them to the fort to await shipping to Washington for "medical" study. The boxed-up heads remained in the fort for weeks, serving as curiosities for the settlers and warnings for the Timpanogos held captive at the fort. One of those Timpanogos was Wakara's teenage nephew Antonga (Black Hawk), who looked on with horror

Ute Prisoners in Fort Utah (1850). Following the Fort Utah Massacre, when dozens of Timpanogos Utes were killed or died of exposure, women and children either took shelter or were imprisoned at the fort. (From Howard Stansbury's Exploration and Survey of the Valley of the Great Salt Lake of Utah [1852]. Courtesy of the General Collection, Beinecke Rare Book and Manuscript Library, Yale University)

as the boxed heads rotted in the warming air, then were dumped in the trash—a gruesome scene Antonga did not forget. To Antonga, these heads were neither trophies of war nor scientific artifacts. They were the remains of kin.[23]

Still, the violence was not over. With Antonga conscripted by the Mormons as a scout, militiamen pursued Old Elk and other surviving Timpanogos into Rock Canyon (which the Timpanogos called "House of God"). Near the canyon's mouth, Antonga and the soldiers found Old Elk's frozen corpse inside a lodge. "Wild Bill" Hickman, the infamous bodyguard of Joseph Smith and Brigham Young, chopped off Old Elk's head and brought it back to the fort, where he hung it up by its hair from the roof of a house (Jim Bridger, Hickman claimed, told him that he'd give him $100 for the head). The militiamen also found living Timpanogos in the canyon, including women and children. As the militiamen began moving the captives back to

"Old Elk and His Squaw." (From Howard Stansbury's *Exploration and Survey of the Valley of the Great Salt Lake of Utah* [1852]. Courtesy of the Smithsonian Institution Archives, Record Unit 95, Box 83, Folder 11, Image No. SIA_000095_B83_F11_014)

the fort, Old Elk's wife, described as the "handsomest squaw in the Ute nation," made a run for it. According to her pursuers, she either fell or jumped to her death when she tried to scale the canyon's steep cliffs, the summit of which until recently was named "Squaw Peak."[24]

It is hard to tally the number of dead from these 1850 massacres. Settler records from the time report the deaths of approximately forty Timpanogos. But that number is almost certainly an undercount. The true total of dead was more likely in the triple digits. Many died from bullets and cannon blasts; dozens of others perished from measles, as well as from starvation and exposure after they were routed from their winter camps. As planned, the militia brought the surviving women and children to Salt Lake City. The captured were initially kept in two tents north of the Bowery, where Wakara had joined the Saints to celebrate the first Pioneer Day the summer before. Within a few days, the women and children were "placed in families as servants to make white people of them," recalled the explorer John Gunnison, who was in Utah as part of Stansbury's survey expedition. When warm weather arrived, many escaped, but not before untold more died of communicable diseases.[25]

A few weeks after the massacres, Young dispatched interpreter Barney Ward to bring news of the violence at the lake to Wakara and the Manti settlers with whom the Ute leader had spent much of the winter. For his part, "Walker is in favor of what we've done," reported Ward. The death of Old Elk helped Wakara become the undisputed "chief of the Utahs." It also shored up Wakara's control over the only space in central Utah that he had yet to dominate outright: the sacred Timpanogos lands and waters in the Utah Valley. What's more, there was no love lost between Wakara and Old Elk and other leaders at Timpanogos Lake, whom Wakara blamed for the murder of his father years before. Still, Wakara was glad to avoid direct conflict with his kin, even those whom he said had betrayed him. Instead, Wakara had indirectly conscripted the Mormons to fight his battles against his rivals. Wakara had also deployed the settlers in order to expand his control over the region's lands. Over the fall and early winter of 1849–1850, in the run-up to the massacres, Wakara helped the settlers establish their first colonies outside the Wasatch Front and on lands long controlled by other Ute bands. Wakara also approved the Mormons' plans to expand into southern Utah along the Old Spanish Trail, which Wakara had dominated for the previous decade. For

Wakara, these outposts would become new trade markets where he would exchange his horses and slaves for Mormon cattle, foodstuffs, guns, and ammunition.[26]

Still, Wakara did not come out of the massacres unscathed. The Timpanogos at the lake killed his son Battee. And many in Wakara's own band contracted measles, including Wakara himself and his brother and second in command, Arapeen. In February 1850, to stave off the illness, Wakara's Utes killed Paiute captives. But the sacrifices did not work, and dozens of Wakara's Utes died. Isaac Morley, leader of the Manti settlement in the Sanpete Valley, nursed Wakara back to health with tea and medicine. A few weeks later, Morley baptized Wakara into the Mormon faith. Over the summer, 126 members of Wakara's band were also ceremonially dipped in Manti's City Creek.[27]

WAKARA SUPPORTED THE MASSACRE OF THE UTES AT the lake and the growth of the Mormon settlements in the Sanpete Valley. He did so not because he lacked love for the Utes' most sacred lands and waters but because he cherished them. Along with his kin Sowiette ("the man that picks fish from the water"), Wakara wanted to wrest control over the fishing and festival grounds from his Timpanogos rivals.

A few weeks after Wakara was baptized in Manti, Wakara sent a letter via Isaac Morley to Brigham Young, urging him to hunt down the massacre's few survivors, including his rival Patsowet. Wakara pressed the Mormon prophet to put Patsowet and other troublesome Indians "out of the way" so that Wakara, other "good Indians" like him, and his new Mormon brethren might "be at rest and peace" and could "lay down and sleep good." The Mormons also alleged that Patsowet killed Joseph Higbee, the only Mormon who had died in the massacre. For his part, Patsowet had objected to Wakara's association with the settlers. "If Walker or others make peace with the Mormons, they [Patsowet and his followers] say they are women."[28]

That spring after the Mormons failed to find Patsowet, Wakara himself tracked his rival to a hideout south of Salt Lake. Wakara then sent for Mormon authorities to arrest Patsowet. The Mormons obliged. They brought Patsowet to the Council House in Temple Square, where he was tried and convicted for killing Joseph Higbee and sentenced to death. The Mormons then took Patsowet outside the city to carry out his death sentence, which was more a lynching than an execution. Settler Hosea Stout recalled that Patsowet was disemboweled. John Gunnison suggested that Patsowet was strangled with a bow.[29]

While he helped the Mormons kill off his last remaining Ute rivals for control over Timpanogos Lake, Wakara pushed the Mormons to concentrate their settlement and trade efforts away from the Utah Valley. In an April 21 letter, Morley reported to Young that Wakara wished to trade horses and enslaved Paiutes, which he had brought east after another raiding expedition in Paiute country and in California the winter before, for Mormon cattle, arms, and blankets. But Wakara wanted this trade fair to take place at Manti, not Timpanogos Lake. Wakara was growing worried about the Mormon sprawl around the lake.[30]

Wakara's worry wasn't without merit. Along the shore of the lake and beyond Fort Utah's walls, the settlers built fences to corral their cattle. The cattle fattened themselves on the rich grasslands. Their heavy hooves also trampled roots, seeds, and berry-producing plants, which supplied key calories to the Timpanogos diet. The ranches and farms, and the footprint of the fort itself, were dug across the Timpanogos' hunting trails, disrupting the valley's game.

But it was the damage to the waters that most threatened the Timpanogos. To build their cabins and fences, the settlers cut down cottonwoods and willows that grew along the river. Those trees kept soil in place so that the water remained clear and cool. The lands also provided food for spawning fish and their offspring in the form of bugs that lived in the trees and fell into the waters. George Bean, who dug the first irrigation ditches in the Utah Valley, noted the changes to the waters wrought by the settlers' arrival in 1849. Though late-spring frosts killed much of the settlers' early plantings, Bean also blamed the "considerable mineral developed [in the water] from irrigating" for the failure of their crops to grow. In August that same year, federal Indian agent John Wilson reported that the Mormon irrigation systems were rapidly drying up the land and damaging Utah Valley's fisheries. Wilson recommended that the government establish an orderly system of emigration to prevent settler population explosion, which he predicted would lead to environmental degradation and the starvation of the Utes.[31]

No system materialized. Instead, the Wakara-backed massacre of the Timpanogos emboldened the Mormons to expand their Utah Valley settlements. As more settlers poured into the valley, they fanned out around the lake to found Lehi, Pleasant Grove, Springville, Payson, Alpine, Spanish Fork, and American Fork—all of which were established in 1850.[32]

These newcomers needed to be fed. And while they tried to adapt their farming practices to Utah's unfamiliar soil, the newcomers fished. Their trolling nets were constantly in the water, Wakara complained to Brigham Young when they met in Provo in May 1852 during the fish festival. In January 1853, the Legislative Assembly of the Territory of Utah passed an act to prevent the "needless destruction of fish" in the lake; the city government of Provo was given jurisdiction over the Provo River. The settlers enacted these provisions not to benefit the Utes but to organize the exploding fishing activities in the valley, which blocked the Utes from the lake and river where they had fished—and managed the fisheries—for generations. The fight for control over lands and waters around Timpanogos Lake grew so contentious that in 1853 a fish fight between Wakara's Utes and Mormon settlers would spark the so-called Walker War.[33]

IN LATE MAY 1850, JUST AS THE JUNE suckers began their spawning run, Wakara and his followers pulled up the stakes of their camp near Manti, where they had spent most of the winter. They loaded their horses with deer and buffalo skins and made the eighty-mile trek along the eastern spine of the Wasatch Front to the fish festival at Timpanogos Lake. On May 22, Young and his own entourage forded the Timpanogos (Provo) River, then swollen from melting snows, to reach Wakara's camp near the abandoned village of Wakara's massacred Ute rivals. With the lake Timpanogos displaced or killed, both Wakara and Young set their sights on taking control of the lakeshore and surrounding Utah Valley.

That morning, Young and other Mormon leaders ducked into Wakara's tent. Once inside, Wakara, his brothers Arapeen and Sanpitch, and his kin Sowiette and Antonga offered their greetings to the Mormon delegation. Young and the Mormon brethren squatted on the ground in a circle. With Huntington serving as interpreter, Wakara opened the conversation with a list of complaints. He felt bad. He had lost eight relations in an ambush from the Shoshones in Wyoming's Wind River Range. Wakara had been unable to defend his kin because he was preoccupied with supporting the Mormons in their fight with the Timpanogos at the lake. Wakara wanted Young to find out who had killed his friends. And he wanted assurances that he could trust Young. "I don't want you to throw me away," Wakara said. The Ute leader—whom Isaac Morley described as having "an eagle's eye, nothing escapes his notice" when it came to the interactions of men—knew Young's promises of friendship with Natives were often conditional and temporary.[34]

"I won't throw you away," Young promised the Ute leader. "We want to smoke the pipe of peace and be friends and make an everlasting covenant," the prophet implored. "You are my brother, let us be brothers." Young then made the same invitation to the rest of the gathered Ute leaders. "We want you all to be brothers." Wakara agreed. "It is done."

Young then requested that Wakara help him transition the Utes to a settler lifestyle. The Mormon prophet asked Wakara to allow his young men to become apprentices to the settlers in house building and farming and allow his children to go to Mormon schools. Wakara said yes. But not here, at Timpanogos Lake, Wakara insisted. He wanted this future Ute-Mormon settlement to be built in Manti. The Ute leader understood that a sizable Mormon presence at the lake would likely further damage the much older and more sacred covenant that the Fish Eaters had with the fish.

Young pressed Wakara to sell his lands to the White settlers. Wakara said no. Instead, Wakara pressed Young to view the land as he did: not as a commodity to be bartered away like horses, skins, clothes, kettles, and slaves but as a homeland that the Utes were willing to share with the newcomers. You can "settle on it," Wakara explained, as long as there is respect and reciprocity. "Mormons love us, we love them." Wakara then called for a break for lunch. There was fresh fish to eat.

After lunch, the meeting moved to the lodge of Sowiette, the Utes' civil leader. Young again gathered the Utes in a round and professed his love for them. "We have come here to settle on your land," Young explained. Perhaps to show that he had some understanding of the Utes' views on landownership, Young continued, "Our father the Great Spirit has plenty of land for you and for the Mormons." Forget about what happened a few months ago when the Mormons massacred Utes in this valley, near this very spot. Instead, Young told the Utes to focus on the future, when they would give up their traveling and hunting in order to build houses, raise grain, and tend cattle like the settlers did. Then, with his hand on Wakara's shoulders, Young declared, "Walker is now my brother." And with his other arm around Arapeen, Young continued, "Arrapine is my brother. Sowiet is a good man."

Filled with enthusiasm for the dawning of a peaceful era, Young then began speaking in tongues. Young's physician, Dr. Samuel

Sprague, joined him, speaking a language that Arapeen identified as Sioux. In the evening, the festivities moved to the relocated fort at Provo. Wakara had come down with a fever from the day's excitement. Dr. Sprague treated him with botanic medicine. Some Utes sat by the fire and gambled. Others sang and danced in a round.[35]

Young's spirit-filled profession of affection for Wakara's Utes was itself a choreographed performance. According to his own recollections, Young left the May 1850 meeting more convinced than ever that the Mormons could not live in peace with even "friendly" Utes like Wakara. Despite the Ute leader's claims that he had received a prophetic message to share the lands with the Whites, Young really wanted Wakara to realize that there was in fact no future for the Utes in the verdant Utah Valley. Wakara should really turn over his lands to the settlers, lest he and the surviving Ute leaders also end up like their rivals, with their heads cut off and boxed up.[36]

Young did not blame Wakara. Young believed that Wakara's refusal to sell the Mormons their lands was the fault of the settlers. Instead of lifting up the Utes to the Mormons' level of civilization, as the Book of Mormon had called them to do, the settlers "by their conduct had placed themselves on the level with the Indians," Young wrote in his journal. Much to Young's disgust, even after the bloody massacres in early 1850, the settlers again participated in the Utes' fish festival games of wrestling, racing horses, and gambling. And they fished and fished and fished alongside the Utes.[37]

In short, from Young's point of view, there had been too much fishing and not enough forting up, farming, and fighting.

IN NOVEMBER 1850, THE CHURCH'S FIRST PRESIDENCY SENT a letter to the church's representative in Washington, DC, Dr. John Bernhisel. The church's highest leaders gave Bernhisel talking points to petition President Millard Fillmore and members of Congress to grant "Deseret" statehood and support their efforts to remove Native Americans from the Mormon settlers' hoped-for homeland.

The letter echoed President Andrew Jackson's infamous 1830 Indian-removal speech. In it, Jackson declared that it was necessary to drive "savages" off their own lands, to make room for "our extensive Republic, studded with cities, towns, and prosperous farms embellished with all the improvements which art can devise or industry execute, occupied by more than 12,000,000 happy people, and filled with all the blessings of liberty, civilization and religion." The church's First Presidency wrote to the Washington-based politicians via Bernhisel,

> Is it desirable that the barren soil of the mountains [and] valleys should be converted into fruitful fields? Let the Indians be removed. Is it desirable that the way should be opened up for a rapid increase of population into our new state or Territory, also to California or Oregon? Let the Indians be removed. We can then devote more time to agriculture, and raise more grains to feed the starving millions desirous of coming hither. For the prosperity of civilization, for the safety of our mail routes, for the good of the Indians, let them be removed.[38]

While Young attempted to enlist Washington to help him rid Deseret of Native presence, at the other end of the country, as he had done for the previous decade, Wakara spent the fall and winter of 1850–1851 raiding horses. Just as much as fishing at Timpanogos Lake, these annual horse raids in Southern California helped shape Wakara into the great Native and American leader he became. And the raids helped shape other people and places of the American West.

Such people and places included Wakara's favorite horse-raiding target: the ranchos of the Lugo family in San Bernardino.

Part III

Wakara's Horse

Chapter 8

Horse Wars

Antonio María Lugo and Isaac Williams clutched their rifles with one hand. With the other hand, they held fast to the reins of their horses, steadying the animals who whinnied underneath.

In October 1845, the two rancheros and a dozen posse members stood guard at the entrance of the sprawling Rancho Santa Ana del Chino in what was then Alta (Mexico-controlled) Southern California. The posse fixed their gaze on the foothills of the San Gabriel Mountains. Any minute, they expected to see dust clouds rise as hundreds of hooves raced toward them.

Lugo and Williams were waiting for Wakara. They had received word that the Ute leader and his cavalry were again making their way west along the Old Spanish Trail. And word was that Wakara intended on, once again, raiding horses from the Lugo family's massive properties.

Antonio María Lugo was the sixty-seven-year-old patriarch of one of the largest landowning families in Alta California. Isaac Williams was a Pennsylvania-born trapper and merchant who had married Antonio María's daughter, María de Jesus. Williams ran Rancho

Antonio María Lugo (1778–1860). Painting by Henri Penelon. Lugo was the patriarch of a prominent *Californio* family, whose ranchos became frequent targets of Wakara and other horse raiders during the 1830s and 1840s. (Courtesy of the Seaver Center for Western History Research, Los Angeles County Museum of Natural History)

Santa Ana del Chino with his father-in-law. In total, the Lugos held more than 250,000 acres of land, stretching thirty miles from modern-day San Bernardino southwest to the Chino Hills.[1]

Lugo and Williams knew Wakara. Since the beginning of the decade, Wakara and his cavalry, comprising fur trappers, Utes, and California Natives, had made annual raids of the California ranchos, including those of the Lugos. They arrived in early fall. For several months, Wakara and his men raided a few dozen horses at a time, almost always at night, then ran their bounties into nearby canyons to avoid capture by *Californio* posses. In early winter the horse wranglers gathered their raided horses on the other side of the mountains, then began the return east on the trail with hundreds, sometimes thousands, of horses and cattle following behind.

In October 1845, word of the imminent arrival of the infamous Ute raider spread as fast as a Spanish colonial horse and his rider could gallop across the valley floors. The Mexican governor at Los Angeles had also learned that Wakara was coming. He called for soldiers and volunteers to arm themselves and defend the *Californios*' livestock against another raiding season led by Wakara. The Lugos would be the first line of defense.[2]

Antonio María Lugo was already a seasoned Indian fighter when he prepared to face down Wakara in 1845. Born in 1778, Lugo spent most of his teens and twenties as a soldier at the Spanish military outpost at Santa Barbara, where he guarded the mission against attacks and revolts from Indigenous California tribes. Junípero Serra founded the mission just a few years before Lugo's birth when the Spanish government charged the Franciscans with establishing strongholds to thwart English and Russian expansion along the West Coast and to spread Catholicism to California's Natives. The Spanish Crown also wanted to develop another source for horses and human labor to power their colonial growth in the American Southwest. To build what would become a network of twenty-one missions stretching from present-day San Diego to San Francisco, the Franciscans created a system intent on taking complete control over Native lives, lands, and resources. With the help of militias like the one Antonio María Lugo served in, the missionaries coerced California Natives to abandon their homelands and lifeways and forced them into captivity and servitude in overcrowded missionary encampments. At night, the padres locked the unmarried "neophytes" in cramped, disease-ridden quarters. During the day, the Natives worked like slaves in missionaries' homes and fields. The padres fed their captives starvation rations. The padres' intent, some scholars believe, was to weaken the neophytes' bodies and spirits so they would accept the gospel—or at least be too hungry to run away.[3]

Still, some Native Californians did run away. Others fought back, as in the famous Chumash Revolt of 1824, during which, for a time, the Chumash took control of the mission at Santa Barbara where Antonio María Lugo had long been stationed. But death due to disease and malnutrition was a more frequent outcome than flight or fight. By 1833, when the missions were secularized and the lands were purchased or given to prominent *Californio* families, including the Lugos, the Franciscans had baptized 81,586 California Natives and recorded the burials of 62,600.[4]

Antonio María Lugo's eight children came of age during this massive emptying of California of its Native peoples, which corresponded with a massive increase in the population of horses. When they founded the missions in the 1770s, Serra's Franciscans brought with them a few dozen Spanish colonial horses—descendants of the horses that the conquistadors had brought from Spain in the early 1500s. In California, the herds grew larger each year as they fed on the region's rich grasslands. By 1820, there were likely over 50,000 horses in Southern California, which, along with cattle herds, destroyed grasses, herbs, and seeds that California Natives had fed upon and managed for generations.

Even for the settlers, the boom in the equine population was not always welcome. Antonio María Lugo's eldest son, José del Carmen, remembered seeing the massive herds of wild mustangs eat up grasses that the ranchos relied on to feed their tamed horses. The younger Lugo recalled watching his father and the vaqueros (cowboys) erect massive corrals to gather the wild horses, which they then slaughtered by the thousands. Despite regular culling, the horse population continued to increase. And as the herds grew, so did the trade caravans that trekked to California from New Mexico, where the desert climate made it harder to raise large numbers of horses. At the ranchos or in the markets in Los Angeles, New Mexicans traded fine blankets—often made with Indian slave labor—for California horses, which the traders then drove back to New Mexico, where they fetched much higher prices.[5]

Wakara and other raiders had shown that stealing horses was cheaper than trading for them. But Wakara needed lots of men to pull off his well-coordinated, weeks-long raiding campaigns. In October 1845, Antonio María Lugo and Isaac Williams heard that they might have to fight 180 mounted men under Wakara's charge.

As expected, on the horizon, Lugo and Williams spotted Wakara riding toward them on his signature caparisoned horse. But to their surprise, trailing behind the Ute leader was a group of only forty warriors. Even more surprisingly, the Utes brought with them women and children.

Wakara broke off from his group and rode to Lugo and Williams. The posse leveled their rifles at the approaching rider.

The Ute leader told Lugo and Williams—almost certainly in Spanish as he was fluent in the language—not to fear.

He explained that he brought with him furs, pelts, and Paiutes. Wakara signaled to one of his lieutenants, who pulled sample furs from a satchel. Another lieutenant pulled forward a Paiute child for the rancheros to examine. Wakara told Lugo and Williams that he wanted to exchange Utah animal skins and humans for California cattle and horses.

Wakara then pointed to the Ute women and children, indicating that he came not to raid but to bring peace, friendship, and commerce.

Relieved, Lugo and Williams gave the signal to lower their weapons. The rancheros invited Wakara to make camp at Rancho Santa Ana del Chino. Wakara accepted, setting up his lodges near Williams's adobe home. Just as they did with the Mormons during their fish festivals at Timpanogos Lake, the Utes and the rancheros traded goods during the day, then at night swapped stories of the trail around a communal fire. Wakara so charmed the California landowners in those early fall days in 1845 that Lugo sent a letter to the governor at Los Angeles telling him to stand down. Wakara and his lodges of families meant no ill, the message read.

But Lugo and Williams soon discovered that Wakara's harmless trading party was a Trojan horse. While he dined with the Lugos and slept on their grounds at their invitation, Wakara was also casing their horse corrals for coming raids. Over the fall and early winter, when the moon lit up the desert sky, Wakara led his warriors on nighttime raids targeting the Lugos' horses and cattle as well as the livestock of other nearby ranchos. He and his cavalrymen quietly opened the corral gates. Then, in unison, they let out yells, breaking the still of the night, to excite the animals out of the gates of the football-field-sized enclosures. Wakara then drove the horses into the nearby hills and canyons, including one that would come to bear the name Horse Thief Canyon. There, other members of Wakara's raiding parties kept the horses fed and watered near the canyons' well-concealed streams.

In February 1846, Wakara, his followers, and their bounty of hundreds of horses and cattle began their return east. Antonio María Lugo's son Vincente rounded up a group of *Californios* and Cahuilla Indian allies to pursue Wakara to the other side of the Cajon Pass. Lugo's posse found thirty of Wakara's men on the banks of the Mojave River. But the posse turned back. Lugo decided against starting a gun fight with the well-armed cavalry. Wakara continued east along a section of the Old Spanish Trail that became known as Walker's Trail.

The raiding season of 1845–1846 would not be the last time the Lugo family tried to chase down Wakara's cavalry and recoup their horses. Over the next few years, the Lugos and other *Californios* would try different approaches to stop Wakara, including threatening to hang him or scalp him if the *Californios* ever caught him.[6]

Wakara was never caught. Instead, a few years later, when they attempted to ride down Wakara after another raiding season, it would be Lugo family members whose necks were in danger of getting stretched at the end of a hangman's noose.

JUST AS THE FISH OF TIMPANOGOS LAKE MADE the Timpanogos Fish Eaters, the adoption of the horse made Wakara's Utes and other Native Americans into horse people. Atop Spanish colonial horses, in the sixteenth century, the Spanish toppled the great Indigenous empires of Mesoamerica. By the next century, Native Americans had begun to develop their own transregional empires that warred, raided, and traded with settlers as well as with other Native horse and nonhorse nations. In doing so, Natives like Wakara's Utes transformed the environment, human population, and political geography of the American West.

The horse allowed Wakara to remain Native. On horseback, Wakara protected his ancestral land and people from rival Natives, including his Numic kin, the Comanches, and from settlers like Brigham Young. The horse also allowed him to become American. Atop his horses, Wakara expanded his territorial reach outside the "earths" of the Great Basin, raiding more horses in California, enslaving nonequestrian Numic peoples, especially the Paiutes of southern Utah, and enriching himself and his followers along the way.

WAKARA'S HORSE EMPIRE MIGHT BE GONE. BUT REMAINS of this empire, including Wakara's horses themselves, continue to shape the American West.

On a cool spring morning in 2018, I went in search of the Sulphur herd of wild horses that roam over a vast, rugged landscape of public land overseen by the Bureau of Land Management (BLM) on the border between Utah and Nevada. Historical evidence and genetic testing indicate that the Sulphur herd of colonial Spanish mustangs descend from the horses Wakara stole from the Lugos and other California rancheros in the 1840s. As the Ute raider moved his herds east, some of the horses escaped. They eventually made their way north where, free from humans and other predators, they reproduced in the remote region of desert and mountains.[7]

The descendants of Wakara's horses have formed a herd of a few hundred that run, feed, and breed on more than 250,000 acres of the Sulphur Herd Management Area (HMA), spread between the 10,000-foot Indian Peak and Mountain Home Ranges. The horses spend hot days in the foothills under the shade of evergreens. In winter, they gallop through sagebrush and salt desert shrubs. Whatever the season, the horses stay close to water. While the herd gets its name from the natural springs spread throughout the HMA, today human-made wells, which fill 1,000-gallon metal tanks, keep the horses watered.

Because the Sulphur HMA covers an area larger than all five boroughs of New York City combined, I knew that I would have trouble finding the horses on my own. In the West, whether it's backcountry skiing in the winter or morel mushroom hunting in the spring, it's best practice to employ a guide before going anywhere unfamiliar. And when it comes to these horses, guides are not in short supply. There is a whole cadre of horse people who care a lot about America's wild horses, and care for the Spanish mustangs in particular, which their self-appointed protectors call "America's first horses."

Even before my rented Kia sedan stopped in the driveway, my guide to the herd, Robert Hayden, a jovial retiree, bounded out the front door of his home, just outside the tiny town of Baker, Nevada. Robert and his wife, Kathleen (her friends call her Kat), split their time between their Baker country cabin, which has more horse stalls outside than bedrooms inside, and their main home in Southern

California. Since the establishment of the Great Basin National Park in 1986, Baker has become the seasonal home to a growing number of mountain bikers and hikers, artists, and wealthy ex-coastals. But many of Baker's "old-time" residents run libertarian, like the Haydens, who in the last two decades have sought refuge from California's high taxes and the "nanny state," as Robert calls it, in the wide-open spaces of what he describes as the last unsettled part of the West.

Battling the nanny state is how the Haydens spend most of their time as wild horse protectors. "We the people, not the government, own the horses," Kat Hayden often says. And thus we the people, not the government, must protect them as part of our heritage. In fact, according to Kat, despite laws requiring the government to care for the horses, left to its own devices the government and its cabal of "professional 'environmental practitioners'" would "manage" these priceless horses out of existence.[8]

And if that happened, the loss to America's past and present would be incalculable. "It was on their backs that the West was won," Robert Hayden yelled to me as we drove south toward the Sulphur HMA, the dry wind whipping through the cabin of his Chevy Silverado. And Hayden is right. The Sulphur horses are descendants of the Iberian barb type, which the Spanish conquistadors brought to the Americas in the 1500s. These horses were well adapted to the American West. Its dry, rugged climate resembles that of the southern Iberian Peninsula where the horses were first bred and battle tested. The last of the *Reconquista* wars of the Old World—which ended with the 1491 fall of the Nasrid kingdom of Granada—occurred on the eve of the *entrada* into the New World. In 1493, as part of Christopher Columbus's second voyage, King Ferdinand and Queen Isabella ordered that ships crossing *Mar Oceano* carry fifteen stallions and ten mares. Their goal was to establish breeding *rancherías* to supply the conquistadors with Iberian horses for their wars of conquest in the West Indies and the rest of central America.[9]

Spanish colonial mustangs, Sulphur Horse Management Area, western Utah. This horse is a descendant of the Spanish colonials that Wakara stole from *Californio* rancheros, including the Lugos, in the 1840s. (Courtesy of Chet Kalinowska)

The horses flourished in the New World. After all, the Spanish did not introduce the horse to the Western Hemisphere—they reintroduced it. *Equus caballus* first evolved in the Americas then disappeared some 10,000 years ago for reasons that remain a matter of debate. Between the early sixteenth and the nineteenth centuries, horses, along with European diseases and guns, became crucial weapons in Spain's conquest and settlement of lands and peoples from Chile to the Rio Grande. Yet, during the same period, Native American peoples, including the Comanches, Apaches, and Utes, built their own equestrian empires as they vied for control over what would become the American West.

Wild horse protectors like the Haydens see it as their patriotic duty to safeguard these historic horses as well as the horses' land, water, and grass from ravenous cattle and sheep, from water-hoarding cities, and from dollar-driven mineral extractors. But the horse protectors

Note the tiger-striped legs on the Spanish colonial mustang. (Courtesy of Chet Kalinowska)

say that the greatest threat to the horses is the governmental body charged with protecting them: the BLM.

In 1971 Congress passed the Wild and Free-Roaming Horses and Burros Act, a law that traces its origins to lobbying efforts on behalf of the declining herds of Spanish descent in western states, including the Sulphur herd. In the decades preceding the act, western ranchers shot wild horses, chased herds in helicopters until they collapsed from exhaustion, and poisoned their watering holes. They also rounded horses up for slaughter to make pet food. The act mandated that the BLM preserve these "living symbols of the historic and pioneer spirit of the West" from inhumane "capture, branding, harassment, or death."[10]

According to the BLM, the act has been too successful. At the time of its passage, an estimated 25,000 wild horses lived on public lands. As of 2021, the BLM estimates, there are over 86,000 wild horses and burros, most on the 175 HMAs spread across the West. That's 59,000 too many horses to meet the BLM's budget and to live in balance with livestock that also call the HMAs home, the BLM declared in a recent report. Left unchecked, the BLM claims, the herds will double in size every four years. Overpopulation leads to overgrazing, growth of invasive grass species, and stress on natural water sources, which leads to horse deaths from starvation and dehydration. Overpopulation also forces the horses off the HMAs and onto roadways, causing horse and car collisions, and into conflicts with ranchers and farmers. Through a combination of fertility controls and adoption programs, the BLM hopes to cut its costs and cull the herds by more than half.[11]

What the BLM sees as a plan to manage the horses, many horse protectors deem a declaration of genocidal war. In September 2016, after a BLM advisory board voted to euthanize tens of thousands of wild horses in the BLM's care, the US Humane Society declared that, if carried through, the recommendation signaled "a sort of 'Final Solution' cooked up by public-land ranchers and their allies." The lobbying group Saving America's Mustangs also viewed the BLM's plans through the prism of Nazism. "Today, the BLM is taking a more modern, yet similar approach to Dr. Josef Mengele. His name is familiar to anyone who knows about one of the most atrocious eras in human history: The Holocaust." Kat Hayden is less hyperbolic. Still, she predicts that BLM's plans to remove horses from HMAs and castrate those remaining on the range will lead to the "erosion of genetic viability." Rather than on a path toward stability, wild horses, especially the most historically significant like the Sulphur herd, would be placed on a "path to extinction."[12]

To the horse protectors, the BLM's horse management is cynical. The BLM fails to maintain the water and food on the HMAs. The BLM fails to prevent ranchers from grazing on land that, by right of inheritance from the horses' forefathers who first settled the lands and by legal mandate, belongs to the horses. The BLM then blames the horses, not the cattle and sheep, for the damage to public lands. And when the herds leave the HMAs in search of resources, the BLM deems it necessary to cull the herd.

So far, the horse protectors have stopped the BLM's culling plan in its tracks. With its smaller roundups, the BLM wants to reduce the Sulphur herd to 250 horses, claiming this to be the top end of sustainability for the Sulphur HMA. The horse protectors don't buy it. They are convinced that the BLM's goal is nothing less than genocide of these historic horses.[13]

The horse protectors agree that the BLM is the enemy of the wild horses of America. They do not agree about what these horses symbolize. To some, the horses are akin to the descendants of America's human revolutionaries: born free and wild on wild and free land. "We identify with wild horses as symbols of our own inherent and inalienable right of freedom," Kat Hayden has written. "Horses have been fundamental to our stock-raising, ranching lifestyle since the times of the Spanish vaqueros in the Southwest, the Mormon immigrants in Utah, and the great drives along the Old Spanish and Chisholm Trails." At best, BLM bureaucrats stifle the liberty of the horses and their patriotic protectors. At worst, they threaten the horses' existence.[14]

To others, these horses are akin, or even literally kin, to Native Americans. Leland Grass, a Diné elder and medicine man, has explained that the horse's body is a sacred manifestation of nature and nature's connection to the Navajo people. "The horse's mane represents dark rain clouds and ensures moisture and well-being to all life forms on Mother Earth and in Father Sky," Grass has written. "Underneath the hooves are arrowheads that ensure the protection of the Diné people and all other life forms." Grass chastised other Navajo leaders, who had backed the government's plans to cull horses on the Navajo Nation, as falling under the spell of "forced assimilation" of Native peoples, similar to when the government cut Native peoples' "hairs and prevented our children from speaking our language. We see this mass execution of our relatives, the horses, as the rotten fruit of a bad seed that was planted in the minds of our children in the earlier days."[15]

Some horse protectors draw parallels between Indian reservations and HMAs, where horses have been crowded into smaller areas that are constantly being invaded by settler sheep and cattle who eat up the grass and drink up the water. The horses suffer; then they are blamed for their own poverty and sickness. What's more, as the Indian boarding school movement separated Native children from their families, the BLM separates horses from their family bands during roundups, actions that, according to horse advocacy organizations, destroy life-sustaining familial connections, making the horses more prone to death due to injury, disease, and despair.

Still, the work of some horse protectors echoes the paternalism of the "Friends of the Indian Movement" of the late nineteenth century as well as Christian missionary programs that started in the late twentieth century. Akin to World Vision's infamous program—that for the cost of a newspaper subscription, Christians can "sponsor" photogenic children from countries in the developing world to ensure they get food and Christian educational materials—Return to Freedom offers sponsorships, billed monthly, for a select group of horses with names like El Presidente, Black Moon, and True. Such sponsorships supposedly support the cost of housing these horses off their HMAs in "safe havens" under the watchful care of adoptive parents.[16]

The Haydens are veterans of the horse wars. They cut their teeth by advocating for the Coyote Canyon herd whose ancestral range is near the Haydens' home in Southern California. According to Kat, these horses are also descendants of the Spanish colonial stock that were brought to California in 1769 when Junípero Serra established the first mission in the region. Some of these horses were then stolen by the Yokuts and Miwok, who mounted them to protect their own territories and peoples. Others escaped, creating the feral herds that the Lugos tried to cull in the 1820s.[17]

Despite their historic importance to California history, Kat says, the government has failed to protect the herd. So, in the 1990s, the Haydens founded the Coyote Canyon Caballos d'Anza, an advocacy group dedicated to "educating about and restoring a tiny segment of the last tribal wild horses in Southern California and [repatriating] them to our historic landscape." Kat has chronicled what she calls acts of "conspiracy and fraud" against these horses by the BLM and state bureaucrats, culminating when officials removed the last members of the herd from their ancestral lands on a state park sixty miles east of San Diego. The state denied wrongdoing, describing the horses it removed as "feral and invasive."[18]

Robert Hayden is a cofounder of Coyote Canyon Caballos d'Anza. But it's Kat who "does the politics," Robert explained to me during our drive to see the Sulphur herd. Kat writes the op-eds, gives talks at historical societies, and lobbies officials to enact protections for the horses and their lands. Robert's work for the horses is manual. He counts the horses, preparing to counter the inevitable calls to cull the herd. He makes sure the water tanks are full and free of algae. On occasion, he drags the carcass of a horse hit on the highway out of sight.

The Coyote Canyon horses, along with all wild horses, are special to the Haydens. They want the horses to be recognized as Native American historic cultural resources and thus afforded the same protections as rock carvings, historic shelters, tools, weapons, and human remains. This is why, at her horse talks, Kat is sure to point out that the Coyote Canyon and Sulphur herds are connected not only to famous settler figures like Serra but also to Native horse peoples. Wakara's horse raiding—which made him in the 1840s, as Kat puts it, "the most wanted man in California"—always shows up in her talks.[19]

But no horses are as special as the Sulphur herd. "It's their blood purity," Robert said. In their veins runs the purest Iberian blood of all the wild horses in North America. In the 2010s, the Haydens even convinced a reluctant BLM to breed the four surviving Coyote stallions, then in captivity, with mares from the Sulphur herd.[20]

Robert told me what to look for in these "pure-blood horses." The Spanish colonials, which some people call Spanish mustangs, are easily identified by their physical features. Their colorations are either "grulla" (blue gray) or "dun" (reddish and chestnut). They have tiger-striped legs and a prominent dorsal stripe and bicolored manes and tails (see photographs on pages 148 and 149). They have curved ears, which resemble a bird's beak, and short backs. But the herd isn't as pure as it once was. "People dump their unwanted horses here, and they've mixed up the lines," Robert said. To ensure the purity, the Haydens have advocated for the horses to be considered a cultural resource of the Great Basin National Park and protected by armed park rangers.

Once we turned off US Highway 21 and into the HMA, it didn't take long for us to spot the herd, then spread out on the foothills of the Mountain Home Range.

We parked the truck. Hayden smiled after peering through a set of binoculars, relieved to see the herd of three dozen adults. He counted three yearlings grazing near their parents.

After ten minutes, we started up the truck to see if we could get a closer look. At the start of the motor, the horses raised their heads. Then they took off in a hurried trot toward the hills. Even over the whirl of the truck engine, we could hear the steady rumble of more than 150 hooves hitting the sandy ground. A large male ran parallel to us. "He's scouting for danger," Hayden explained.

TODAY, THE SULPHUR HERD IS FERAL. THESE MUSTANGS have forgotten the time not so long ago when their ancestors formed a partnership with humans that changed the American West.

In the long-established narrative of this history, the Spanish get the credit for bringing the horse back to America and, atop the horse, leveling Mesoamerican empires to make way for European conquest. American cavalries and pioneers get the credit for "taming" the American West and bringing the remaining wild Indians and wild landscape to heal. More recently, scholars have given credit to Native horse nations, like the Utes and Comanches, for creating their own horse empires, which helped loosen the Spanish and later Mexican grip over the Southwest and which allowed American armies to march into already-vanquished territories in Texas, New Mexico, and California. But arguably there was no more consequential union of human and horse in North America than that of Wakara and the Sulphur herd's ancestors.

To understand how Wakara and his horses came to dominate the American West in the 1840s, we need to explore the millennia-long evolution of the horse and human partnership. This story, like the cover-up of Wakara's life and legacy, has long been written less as history and more as myth. After all, those who have claimed to be the originators of horse mastery have often claimed to be members of the master race, religion, and nation.

Chapter 9

We've Always Had the Horse

Forrest Cuch and I entered the workshop of Brigham Young University's Museum of Paleontology in Provo, Utah, in the summer of 2023. Fossils from dinosaurs and ancient mammals were stacked from floor to ceiling. The tangy smell of dust and plaster hung in the air. Undergrads were perched on work benches, removing debris with tiny brushes from a set of bones of indeterminate origin. The remains of the "Lehi Horse" were laid out on a folding table in the center of the workshop.

In the fall of 2017, a couple doing landscaping at their home in Lehi, Utah, on the northern shore of Utah Lake, unearthed an almost complete horse skeleton. She (testing revealed that the horse was female) was buried so deep in Bonneville sands that the paleontologists first called to excavate her believed she was from the last ice age some 16,000 years ago. The discovery of an ancient horse was such exciting news that *The New York Times* published a story about it. But when archaeozoologists and anthropologists examined the skeleton, they realized that this horse was even more special than first thought. This horse wasn't ancient—she was modern, an *Equus caballus*. Radiocarbon dating indicated that she died in the 1700s or 1800s.[1]

In the workshop, Dr. Isaac Hart, then an anthropologist at the University of Utah, expert on the history of horse domestication, and coauthor of a study of the Lehi Horse, picked up a set of vertebrae. He turned the yellowish-brown bones over in his hand to show the cracks in her back.

"See the fractures here?" Hart ran his fingers over the lines in the bones. "That indicates that she was clearly used for riding." The fractures meant that Native Americans rode her before the Spanish introduced framed saddles to Native horse culture. Hart then picked up the right femur. "Bone on bone. She had arthritis and osteoporosis. Every step must have been excruciating." The question is then, if she was so lame, why keep her alive? "Perhaps to breed her," Hart explained. "That and she clearly was loved."

"She might have served a religious purpose," Forrest Cuch, Wakara's descendant, chimed in. "Maybe she was a healer." Cuch works with his own stable of equine therapy horses on his ranch on the Northern Utes' reservation in the Uintah Basin. "Horses are very spiritual beings. And they are sacred beings for us Utes," explained Cuch. When the Lehi Horse died at the age of about twelve years, she was buried by her caretakers with a reverence similar to that shown a human loved one.[2]

Born in 1815, Wakara came of age when the Utes around Timpanogos (Utah) Lake were becoming equestrian. In the 1840s, Wakara told Dimick Huntington that his father had bought the band's first horse from Spanish explorers. But other written sources indicate that Wakara's recollection about when the first horses came to the Utah Valley might have been off by a few decades. In their journals from 1776, Francisco Atanasio Domínguez and Silvestre Vélez de Escalante made no mention of the Utes at Timpanogos Lake having horses, though the Utes were well acquainted with horse raids from their

Numic kin, the Comanches. By 1805, ten years before Wakara's birth, other visitors reported that the Timpanogos were raising horses in the valley. Still, Wakara's story of the Timpanogos' first horse hints at a transitional period when the Fish Eaters also became horse riders, and soon after that, one of their own—Wakara—became the most infamous horse raider in the West.

The discovery of the Lehi Horse, along with studies of other domesticated horse remains throughout the American West and Great Plains, has exploded long-received narratives that European conquistadors and settlers not only reintroduced horses to the Americas but also shaped how Native Americans integrated them into their own cultures. There is mounting evidence that, hundreds of miles away from European settlements and decades before European penetration into Native homelands, once the horse reached them, Native Americans, including Wakara's Timpanogos and other Indigenous peoples around what is today Utah Lake, developed their own horse cultures.

Most of the horses on whose backs Wakara dominated the American Southwest in the 1840s were Spanish colonial horses or their wild kin, Spanish mustangs. The Lehi Horse was not a Spanish horse. She was too small, standing no taller than a small pony. But Wakara's Utes might have learned to ride, rear, breed, and care for horses on the back of the Lehi Horse and others like her. In that sense, the Lehi Horse might have been the mother of Wakara's horse culture.

THE LEHI HORSE REPRESENTS THE END OF THE story of how Wakara became one of the greatest horsemen of the American West. To understand that end, we need to meet the ancient ancestors of *Equus caballus* and the humans who first domesticated them.

Equus—the genus of modern horses—first evolved on the American continent about four million years ago. *Equus* was the size of a modern pony and looked very much like its contemporary descendants, with long legs and fused leg bones, a big brain, and one toe. Some 2.6 million years ago, glacially formed land bridges allowed some *Equus* species to migrate across the seas, where the genus continued to thrive and diversify. By 500,000 years ago, *Equus* was on every continent and in every biogeographic realm, save for those of Australia and Antarctica. In Africa, *Equus* evolved into various species of zebras. In Asia and the Middle East, *Equus* became the onager (wild ass). The wild species of horse (*Equus ferus*) was the last to leave North America, some 200,000 years ago, spreading throughout the continents, including South America and Eurasia.[3]

The age of the horse birthed the age of man. Once humans learned to harness horsepower—riding behind horses on chariots or mounting them—humans explored and settled greater distances. And these equestrians traded, mated with, warred with, and enslaved other human populations, spreading languages, religions, genes, and diseases across the globe. The domestication of the horse also led to rapid advancements in horticultural and herding technologies, which in turn helped feed more people, leading to population booms, more complex social and political organizations, and advances in linguistic sophistication. Or, as anthropologist David W. Anthony has famously suggested, the horse begot the wheel and language as we know them today.[4]

Yet archaeologists and anthropologists have debated, often fiercely, when, where, and by whom the first horses were domesticated. This debate has long been shaped by politics as much as scholarship. After all, ethno-national pride was at stake. Those nations and peoples who could lay claim to being the first humans to harness and mount horses could claim to be the descendants of the creators of much of global human culture, most notably of Indo-European languages, which scholars have long thought spread with the horse.

From English and French to Kurdish and Punjabi, close to half of the world's population speak Indo-European languages.

In the late-nineteenth century, to justify British global conquest and unify their empire around a shared origin myth, scholars at Oxford and Cambridge argued that the English were the true descendants of the Aryans, the name ascribed to the authors of the *Rig Veda*, the most ancient religious texts written in an Indo-European language. At the turn of the twentieth century, linguist and archaeologist Gustaf Kossinna argued that the original Aryan homeland was in Germany, where he claimed prehistoric Germans were the first to domesticate the horse, the first to develop an alphabet, and the first to make bronze. Kossinna also argued that with their horses and superior metallurgical and linguistic technologies, the Germans spread Aryan culture throughout the rest of Eurasia, enslaving pedestrian peoples they encountered, then forcing them to adopt Proto-Germanic language and culture—or die resisting.[5]

Kossinna's nationalistic project provided the mythic claims of an innately German Aryan racial and cultural superiority that undergirded Nazi ideology. Adolf Hitler cribbed from Kossinna's work in *Mein Kampf*, arguing that the Aryans' greatest strength was their ability to "tame" and subjugate animals—both horses and "inferior men"—further propagating a pure race and a purified nation. The Nazis funded excavations in Germany as well as in Greece—long considered the birthplace of Western culture—where Nazi archaeologists claimed to have unearthed artifacts from an Indo-Germanic migration dating back 10,000 years. "In all this troublesome business" of archaeology, the architect of the Holocaust, Heinrich Himmler, said, "we are only interested in one thing—to project into the dim and distant past the picture of our nation as we envisage it for the future."[6]

For Hitler, Himmler, and Kossinna, archaeology was a tool to forward the Fatherland's fascist goals. In 1941, when German armies marched into a fallen Paris, in the shadow of the Eiffel Tower, Hitler announced that the world should ready itself for a 1,000-year reign of the Third Reich. Be not afraid, Hitler and his henchmen intoned, for they came not to destroy. They came to liberate and reunify the Aryan race that Germans had first spread on horseback throughout the Indo-European world millennia before.

By the mid-twentieth century, a consensus emerged pointing to the Eurasian steppe as the original site of domestication. Again, world politics—this time the Cold War—impeded the pursuit of definitive answers. Only after the fall of the Berlin Wall were scholars outside the former Soviet Union able to gain access to Eurasian sites, where archaeologists and anthropologists found evidence of domestication dating as far back as 6,000 years ago. By studying teeth and jaws of ancient ridden horses that indicated damage from metal mouthpieces, the scientists argued the first equestrians might have mounted horses to better manage and expand sheep and cattle herds and raid nearby pedestrians.[7]

Yet recent advancements in genetic testing suggest that the domesticated horse had many mothers. That is, domestication did not begin when a few wild horses were captured and bred in a limited geographical region to produce horses that then spread outward to other parts of the world. Instead, different human communities captured and bred different horses from diverse wild herds. What's more, the latest DNA studies suggest that instead of spreading alongside the ancient wheel and Indo-European languages, the ancestors of the modern horse spread as part of the early Islamic conquests of the eighth and ninth centuries. Ironically, these findings suggests that the forefathers and foremothers of the horses that the Spanish Crown used to reconquer the Iberian Peninsula from Muslim Moors in 1491 were used eight centuries before by Islamic Arabs to conquer Christian Hispania.[8]

The precise origins of domesticated horses remain a source of some debate. Not debatable, however, is that when introduced to knowledge of how to become equestrian, nonhorse people have long been highly motivated to become horse people. Those who remained on foot might not have remained *at all* for long. In other words, prehistoric equestrians used the horse to remove and enslave the peoples whose land they took by force. As would be the case in the early American West, raiders on horseback like Wakara often usurped lands, resources, and even people of the pedestrians they encountered, replacing the conquered's cultures and genes with their own.

SUCH POLITICAL AND RACIALIZED DEBATES ABOUT WHEN AND where the first horse was domesticated echo in debates about when and where Native Americans adopted the horse.

The conventional narrative has long held that the Spanish returned *Equus caballus* to North America in the early 1500s. The conventional narrative has also long held that Native Americans domesticated the horse only after they came into direct contact with European conquerors and settlers from whom they adopted horse cultures of riding, breeding, trading, and raiding. But recent studies, including of the Lehi Horse, show that this story, based on written records from European conquerors and settlers, covers up a more complex history in which Native Americans became master horse people independent of European influence and shaped the history of the American West as we know it today.

In 1492, Christopher Columbus infamously "discovered" the "West Indies" with a fleet of three ships, which carried just eighty-seven men and were stocked with little food and water. Dehydrated and suffering from scurvy, the crew contemplated mutiny before they reached the island they called Hispaniola. On his second voyage in 1493, Columbus returned with an armada of seventeen ships, carrying 1,500 men, including a dozen priests, along with mules, pigs, cattle, chickens, goats, and sheep. Columbus also brought ten mares and fifteen stallions. Perhaps second only to the trillions of microscopic pathogens that Columbus brought to the New World, these horses proved to be the most consequential import of the Columbian Exchange. Over the next 350 years, new equestrian empires—including those of the Spanish as well as of Natives like the Comanches, Apaches, and Wakara's Utes—would be built atop the progeny of the Spanish conquistadors' original horses. Old pedestrian empires would be crushed underfoot.

For this conquest of the New World, not just any horses would do. Writing to the Spanish sovereigns detailing the successes of his second voyage, Columbus requested that the horses sent west be of the high-quality breed used in the wars against the Moors. Not coincidentally, in this same letter, Columbus also established the transatlantic trade in "Indian" (*Indios*) slaves—a trade that would become intricately connected with the return of the horse to the Americas. Columbus proposed to enslave Indians to supply the expeditions with much needed labor. He also proposed to send some enslaved back to Spain. There they could be trained in the Spanish language and the Catholic catechism, then sent back west to become cultural ambassadors who could help speed up the Christianization and civilizing of the Natives.[9]

When Columbus's men unloaded their cargo off the coast of Hispaniola in 1493, the Taíno people were horrified by the huge four-legged beasts, which they feared might feed on human flesh. Within a few months, these horses, along with their riders and 200 foot soldiers, had routed the Taínos in the first battle of conquest in the New World that utilized horses. Scholars estimate that there were several hundred thousand Taínos before Columbus arrived in Hispaniola. By 1548, war waged on horseback, along with displacement and disease, had reduced the Taíno population to less than 500.[10]

During the first decade after the Spanish arrival in the New World, the Crown granted Columbus's request that Iberian pure-blooded broodmares be included on every ship headed to the West Indies. The monthslong voyages were not easy for these horses. In rough weather, they slammed into rings and ropes that kept them hobbled, leaving their bodies bruised and ribs broken. Absence of shade left their skin sunburned. When the winds failed, suspending the ships in seas of glass, sailors were sometimes forced to throw horses overboard to save fresh water for themselves. Some scholars believe that the phrase "horse latitudes," which became common in nautical parlance during the sixteenth century, originates from these unfortunate horses' watery graves.[11]

Within thirty years of the opening of the Columbian Exchange, the shipments of horses from Spain stopped for two reasons. First, the Crown grew worried that the horse exports threatened the supply of high-quality war horses in Spain, which the monarchs believed were needed in their continued fight against the Ottomans. Second, the horse farms in the West Indies were producing more than they needed, to the point that the horses bred in Hispaniola were sent to establish breeding farms in Puerto Rico, Jamaica, and Cuba.[12]

ON FEBRUARY 10, 1519, HORSES RETURNED TO THE American mainland when Hernán Cortés left Cuba to conquer Mexico and seize Aztecan gold. Cortés's expeditionary force of eleven ships and 350 men brought with it at least sixteen horses. It would have brought more, the expedition's chronicler Bernal Díaz del Castillo wrote, but the transportation costs were too high, making the horses "worth their weight in gold."[13]

Soon after their return to the American continent, these horses and the Cortés-led Spanish conquistadors vanquished Mesoamerican armies who had never faced such a fierce tandem. During the final siege of their capital, Tenochtitlán, in 1521, the Mexicas (Aztecs) cut open captured horses and horsemen, perhaps hoping that such

The Capture of Tenochtitlán, 1521. Note the prominence of the Spaniards on their horses as Cortés and his cavalry attack the Mexica capital. (From *Conquista de Méxica por Cortés* [ca. 1650s], unknown artist. Courtesy of Jay I. Kislak Collection, the Library of Congress)

bloodletting would stave off the fall of their city. But the sacrifice did not work. On August 13, 1521, Tenochtitlán (now Mexico City) fell to Cortés. August 13 became the feast day of St. Hippolytus, the patron saint of horses. As Díaz del Castillo wrote, the horses and their riders "behaved so valiantly that, next to God, they guarded us most." The expedition mourned the loss of sixty horses more than it did the 860 Spanish soldiers who died during the conquest—a conquest that likely killed tens of thousands of Mexicas.[14]

In spring 1598, Don Juan de Oñate, accompanied by hundreds of men and horses, crossed the *Río del Norte* (Rio Grande) and claimed the land in the name of King Philip II of Spain and the Holy Catholic Church. In doing so, two decades before the founding of Plymouth Plantation, Oñate created the first permanent European settlement in the lands that would become the United States. Perhaps while sitting astride his horse, Oñate declared that the Natives were vassals of the Crown and were expected to recognize him as their temporal lord and the Franciscans who accompanied the expedition as their spiritual fathers. Still, Oñate acknowledged that more than official decrees, the horse and the gun separated his nascent Spanish settlement from the Natives. Colonial law forbade giving Natives access to these weapons of conquest.[15]

In the late 1630s, a smallpox epidemic killed one-third (some 20,000 people) of the Puebloans in Spanish-controlled New Mexico. Governor Luis de Rosas needed to replace the Puebloans who worked as slaves in the *obrajes* (textile workshops) that refined the region's cotton and wool. In the first documented Spanish encounter with Ute peoples, Rosas and Spanish soldiers rode north and waged war against the "Utaca" nation, after which they returned to Santa Fe with eighty captives. Many of the Utes, along with Apaches whom Rosas also enslaved, ended up working in the *obrajes*. Others were sent south to work in the silver mines of Mexico. In 1640–1641, a violent power struggle between the governor and the Franciscans for control over Indian missionary work and trade left Rosas deposed, excommunicated, and then assassinated.[16]

Disease, drought, and poor maize production ravaged Pueblo communities in the 1660s and 1670s. In violation of colonial dictates forbidding Native religious practices, some Puebloans still performed corn dances in hopes the *katsinam*—spiritual messengers between Puebloans and the gods—would restore the rains and fertile soils, which the Puebloans believed the Corn Mothers took with them when other Puebloans accepted Christianity. In response, the colonists arrested and tortured more than a dozen Puebloan medicine men and executed a few. In turn, in 1680 Popé, a Pueblo Tewa religious leader with millenarian goals to return his people "to the state of their antiquity" by driving the colonists from their lands, organized 8,000 Native warriors, mostly Puebloans but also Apaches and Utes, into one of the first pan-Indian resistance movements in American history. Among the Natives' first acts in what became known as the Pueblo Revolt was to seize the colonists' horses, which one Spanish colonist called "beasts for the defense of the Kingdom." The warriors overwhelmed the horseless Spanish forces, killing hundreds of colonists and driving thousands out of the colony. After the revolt, as sedentary horticulturists, the Puebloans had little need for horses. They killed some, freed others, and sold or gave away the rest to neighboring tribes, including the Utes.[17]

Popé's prophecies that Spanish expulsion from Puebloan homelands would sprout grand harvests of Indian maize, beans, and fruits failed to materialize. Within a year, drought and poor governing led to civil war. Popé was deposed. The power vacuum was made worse by equestrian Utes and Apaches who raided the pueblos to acquire more horses and enslave Native captives. In 1692, when Diego de Vargas, along with sixty Spanish soldiers and 100 Native allies, marched north from their exile in Mexico and into Santa Fe, they met little resistance.[18]

Most historical narratives of the American West point to the Pueblo Revolt of 1680 as the catalyst for the spread of horses among Native peoples. Relying on written records that center Europeans as history's protagonists, historians have argued that the flow of horses following the revolt to neighboring peoples to the north, especially to the Utes, led to a swift adoption of horse culture. Natives became horse people so fast, the prevailing narrative has held, because they learned directly from the Spanish.[19]

Generations of Native knowledge keepers and oral historians, including Utes, Shoshones, Comanches, and Lakotas, have insisted that they had the horse long before Europeans arrived in their homelands. In fact, some tribes insist that they've always had the horse. As Yvette Running Horse Collin (Oglala Lakota Nation) claimed in her groundbreaking study of oral histories of Native-horse relations, her people and the horse have been together "since time immemorial."

Settler scholars have largely discounted such assertions because of the medium—the oral word matters less than the written word in conventional historical narration—and because of the message: that Native people developed their own horse cultures independently of European influence.[20]

Yet recently the long-disregarded histories of Native peoples and their horses have gained mainstream acceptance. The main catalyst for this change was the findings of a study published in *Science* in March 2023, which made international headlines. The authors of the study combined oral histories from the Pueblo, Pawnee, Comanche, and Lakota Nations with archaeological evidence, radiocarbon dating, and DNA analysis of horse remains that indicated signs of human interaction and care. The authors concluded that as early as the mid-sixteenth century and hundreds of miles away from the northernmost Spanish settlements, horses and Native horse culture spread along Native trade and alliance routes, changing these routes and peoples along the way. In other words, the spread of horses across the continent had nothing "to do with European people other than that first horse off the boat," explained William Taylor, the study's lead author. Carlton Shield Chief Gover (Pawnee), a coauthor of the study, explained how oral traditions highlight the process that Native peoples went through—far away from Europeans and their written archives upon which previous Native horse histories were based—to adopt the horse. "Even in language, [the horse] shows up as 'what is this?'" explained Chief Gover. In Pawnee "horse" translates to "new dog." The Comanche called horses "magic dogs."[21]

WAKARA'S TRIBAL ANCESTORS IN TODAY'S WESTERN COLORADO were among the first Native peoples to get horses, probably in the 1640s. Before they mounted the horses, Eastern Utes used them as big dogs, pulling travois that supplied their traveling bands that crossed the lower plains following bison herds. Riding soon followed. The Utes found that these nimble-footed and compact horses were well suited for days-long rides over the central Rockies' rough terrain, which was similar to the semiarid plains and mountains of southern Spain, where Spanish colonial horses were first bred. The region's rich grasslands allowed the horses' numbers to grow rapidly during the rest of the seventeenth century.[22]

On the backs of these horses, the Utes defended their homelands against raiding from the Spanish. They also began to move beyond the Lower, Middle, and Upper Earths of their homelands. To the east, the Utes were among the first Native peoples to hunt bison on horseback in the western Great Plains. To the south in New Mexico, the Utes began their own raids to steal more horses and cattle. In response, the Spanish built colonial adobes with fortified windows that they could quickly close when they saw Ute raiders approaching. To the north, in what is today Wyoming, the Utes encountered bison-hunting Shoshones. One group of Shoshones eventually split off to become Comanches. Some scholars have suggested that intermarriage among the Utes and the Proto-Comanches might have facilitated the transfer of knowledge of how to feed, breed, and ride horses—including how to ride to raid. The horse bonded the Utes and Comanches together, creating a trading and diplomatic alliance in the decades before the Pueblo Revolt. Through their alliance with the Utes, and through their mastery of the horse, the Comanches created an economic, cultural, and military empire that by the mid-eighteenth century enabled them to displace the Apaches for control over the southern Great Plains. The *Comanchería* stretched from southern Texas to central Kansas and Oklahoma, from eastern New Mexico to southern Colorado.[23]

The dominance of the Comanches was so pronounced that their alliance with the Utes had dissolved by the 1750s, as the Comanches no longer needed the Utes as raiding and trading partners. The

Comanches even expanded into the Ute homelands, including into the Utah Valley. In response to Comanche raids, the Utes went south to seek peace and protection from the Spanish. The Ute-Spanish alliance ushered in greater trade and contact between the settlers in New Mexico and Wakara's ancestors in the Utah Valley.

In the summer of 1776, with a mandate to establish an overland route between Santa Fe and the recently established missions in California, the Domínguez-Escalante expedition traveled into Ute territory, guided much of the way by two Timpanogos. By early fall, the expedition reached Utah Valley, where the padres reported finding a large freshwater lake, picturesque rivers, streams full of fish and waterfowl, and fields and mountains full of grasses and game. Still, the journey to the center of the Timpanogos world was not without worry. The padres' Ute guides begged them to turn around, concerned that the Comanches, who had established raiding outposts on Ute lands, would massacre them. When the Timpanogos in the Utah Valley first saw the padres on horseback approach their homelands, they lit smoke signals to warn others of the arrival of potential raiders. The Utes also burned pastures to deprive the would-be raiders of grasses they needed for their horses. The Ute guides soon convinced their Timpanogos kin of the padres' good intentions. The padres then spent a few days preaching to the Timpanogos, including to their leader, Turunianchi, whom some believe to have been Wakara's grandfather. According to Escalante, the Timpanogos invited the padres to come back and baptize them into the Catholic faith. But perhaps the Timpanogos wanted the padres to return with horses and guns, more than religion, so that they could protect themselves from raiding Comanches.[24]

Escalante and Domínguez did not mention seeing horses when they visited the Utah Valley in 1776. Still, the recent discovery of the Lehi Horse reinforces the idea that, away from the view and written recordkeeping of settlers, the horse became an integral part of Native culture in central Utah. The Domínguez-Escalante expedition did not travel north to what is today Lehi, Utah. If it had, the explorers might have seen Native peoples raising horses. The land between Timpanogos Lake and the Great Salt Lake was the homeland of the Cumumba Utes, the people who "speak two languages," because they frequently intermarried with the Shoshones.[25]

The Timpanogos learned to ride, rear, and care for horses soon after the Domínguez-Escalante expedition and within a generation before Wakara's birth, most likely from other Numic peoples. Perhaps they learned from the Cumumba Utes to their north or from their Eastern Ute kin who used the deep canyons cut into the Wasatch Mountains to ride through the Timpanogos' homelands on their way to hunt bison in the Wind River and Uintah Basins.[26]

The Timpanogos also became equestrian because they had to. The Fish Eaters had previously been happy to live off the bounties of the lake and rivers they managed for generations. But increasing raids from Comanches meant they had to adapt to the times. The first written record that the Timpanogos had become horse people speaks to the Comanches' influence on Timpanogos horse adoption. In 1805, the governor of New Mexico penned a series of letters in which he wrote that the "Yuta interpreter," peace broker, and trader Manuel Mestas had gone north to recover Spanish horses whom the Spanish suspected the Timpanogos of stealing. In fact, the Comanches had first stolen the horses. Then the Timpanogos stole these horses from Comanches during their ongoing inter-Numic conflicts.[27]

The Timpanogos also became horse people because they could afford to. Unlike their Paiute kin, who scavenged in the calorie-poor deserts of the southern Great Basin, the Timpanogos lived in the calorie- and water-rich Utah Valley. The same waters that supplied the Timpanogos with fish watered the grasslands. On these grasses, and in the care of the Timpanogos, the horses thrived. Two decades after Mestas went north in search of stolen horses, in August 1826, fur trapper Jedediah Smith observed that the Timpanogos had become skilled horsemen who moved through the rugged country with ease. In contrast, when a horse roamed into Paiute territory, they killed it. They did so to eat it and prevent it from eating the grasses upon which the Paiutes fed "like cattle," observed fur trapper William Wolfskill in 1830 when he crossed the path that Smith had mapped from New Mexico to California in the late 1820s and which became part of the Old Spanish Trail.[28]

The Timpanogos viewed the horse as more than food or another mouth to feed. They understood it as a vital technology, which at once expanded and shrank their world. Like the railroad and telegraph in the nineteenth century, the horse increased the distances the Utes could travel and collapsed the time needed to do so. With this technology, the Timpanogos conducted more trade with New Mexico. In a matter of days, instead of weeks by foot, they could ride to and from markets in Santa Fe and Abiquiú, where they traded for food, blankets, metal goods, and weapons that they incorporated into their fishing, hunting, and raiding practices. During Wakara's lifetime, the Timpanogos began to venture north to hunt bison and to raid for captives among the northwestern Shoshones. And to the southwest, they began to hunt the pedestrian Paiutes who would become Wakara's greatest source of slaves.

The meaning of the horse also changed. Wakara's Timpanogos used the horse to be Native: to hunt bison, to protect their territory, to trade with Natives and settlers, to raid like their Comanche kin. Yet Wakara also used the horse to become American—always looking to expand control over land, people, and capital. For Wakara, horses in part became a commodity to exploit and grow his empire of horse and human flesh. Wakara's horses made him rich and powerful. But his horse raiding also put him at risk of an early grave.

Chapter 10

Land Pirate

THE WEATHER WAS FINE in southern Utah during the first week of March 1851. Watered by the snowmelt from the mountains, grasses pushed through the earth and fed on sunrays that grew stronger each day.

Despite the good weather, Wakara was in a bad mood when he and seventy warriors arrived at the Mormon settlement then called Fort Louisa. With Wakara's blessing the Saints had founded the outpost, named after one of Brigham Young's plural wives, the year before on the Old Spanish Trail.

Wakara explained his sour mood to the leader of Louisa, Apostle George A. Smith, as they smoked a pipe in Smith's one-room cabin. Between puffs, Wakara told Smith, the cousin of church founder Joseph Smith Jr., that just as they had done for the past decade, he and his cavalry had spent the previous months in California stealing horses from the Lugos and other rancheros. But this season, Wakara had sent his brother Sanpitch (also called Sanpete) to lead the raids.

At first, the raiding had gone to plan, Wakara told Smith. The raiders hid out at Isaac Williams's home. Williams, who had married one of the Lugo daughters, ran the family's massive cattle and horse ranches in the San Bernardino Valley. But Williams became a turncoat. In exchange for their promise not to steal his livestock, Williams housed Wakara's warriors throughout the fall of 1850 and even kept their presence a secret from his in-laws. Over the course of several weeks, Sanpitch and his raiders stole horses by the dozens, hiding them in the canyons west of San Bernardino until they had gathered more than 1,000 head. As they began their trek home, a posse pursued Sanpitch's men over the Cajon Pass. During a fight, Sanpitch's warriors killed one of the Lugos' soldiers. Still, the *Californio* posse recovered all but 120 horses, far fewer than the haul of 1,000 Wakara had grown accustomed to.[1]

Wakara told Smith that he planned to head back to California. A yield of 100 head—the rest had escaped or died during the trek across the mountains and deserts—was not acceptable. Each horse not stolen cost Wakara a rifle, or several pounds of flour, or an ox. Even a worn-out horse could be traded for a young Paiute if her parents were hungry enough. But Wakara's Utes had also grown hungry—forced to rely more and more on trade in beef, bread, and slaves—because of the increasing damage to their hunting and fishing grounds that the settlers wrought.

Smith cautioned Wakara not to go back to California. The situation had changed since he began raiding the Mexicans a decade before. First, the Mexicans weren't Mexicans anymore, Smith explained. They became Americans after the United States annexed California in 1848. And the Americans sent soldiers, including the Mormon Battalion, to guard the Cajon Pass with the mandate to stop Wakara's raiding. Second, these well-armed soldiers were not the Lugos' motley posses whom Wakara had bested during previous raiding seasons. The army soldiers would not just take back the stolen horses. If they caught him, Smith told Wakara, they were likely to scalp or hang him.[2]

A few days after they smoked the pipe in Smith's cabin, the Mormon apostle made clear that Wakara need fear not just American troops in California but also Mormon militias in Utah. As they had done at Fort Provo a few years before, the Fort Louisa settlers fired a warning shot with their cannon toward the Utes' lodge, "producing desperate fears with the Indians," wrote George Smith in his journal. Having achieved the desired effect, Smith instructed the cannoneers to point the big gun in another direction. At least for now.

Soon after, Wakara and his troops accepted Smith's invitation to inspect the fort, which they did, Smith recounted in his journal. Atop their well-appointed horses, they "cut a considerable show in their warlike dress." After these mutual displays of force, Smith showed Wakara John C. Frémont's map, which Wakara likely helped Frémont create when they met in 1844 and which the Mormons had used to navigate to Utah in 1847. Still, when he saw the map, Wakara shook his head at its inaccuracies. Wakara used a pencil to mark corrections, drawing the Sevier Lake and its tributaries and the surrounding mountains. Wakara explained that the proper name for the Sevier River and Lake was "parvine" or "trout" in English. Wakara also told Smith that the proper name of "Little Salt Lake," which was near the settlement of Louisa, was Parowan. Soon after Wakara's topographical corrections, the settlement changed its name from Louisa to Parowan.[3]

Wakara knew this land better than anyone. For the past decade, these lands had been where he built his empire of horses and slaves and his reputation as the most feared man on the Old Spanish Trail. Wakara wanted to go back to California not just to raid horses but to uphold his status as the "Napoleon of the Desert," as the mountain man turned Mormon missionary to the Indians Daniel Jones called him. He was "a great strategist, often out-generaling those he had to meet in war or whom he designed to plunder," Jones later wrote. As much as a military leader, Wakara acted like the captain of a pirating ship who kept his men by his side by gifting them with goods, horses, and enslaved captives. Dimick Huntington even called him a "land pirate."[4]

These pirates of the Great Basin traveled across seas of deserts. Each fall and winter, they raided rancheros, captured Paiutes, and exacted tolls on caravans and expedition parties that passed through Wakara's lands. Each spring, they returned to their oasis at Timpanogos Lake to rest, regroup, and count up and divide their spoils. And each summer, they hunted bison in the western Great Plains.

WAKARA WAS NOT THE FIRST HORSE RAIDER TO target California horses. Almost as soon as the Old Spanish Trail opened in the early 1830s, fur trappers became horse traffickers. Famed mountain men, including Joseph Walker, Thomas "Pegleg" Smith, and Billy Williams, raided Spanish colonial horses raised at the massive ranchos in Southern California. The largest and most infamous horse raid occurred in 1840. That year, Pegleg Smith, Jim Beckwourth, and 150 Native allies, including Wakara and other Utes, stole horses across the whole of southern Alta California—from the Lugos in San Bernardino in the California interior west to the San Gabriel Valley in Los Angeles, and from San Juan Capistrano north to San Luis Obispo. After several coordinated attacks over weeks, the raiders drove their captured horses over the Cajon Pass and back along the Old Spanish Trail.[5]

According to Pegleg Smith's account, Wakara led the attacks at San Luis Obispo. At night, he and other raiders snuck into the mission's corrals, opened the gates, and ran off with hundreds of horses. In response, the prefect of Los Angeles released prisoners from local jails to bolster the posses' numbers. These posses, which included the Lugos, pursued the horses and raiders into the deserts east of Los Angeles. But Wakara's raiders evaded capture due to their knowledge of the Mojave and Yukot trails. In fact, by chasing Wakara into territory that they did not know, the posses brought more horses to the raiders. When the *Californios* rested their exhausted horses at a watering hole, the raiders stole them, forcing the posses to walk back to Los Angeles on foot with their heads hanging low.[6]

In 1842, fearing imminent attacks, Antonio María Lugo and his son-in-law Isaac Williams, along with other rancheros, petitioned the local government to authorize them to launch preemptive attacks on Natives coming over the trail. To thwart raiders from even reaching the horse corrals, a militarized outpost was established at the mouth of the Cajon Pass. With the promise of land to raise their own herds, in the early 1840s the rancheros also enticed New Mexicans, including Lorenzo Trujillo and his family, to move to California. The *Californios* hoped that the New Mexicans would serve as buffers against Wakara's raids. The Trujillos were intimately familiar with Wakara's Utes. For generations, the Utes had come to their villages, notably Abiquiú and Taos, to trade and raid. The rancheros gave the Trujillos land east of the Lugos' ranchos in San Bernardino. The Trujillos paid for this land with their flesh and blood. During one raiding season, three of Lorenzo Trujillo's sons pursued Wakara's raiders into the mountains. A battle ensued. One son was shot in the back with an arrow, another was shot through the nose, and the third was shot in the right foot. The sons survived and recaptured some horses.[7]

By the fall of 1845, the Lugos thought they were prepared to rebuff Wakara's raiders. When Williams heard that Wakara was on his way to San Bernardino with scores of armed cavalrymen, he sent word to the Mexican governor, Andrés Pico, in Los Angeles. The governor sounded the alarm, raising a posse of *Californios* and Native allies. But when Wakara arrived with his trade delegation made up mostly of families, Lugos and Williams called off the reinforcements.[8]

The *Californios* should have known better than to trust appearances. Before the 1840 raid, Jim Beckwourth visited the rancho, pretending to search the area for sea otters, whose pelts were then in high demand. In fact, Beckwourth was scouting out the ranchos ahead of his planned raids with Pegleg Smith. In late 1845, it was Beckwourth and Pegleg's onetime raiding partner, Wakara, who came to the Lugos rancho pretending to be a peaceful trader. But just as in 1840, by moonlight over the next few months, Wakara and his raiders, who were hiding in the nearby hills, broke into the Lugos' corrals and ran horses into the canyons to the east. They then rounded up the horses on a trail on the Mojave River that would come to bear Wakara's anglicized name.[9]

In early spring 1846, Wakara prepared for the long journey home. Out of reach of the *Californios*' posses, Wakara and his raiders, who had spread out to attack various ranchos, gathered on the eastern side of the San Bernardino Mountains over the Cajon Pass. There, they slaughtered cattle, turning fresh meat into jerky, which would be their main source of calories during the monthslong journey to Utah. They timed their departure to set off before the New Mexico–bound trading caravans—known to eat up the grasses and brown up the waters with their own herds—began their trip back to Santa Fe.[10]

Despite these preparations, the trek drained the bodies of men and beasts. Wakara's cavalry ran their herds from low-lying Southern California plains over mile-high mountain passes. In spots, the trail narrowed to a single track. Rocks and roots rose up to trip hoofed feet. Horses that broke legs were left to die where they fell. Those that survived the mountains faced the desert, where hot, dry air sucked water and salt from their bodies. In the 1840s, one explorer reported that horse carcasses were so numerous east of what would become Las Vegas that the bleached-white bones served as cairns along the trail. Overuse by overland travelers turned life-giving springs into homes for parasites that feasted on the already-weakened horses. Other horses left the herd in search of water and grass in the mountains; their descendants make up the Sulphur herd of today.[11]

Once they arrived in southern Utah, Wakara's horses, then as much skeleton as muscle, began a season of recuperation. The horses and their human minders spent the next few months "chasing grass," as the historian Elliott West has described it. They migrated north in sync with the grasses that pushed through the plains of melting snow. These grasslands were maintained by careful Indigenous resource management. On their way to California the previous fall, Wakara's Utes had set fire to select sections of prairies. These controlled burns promoted more robust grass growth the next spring. While the horses fed on grasses, Wakara raided and traded with the region's Paiutes. He exchanged women and children for horses too weak to make the final leg of the journey but would make a fine meal for the Paiutes whose diet usually consisted of roots, berries, and small game. Leaving Paiute territory near what is today St. George, the horses continued to eat their way north to the Sevier Valley, then to Wakara's birthplace around Spanish Fork, and then, by the start of the spawning season, to Timpanogos Lake for the fish festival.[12]

The fish festival was a feast for the horses too. They fattened themselves on the sweet, plentiful grasses around the lake. When they weren't eating or mating, the horses raced across open fields, strengthening their legs and hearts. In late summer, the fastest and strongest went north for the bison hunt along the Green River in northern Utah and southern Wyoming. Unlike their Colorado kin, Wakara's Fish Eaters never relied solely on bison for food or trade. Still, bison were an integral part of their diets and culture. During the bison hunts, while the Ute men hunted, Ute women turned bison hides into clothing, bags, horseshoes, and tent canvas. Wakara's seasoned raiders and fresh horses filled out these hunting parties, for which Wakara was compensated with the choicest bison meats and pelts. The hunts took the Utes into the Great Plains Indians' territory. Wakara would later tell George Bean that he had scars "all in front, and not on his back"—in other words, that he had never run from a fight with the Sioux, Shoshones, Arapahos, Cheyennes, and Crows.[13]

By late summer, Wakara and his hunting parties returned home to Utah. The horses recovered from chasing bison by eating late-summer grasses. The Utes took to their feet. The men hunted game. The women gathered meals of berries, nuts, and roots. After the horses rested, Wakara traveled south to New Mexico and Navajo country to trade horses, pelts, and Paiute captives. The slaves were the most valuable commodity, especially if the slave was young and female. Still, the New Mexicans also paid top dollar for Wakara's horses since New Mexico lacked the grasslands that could sustain breeding herds. After trading in New Mexico, Wakara needed more horses. By November, with the weather turning cold, Wakara, his cavalry, and his remaining horses began the trek back to California to raid again. He captured more than a few Paiutes along the way.[14]

TWO SPRINGS BEFORE THE 1845 RAIDS, IN MAY 1844, Charles C. Frémont and his company were riding north to map the Salt Lake Valley when they met Wakara near the Sevier River. Wakara and his band were making their way south to collect tribute from the expected caravans returning from California on the Old Spanish Trail.

Frémont, then thirty-one, handsome, dark haired, and slight—five feet, eight inches tall in boots—was a skilled topographer. He honed his mapmaking skills as part of the topographical corps that had charted the Cherokee Nation's lands in Georgia ahead of that people's forced removal in 1838. Through this work and his later explorations of the American West, Frémont became a general in the informal army of Manifest Destiny—the doctrine that America was destined to rule from the Atlantic to the Pacific. Western boosterism was a family affair; his father-in-law and chief benefactor,

Missouri Senator Thomas Hart Benton, was the nation's most prominent advocate of western expansion.

During his first expedition in 1842, Frémont and his company followed the well-established Oregon Trail along the Platte River, then turned north to study the Wind Rivers, the homelands of the Shoshones. There, they scaled what Frémont mistakenly believed was the Rockies' highest peak and where, legend has it, he planted an American flag. After returning to Washington, Frémont and his wife, Benton's daughter Jesse Benton Frémont, composed a report of the epic journey, which they published in 1843 as *A Report on an Exploration of the Country Lying Between the Missouri River and the Rocky Mountains on the Line of the Kansas and Great Platte Rivers.* Despite its awkward title, the report became a national sensation. Excerpts were printed in newspapers throughout the nation, making Frémont and his trusted guide, Kit Carson, celebrities rivaling Meriwether Lewis and William Clark. The public ate up Frémont's stories of life on the trail and colorful descriptions of his encounters with the West's wild things, including bears, bison, and Indians. But, to borrow from historian Will Bagley, Frémont did "what he always did best: following the tracks" laid down by others, including fur trappers, missionaries, and Native peoples. Frémont's genius lay in writing those tracks down on paper and marketing his adventures to the masses. As Frémont's legend grew, the popular press named him "the Pathfinder" after James Fenimore Cooper's fictional frontiersmen. In 1856, Frémont would run for president on the exploits of his western expeditions (there would be five in total). A campaign banner reenacted and embellished Frémont's "planting the American Standard [flag]" atop the peak that would come to bear his name in the Wind River Range. In the image, Kit Carson looks on from below, while Frémont tips his hat to the east, inviting settlers westward.[15]

"Col. Frémont Planting the American Standard on the Rocky Mountains." Woodcut campaign banner by Baker & Godwin (1856). Frémont and Wakara met in May 1844 while Wakara and his cavalry patrolled the Old Spanish Trail and charged tribute, including from Frémont, from those traveling on it. Wakara also likely supplied Frémont with directions and descriptions of the Southwest, which Frémont and his cartographers then drew onto their maps. In 1856, Frémont became the first presidential candidate of the newly formed Republican Party, in large measure based on his popularity as a western explorer and general in the Mexican-American War. (Courtesy of the Library of Congress)

The popularity of Frémont's expeditions catalyzed large-scale western emigration. During the so-called Great Migration of 1843, close to 1,000 emigrants traversed the Oregon Trail. Many made the trip with Frémont's report and maps stuffed in their sacks. Over the next two decades, before the completion of the transcontinental railroad, thousands more followed the trail to settle the fertile plains and valleys of the Northwest, to pan for gold in California, and to find refuge from religious persecution in the Great Basin.

When Wakara and Frémont met in May 1844, the two men took the measure of each other. Though neither was physically imposing, both saw themselves and each other as great men of the West. Wakara reportedly told Frémont that he had heard of his expedition of 1842, which had taken the Pathfinder across Wakara's bison-hunting trails. And Frémont had heard of Wakara and his cavalry's raiding exploits in California and their practice of charging a toll for safe passage through Ute country. As Frémont wrote in his journal, "Instead of attacking and killing, they affect to purchase—taking the horses they like, and giving something nominal in return." Frémont experienced this toll taking firsthand. Wakara gave Frémont a Mexican blanket, while Frémont reluctantly surrendered a much more valuable blanket that he had purchased in Vancouver, likely a famed Hudson Bay point blanket. Charles Preuss, Frémont's Prussian-born cartographer—who actually drew Frémont's map of the Great Basin, which later explorers, including the Mormons, followed as if their lives depended upon it—remembered that the two leaders disagreed about the fair value of the exchange. "'You are a chief, and I am one too,'" Preuss recalled Wakara telling Frémont. "'It would be bad if we should evaluate exactly the price of one or the other.'"[16]

After their brief encounter, the two "chiefs" parted ways. Wakara went south to collect more tolls. Frémont headed north to take the measure of Wakara's land dominated by Timpanogos Lake. Frémont got some things right about the lake: "Its greatest breadth is about 15 miles . . . almost entirely surrounded by mountains, walled on the north and east by a high and snowy range." But he got other details wrong—for example, proclaiming that the lake directly connects to the Great Salt Lake, when what the Mormon settlers would call the Jordan River connects Utah Lake with the Salt Lake. Wakara would correct these, among other inaccuracies, on George A. Smith's copy of Frémont's map during Wakara's stop in Parowan in March 1851. Frémont's description of Timpanogos Lake as an untouched wilderness ripe for cultivation and exploitation would attract the Mormons to the region. In 1845, as they prepared to flee Illinois after the assassination of their first prophet, Joseph Smith Jr., and his brother Hyrum, in church newspapers the Mormons published excerpts of Frémont's visit to "Euta" Lake and made plans to send their Vanguard Company to the region.[17]

THE VANGUARD COMPANY'S ARRIVAL IN UTAH IN JULY 1847 brought profound changes to the lives of the Ute people. Yet, in the decade before, Wakara's horses were already changing the *Nuche* (the People). Some of these changes were noted by passing explorers. However, much like the adoption of horses by the Utes and other Native peoples, these changes occurred out of settler sight and away from pen-and-paper recordkeeping. Before Wakara, there had been horses and horsemen among the Western Utes. And before Wakara, there had been Ute horse raiders in California. Still, Wakara's unprecedented raids in the 1840s brought more horses than ever into the Timpanogos homelands. And with these larger, healthier herds came changes to Wakara's Utes' way of life.

The horses changed what Wakara's Utes ate. To be sure, even after they adopted the horse, the Timpanogos centered their diets on Utah Valley's native plants and game and the fish that swam in the valley's lakes and rivers. Still, the horses allowed them to hunt more bison farther away from their homelands, as well as to trade in New Mexico and to raid in California. This expanded trade added more beef and settler grains to the diets of those Utes who followed Wakara on his seasonal trading and raiding. In their food storage and on their bodies, Wakara's Utes carried these surplus calories. Thomas Bullock recorded the heights and weights of the leading Utes in August 1852. Sowiette weighed 158 pounds and was 5 feet, 8 inches tall. Wakara's brother Peteetneet was 144 pounds and stood 5 feet, 5 ¼ inches. Wakara was stouter than the rest. He weighed 164 pounds and was

5 feet, 7 ½ inches tall. By today's body mass index, Wakara would be considered borderline overweight.[18]

The horses changed how and where Wakara's Utes lived. Silvestre Vélez de Escalante observed in 1776 that most Western Ute bands built their homes using brush shelters. By the 1840s explorers recalled that Wakara's Utes' lodges resembled the animal-skin tepees of the Plains peoples. These portable lodges reflected Wakara's Utes' new practice of migrating seasonally hundreds of miles from their homelands to raid, hunt, and trade. The horse also increased the number of people in Wakara's entourage. Instead of small nuclear families who reunited seasonally with other family units to hunt and fish, Wakara's main lodges included several wives and children, along with his brothers Sanpitch and Arapeen and their families, who spent most of the year together. According to one settler's recollection, along with humans, Wakara's entourage included 120 horses and several goats, sheep, cows, and oxen. He also had what was described as a "performing bull" to sire more cows.[19]

Wakara's horses also brought settler goods into his people's lives. These items included fine knives, horse tack, and blankets woven in New Mexico like the one he traded to Frémont. Wakara and his men were also well armed with long guns and pistols. Wakara himself carried a shotgun, a rifle, and a pistol. Wakara's clothing also reflected his status as the most cosmopolitan Native leader of his era. "His dress is a full suit of the richest broadcloth, generally brown," recalled one observer in 1850, "cut in European fashion, with a shining beaver hat and fine cambric shirt." Wakara's cavalry's ornate uniform included their "richly caparisoned horses, with their embroidered saddles and harness, [which] shine and tinkle as they prance under their weight of gay metal ornaments."[20]

Wakara's Utes' dress—of both horses and horsemen—was not just a show of wealth. It was a display of power. Wakara armed and appointed his cavalry with the purpose of convincing the caravans on the Old Spanish Trail to give Wakara what he wanted without the need for actual violence. The most vivid description of Wakara's dominance over the trail came from the artist and explorer Gwinn Harris Heap, who was in Utah in 1853 during the outbreak of the "Walker War":

> Having an unlimited supply of fine horses, and being inured to every fatigue and privation, he keeps the territories of New Mexico and Utah, the provinces of Chihuahua and Sonora, and the southern portions of California, in constant alarm. His movements are so rapid, and his plans so skillfully and so secretly laid, that he has never once failed in any enterprise, and has scarcely disappeared from one district before he is heard of in another. He frequently divides his men into two or more bands, which, making their appearance at different points at the same time, each headed, it is given out, by the dreaded Walkah in person, has given him, with the ignorant Mexicans, the attribute of ubiquity.[21]

Wakara's horses made him into a living legend in the annals of American explorers and settlers. His horses also changed his status within his own band. Beyond their well-established fish "captains," in the generation before Wakara's rise, the formation of larger bands within the Timpanogos required more complex sets of hierarchies and responsibilities, including the establishment of political, hunting, and war captains. According to settler recollections, during periods of conflict, Wakara filled the role of "war chief" or "war captain" within the Timpanogos Band while Sowiette served as the "civil" or "political" leader.[22]

Members of Wakara's entourage also benefited from their association with the Ute leader. Horses among Wakara's Utes were held as private property, which allowed Wakara's men to accumulate their own wealth and status. In August 1843, during the bison hunting season, Theodore Talbot, who was leading a detachment of Frémont's second expedition, met the Ute leader near Fort Bridger in Wyoming. According to Talbot, Wakara was not just knowledgeable about trading "with the Whites, and reselling goods to such of his nation as are less skillful in striking a bargain." Wakara also knew that to keep his men happy, he had to spread the wealth. As Talbot put it, "He is not at all brave, but sustains his position by judicious presents to his principal men," presents that took the form of horses, trade goods, cash, and slaves.[23]

Despite the assessment of Talbot's boss, John C. Frémont, that central Utah was an unspoiled Eden, Wakara's horses also brought changes to Wakara's homelands and to the plants and animals who lived there. Seasonal migration was good for the horses; chasing grass allowed Wakara's Utes to maintain their expanded herds throughout the year. But these larger herds depleted resources upon which other animals depended, including the largest fauna in the eastern Great Basin, the American bison. In 1841, the Ute leader Want-a-sheep (Wanship), a kin of Wakara, told the trapper Osborne Russell that he remembered when the bison grazed in large numbers on the grasses north of Timpanogos Lake. In 1848, Parley P. Pratt described the "parks" to the northeast of the lake as full of antelope but also replete with bison skeletons. With the influx of horses, Wakara's Utes likely hunted the small northern Utah bison herd to extinction. The destruction of that herd meant that Wakara's Utes relied even more on their horses to travel farther away from home during bison hunts.[24]

From bison down to the smallest plants that the increased number of hooves crushed, Wakara's horses left the land changed. In part to ingratiate themselves with the settlers whom they hoped would protect them from Wakara's raiding, many Paiutes and some Utes, like Kanosh's Pahvants, turned to agriculture and animal husbandry. Most of Wakara's Utes showed much less interest in turning their homelands into fields for grazing cows and fenced-off rows of crops. And yet, while many refused to "throw the dirt," as some called farming, Wakara's Utes did chase grass. They also created grass through, among other practices, controlled burns as they migrated to California in the fall.[25]

The horse changed the Utes from the inside out, altering their diet, dress, economics, and social structures. The horse changed how they organized hunts, how far they raided, and what they valued. But it also changed them from the outside in. That is, the horse put the Utes into greater contact with settlers, including New Mexicans in Abiquiú and the *Californios* in San Bernardino. The horse also put Wakara's Utes into greater contact with other Great Basin peoples, contact that led to hardening of ethnic distinctions among Numic peoples.

The Utes, Paiutes, Shoshones, and Comanches were once kin. When Uto-Aztecan peoples migrated into the southern Great Basin around 1000 CE, the people who became southern Paiutes made their homes in the dry climate of southern Utah and northern Arizona. The people who became the Utes moved into the mountains, basins, and plateaus of Colorado and Utah, where water and water-dependent food, including fish, were more plentiful. In these regions, the Proto-Utes as well as the Shoshones lived in sync with these water-based seasons. In spring and summer, they camped near lakes and rivers, hunting antelope and deer and harvesting wild plants and fruits. In fall and winter, they moved south to lower elevations, where they hunted and lived off their stored foods. Yet, at least until the eighteenth century, distinctions among the Utes, Paiutes, and Shoshones remained fluid. Their languages stayed mutually intelligible. They shared origin stories. And their boundary lines remained blurred, leading to trade, quarrels, captivity, and intermarriage.[26]

The arrival of the horse changed how these Numic peoples saw each other. The horse at first unified the Utes and the Comanches. The *Nuche* and the *Numunu* established military, marriage, and trade alliances. By the mid-eighteenth century, the horse had led to their separation. The Comanches' expanding empire forced the Utes out of the plains and into the mountains. The Comanche empire also meant that, in the pre-equestrian generations before Wakara's birth, the Western Utes were no longer isolated in their hard-to-reach valleys surrounded by almost impassable mountains. As such, the first empire to threaten the Utes of the Utah Valley was not European in origin but Comanche. During their 1776 visit to Timpanogos Lake, after Francisco Atanasio Domínguez and Silvestre Vélez de Escalante's Timpanogos guides convinced their bandsmen that the padres meant no harm, Wakara's grandfathers saw the Spanish as potential liberators from the raiding tyranny of their Comanche Numic kin.[27]

Escalante expected it would be the Spanish who would create a large "province" on the Timpanogos' lands. Yet, by 1845, it was Wakara who made Utah Valley the center of a vast and powerful Native empire of trade in horses and enslaved Natives. This empire's reach stretched south to the capitals of northern New Mexico and west to the California coast. With this empire of raiding and trading, Wakara drew more distinctions around the Ute identity and territorial boundaries. Before the horse arrived in Utah, some Shoshones and Utes, like the Cumumbas of the Weber Valley, were allies and intermarried. But the lines between Utes and Shoshones hardened when, in the 1840s, Wakara's larger herds of horses meant that during hunting trips, he frequently came into conflict with bison-hunting Shoshones. These conflicts set off a series of reciprocal raids between Wakara's Utes and the Shoshones that continued well past the arrival of the Mormons in 1847.[28]

But the horse created the biggest distinction between Wakara's Utes and the Paiutes to their southwest along the Old Spanish Trail.

During his return trips from horse raiding in California, Wakara "hunted" the Paiutes, observed explorer James A. Bennett in 1851. This season of human hunting was timed for the spring when the Paiutes were "poor and weak" after eating up their winter stores. Wakara sometimes offered "used-up horses" from the California raiding season to the Paiutes as payment for captives, recalled Daniel Jones.[29]

During his 1844 expedition, John C. Frémont drew distinctions among Utah's Native communities based on more than who was equestrian and who was pedestrian. Frémont observed that Wakara's Utes lived in larger communities near lakes and rivers that supplied them with fish and that watered large grasslands where the Utes hunted deer and antelope. In contrast, the Paiutes lived in single-family units in the deserts and fed off seeds, insects, and roots. Even without the horse, food sources—meager desert fare compared to richer and more plentiful fish and game in the Utah Valley—created cultural distinctions among the Great Basin's peoples.[30]

Still, in Utah the horse made differences of degree into distinctions of kind. On the horse, Wakara's Utes became predators; the Paiutes became prey.

IN MARCH 1851, WHILE WAKARA WAS IN PAROWAN complaining to George A. Smith about that season's poor horse-raiding harvest, in Los Angeles the brothers Chico and Benito Lugo sat in a jail cell. Earlier in the year, while guarding the Cajon Pass against Wakara, a US Army company had come across the bullet-ridden bodies of an Irishman named Patrick McSwiggen and a Creek Indian named Sam. Soon after, Chico and Benito, teenage sons of José María and grandsons of Lugo patriarch Antonio María, were arrested for murder.[31]

The brothers awaited trial, under threat of the hangman's noose, in a jailhouse perched on a hill overlooking Los Angeles, then no more than a few dozen adobe homes and shops gathered around a dusty, sun-drenched central plaza. Chico and Benito likely cursed Wakara's name. After all, the murders occurred when the Lugo brothers joined their uncle José del Carmen Lugo in a posse tasked with recovering horses that Wakara's men, led by Sanpitch, had stolen from the Lugos' Rancho San Bernardino during the 1850–1851 raiding season. The posse had been successful at recouping most of the horses—but not without violence. One of the posse members said that the Lugo brothers had killed McSwiggen and Sam because they believed the Irishman and the Creek were allied with Wakara.

The Lugos probably blamed Wakara for more than the loss of their horses and freedom. They blamed Wakara for the loss of their country. In the mid-1840s, the Comanches' relentless raids had left much of New Mexico and Texas depopulated and defenseless against advancing US armies, making it easier for the United States to annex Texas. Likewise, by 1846 and the start of the Mexican-American War, Wakara's raids had eroded Mexican California's defenses to the point that within a year of the outbreak of hostilities, then US Army General John C. Frémont was able to rush into California, muster Americans into a company of soldiers, march into Los Angeles, and force Mexican officials to surrender. After the capitulation papers were signed, José del Carmen Lugo assisted Frémont in gathering up escaped horses abandoned by the defeated Mexican army. José del Carmen also served as a mayor (*alcalde*) of Los Angeles and a justice of the peace. But soon after, he was replaced in these roles by Anglo-Americans who began to flood into California.[32]

In the early 1850s, the trial of the Lugo brothers became a proxy fight between the new Anglo-American overlords, who made up only 10 percent of Los Angeles' population, and the Spanish-speaking *Californio* majority. The Lugos and other *Californios* believed that the charges against Chico and Benito were trumped up, the result of coerced witness testimony orchestrated by American lawmen whose real goal was to drive the *Californio* rancheros off their valuable lands in the San Bernardino Valley. By mid-1851, the Lugo affair had Los Angeles on edge. The Lugos wanted to free their sons who languished in jail. The Americans wanted to see them strung up by their necks. Making matters worse was the arrival of John "Red" Irving and his gang. A former Texas ranger and a cavalryman in the Mexican-American War, Irving offered to break into the jail and free the boys if the Lugos would pay him $10,000. When the Lugos refused, Irving threatened to kill the boys himself.

A short time later, after the state's key witness fled, the Lugo boys were released. Fifty mounted *Californios* escorted them home to San Bernardino. Irving and his men followed. After a daylong gunfight with the Lugos and their Indian allies, all but one member of Irving's gang was dead. The American magistrates in Los Angeles ruled that the killing of the Irving gang was justified, and the charges against the Lugo brothers were dropped. Still, the Americans got what they wanted. José del Carmen Lugo sold Rancho San Bernardino for $77,500 to a group of Mormon settlers led by Amasa Lyman. Lugo explained that he had sold the land so that his family's lives "need not be in constant peril" as they had been for the previous decade due to Wakara's raids and Anglo-American aggression. After retiring in Los Angeles, José del Carmen Lugo died penniless after another land deal went bad.[33]

The Lugo sale to Lyman was not the first time that the Mormons contributed to the end of *Californio*-era California. In late January 1847, a few weeks after Mexican Governor Andrés Pico signed articles of capitulation to General Frémont, the Mormon Battalion—the only military unit in American history whose members came exclusively from one religious community—arrived on the West Coast. The year before, the battalion's 500 men had been recruited to fight the Mexicans. But after a grueling 2,000-mile march from Iowa, where the Mormons were quartered awaiting their trek to Utah, the battalion arrived too late to fight. Instead, a battalion company was dispatched to the Cajon Pass to guard against Wakara's raiders coming across the Old Spanish Trail.[34]

In the early 1840s, the Lugos and their Indian allies were faulted for failing to stop these raids. After the Mexican-American War, the battalion was celebrated for deterring Wakara. But the Lugos got too much blame, and the battalion got too much credit. One of the reasons Wakara's raids slowed but did not stop after 1848 was that back home in Utah, Wakara was preoccupied with more profound changes to his homeland, this time spurred by the arrival of the Mormons in the summer of 1847.

In part, Wakara himself was responsible for these changes. Fearing Wakara's well-mounted Utes, the Mormons abandoned their plans to settle on the water-rich grasslands around Timpanogos (Utah) Lake. Instead, they built their settlements on the space between Shoshone and Ute lands in the Salt Lake Valley. When the Mormons expanded south around the lake starting in the spring of 1849, they did so with Wakara's blessing. Soon after, Wakara condoned the Mormon massacre of his Timpanogos rivals. At the same time, Wakara helped the Mormons settle Manti in the Sanpete Valley on lands that weren't actually his but belonged to "digger" Utes who didn't have horses and thus could not put up a fight. Soon after that, Wakara invited the Saints to settle at Parowan, near one of his favorite camping spots on his way to and from California.

Wakara turned these new settlements into horse-trading hubs. In summer 1848, Wakara brought hundreds of horses to Salt Lake, where the Saints traded guns and clothing for them. The Mormons expressed worry that buying stolen horses might disrupt the peace they had established with the *Californios* at the other end of the trail. But the Mormons also needed fresh horses. So Mormon settlers in Salt Lake, and later in Provo, Manti, and Parowan, bought them anyway. The Mormons were not the only market for Wakara's horses. In the late 1840s, thousands of Americans and foreign emigrants crossed the Great Basin, making their way to California in search of gold and greener pastures. Some forty-niners who purchased horses from Wakara speculated that the Mormons encouraged Wakara to conduct his California raids so that Utah would have fresh horses for local settlers and for westbound travelers and so that the Mormons could serve as intermediaries and earn a cut of the profit. With or without the Saints' help, more than a few of the horses that Wakara had raided in California in previous seasons returned west underneath the hundreds of forty-niners who visited Mormon settlements in Utah, trading guns, powder, and cash for Wakara's fresh mounts.[35]

This increase in customers meant Wakara needed to increase his horse supply. Contemporaneous written records from California are silent about the raiding seasons of 1846–1847, 1847–1848, and 1848–1849. But the fact that he had fresh horses to trade with the Mormons and the forty-niners indicates that during these years Wakara continued his raiding. Still, the increased foot and hoof traffic on the road between Utah and California made raiding more treacherous. By 1850 Wakara was forced to break up his raiding parties into smaller units and delegate leadership to his lieutenants, as he did with Sanpitch for the 1850–1851 raiding season.

Wakara was disappointed with Sanpitch's leadership of that raid. Yet the 100 or so horses Sanpete brought back to Utah were perhaps among the last horses Wakara would steal from California. Soon after the end of the Mexican-American War, the Old Spanish Trail, which for decades connected Mexican hubs in Santa Fe and Abiquiú to Mexican Los Angeles, was replaced by a new, larger American road. This new road connected the newly formed (mostly) Anglo-American settlements in Salt Lake with an increasingly Anglo-American Southern California. In 1848, bringing supplies back from California, veterans of the Mormon Battalion were the first to blaze this wagon road. Over the next few years, forty-niners and California-bound Mormons passed back and forth on the road. In 1851, the former

Rancho San Bernardino, which Wakara long terrorized, became a port of entry for the westbound travelers and a center of trade. This steady traffic also meant that the Mormons in Utah no longer needed to rely on Wakara's raiding to refresh their supply of horses.[36]

As the market for his horses in Utah was drying up, Wakara's horse raiding remained more than a nuisance in California. The 1851 raid resulted in not only the loss of horses but also a wave of unrest, notably the arrest of the Lugo brothers under suspicion of murder and the subsequent killing of Red Irving and his gang. Hoping to snuff out this tinderbox sparked by Wakara's raiding, in early 1851 the US Army placed a company of fifty rangers to guard the Cajon Pass, a formidable-enough force that word of it reached George A. Smith in Parowan. In March of that same year, Smith relayed to Wakara the dangers that such a company posed to his scalp and neck, were he to return west to steal more horses.

Along with warnings of a bigger stick at the Cajon Pass, the Mormons gifted Wakara carrots to dissuade him from returning to California. The day of the spring equinox in March 1851, in Parowan George A. Smith gave Wakara and his brother Peteetneet a letter of recommendation, which granted the Ute leaders free passage through Mormon settlements as they made their way north to the fish festival. The certificate also informed settlers to whom the Ute leaders showed the document that "they should be treated as friends, + as they wish to trade Horse[s,] Buckskins & Piede children. We hope them success prosperity & good bargains." Over the spring and early summer, Wakara and his lodges moved north along the Wasatch Front, fishing and trading horses and Paiutes along the way. On June 9, Mormon leaders, including Brigham Young, visited Wakara's camp near Salt Lake City and ordained him, Arapeen, Sowiette, and Unhoquitch elders in the church.[37]

After his ordination, Wakara and his followers trekked south, gathering provisions from the Mormon settlements he had helped found in previous years. In late June 1851, in Provo Wakara's horses fed on the wheat fields that the settlers had planted on the Timpanogos' fish festival grounds. By September, Wakara was near Manti, where his people helped themselves to wheat from the settlers' fields and stores. By late November, Wakara and his lodges were in Parowan. There, George A. Smith reported that the settlers feted the Utes with a Thanksgiving-like feast of pumpkin, squash, potatoes, meat, and bread, the leftovers of which Wakara's people carried south with them. That fall, Wakara's destination was not the ranchos in San Bernardino. Instead, he was headed to what is today Arizona to trade Mormon wheat for Navajo sheep.[38]

The Mormons' expansion on his lands and control over the road to California meant that, instead of spending seasons fishing, chasing grass, and raiding horses, Wakara had to rely on receiving such gifts of food as well as stealing grain and trading for livestock.

NONE OF THIS MADE WAKARA HAPPY. THE NEXT year, when he met with Brigham Young in Provo in May 1852, Wakara complained that the settlers were overfishing with their trolling nets. Worse, the Mormon bread that the hungry Utes were forced to eat because they could not get fish made his people sick.[39]

When Wakara set up camp at the mouth of the Provo River just before the run of the June suckers, the settlers complained that Wakara's horses, which he paddocked in the settlers' fields, were again trampling on their grains. Provo leader Isaac Higbee reported the growing conflict in a letter to Young. Higbee explained that when he told Wakara he needed to relocate his camp, Wakara held his ground. "He does not feel disposed to go at the present or without being paid for it," Higbee reported. In response, Brigham Young offered some accommodations. Young told Higbee to take Indian interpreter George Bean to Wakara's camp and tell him "he can stay" if he removes his horses from the Mormons' fields. Young recognized that continued interference with the fish festival could lead to open conflict, which Young was not (quite) ready to take on.[40]

Still, this disruption of his fish festival and the end of his horse raiding meant Wakara was forced to rely not only on settler grains and cattle but also on another commodity: enslaved Natives.

Part IV

Wakara's Slave

Chapter 11

"The Saddest-Looking Piece of Humanity"

In the fall of 1847, either strapped to a horse or forced to walk through early snows, Pidash, an enslaved Native woman, was brought by her Native captors to the Salt Lake Valley, then a borderland between the Shoshone and Ute homelands. A Paiute or Ute—knowledge of her tribe of origin has been lost to history—Pidash had been with her captors for some time. Her father had died a few years before. Her mother remarried. Her stepfather then sold her to the Ute medicine man and slave trader Baptiste, Wakara's brother.[1]

Pidash was starving. Though she was in her late teens, her body was so gaunt that she was later mistaken for a child. She might have passed in and out of consciousness from fatigue as Baptiste set up camp in the foothills of the Salt Lake Valley's northern mountains, pitched the tents, and lit a fire.

Pidash came to when her captors cut into her forehead and limbs. She screamed in agony when they stuck knives heated in the fire into her wounds. Her blood spattered on the hard-packed snow blanketing the valley floor.

Baptiste's torture of his captive was heinous. But it wasn't without precedent. To convince reluctant buyers in New Mexican slave markets to purchase enslaved Natives they brought for sale, Baptiste and Wakara's ancestors had also publicly tortured, even killed some of their human wares until would-be buyers relented. The torture had another purpose. Baptiste wanted to get the attention of the settlers inside the two-room log cabin a stone's throw from their camp.

Baptiste's calibrated torture worked. Hearing cries that shattered the crisp morning air, Lorenzo D. Young, the younger brother of Brigham Young, stepped out of the cabin door to see what was going on. Lorenzo, then forty years old, called his ten-year-old son John to his side. He told John to run the mile southwest and fetch help from the fort.

Like the rest of the Mormon settlers who arrived in the Salt Lake Valley in the summer of 1847, Lorenzo Young built his first house inside the Old Fort, with defenses against expected Native attackers, not comfort, the main factor in its design. But Harriet, one of Lorenzo's three wives, suffered from tuberculosis. She believed that her coughing would subside if the family moved out of the stuffy, communal quarters to higher ground. By late fall 1847, Lorenzo had finished the cabin—the first settler home built outside the fort—next to a stream fed by snowmelt from the canyon above.

In a few years, the cabin would be leveled to make room for the Beehive House—one of Brigham Young's many mansions, which sits to this day on the edge of Temple Square in Salt Lake City. But in 1847, Baptiste targeted the isolated cabin for trade, not attack.[2]

Baptiste said as much to Barney Ward, whom John Young, along with a few others, fetched from the fort. Ward, a mountain man who had learned Numic from his Shoshone wife, served as the interpreter between Baptiste and the Saints gathered at Lorenzo Young's cabin. Baptiste offered two captives for sale, Pidash and a teenage boy. The

Sally Kanosh (ca. 1830–1878). Carte de visite by Charles Savage (ca. 1872). (Courtesy of the University of Utah Special Collections)

Saints refused the offer. Baptiste threatened to kill the captives if the Saints did not buy them. The Saints still refused.

Baptiste made good on his threat. He killed the boy and, according to some recollections, began to torture Pidash anew. The Saints stepped in. Charles Decker, who was married to Brigham Young's daughter Vilate, exchanged a rifle for the girl.[3]

Charles took Pidash to Lorenzo and Harriet's cabin. "She was the saddest-looking piece of humanity I have ever seen," John Young recalled in his memoirs. "All the fleshy parts of her body, legs, and arms had been hacked with knives, then fire brands had been stuck into the wounds." After this inspection, Harriet washed her, tended to her injuries, and clothed her. Harriet also gave her a new name,

Sally, likely after Barney Ward's Shoshone wife of that name. Then Charles Decker took her back to the fort and gave her to his sister Clarissa, Brigham Young's sixth plural wife, who was about the same age as Sally.[4]

SALLY BECAME THE FIRST OF MANY ENSLAVED NATIVE Americans sold by Wakara's Utes to the Mormons. But she was far from the first of Wakara's slaves. Generations before Euro-Americans arrived in the American Southwest, in conflicts over territory and resources, Wakara's ancestors enslaved other Native peoples; Wakara's ancestors were enslaved as well. The arrival of the horse allowed Wakara's Utes not only to steal more horses in California but also to increase their raids against their nonequestrian Numic kin, the Paiutes in southwestern Utah, and against other equestrians, including the Shoshones and Navajos. Wakara and other Utes sold their captives in slave markets from Abiquiú to Los Angeles and in between.

In 1847, the settlers' arrival expanded Wakara's horse and slave markets. While they welcomed Wakara's horses, the Mormons only bought Wakara's slaves after their consciences had been tortured.

Or so they said. In late 1851, Mormon officials arrested a New Mexican named Don Pedro León Luján for trafficking in Indian slaves in Utah without a proper license. While Luján was put on trial, the real target was Wakara. The Utah Territory did not yet have legal authority to try Wakara for Indian slave trading, because Wakara was ostensibly a Utah resident. Still, during the trial against Luján, Brigham Young testified that "Indian Walker" had for years trafficked in Indian children, whom he treated worse than his horses. "I have seen Walker's slaves so emaciated they were not able to stand upon their feet," Young explained. "He is in the habit of tying them out from their camps at night, naked and destitute of food unless it is so cold he apprehends they will freeze to death. In that case he will give them something to sleep on, lest he should lose them." At the trial, Young also recounted the horrors of Sally's purchase as the prime example of the savagery of Wakara's slaving, including the use of torture to exact higher prices from would-be buyers. Young testified that, having passed from the clutches of Baptiste and into the loving embrace of the Saints, Sally "has lived in my family ever since, has fared as my children, and is as free."[5]

Young lied. Sally was not treated as one the fifty-seven children Young would eventually sire with sixteen of his fifty-six wives. She never lived "free."

Instead, for most of the three decades she lived with the Youngs, Sally rose before dawn to cook, clean, and care for the dozens of children who also lived in Young's Lion and Beehive Houses—houses built on the spot where Charles Decker had purchased her from Baptiste. She was labeled a "servant" in census records; there is no record that she was ever paid for her "service." Despite Young's claims that she became one of his family, on these census records Sally's surname was not Young but "Indian."[6]

Brigham's lie about Sally became law. In early 1852, the Mormons used the story of Sally, and their accounts of Wakara's slaving more broadly, to pass legislation that outlawed Wakara's trade in Indian slaves. In the same law, the Mormons legalized their participation in the trade. Their justification was that God brought the Saints to Utah, in part, so they could buy Indian slaves in order to free, Christianize, and civilize them.

Young's lie also became lore. Those who wrote the official narratives of Native-Mormon relations in Utah created on paper the "Indian Walker" that Young described while testifying against Luján in 1851: a vicious and unredeemable savage who preyed on the weak. Creating this Indian Walker on paper allowed the Saints to portray their own efforts to end Wakara's flesh-and-bone slave trade as a righteous campaign against evil.[7]

There is no doubt that the people Wakara captured and sold feared him. Oral histories collected in the early twentieth century from Paiute elders whose bands Wakara targeted recalled that even the mention of Wakara's name struck terror in their hearts decades after Wakara's death. Likewise, there are written records of Paiute parents being forced to "sell" their children to Wakara in exchange for a horse to eat. Later, when they settled on Wakara's lands, the Mormons also claimed that Paiute parents gave their children to the Saints for food and protection from slavers like Wakara.

Yet, to justify their own participation in the trade, Mormons almost certainly exaggerated the savage treatment that Wakara and other Ute slavers inflicted on their captives. And written and oral histories show that the Mormons practiced Indian slavery—sometimes in ways that rivaled Wakara's transactional brutality—before they purchased Pidash and long after Wakara's death. The Mormons brought to Utah at least one Indian "servant," the Cherokee woman Peninah Shropshire Cotton Wood, whom the Wood family had acquired back east. Though in Mormon records Peninah officially entered a plural marriage (albeit with a man twenty-seven years her senior), some family historians remember her as more slave than wife. Likewise, for a time the Mormons aligned themselves with Wakara's slave trading. They saw him as a fellow priesthood holder and the bearer of a letter of recommendation that required settlers to trade for Wakara's horses, buckskins, and Paiute children. Thus Wakara, who according to one witness had turned from "reddish olive" to "white" after being baptized, was an ally in the Mormons' goal of removing Natives from land that the Mormons believed was theirs by divine right. The women and children—most of the men, we will see later, would be killed—would be placed in Mormon homes so that they too could be made White.[8]

For some enslaved, this process of whitening was figurative. But it could also be literal. To be sure, many of Wakara's slaves found death in the form of communicable diseases in Mormon homes. Of those who survived, many, if not most, remained as Sally did—as slaves by other names. As laborers, field hands, and house servants, they constructed the very buildings and farms that dug up their hunting grounds and dirtied their fishing waters. Still others were given the name "sister wives." Their wombs became sites of work in birthing members of the Mormon body of Christ. In written family histories, most remembered their White Mormon fathers and forgot their Native mothers.[9]

After thirty years as a servant in the Mormon prophet's homes, in 1877 Sally once again changed hands. Young gifted her to Kanosh, the leader of the Pahvant Utes, and she became one of Kanosh's plural wives. Sally died within a year of the marriage. She was buried not among her husband's Ute kin on Walker's Mountain but in the settlers' cemetery in the town of Kanosh. The *Deseret News* story of her funeral reports that Sally was given "a kind and Christian burial." Overseen by local Mormon women, the ceremony contrasted "with the rude manner of disposing of the Indian dead," perhaps a reference to Wakara's infamous funeral ceremony. According to the *Deseret News*, Sally's burial—she was dressed in temple robes that Young, who had died a few months before, had given her—marked the completion of her transformation from Indian savage to Mormon wife. "Beneath the tawney skin," the report concluded, "was a faith, intelligence, and virtue that would do honor to millions with a paler face."[10]

I FIRST MET RICK AND RENA PIKYAVIT IN the summer of 2018 at the Fish Lake Lodge, a rustic retreat located on an alpine lake tucked into the southern Wasatch Plateau. Rick and Rena are elders of the Kanosh Band of Paiutes, which Sally's husband, Kanosh, founded in the 1860s.[11]

Two centuries before our meeting, Fish Lake had been a gathering place for various Ute bands, who, like their kin at Timpanogos

(Utah) Lake, feasted on the bountiful fish that they harvested every spawning season. Fish Lake was also part of the "northern cutoff" of the Old Spanish Trail, which Wakara and other Utes traversed to access their homelands in the Utah Valley, bringing with them the horses and enslaved Paiutes they captured during raiding seasons in California and southern Utah. Today, every summer thousands of people gather at the picturesque, high mountain lake, about a mile wide, five miles long, and 8,848 feet above sea level. They come to fish the native trout as well as the invasive perch.

Rick and Rena know Fish Lake intimately. For decades, they worked alongside archaeologists on digs and surveys at the lake and other locations in Utah. Yet, echoing many Indigenous scholars, most notably Vine Deloria Jr., Rick and Rena are skeptical of archaeology. They describe the science as "biased and subjective," more often serving to reduce Native people to an ancient past, instead of seeing them as part of the present. Still, kneeling in the dust and mud and sifting through pans of rock, Rick and Rena have done the painstaking work of making sure Native perspectives are included—and sacred sites are acknowledged (and protected)—in the written, governmental reports that archaeological surveys are required to produce, most often to clear the way for more roads and more settler American developments.

Rick and Rena are also historians. They keep their ancestors' histories alive by retelling their stories and practicing their ways of life. Rick describes himself as "traditional." At our first meeting, to illustrate that point, Rick pointed to his long, thick, salt-and-pepper ponytail, signifying that he had resisted the centuries-long pressure on Native men to cut their hair. For more than a decade Rena worked at Utah's Fremont Indian State Park and Museum, where she taught classes on Indigenous history and foodways.

In addition to being educators and history keepers, Rick and Rena are also advocates and practitioners of Native people adopting Native children across tribal lines. Such work is in the DNA of their band; Kanosh's Utes and Paiutes from central Utah formed their community after most of Kanosh's fellow Utes were forced onto the Uintah Reservation and after slavery, disease, and environmental destruction of their homelands displaced the Paiutes of southern Utah. Though Rick's grandmother was Ute, he is not a direct kin of Wakara. The rest of his family is Paiute. Rena is Apache and Diné. But through their work defending their ancestors' connections to the land and Native sovereignty, including the sovereignty of the future generations embodied in adopted Native children, they are spiritual descendants of Wakara and Kanosh, their band's founder.[12]

In 2018, the Pikyavits agreed to meet me at Fish Lake so we could discuss Wakara's legacy—notably, the history of Wakara preying on Rick and Rena's Paiute tribal ancestors.

As we sat in the conference room, framed with picture windows overlooking the bright blue lake, I shared with Rick and Rena what I had read in settler narratives on Indian slaving in Utah: how Paiutes like Sally's family sold their children to slavers like Baptiste and Wakara, who then sold them at trade fairs in New Mexico or to the Mormons. I also shared that I read that Paiute parents also sold their children directly to the Saints. They did so to avoid, the settlers' records claim, the trauma Sally faced as a captive of Ute slavers.

"Wakara was the greatest warrior in Utah. He did what he had to do to protect his land and his people," Rena told me, a view that did not surprise me. What she said next did. She told me that it was wrong to remember Baptiste and Wakara for having "abused other Native Americans," including enslaving Paiutes. "He wouldn't do that because he dedicated his life to defending his people."

Rena went even further. She rejected out of hand the history of Indian slavery. She told me the whole "history was made up by White historians." She pointed her finger at me when she said this. The history of Indian slavery was written down first by White settlers, then reprinted in books written by White settler historians to make Native leaders like Wakara into inhumane savages so that they could justify "taking our lands."

Rena concluded by challenging not only the historical claim that Utes like Wakara participated in Indian slavery but also the notion that Paiute parents traded their children to settlers. "We would never sell our children!" Rena proclaimed, with the force of a mother and grandmother who has dedicated her life to protecting her own children and children not necessarily related to her by blood.

At our first meeting, I saw Rena's rejection of the history of Indian slavery as creating an unbridgeable impasse between the written word and the oral record, between settler "history" and Native "storytelling." But in later meetings with Rick and Rena, during which our mutual trust increased, Rick challenged me to think about the "very words you use to write our history."

Inspired by Rick's challenge, I've come to see that the juxtaposition of the written narratives, which insist that Ute slavers and Paiute parents participated in Indian slavery, with Rick and Rena's oral histories, which insist that they didn't, points not to an impasse but an opening. An opening that leads to a deeper, more nuanced narration of Indian slavery and Natives' roles within it.

Other scholars have forwarded similar views that the history of Indian slavery blurs carefully curated lines between slavery and freedom and between Native and settler. Historian Andrés Reséndez has argued that with the concept of "Indian slavery" we have a failure of definitions. In the Western Hemisphere, "the very word 'slavery' brings to mind African bodies stuffed in the hold of a ship or white-aproned maids bustling in antebellum homes." Such images create "historical myopia" that conflates slavery with the "African slavery" practiced in the American South before the Civil War.[13]

But the Americas were home to indigenous forms of slavery well before the arrival of the first enslaved Africans to Jamestown in 1619. And "Native Americans were subjected to a parallel system of bondage as degrading and as vast as African slavery," Reséndez has argued. Indian slavery took place in every major region and was present before the arrival of explorers, conquerors, and settlers. And it continued well after the legal abolition of its African counterpart in the mid-1860s. Reséndez estimates that between 1492 and the twentieth century, 2.5 million to 5 million Native people were enslaved for some or all of their lifetimes.[14]

In the mid-nineteenth century, African chattel slave labor built the wealth of the planter class of the American South, as well as much of the wealth of Northern industrialists in whose factories Southern cotton was transformed into textiles. In part, Indian slavery built the wealth and infrastructure of the American West directly through Indian labor. But Indian slavery also created the West when Spanish, Mexican, and later American settlers used it to break up Indigenous families and ready the West for settler colonial invasion.

Native slavers like Wakara and Baptiste also grew their wealth, power, and territory by practicing what I call "settler Indian slavery," which like African chattel slavery viewed enslaved bodies as commodities from which to extract wealth. And like Southern slave owners, Wakara and other Ute slavers calibrated physical violence, or threats of it, to maximize the price slaves fetched in trade and to maximize labor output. They also restricted their slaves' diets to minimize cost.

Yet Wakara's participation in Indian slavery was more complicated than the inhumane abuse captured in the settlers' written records. As James F. Brooks, among others, has demonstrated, Native "captives" could become "cousins"; captives sometimes became adopted members of the band or tribe that enslaved them. Like the history of the Native adoption of the horse, these transitions from captive to kin were recorded in oral histories. But such transitions from slave to family occurred out of earshot of the keepers of the settler archives on which most of what scholars have written about Wakara's slaving has been based.[15]

For example, oral family history claims that at least one of the Paiute slaves who was killed to accompany Wakara in his grave was an adopted child. Oral family history also suggests that at least one of the adult women who was killed to accompany him in his grave was born a Paiute. But it seems likely that not all Paiute-born family members were sacrificed to join Wakara on Walker's Mountain. Sometime after Wakara's death in 1855, at least one of Wakara's surviving wives, Peaweeds, joined the Paiute Koosharem Band, perhaps returning to her family of origin. Likewise, the children of Arapeen, Wakara's heir, also joined the Koosharem Band.[16]

Listening to the keepers of oral histories, which challenge the written archive on Indian slavery, forces us to think beyond our binary Black/White, North/South views of slavery to consider something messier and unfamiliar: a "Native Indian slavery" that sometimes even approached kinship.

This Native version of Indian slavery also challenges received notions of race and tribe. In the context of Wakara, it challenges the definitions of what it means to be Ute and Paiute.

It is not a new observation that tribal boundaries were fluid before the arrival of settlers, who, to divide, conquer, and displace, drew lines of geography and race between tribes that were often, to one degree or another, kin. Still, there is ample evidence that before and even after the arrival of settlers, individual Natives moved between Paiute and Ute bands. Captivity was one way a Paiute could become a Ute. So was marriage. Before her stepfather traded her to Baptiste, Pidash (Sally) was either a Paiute or a nonequestrian Ute. Sally became a Ute when she married Kanosh. Wakara himself gave a Paiute child whom he had captured or purchased to his fellow Ute leader Kanosh. That "adopted" son, John, was the only child of Kanosh to have his own family.

The settler state imposed fixed distinctions between the tribes in the form of law and in the form of reservation lands upon which the tribes were forced to resettle. But ironically, the settler state was also another way a Ute became a Paiute.

For example, at least two daughters Wakara fathered with his wife Peaweeds married Paiute men. To this day, their descendants are enrolled members of Paiute bands. Take another example: Kanosh, the Mormons' favorite Indian ally, was born a Pahvant Ute. But he refused to move to the Ute reservation in the 1860s. Because he cut his hair, was baptized a Mormon, and became a landowning farmer, the settlers let him stay in central Utah. There he became the founder of the mixed Ute and Paiute community that is today the Kanosh Band of Paiutes. Still, because historians have often been locked into fixed ideas about tribal identities, many scholars of Native-Mormon relations, including myself, have misidentified Kanosh as a Paiute.[17]

Conceptualizing a Native form of Indian slavery goes even further: It leads to a blurring of the boundaries between Native and settler identities. Wakara's own family captures this boundary blurring. Oral family history, combined with DNA and genealogical evidence, strongly suggests that Wakara himself gave at least two of his own children to the Mormons in the early days of the Manti settlement to build kinship with the settlers. The children Wakara gave to the Saints grew up to marry White Mormon men. As I discuss later, in exchange, Wakara asked for and received (for a brief time) the infant son of Isaac Morley, with whom Wakara cofounded the Manti settlement. Wakara also expected to receive a "White" wife—though he never did.

REIMAGINING NATIVE INDIAN SLAVERY AS A COMBINATION OF captivity, bondage, brutality, and (sometimes) kinship challenges the idea that Paiute parents "sold" their children to the Mormons, an idea that Rick and Rena reject. "Would you ever sell your child?" Rena asked me in 2018. And pointing at me, she asked, "Why do *you* think we would do that?"

To be sure, there are accounts of Paiute children passing from Paiute parents into the hands of Mormons. And sometimes the Mormons gave these Paiute parents food at this point of "sale." But the question remains, did the Paiute parents choose to sell their children?

In late 1850, following the new Mormon wagon road, George A. Smith led a group of Mormons south on their way to establish a settlement and missionary outpost to the Paiutes in southern Utah near Wakara's Old Spanish Trail. The day after Christmas, Smith discovered that his ox "Bailey" had been shot full of arrows. The settlers dressed the ox's wounds with turpentine and salt and covered it with a buffalo robe to guard against the cold. The expedition's thermometer read sixteen degrees below zero that morning. But to no avail. The next day, Smith ordered that Bailey be "knocked in the head, out of his misery." A Mormon cavalry then rode down two Paiutes, a man and a boy about the age of twelve, likely a father and his son. The settlers forced the pair back to camp. Smith called the man a "scoundrel" for shooting the ox. The Paiute man denied the accusation, but still he "turned very pale for a Red Man, and sent up an Indian cry for the ox," Smith wrote in his journal. Smith related that he told the man "it was too late to cry, but if he would let me have the boy, he [the father] might have the ox" to eat. The Paiute "readily agreed" to this offer. "I told him the boy should be well fed comfortably clothed and made a man of him if he would be a good boy." The father accepted and said "he wanted to see him dressed like a white man" if he ever saw him again.[18]

Almost two centuries later, Rick and Rena, tribal descendants of this Paiute father and son, warn us to be suspicious of such written records in which Natives speak and act as the settlers wished they would: a "paper Indian" father talking in the archive, so that the Saints could do what they wanted to do with his flesh-and-bone son.

Rick and Rena's rejection of the idea that the Paiutes would participate in such a sale leads us to consider that Paiute parents were forced into a settler colonial Sophie's choice. They could relinquish some children to the Saints and get meat to feed other children, or they could have children taken by force as punishment for a perceived offense—shooting the ox Bailey, for example.

Redefining Native Indian slavery through oral history points back to what Rick and Rena told me was Wakara's central motivation: preserving his people, the Utes, and their connection to the land—even at the expense of Paiutes.

With his fisheries under threat from Mormon settler expansion around Timpanogos Lake, and with his horse raiding constrained by US militiamen and later Mormon settlers in San Bernardino, in the early 1850s enslaved Paiutes became the last commodity Wakara had left to trade. The Mormons became his market of choice and soon, by the Saints' own hand, his market of necessity. The same winter that Smith exchanged Bailey's meat for the Paiute boy, with Wakara's blessing and guidance, Smith established the settlement Louisa (Parowan) along the Old Spanish Trail. And that winter, while Wakara's brother Sanpitch was in California stealing horses from the Lugos, Wakara was in southern Utah enslaving Paiutes.

Before we can explore how Wakara and the Mormons became partners in enslaving Paiutes at places like Parowan, Provo, and Manti, we need to visit grand capitals of empires, from Granada in Spain to Tenochtitlán in preconquest Mexica, as well as small settlements, from San Carlos in California to Abiquiú in New Mexico. In these disparate places emerged ideas and practices of settler Indian slavery that transformed the American West by ripping Natives from their homelands and commodifying them—based on the price their (most often young, female) bodies could fetch at trade fairs and based on the value of the labor that their (most often young, female) bodies could perform with their feet, hands, and wombs.

Chapter 12

"Gold and Silver and the Richest Treasure"

It was fair season in 1775. The plaza of Abiquiú Pueblo, a dry, dusty square built on the mesa above the Río Chama and anchored by the Church of Santo Tomás, was abuzz with the sounds of neighing horses, bleating cattle, wailing slaves, and bargains being struck.

A small mission town fifty miles northwest of Santa Fe, Abiquiú was established about twenty-five years before to bring Christianity to the Puebloans and to bring stability to the New Mexican frontier, which for the previous half century had been under constant threat of horseback-raiding Navajos, Utes, and Comanches. Trade had brought some peace to the region. Making people rich tends to make them less interested in war.

Just as crisp air arrived in the desert each fall, "heathens of the Ute nation" also arrived, Padre Francisco Atanasio Domínguez explained in a report he wrote after a tour he took of the New Mexico missions before he and Silvestre Vélez de Escalante left for their 1776 expedition into the Great Basin. Abiquiú did not host the largest fairs. Taos, about seventy miles to the east, was bigger and more popular with the Comanches. But the Utes came to Abiquiú because it was closer to their homelands.[1]

The trade fairs were the high holy days of commerce. For most of the year, it was illegal for settlers to trade directly with Natives, though this did not stop them from illicit intercourse with their Ute neighbors to the north. Still, each fall, Spanish prefects licensed fairs to allow the Utes to come to town and trade in the full light of the law.

The Utes arrived with their horses weighed down with deerskins and buffalo meat, which they exchanged for more horses. Fifty years later, in the 1820s, the opening of the Old Spanish Trail would allow them to procure horses from California. But in the 1770s, the Utes needed fresh mounts to hunt bison and to protect themselves against raids from Comanches and Spanish settlers. The Utes also sought Spanish maize, corn flour, blankets, pottery, and metal tools. Renowned for their tanning skills, in the Abiquiú plaza Ute traders could exchange a fine Ute hide for a good horse or two hunting knives. Still, deals went bad so frequently that officials posted guards to watch over the fairs, lest disputes turned violent and weapons were drawn to cut down limb and life.[2]

The Utes brought with them other flesh to trade: "little captive heathen Indians," as Domínguez described them. The slave-trading component of the annual fairs was so well established that the weeks in early fall when they occurred became known to some as the "month of slaves."[3]

And herein, a deep irony also hung in the air in Abiquiú in the fall of 1775, an irony that went unspoken. Many of the residents of the pueblo who purchased the Utes' little captives were themselves descendants of formerly enslaved Natives. As recently as the generation before, during wars with other Natives, many of the parents of the current Abiquiú residents had been captured from nearby Puebloan tribes, as well as from the Great Plains tribes hundreds of miles away, and sold into bondage in New Mexico.

Indian slavery in the Americas, particularly in what became the American Southwest, existed long before the arrival of Europeans.

Still, Europeans brought their own ideas of slavery to the New World, which led to the creation of an Indian slavery that was neither European nor Native but settler American.

Settler Indian slavery commodified bodies to extract labor and profits, while Native Indian slavery was often performed to establish or renew connections to the land and to people. Over time, some Spanish, Mexicans, and Anglo-Americans also participated in forms of Native Indian slavery, which were culturally specific and often geared to create kin networks across tribal and racial boundaries. But Natives like Wakara's Utes also adopted settler Indian slavery by adopting European ideas of race and commerce.

THIS SETTLER FORM OF INDIAN SLAVERY SPREAD ACROSS the North American continent in concert with the spread of Euro-American conquest. During the colonial era, settlers in New England enslaved Native peoples who resisted the seizure of their lands, shipping many to the Caribbean, where they joined enslaved Africans working sugar plantations. In the last decades of the seventeenth century and the beginning of the eighteenth century, Charleston, South Carolina, shipped out more Native Americans from its port than it imported Africans. By the early nineteenth century, African slavery had replaced Indian slavery on the Eastern Seaboard. Settler Indian slavery had served its main purpose, uprooting Native peoples from their lands to make way for settler conquest. Out West, settler Indian slavery was present a lot longer. The Spanish introduced it to the American Southwest in the 1500s, and it lasted there until at least the second half of the nineteenth century.[4]

The *Reconquista* of the Iberian Peninsula in the late fifteenth century helped not only to train Spanish horses to conquer the Americas but also to train Spanish religion, law, and economics to enslave Natives in what would become New Spain. In 1492, the archbishop of Granada gave the conquered Moors a choice to become Christian, leave the country, or face the sword.

Likewise, in 1510 the Council of Castile first issued the *Requerimiento*. The document, which conquistadors read when they first encountered new Native populations in the West Indies and Mexico, stated that under the pope's authority, Natives were required to acknowledge the Catholic Church "as the Ruler and Superior of the whole world" and to accept the Spanish Crown as their legal sovereign. If they did so, then the conquerors "shall leave you, your wives, and your children, and your lands, free without servitude." But if the Natives refused, the seizure of the lands and the enslavement of their "wives and children" would follow with the force of Spanish law and weapons of war.[5]

When Hernán Cortés landed in what would become the Gulf of Mexico in 1519, he read the *Requerimiento* to Native onlookers. But Cortés did not expect that it would convince anyone to bend the knee. Instead, he expected to find Natives ready to protect their lands with force. So Cortés requested authorization from the Spanish Crown to respond to resistance with warfare and to make captured Natives into *esclavos de guerra*, or "war slaves." The Crown agreed. But the Crown also wanted its cut. Records indicate that in 1521 and 1522, soldiers who overthrew the Aztecan capital Tenochtitlán paid taxes on more than 8,000 slaves to the monarchs. The Mexica also took slaves during the battles. But instead of paying taxes to a colonial state an ocean away, Mexica warriors sacrificed Spanish soldiers to Mexica gods, in hopes that the gods would protect their lands from the invaders. This difference in how the Spanish and the Mexica used their slaves during the battle for Tenochtitlán hinted at what would become the difference between settler and Native Indian slavery.[6]

First came the *Requerimiento*. Then came marriage as a tool of conquest of the New World. In Spain during the 1490s, as the frontier of Granada moved southward, captured Moorish women were forced to convert to Catholicism, marry their abductors, and serve as intermediaries between the conquistadors and the conquered. Some two decades later, Tabasco Natives gave twenty enslaved women to the Spaniards soon after they arrived in the Gulf of Mexico. Among them was the Nahua woman known as La Malinche (Malintzin), who became Cortés's interpreter and consort. Thousands of similar unions followed. The Spanish Crown and the pope hoped that such Spanish-Native marriages, and the children they produced, would speed up conversion to Catholicism among the Natives.[7]

The Spanish not only introduced Catholicism and Catholic marriage as a tool of enslavement and conquest. They also introduced a new form of slavery to the New World. Before the Spanish conquest, bondage and captivity among Indigenous peoples of Mesoamerica were culturally specific and ritualized. Among the Mayans and Aztecs, captives of wars were forced to work the lands of their captors or were sacrificed to appease local gods. Women and girls were often forced into concubinage or marriage with their captors. Aztecans found guilty of crimes against their own communities—from rape and illegal hunting to embezzlement of common goods and breach of common trust—could be sentenced to periods of enslavement. Yet, with the arrival of the Spanish, this precontact Indian slavery, which served to bond Natives to their lands and to their peoples, was replaced by a broader category of *esclavitud*. Native bodies, like their African counterparts, became commodities, uprooted from their homelands and shipped long distances to perform extractive labor.[8]

For example, Juan de Oñate's 1598 expedition into what became New Mexico failed to find mythical gold and silver. But the expedition still produced riches. Oñate parceled the pueblos into *encomiendas*, the feudal system imported from Spain following the *Reconquista*. In exchange for their Catholic education and military protection, non-Christian conquered peoples were required to work for the conquistadors in fields and textile shops. Oñate also became the first in a series of Spanish governors in New Mexico who extracted Natives from the pueblos and from nomadic bands in the Southwest, including from the Apaches and Utes, and shipped them south to central Mexico. There, the enslaved worked the massive silver mines, which produced, between the sixteenth and eighteenth centuries, twelve times as much silver as the gold rushes of the mid-nineteenth-century United States, and which propelled the Spanish peso to become the world's first global currency. This was *esclavitud* in action. Extraction of Native bodies from Native lands fueled extraction of native resources from Native lands, which fueled the creation and expansion of global empires.[9]

New Mexican Natives did not sit by and accept enslavement, dislocation, and destruction of their culture. To be sure, the 1680 Pueblo Revolt was, in part, an effort to rid Puebloan lands of all symbols of Catholic and Spanish dominance and presence. Under orders from Popé, the Puebloans razed churches and burned paintings and statues of Christ and the Virgin Mary. Diving into rivers, they ritualistically washed themselves with the native root *amole* to remove the holy oils they had been immersed in and remove the names imposed on them during their coerced baptisms. They also destroyed Spanish wheat, citrus fruits, and peaches and replaced them with native maize, beans, watermelons, and cantaloupes. Still, as Andrés Reséndez has argued, the revolt was a Native insurrection not just against the imposition of a foreign religion and culture but also against *esclavitud*. The Puebloans refused to accept Spanish bondage and exploitation—both in the textile sweatshops of New Mexico and, increasingly during the seventeenth century, in the forced migration to the southern silver mines.[10]

SINCE THE BEGINNING OF THE EUROPEAN CONQUEST AND colonization of what became the American Southwest, Natives not only resisted bondage and slavery but also participated in it. After the Pueblo Revolt, in the eighteenth and nineteenth centuries, the Utes and the Comanches—sometimes in alliance, sometime as antagonists—used horses, firearms, and slavery to expand territorial control, amass wealth, and, to some extent, differentiate themselves from other Numic peoples.

In the late seventeenth century, the Pueblo Revolt was so disruptive to the extractive industries of New Spain that the Spanish Crown made it illegal for its representatives to traffic in Indian slaves. The Comanches and Utes stepped into this void to become the region's dominant slavers, often targeting Navajos and Apaches. The Comanches and Utes also traveled into the plains on their bison hunts, where they enslaved Plains peoples, then brought them to market in Santa Fe, Taos, and later Abiquiú.

In colonial town squares, Catholic missionaries claimed to have witnessed Native slavers torturing their captives, setting the precedent that Wakara and Baptiste employed in Utah. In 1761, friar Pedro Serrano described a particularly gruesome form of torture: public and serial rape. "When these barbarians bring a certain number of Indian women to sell," recalled Serrano, "before delivering them to the Christians . . . if they are ten years old or over, they deflower them and corrupt them in the sight of innumerable assemblies of barbarians and Catholics . . . and saying to those who buy them . . . 'Now you can take her—now she is good.'"[11]

In their church records and in their letters back to Spain, Spanish settlers claimed to be horrified by such barbarity. In response, despite legal edicts not to do so, padres in New Mexico argued that it was their Christian duty to buy ransomed captives in order to free them, immerse them in Spanish culture, and convert them to Catholicism.[12]

Yet, by the mid-eighteenth century, during annual fairs in New Mexico, Ute and Comanche slave traders were often feted as visiting dignitaries, not unredeemable barbarians. Their horses were quartered, and their personal safety was guaranteed by local magistrates. The slavers received such deference and honor, explained one New Mexican governor in 1752, "because of the favorable results which their trade and good relations bring to this province," including long-sought peace between the Spanish and the Utes. Once purchased, "Indian slaves," recalled one Franciscan, became the "gold and silver and the richest treasure" of Spain's New World empire.[13]

The value of this treasure was gendered. Spanish colonial laws written after the Pueblo Revolt established Catholic "just war" as the main way settlers rid the land of male Natives. Buying ransomed women and children captured in warfare—both those wars that Spanish waged directly against Natives and the intertribal wars that the Spanish promoted—served to "detribalize" Natives, breaking up families so that new generations could not be produced. Women and children also made better slaves in the factories, fields, and bedrooms of New Mexican settlements. The gendered nature of the slave trade shows up in the parish records at Abiquiú, where more than nine in ten of the captives sold by Utes, whose age at baptism was recorded, were girls age fifteen or younger. Wakara's Ute and Comanche slaving predecessors were handsomely paid for these human wares. "If it is an Indian girl from twelve to twenty years old," wrote Domínguez of the 1775 slave trade fair at Taos, then the trader can get "two good horses and some trifles in addition, such as a short cloak, a horse cloth, a red lapel. . . . [I]f the slave is male, he is worth less."[14]

Since slavery was officially illegal in the Spanish colonies, in the Catholic parish records that served as the colonial archives, the purchased Indian captives were often labeled *criados*, from the verb *criar*, meaning "to rear." After they were bought, baptized, and given Catholic names, the *criados* were placed in Spanish households to be Christianized and civilized. They were also promised that they would eventually be freed after a period of indenture. Not surprisingly, such promises were rarely kept, often leading to perpetual servitude and emotional, physical, and sexual abuse.

Still, some *criados* took their fates into their own hands using the cultural resources they had acquired, including knowledge of the Spanish language, Spanish law, and Spanish gendered expectations. In 1763, two enslaved women wrote to the New Mexican governor, complaining that their masters had not properly trained them in the Catholic faith. They had also been forced to tend sheep, which they considered a job for men. While shepherding, one of them had been raped. In response, the governor removed the two women from their first master and placed them in another home "where they might be instructed in the Christian doctrine and customs, and be fed and clothed through household chores appropriate to their sex."[15]

Other *criados* and their often mixed-race offspring, issue of purchased Native girls and their Spanish fathers/masters, escaped captivity and banded together, sometimes living in the mountains on the northern frontier of New Mexico. While the friars labeled them "apostates," these detribalized Natives called themselves *los genízaros*, the Spanish word for janissary, which originally referred to war captives conscripted to fight for the Ottoman sultan. As the Puebloan population collapsed due to disease and starvation, the population of *genízaros* exploded. Some scholars believe that by the dawn of the nineteenth century, *genízaros* accounted for one-third of the population of New Mexico.[16]

Many *genízaros* were shunned by the Puebloans. And the Spanish denied them citizenship. In response, the *genízaros* formed themselves into a new, in-between people and declared themselves not subject to the Spanish *casta* laws that forbade Indigenous peoples from owning land. They also formed new, in-between places. In 1752, the New Mexican governor granted thirty-four *genízaro* and Hopi families 16,000 acres of land around the Río Chama. In exchange, the residents of this new *genízaro* town, Santo Tomás de Abiquiú, pledged to defend the northern frontier against Comanche, Apache, and Ute raiders. The founding families of Abiquiú built homes, raised crops, and manufactured goods. In their town square, they traded with Spanish settlers and Utes, making Abiquiú the hub of the Spanish-Ute alliance, which enriched both sides through extensive commerce in skins, horses, and enslaved humans.

Historian Ned Blackhawk (Te-Moak Tribe of Western Shoshone Indians of Nevada) has described Abiquiú as Spanish New Mexico's "gateway to the northwest." In particular, it was a slaving gateway. During the month of slaves in 1775, Domínguez witnessed how Wakara's Ute predecessors brought to Abiquiú animal meat, hides, and captives that they had captured the previous spring when they raided Paiutes, Navajos, and other Great Basin Native peoples. The fall harvest of slaves was then processed in the New Mexican slaving system by ritually turning Indians into Catholics. In the last decades of the eighteenth and the first half of the nineteenth centuries, records of the Catholic parish at Abiquiú were replete with references to "Yuta" children who were baptized with Spanish settlers serving as their *padrinos*, or "godparents." As Ned Blackhawk has argued, such references to "Ute" and "Yuta" in the church records did not mean these children were Ute in origin. Most likely they were captured by Utes who sold them to the Spanish. Likewise, references to "godparents" in church records provided a gloss of Catholic paternalistic propriety over what the Spanish really were to these children: their masters.[17]

Before they were purchased and placed into Spanish households in Abiquiú, some enslaved were subjected to rituals of public torture. In August 1805, Padre José de la Prada scribbled out an urgent dispatch to the New Mexican governor, describing the conditions of a woman whom the Utes had captured from the Navajos, then tortured—evidenced by arrow-point wounds covering her body. Because he was a man of faith and thus "moved by charity" to save "her from the tyranny of the Utes," the padre had no choice but to break the law against purchasing Indian slaves, he wrote to the governor. In exchange for the woman, whom he named María, the padre gave the Utes several horses, a mule, and 100 pesos in cash.[18]

María's torture was not unique. According to Spanish archives, public torture, branding, whippings, and even beheadings were common spectacles in New Mexican slave markets. Just as the Latter-day Saints would argue a century and a half later, the Utes' torture, explained Padre José de la Prada, was calibrated to enliven Christian sympathies and to increase the price they could demand for the women and children they brought to market.[19]

In the second half of the eighteenth century, settler Indian slavery also contributed to the making and unmaking of people and places in California, the northwestern edge of the Spanish empire in the Americas.

As in New Mexico, the Franciscan missions in California were ostensibly founded to convert the area's Native population to the Catholic faith and civilize them in Spanish culture. Once they were baptized, Natives became, by special decree from the viceroy of New Spain, wards of Junípero Serra's Franciscans. "Just as a father of a family has charge of his house and of the education and correction of his children," proclaimed the decree, the padres were charged with "the management, control, and education" of their Indigenous spiritual children to prepare them to become Spanish subjects who would eventually farm the land independently of Spanish overseers. California Natives under Serra's care practiced their future self-sufficiency by constructing, without pay, most of the built infrastructure and raising most of the agricultural produce of colonial California.[20]

But the Franciscans did not free the Natives in their charge. After all, Serra viewed them as *gente sin razón* ("people without reason") who proved their incapacity for self-rule with their frequent insurrections. The spiritual fathers had no choice but to give their insolent children "corrections," including putting them in stocks and flogging them in mission squares. The Natives received these punishments for infractions ranging from talking back to priests and missing mass to desertion, gambling, and participation in Native religious rituals.[21]

Serra himself understood that public torture against one Native needed to be calibrated to produce the desired effect in others. In 1775, a group of Natives who had fled the Mission San Carlos Borromeo near Serra's headquarters at Monterey were recaptured and imprisoned. The governor overseeing the mission carried out Serra's command that runaways should suffer "two or three portions of whippings on different days," so that the punishments would serve as "a warning" and "may be a spiritual benefit to all." However, the benefits of such torture, as well as the labor produced by Natives, flowed to the missions themselves—and the mission fathers—not to the missionized. At the height of their wealth in the 1820s, the missions owned hundreds of thousands of sheep and cattle and tens of thousands of horses and mules. All this wealth would become a target for Wakara's raiding in the decades to come.[22]

Like in New Mexico, *esclavitud* combined with settler farming and ranching to detribalize California Natives. To make way for settler row crops, California Natives were forced to dig up soil and tend to horses and mules that trampled the local grasses and seeds that fed native Californian game, waterfowl, and other mammals—animals upon which Native Californians had relied for generations to feed themselves. In exchange for their labor that destroyed their own homelands, they received meager rations and frequent rounds of torture.

In 1776, Escalante and Domínguez's search for an overland route to Junípero Serra's Spanish missions in California was unsuccessful. But the padres' *entrada* into Ute homelands established steady contact between the people of northern New Mexico, especially the *genízaros*, and Wakara's Utes. Along with their Timpanogos guides, on their expedition the padres brought with them two brothers, Lucrecio and Andrés Muñiz, who were *genízaros* reared near Abiquiú who might have been of Ute origin, spoke Ute, and had frequently traded with the Utes.[23]

The *genízaro*-Ute intercourse strengthened the Spanish-Ute alliance, which provided trade and defenses against Comanche raiders for both the Utes and the Spanish settlements. The Utes came south for food, metals, guns, clothing, and, until the Old Spanish Trail opened in the 1820s, horses. The Utes brought with them flesh—animal skins and Native slaves. The Spanish traveled north into Ute territory for slaves and animal skins. Yet, because it was illegal, trading remained clandestine, only making a mark in the colonial archives when the traders were caught and tried for their offenses.[24]

Wakara was born and came of age in the first decades of the nineteenth century when the annual cycle of raiding, trafficking, and trading between Abiquiú and Ute country continued to grow. In the spring, as an apprentice slaver, Wakara watched the newly equestrian Timpanogos capture winter-thin Paiutes to trade with the Spanish who arrived in central Utah as regularly as the spawning fish in Timpanogos Lake. In the fall, during the month of slaves, young Wakara rode south to the fairs at Abiquiú and Santa Fe where the Utes sold more slaves.

During these decades, the *entrada* of the Spanish, combined with the arrival of the Spanish horse and Spanish *esclavitud* to the Timpanogos homeland, changed the relationship between the Utes and their Numic neighbors, the Paiutes. The Utes began to see the Paiutes less as kin to trade with, war with, enslave, and on occasion marry. Instead, to the Utes, the Paiutes became commodities, which they extracted from Paiute families and Paiute lands, strapped to their horses or marched by foot south to Abiquiú, where they were exchanged for Spanish horses, blankets, guns, and grains.

Wakara was a teenager when, in the late 1820s, American mountain men and merchants from Abiquiú blazed and mapped the last section of the Old Spanish Trail through Ute country to California. The completion of the trail realized Spain's longtime quest to connect its settlements in *Nuevo México* with the California coast—a quest that Domínguez, Escalante, and their *genízaro* and Ute guides had inaugurated a half century before.

But New Spain was no more. Mexico won its revolutionary war against the Spanish Crown in 1821. Under the hooves of newly independent Mexicans, along with American fur trappers, mountain men, and Native raiders, the Old Spanish Trail became more than just a horse trail. It became a transregional slave-trading crescent—a landlocked Indian version of the transatlantic African slave trade. At the center of this crescent in central Utah and northern New Mexico, captives were stolen from their homelands, then shipped to both ends of the crescent along with, and in exchange for, trade goods, horses, and other livestock. Census records indicate that by 1823 in New Mexico, approximately 5 percent of households had a slave (*criado*) or servant (*sirviente*). By the 1830s, between 10 and 20 percent of *Californio* households had a Native captive living under their roofs.[25]

In the fall, Abiquiú became the eastern departure point for California-bound seasonal caravans—moving villages of 100 traders and scores of mules and horses weighed down by slave-produced blankets from New Mexico's textile shops. On their way west, they traded these goods to the Navajos and Utes for horses. After a month of bartering trade goods for horses, early in the new year the caravans returned to New Mexico, timing their trip home to coincide with not only the emergence of the spring grasses but also the starvation of the Paiutes. As the English explorer Thomas J. Farnham described it in 1839, when caravans and slavers reached the Sevier River, they exchanged a horse or two for young Paiute women and children, whom they then "fattened, carried to Santa Fe and sold as slaves." In the slave markets, slavers rarely had to resort to torture to get their desired price. As the mountain man turned Mormon Daniel Jones put it, New Mexican purchasers and Native slavers "were as fully established and systematic in this trade as ever were the slavers on the seas."[26]

WAKARA BECAME THE MOST FAMOUS OF THESE "SLAVERS on the seas" of deserts and mountains of the Old Spanish Trail. His rise to become the greatest slave trader in the American West coincided with his emergence as the region's greatest horse thief. Baptismal records of captives in Abiquiú indicate that the Ute slave trade reached its peak in the 1840s, the same time as Wakara's horse raiding peaked.[27]

There was a season for each of Wakara's professions. In the fall, on his way to California, Wakara spent some time hunting Paiutes. When he and his men rode into a Paiute camp, women and children hid in the sparse underbrush, while older men approached the riders. Wakara and the elders bargained, or Wakara stole the Paiutes he wanted, killing the men who tried to stop him. Wakara then took his captives to California, where during late fall and winter, he engaged in the horse-raiding season. Even if the raids did not go well, the trip to the West Coast would still be successful as Wakara traded slaves for Spanish colonial horses.[28]

Still, early springtime was Wakara's favorite slaving season. Wakara was not above deploying violence to capture his slaves. But he preferred to get Paiutes through their empty stomachs instead of filling their bodies with lead. On his return from California, once he reached southern Utah, while his road-weary horses fed on spring grasses, he found the Paiutes starving after they had exhausted their winter food supply. So they "would sell their own children for a horse and kill and eat [it]," recalled Daniel Jones.[29]

Not all members of Paiute families agreed with the decision to trade away their offspring. In the 1910s and 1920s Paiute elders recorded oral histories of the lengths the mothers of the would-be enslaved went to in order to shield their children from Wakara's raiding. One such mother "seized her child that had already been traded to the Navajos and had fled into the hills," recalled one Paiute elder. "She was chased around for several days by Walker's warriors and the purchasers and was finally trapped on . . . a high promontory that jutted out into the river. As the Indians rushed upon her she threw her child off the cliff down into the swollen river and killed it."[30]

In the 1840s and early 1850s, Wakara's slaving was so brutal that some Paiutes welcomed the arrival of the Mormons, hoping that the settlers would protect them against Wakara. Yet the cost of Mormon protection would often be a Paiute child, whom the Saints would "adopt."[31]

Wakara also welcomed the Saints when they came marching into Utah in 1847. He saw them as another market for his horses and slaves. The Saints welcomed Wakara's horses. It took some convincing, the Mormons claimed—namely, being forced to witness Wakara's kin torture their captives—but soon the Mormons also accepted Wakara's trade in Native slaves. At least until they could take over the trade themselves.

Like the Catholics in New Mexico, the Latter-day Saints would often deploy a settler version of Indian slavery, using religion, race, and the law to justify their own slaving. This settler Indian slavery was also a means to the Saints' end: removal of Natives from Native lands to make room for their growing Zion in the Intermountain West. Still, on occasion, the Mormons also practiced a kind of Native Indian slavery: Like that of Wakara and other Natives, their trade in slaves sometimes created kinships between themselves and Natives, with the goal of converting and assimilating them into their earthbound and eternal families.

Chapter 13

"A New Feature in the Traffic of Human Beings"

It had snowed the night before. The temperature on the camp's thermometer read ten degrees. The clouds blocked the morning sun, which in early December 1849 seemed unwilling to rise past the ragged mountains east of the expedition's camp a few miles north of the Sevier River.

Parley P. Pratt stood by the fire. His cold hands wrapped around a tin cup, trying to absorb warmth from a thin brew of camp coffee. The Mormon apostle was leading an exploratory party through central Utah, scouting locations for new settlements and mission outposts to Native Americans. The fire spat, then sizzled when Pratt tossed his coffee dregs onto the orange coals. He then barked an order to get a move on.

At twenty minutes to nine, horses and men shook the cold from their bones and readied themselves to restart their journey south. Just then, the wagon drivers yelled, "Whoa!" and tugged the reins of the oxen pulling the wagon.

Wakara and another Ute rider cantered into the camp. Wakara did not dismount. He told Pratt that he had dreamed of their meeting.

He wanted to trade with the Saints. But not up here. The ground was too cold, hard, and barren. Wakara beckoned the Mormons to follow him down the Sevier River to a bottom. There they could find good feed for their animals. Pratt and his men obliged.

When they reached the place that Wakara had designated, Pratt's party made camp with Wakara. As they erected tents and built fires, the Mormon apostle took note of Wakara's impressive party "consisting of men, women, and children, cattle, slaves, and dogs." Ever since they had purchased Sally from Wakara's brother Baptiste two years before, Pratt and the rest of the Mormon settlers had accepted that slave trading was as much a part of Wakara's culture as was fishing in the spring and horse raiding in the winter.[1]

The next day, bitter cold wind blew in from the west. Despite the bad weather, trading commenced. The Utes brought many fine horses to sell, Pratt and others remarked. The Mormons and the Utes also traded information. With Dimick Huntington serving as interpreter, Pratt asked the Ute leader where the Saints should go next to settle; the fall before, Wakara had helped them establish the first settlements outside the Wasatch Front in the Sanpete Valley at Manti.

Wakara examined a map that Pratt pulled out, almost certainly a copy of John C. Frémont's map that the Saints followed when they first trekked to Utah two years before. Another member of Pratt's expedition, Robert Campbell, wrote in his journal that the Mormon explorers were astonished that, "like an experienced geographer," Wakara pointed out key features on the map. Directing the Mormons' attention to the southwest, Wakara described fecund land near the Rio Virgin, a name that Frémont gave to the river when he traversed the tributary of the Colorado after he first met Wakara in 1844. Wakara knew the river well. It was one of his favorite slaving fields. The Old Spanish Trail followed the river across the homelands of the Paiutes, where it runs through what is today Zion National Park to St. George and to the Mormon Plateau in present-day Nevada.[2]

In fact, just before meeting Pratt, Wakara had come north from a season of slaving in Paiute country. That winter, the road to California had been too full of forty-niners and US Army companies to raid horses. So Wakara spent some of the fall raiding Paiute camps and trading among the Navajos for blankets, horses, sheep, and slaves. Wakara reported to the Saints that Paiutes were dying off so fast that a whole lodge-full might perish in one night. The cause of the Paiute die-off was likely measles, which Wakara might have introduced during raids on his way to California the previous fall. Wakara's band was also sick, having been exposed to measles either by the forty-niners with whom Wakara traded horses or by the 200 settler families who poured into Sanpete Valley in the fall of 1849.[3]

While at Wakara's camp on the Sevier River in early December, Robert Campbell recalled hearing Wakara's Utes "making medicine." He saw them "suck one another's feet, [and] forehead[s]." None of this sucking worked. Nor did the sacrifice of a dog. The next day, at Wakara's request, Pratt, Huntington, and Daniel Jones, who was also part of the expedition, prayed to "rebuke" the measles and laid hands on the sick. The prayers did not seem to work either. So the Utes sacrificed a Paiute boy they had recently bought for a gun.[4]

Measles, hunger, and cold continued to decimate Wakara's Utes over the next few months. The Mormons at Manti continued to supply their Ute neighbors with food and medicine, supplies that the poorly provisioned settlers could scarcely afford to part with. When Mormon cures also failed to stop the disease, the Utes sacrificed more Paiutes. Still, Wakara made clear that he was grateful for the Saints' medicine, telling Isaac Morley in February 1850 that more Utes would have died had it not been for the Saints. Wakara also told Morley that he wanted Brigham Young to send him more grains from Salt Lake and to send men to teach his people how to raise their own. For these grains and services Wakara would exchange some of his fine horses.[5]

When the snows melted on the road that Wakara helped cut between Salt Lake and the Sanpete Valley, Young sent Wakara 306 pounds of cornmeal, ten bushels of wheat, and twenty-five pounds of rice. Young did not send the whiskey that Wakara had also asked for. The cost for this shipment, $119.75—the equivalent of two of Wakara's fine Spanish horses or one female Paiute—was debited from Wakara's account in Salt Lake City. Wakara perhaps expected to clear this debt when he traveled through the Salt Lake and Utah Valleys on his way to the fish festival in a few months' time.[6]

Young was willing to give the Utes supplies. Feeding them was cheaper than fighting them, was Young's policy toward the Utes in the first few years of Mormon Utah. But Young also believed that fighting was inevitable. As he did with the settlers at Provo, Young warned the settlers in the Sanpete Valley not to trade guns to the Utes. Young explained that these "weapons of war" in the hands of Indians, when their "hearts" had not been fully redeemed, would force the Mormons to kill more Utes, as they had already done that February at the Fort Utah Massacre.[7]

THAT SPRING, AS THE SUN ROSE HIGHER EACH day and the grasses pushed through the earth to meet it, Wakara sought to exchange more than foodstuffs, horses, and Paiute children with his new neighbors in the Sanpete Valley.

In early March 1850, a few weeks before Isaac Morley would baptize him in Manti's City Creek, Wakara rode to Morley's cottage. As payment for allowing the Saints to settle on Ute land, Wakara demanded that Morley turn over an infant son to whom Morley's wife, Hannah, had given birth the year before. According to a Morley family historian, one of Wakara's "squaws" coveted the boy, described as having "large laughing brown eyes and curly brown hair." Hannah fainted at the thought of parting with her child. Morley offered his own life to Wakara if the boy could be spared. Wakara would not budge, threatening to destroy Manti if his demand wasn't met. Morley relented, telling his family, "It is better to lose our baby than the whole settlement and the boy too." After turning the boy over to Wakara, the Morleys prayed all night for their son's safety. And, according to family history, their prayers were answered. The next morning, Wakara and his wife returned the boy, "very dirty, uninjured, and happy to see his parents." Wakara explained that his change of heart arose out of respect for Hannah's feelings. "Your squaw feel bad," he told Morley. "We bring him back."[8]

Again, we should be suspicious of one-sided stories authored by settler narrators that cast Wakara and the settlers in their usual roles of savage and Christian, the whims of the Indian "squaw" mollified only through demonstrations of White motherly love. And yet other family histories suggest that Wakara's request for the Morley's infant might have been, from Wakara's point of view, a request for reciprocity, not an extortion payment. That same year, a young Ute girl named Waddie began living in the Manti household of James and Deborah Leithead. The best-known account of how Waddie ended up with the Leitheads claims that the girl's father was a Ute leader whose wife had died. Because the leader could not remarry until he parted with Waddie, he traded her for a gun and a blanket to another settler family. After that family left for Canada and could not keep her, the Leitheads adopted her, renaming her Nellie. Family history claims that the Ute leader who was Waddie/Nellie's father was Sanpitch, one of Wakara's brothers. But recent DNA evidence and extensive genealogical records conducted by Nellie's living descendants suggest that Waddie's father was Wakara. Such claims reframe Wakara's request for the Morley's son as a ritual of exchange of children among the Sanpete Saints and Wakara's Utes. Wakara's family history and genealogical records also suggest other female relatives of Wakara ended up in settler homes. Wakara's kin Mountain Fawn married Wakara's longtime raiding partner Thomas "Pegleg" Smith, who is said to have had two other Ute wives.[9]

This Native form of Indian slavery was a means by which Wakara wanted the Mormons and the Utes to become kin. And since Wakara traded his female relatives to the Saints and to raiding partners, he expected the settlers to do the same. "I would like to know if you have ever given Walker encouragements of a Mormon woman for wife," Isaac Morley wrote to Brigham Young in a "confidential" letter dated April 13, 1850, a month after Wakara's baptism in Manti. "He has intimated this idea to our interpreters here."[10]

At least on its surface, this idea wasn't far-fetched. Echoing the practice of Spanish men marrying enslaved Native women, since the Mormons first arrived in Utah, Young had encouraged Mormon men to "marry wives of every tribe," which would speed up the redemption, and whitening, of the Indians. But the idea that White Mormon women would marry Ute men was, to the settlers, so scandalous—and Wakara repeated the request so frequently—that it became a laugh line. "Walker himself has teased me for a white wife," George A. Smith, the founder of Parowan, told the faithful gathered at the Tabernacle in Salt Lake City in October 1853, during the height of the so-called Walker War. "And if any of the sisters will volunteer to marry him, I believe I can close the war forthwith."[11]

MORMON WARS AGAINST UTES ALSO MADE SLAVES. IN early 1850, the Fort Utah Massacre left dozens of Timpanogos warriors dead, including Wakara's rivals. On February 14, 1850, Young instructed the Nauvoo Legion's General Daniel Wells to bring the survivors, most of whom were young and female, north to Salt Lake. Many were placed in Mormon homes. As they did with Sally, the Saints claimed that these captives were treated as well as their own family. But visitors to Utah described a different condition. One California-bound emigrant who passed through Salt Lake in the summer of 1850 described the thirty Ute women and girls as being "held in slavery by the Mormons."[12]

While he approved of the violence at Fort Utah, some of Wakara's male relatives were killed. And some female relatives were captured, including a girl the Mormons called Viroque, who was "adopted" into the household of settler Joel Hills Johnson. In June 1854, after the end of the so-called Walker War, Wakara visited Brigham Young in Salt Lake to demand that Viroque, who he claimed was his sister, be returned to his family. Soon after, Viroque moved to Salt Lake. But she did not return to Wakara's family. Instead, at the age of fourteen she became the plural wife of the forty-three-year-old Almon Babbitt, who was already married to two of Johnson's sisters, Julia and Delcana. On February 21, 1855, less than a month after Wakara's passing, Viroque died. To soften the loss, Johnson gave an Indian boy, whom the settlers named "Sam," to his sisters.[13]

In summer 1850, Wakara's wars against Natives also resulted in slaves. Defying Young's calls for peace between the Shoshones and Utes, after trading horses and likely Paiute slaves with the Mormons at Timpanogos Lake, Wakara, his brother Arapeen, and forty raiders left the fish festival. They headed north. Though they followed their bison trails, they were on the hunt not for bison but for Shoshones, whom Wakara blamed for killing eight of his relations earlier that year.

On the morning of June 27, Wakara and his warriors ambushed two sleeping Shoshone villages camped at Yellow Creek in what is today southwestern Wyoming. They scalped the men, set the lodges ablaze, and captured the women and children. Wakara then returned to Manti "laden with plunder, prisoners and scalps," recalled Adelia Cox Sidwell, a chronicler of early Mormon Sanpete Valley. Wakara offered the Shoshones for sale that summer, though there is no record of Mormons making purchases. The Utes interrupted their celebration for another visit to Manti's City Creek. There, in the spring waters, 108 Ute men and 18 Ute women were baptized into the Mormon faith on July 7, 1850.[14]

In the early 1850s, the Mormons turned Timpanogos Utes into slaves of war, in part to demonstrate their power and dominance over their captives and to expand their territorial control. Wakara did the same to the Shoshones whom he captured. Sometimes Wakara and the Mormons turned other Numic people, the Paiutes, into members of their own families. At other times, these Paiutes became forms of currency exchanged for food, trade goods, and cash. At Manti, Adelia Sidwell's mother, Elvira Cox, bought a seven-year-old Paiute girl for some bacon and a few pounds of flour. At Parowan, in March 1851, after Wakara's raiding season in California, George Brimhall recalled that the Ute leader brought to market "three little Indian children prisoners which he tied to the sagebrush to feed on grass, which they did with a good relish." Disappointed that his horse-raiding season had netted only 100 horses, Wakara traded each of the children for a fresh horse. Brimhall would later write about the horrors of "Devil Walker, who held despotic sway over all the tribes between the Rocky and Sierra Nevada Mountains, north from Provo waters and south to the great Colorado." But contemporaneous records indicate that at least some Mormons in Parowan admired Wakara. After having spent several days with the Ute leader, George A. Smith described him as "very much of a gentleman in manners and one of the most intelligent Indians I ever saw." Wakara gave Smith two buckskins. In return, Wakara received one cow from the settlers' limited supply.[15]

In the early 1850s, the Mormons and Wakara became partners in the trade of Paiutes, though they had different ends for their shared means. Wakara saw the Mormon settlements as markets for his slave trade, upon which Wakara had to rely even more since horse raiding in California had become increasingly dangerous. The Mormons bought slaves from Wakara with the goal of turning "Indians" into

"Lamanites." "The Lord could not have devised a better plan than to have put us where we were," Brigham Young told the settlers gathered under a thatched-roof bowery in Parowan on May 12, 1851. "Buy up the Lamanite children [as fast as you can]," Young continued. Baptize them, "educate them and teach them the gospel." Citing the Book of Mormon's most infamous passage (2 Nephi 30:6), Young declared the Saints' efforts to assimilate the Paiutes would ensure "that many generations would not pass ere they should become a white and delightsome people."[16]

The Mormon people followed their prophet's command. "Many of the inhabitants of this Territory have purchased for a trifling sum children," wrote Associate Territorial Justice Zerubbabel Snow in early March 1852. The settlers bought Paiute captives from Wakara, then later, directly from Paiute parents. Historian Michael Bennion, who compiled a database of over 400 Native children in Mormon homes in the nineteenth century, calculated that 56 percent of "adopted" children came from trades with raiders like Wakara, Arapeen, Baptiste, and Peteetneet. At least in 1851, the Mormons condoned such trades. In the letter of recommendation he gave to Wakara and Peteetneet in March 1851, George A. Smith wished the Ute slavers "prosperity and good bargains," as they moved from Parowan to Manti, Provo to Salt Lake, trading their horses and "Piede children."[17]

Judge Snow's claim that purchased Native children were treated as "fair [*sic*] as their own children" is more suspect than his claim that the settlers paid a "trifling sum" for them. These Paiute children provided invaluable labor for pioneering settlements rushing to erect vital agricultural, housing, and defensive infrastructure. The purchased Paiute children in Parowan tended their adopted parents' gardens, kept house, built fences, and plowed fields. Following the dictates of Brigham Young to "fort up" the settlements against the war with Wakara that Young would instigate, the Paiutes also assisted their "parents" in fortifying settler towns.[18]

The Mormons weren't the only settler slavers in Utah. The century-old exchange between the Utes and New Mexicans continued after the Mormons' arrival in 1847. As the Utes gathered for their fish festival, New Mexicans traveled north to Timpanogos (Utah) Lake. There, they traded guns and ammunition for Paiutes. Officials in New Mexico, then a US territory following the Mexican-American War, tolerated, if not tacitly endorsed, the slave exchange with Utah. In 1850, New Mexico's superintendent of Indian affairs, James S. Calhoun, issued a license to José María Chávez to trade with the "Ute Nation of Indians." Due to his trade with the Utes, Chávez became one of Abiquiú's richest residents. Oral tradition holds that one of the rooms in his large home was called the "Ute room," where Utes, likely Wakara himself, lodged during slave-trading fairs. The home later became the residence of New Mexico's most famous painter and booster, Georgia O'Keeffe.[19]

The Mormons also bought slaves from New Mexicans. After serving in the Mormon Battalion in California, Thomas S. Williams settled in Salt Lake where he established a trade-goods store. When he traveled between Utah and California, where he procured cookery, food, tobacco, coffee, and liquor to sell in his store, Williams also bought humans. Family history claims that on one trip west, Williams paid some $1,600 to New Mexicans for a dozen children whom the New Mexicans had recently captured from their Paiute parents. Williams gave one of the children, then between the ages of five and eight, to his daughter Caroline, who was a few years the girl's senior. Caroline renamed her Viroque. Family histories recall that Viroque became a beloved domestic who married a White settler, then died at around twenty-four, likely during childbirth.[20]

At the end of 1851, the Mormons moved to end the slave trade between New Mexico and Utah. They wanted to become the only market for Wakara's slaves.

In December of that year, a Mormon posse arrested Don Pedro León Luján and other Mexican traders at their camp near Manti, then confiscated the New Mexicans' horses and Native captives. A *genízaro* from Abiquiú, Luján was charged with trading with the Utes without a license, though the New Mexican claimed he had a license issued by James Calhoun. In November, before his arrest, Luján had even tracked Young to Manti to get a license. Young denied Luján's request and prohibited him from trading in Indian captives, which Young suspected was his real purpose.[21]

Young was right. After Luján's arrest, Arapeen told settlers at Manti that Luján had been trading with him and other Utes for years. Census records from Abiquiú showed that Luján christened two Native servants whom he had acquired in Utah as far back as 1833. But Luján's claim that Young denied his application for a license "on the ground that he was not a Mormon" was also right. The Saints wanted to take over the trade in order to speed up the redemption of the few (young, female) Natives who could be saved and speed up the removal of the vast majority of (male) Natives the Mormons believed could not.[22]

At Luján's trial, Young acknowledged that the Saints bought Indian children from Ute slavers. But Young claimed that they did so "to obtain their liberty, and to save them from starvation, abuse and even death." To illustrate, Young recounted the story of Sally's purchase in the fall of 1847—how Baptiste killed the captive boy to compel the Saints to buy Sally and how, after this trade, Sally lived with the Young family with the same rights and freedoms as Young's other children. In truth, at the same time Young was giving his testimony, Sally was laboring as a servant just a few hundred feet away. Perhaps she was on her hands and knees scrubbing the floors of Young's home or bent over a woodburning stove making dinner for Young's growing brood of offspring.[23]

During Luján's trial in January 1852, Young made clear that the Mormons really hoped to stop the slaving of "Indian Walker." The racial transformation that occurred during Wakara's March 1850 baptism—emerging from the waters of Manti's City Creek "as white as" any Mormon settler—had not stuck. Instead, Wakara continued to "traffic" in enslaved Paiutes. "He offers them for sale, and when he has an offer that satisfies him in the price, he sells them; and when he cannot get what he thinks they are worth, he says he will take them to the Navaho Indians, or Spaniards, and sell them, or kill them which I understand he frequently does."[24]

Luján lost. An all-Mormon jury found him guilty of trading with the Utes without a license. He was fined $500, and his slaves were confiscated and placed in Mormon homes. Wakara lost too. Following the trial, the Mormons began to curtail the 200-year history of slave trade between New Mexico and central Utah, which Wakara had increasingly relied on to amass his wealth and power and to feed himself and his people. But this trial did not end the slave traffic between New Mexico and Utah. Census records from 1870 indicate that Luján acquired at least two more Paiute boys several years after the trial.[25]

The trial was the beginning, not the end, of the Mormons' efforts to monopolize the trade in Indian captives. On the afternoon of January 5, 1852, Brigham Young, the ex officio governor and commissioner of Indian Affairs of the Utah Territory, delivered a speech to a joint session of the Legislative Assembly of the Territory of Utah. Built at the southwest corner of Temple Square, the Council House was a stone's throw from Young's home, where Sally might have been preparing dinner or sweeping the snow that had fallen during the day off the front porch. In the speech, Young explained his continuing efforts to prevent traffic in Indian slaves, including the then-ongoing trial against Luján. Still, the prophet could not do it all himself. It was time for the legislative assembly to spell out laws against slavery.[26]

"My own feelings are, that no property can or should be recognized as existing in slaves, either Indian or African," Young explained to the all-Mormon legislative assembly. On "African" slavery, Young's actions belied such abolitionist-sounding claims. Three enslaved Black men, Green Flake, Hark (Lay) Wales, and Oscar (Crosby) Smith were part of Young's famed Vanguard Company of 1847. In 1850, hoping to avoid embroiling Utah in the national fight over slavery, the Mormons claimed on federal slave schedules to have sent twenty-six enslaved Black people to the nascent Mormon settlement at San Bernardino. But not all twenty-six went west. Hark Wales's wife and child stayed in Utah, breaking up the family. Still, Young insisted that as descendants of the biblical villains Cain and Ham, people of African descent were by God's commandment to remain in a state of "servitude" until God, not man, saw fit to free them from their accursed state. And in early 1852, the legislative assembly passed a law that sanctioned a form of African chattel slavery in the territory, which provided legal protection to the few Mormons who brought slaves to Utah. As for Indian slavery, Young believed that White citizens of the territory should purchase Indians so long as the Paiutes continued to sell and gamble away their children, Young explained—and so long as slavers like Wakara continued to capture Paiutes, sell those they could, and slaughter those they could not.[27]

Young thus proposed "a new feature in the traffic of human beings." The Mormons would purchase Indians "into freedom, instead of slavery." In this way "many a child [would be] redeemed from the thralldom of savage barbarity," Young explained, "and placed upon an equal footing with the more favored portions of the human race." Since such purchases would cost the cash-strapped citizens of the territory something—Charles Decker's rifle, Elvira Cox's bacon and flour, Thomas S. Williams's $1,600—Young called for a system that allowed the settlers to be compensated for the debts they incurred. While Young spoke these words, Sally might have been emptying the Young family's bedpans.[28]

On March 6, 1852, the legislative assembly passed "An Act for the Relief of Indian Slaves and Prisoners," which turned Young's vision into law. To save the Natives from themselves and from slavers like Wakara and Luján, in the law's preamble the legislative assembly claimed that it was "the duty of all humane and Christian people" to intervene and "to extend unto this degraded and downtrodden race, such relief as can be awarded to them." This task fell to the white Mormons of Utah because the US Congress had failed to move Indians to reservations, a dereliction of duty that left the "Indian title to the soil [of Utah] . . . unextinguished." The act empowered Utah's White settlers to recoup their purchase costs through indentured servitude of the purchased for up to twenty years of labor, twice as long as the maximum allowed by the law in New Mexico. It also required the purchasers to file an indenture agreement with county officials. "Masters" of captives between the ages of seven and sixteen were required to send their servants to school and to clothe them to the standard of their own "condition in life."[29]

Before the passage of the act, Mormons often acquired captives through Indian wars, as was the case for the Ute women and children captured after the Fort Utah Massacre in early 1850, or by purchasing them from Ute slavers, as they did in the case of Sally. Following the passage of the act, by purchasing slaves directly from the Paiutes, the Mormons sought to cut Wakara and other middlemen out of the slaving economy. In March 1852, Zerubbabel Snow, the judge who oversaw the Luján trial, explained to the US secretary of the interior that Wakara's raids left the Paiutes in perpetual fear. The increased foot, horse, and cattle traffic over their lands during the 1840s and early 1850s also destroyed their traditional hunting and foraging grounds. The Paiutes thus traded away children to the Mormons for food and weapons to protect themselves from Wakara's raiders. By 1853, many of the 100 tidy homes in Parowan were ornamented with fruit trees, vegetable gardens, and Paiute children.[30]

Still, many Mormons claimed that Natives used violence to coerce them into trading for humans. Take the case of one purchased Native child, "Sarah" Benson of Parowan. According to Benson family history, in September 1853 a Paiute man and woman came to the home of Richard and Pheobe Benson. The Paiute couple demanded to trade a three-year-old girl, perhaps their own child or one they had kidnapped from another tribe, for a blanket and some food. The Bensons refused. The Paiute man then put a knife to the child's neck, threatening to kill her if the deal wasn't made. The Bensons relented. Within days of the sale, Richard Benson submitted an indenture agreement to the Parowan courthouse, which stated that "Sarah" "voluntarily bound herself to live and serve" him until she reached the age of her majority. Family history claims that Sarah assimilated into the Benson family. She played, did chores, and attended school alongside her White siblings. The only thing she was not permitted to do was knead bread "with her little brown hands" for fear that somehow her color would contaminate the dough. At the age of sixteen, Sarah married Henry Harrop, a French-born Mormon convert, with whom she had several children. After moving to Arizona in 1880, Sarah died due to complications from giving birth to twins. The two children also died.[31]

Some purchased children became plural wives of their purchasers. In the 1850s, a seven-year-old girl, Maraboots, ended up in the household of missionary to Natives Ira Hatch after her father, a Navajo leader, sold her to Hatch for an undisclosed price. Maraboots was half Paiute. After her mother died, the Navajo leader knew that if he took Maraboots back to his clan, she would be treated as a slave. Within a few years, Hatch married Maraboots, whom he renamed Sarah. Sometime between 1855 and 1857, Hatch's missionary partner, Jacob Hamblin, often called the "Apostle to the Lamanites," purchased two Paiute girls. They were renamed Eliza and Ellen. Hamblin's plural wives raised the two girls until Hamblin married Eliza when she was a teenager. Hamblin and Eliza were sealed together in eternal marriage in the Endowment House in Salt Lake City on

February 14, 1863. Their marriage did not last. Eliza ran back to her band of origin, the Shivwits. She married a Paiute man and had at least one son with him.[32]

It is a matter of debate how the purchased were treated by their purchasers. Some scholars have concluded that "indentured" Native children in Utah became more assimilated into their families than Natives purchased into settler homes in New England, New Mexico, and California. Still others argue that these indentured children were treated, at best, as second-class citizens and, at worst, as chattel slaves.[33]

What is clear is that these children performed uncompensated labor. The accounting for this labor was kept in the heads or written ledgers of their masters/parents—much as it was for Black sharecroppers in the post–Civil War South and the *genízaros* in New Mexico under debt peonage. The balance sheets, in other words, turned from red to black only when their parents/masters saw fit. Other written records suggest that many Mormon parents/masters failed to follow the law and send their Native children to school. According to the 1860 census in Utah, more than half of the Native children listed as living in Mormon homes had received no formal education. Despite claims that she attended school, the 1870 census from Parowan indicates that Sarah Benson Harrop could neither read nor write. Still, census records do not capture all the lives or deaths of purchased Native captives. Most of the 400 Native children whom scholars have documented living in Mormon homes show up in just one census, that of 1870. Many of those absent from other records had likely died of measles, diphtheria, or even colds before their short lives were recorded in a census. Two years after the 1870 census was taken, Kanosh told visitors in Fillmore that disease had killed all but one of his children and most of his other relatives.[34]

The Mormons hoped that the "Indian" would die out inside the few Natives who survived these plagues. That is, they hoped assimilation would lead to Native cultural and racial genocide. As Brigham Young explained to the Parowan settlers in May 1851, by buying up the Lamanite children, the Saints would fulfill the Book of Mormon's prophecy of turning Indians into White Mormons. Young even put a Mormon spin on what would become the governing philosophy of the late-nineteenth-century Indian boarding school movement: Kill the Indian, save the man. "The Indians would dwindle away, but let a remnant of the seed of Joseph be saved."[35]

This Mormon version of settler Indian slavery removed the mothers of the next generations, the future keepers of Native land and of Native histories, with the goal of making room for more settlers. Such work occurred in the farms, fields, and bedrooms of Zion. Such work also occurred in written records. In the 1880 census in Apache County, Arizona Territory, Sarah Benson Harrop and Henry Harrop's six children were listed as "1/2 I[ndian]." But by 1910, Sarah's daughter, also named Sarah, was listed as White, as were all her children in the home she shared with her husband, Josh Sweat, in Maricopa County, Arizona. Sarah Benson Harrop's grandson Carlyle Harry Sweat was listed as "Caucasian" on his draft registration card for World War I.[36]

The racial transformation of Wakara might not have stuck in his lifetime, but it did in the generations after him. In the 1880 census in Escalante, Utah, Wakara's grandchildren through his daughter Waddie/Nellie and her Italian husband, Daniel Justet, are listed as 1/2 "I[ndian]." By the 1910 census, they are listed as "W[hite]."[37]

WAKARA SPENT MUCH OF THE FALL OF 1851 among the Navajos, Hopis, and Pimas in what is today northern Arizona. For their maize and clothes, he traded sheep, horses, and almost certainly Paiutes, who would be set to work managing herds, tending fields, and weaving blankets in Arizona. Some newspapers claimed that Wakara also rode, or sent another lieutenant, to California for fresh horses. The *Los Angeles Star* reported that during the first months of 1852, Wakara's cavalry had taken 300 horses and planned to take another 1,000 the next raiding season. In the spring of 1852 Wakara had not been able to trade slaves with New Mexicans. After the conclusion of the Luján trial and the passage of the Act for the Relief of Indian Slaves and Prisoners, Wakara was forced to rely even more on the only market left open to him: the Mormons.[38]

In April 1852 Wakara was headed to Timpanogos Lake for the fish festival and the annual trading fairs for horses and slaves when he received a letter from Brigham Young. The Mormon prophet addressed it to "Capt[ain] Walker, Chief of the Utah," not "Indian Walker," as Young had called him derisively during the Luján trial and in his speeches in support of the Indian slavery act. The Mormon prophet explained that when he arrived at the lake, Wakara would be welcomed as a brother in the Mormon gospel, but that this brother could no longer trade directly with White men. Young wrote that Wakara would first have to sell his horses to a Mormon, "perhaps friend Dimick [Huntington]," who would then sell them to settlers and to the emigrants on their way to the West Coast. Young also informed Wakara that the Mormons had moved the location of his trading fair "a little northwest of Utah Lake" and thus away from where the settlers had planted their fields of wheat and where during previous springs, much to the chagrin of the settlers, Wakara's horses had been set free to feast on soft sprouts.[39]

In his instructions to Wakara, Young made no mention of trade in slaves. By then, the settlers sought to follow the dictates of the new law: to buy Indian children from parents in Paiute territory near their settlements. According to Daniel Jones, who served as an interpreter for the New Mexicans during the trial of Luján, these efforts to stop Wakara's trafficking in enslaved Paiutes "helped to sour some of Walker's band." They were so sour that they returned to torture to compel trade. Jones recalled that during the fish festival of 1852,

> When they came up and camped on the Provo bench, they had some Indian children for sale. They offered them to the Mormons who declined buying. Arapine, Walker's brother, became enraged saying that the Mormons had stopped the Mexicans from buying these children; that they had no right to do so, unless they bought them themselves. Several of us were present when he took one of these children by the heels and dashed its brains out on the hard ground, after which he threw the body towards us, telling us we had no hearts, or we would have bought it and saved its life. This was a strange argument, but it was the argument of an enraged savage.[40]

Wakara and his band spent the rest of the summer in the Sanpete and Salt Lake Valleys trading horses. In early August, he and other Ute leaders also accepted an invitation to visit with Mormon leaders in Salt Lake City. During their visit, General Daniel Wells weighed and measured the bodies of Wakara, Sowiette, and Peteetneet—sizing up the very Utes who would lead a war against the Latter-day Saints, if one was in the offing. In early September, at the behest of Young and federal Indian agent Jacob Holeman, Wakara, Sowiette, and thirty-four Ute lodges were back in Salt Lake for a peace parley with the Shoshones. The Utes' longtime enemies arrived with twenty-six lodges of their own, led by the famed Shoshone leader Washakie. The month before, more violence had broken out when the Shoshones had attacked a band of Utes, killing twenty.[41]

The Mormon leadership was ambivalent about this infighting. Indian-on-Indian violence helped to rid the land of troublesome Natives but also risked pulling the settlers into harm's way. During the meeting in the lower room of the Council House in Temple Square, Washakie and Wakara passed the peace pipe. At least for a time, the generational enemies seemed to agree to set aside their own grievances; they recognized the growing threat to their lands and lives that the settlers presented. Still, before departing, Washakie told Wakara that he also expected to be compensated for the Shoshones whom Wakara had massacred in the summer of 1850. Wakara bartered Washakie down from the ten horses he requested for the ten Shoshones who were killed. Wakara promised to give nine, though he explained that he did not have those horses at the time. Wakara said that he planned on raiding or trading for horses that winter and would bring the promised mounts to the Shoshones next spring.[42]

There is no record that Wakara kept his promise. And peace did not prevail. Two years later, it was the Shoshones who paraded through the streets of Mormon settlements with Ute scalps on polls.[43]

WAKARA SPENT THE WINTER OF 1852–1853 AGAIN AMONG the Navajos and Hopis, with whom he likely traded Paiutes he captured on the way south for Navajo sheep and cattle. Once again, that winter there were "Indian rumors" out of California that Wakara and his Utes were "lurking about the Cajon pass," waiting for a chance to raid horses, reported the *Los Angeles Star* on Christmas Day 1852. The *Star* reminded its readers that stealing horses was a hanging offense. "It seems surprising," the paper concluded, that Wakara's "depredations have not, ere' this, met with summary punishment."[44]

The records are in doubt as to whether in fact Wakara did go to California that winter. Not in doubt is that Wakara's Utes once again raided Paiutes. On their return north in early January 1853, Utes attacked a Paiute camp near Iron Springs, killing or wounding twenty Paiute men and taking at least that many women and children prisoner, reported John D. Lee, then head of the Indian mission at Fort Harmony. Through this mission, the Mormons hoped to bring their gospel directly to the Paiutes and to bring Paiute children directly into Mormon homes. Lee allowed a few Paiute families who escaped the Ute raid to set up camp within Fort Harmony's walls. They did so in exchange for their labor and, though Lee did not report so explicitly, likely for their littlest loved ones. Lee and other members of the southern missions would later trade ammunition and guns for Paiute children.[45]

A few weeks after the raid, Wakara and sixty Utes arrived at Fort Harmony. Wakara hoped to trade and mend fences. Horses from Wakara's brother Peteetneet's band had been grazing in wheat fields near Parowan, which upset the settlers. During the visit, Wakara pledged to respect the settlers' private lands and keep reins on the Utes' horses. In return, Lee threw a "festival" in Wakara's honor. To demonstrate the civilizing influence that the Saints had on the Indians in his care, Lee told Wakara that some of the festival's meals had been prepared by the Paiutes. As for the recent massacre, Lee recalled that Wakara "declared his hands was [*sic*] clear of the blood of the Piedes that had [recently] been shed by his nation." The Paiutes, also camped in the fort and forced to serve the Ute leader his festival meals, likely would have objected to Wakara's characterization of his treatment of them—if they had been asked. Nevertheless, the meal and the camaraderie on display in January had a salutary effect on Wakara, Lee reported. At the end at the festival, Wakara "turned to me and said this looks like true friendship."[46]

ONCE AGAIN, DISPLAYS OF CAMARADERIE DID NOT LAST. If the Mormons had their way, spring 1853 would be Wakara's last slave-harvesting season. And they put arms toward that end. In April, Commander William Wall, a thirty-two-year-old, North Carolina–born military leader and lawyer who would father some thirty-nine children with his several plural wives, also visited Fort Harmony. While making the rounds of the southern settlements and Indian missions, Wall had in his pocket an executive order from Brigham Young to prepare Mormon settlers for war with the Utes. Paiute leaders had told him that they were still afraid of Wakara, who continued to steal their children and sell them in New Mexico. In response, Mormon missionaries and military leaders promised to supply them with guns and ammunition and protect them from Wakara—if, that is, the Paiutes pledged to assimilate into Mormon culture. Captain Wall found the Paiutes who had fled Ute raiders the winter before "perfectly under the control of Major [John D.] Lee—they seem honest, industrious, obedient, and anxious to conform to the manners and customs of the whites." Paiute leaders also invited the Mormons to settle on their lands, teach them to raise grain, and fight against Wakara's raiding.[47]

That spring the Saints also set out to stop New Mexicans and California-bound travelers from selling arms to Wakara. In April, a Mormon posse from Parowan rode down a group of emigrants who had traded rifles and powder for a Paiute boy. Wakara was incensed. He and his cavalry rode down the Mormon posse near his camp south of Parowan. There, Wakara and his men leveled their rifles at the Saints and ordered them to stop pursuing their clients. They also proclaimed that "the Americans were good, that the Mormons were not good, and that Brigham was not good."[48]

During his tour of the southern settlements a few weeks later, Wall met Wakara in person. "Walker was willing to live in peace," Wall reported to Salt Lake City, "if he can have his own way in stealing other Indian children to sell them to the Mexicans, for guns and ammunition." Wakara would also accept peace if the Mormons gave him arms in exchange for his captive children.[49]

Still, news of Wakara's men leveling guns at the settler Saints and threatening violence if he didn't get his way was music to Brigham

Young's ears. In early May, Young stepped up to the pulpit of the Tabernacle in Temple Square. Young told his faithful that he was finally ready for war with Wakara. And they should get ready too. "If you wish to know what you must do hereafter, I will tell you in a few words—keep your powder, and lead, and your guns in good order."[50]

Part V

Brigham's War

CHAPTER 14

A Massacre at Nephi

THE WIND BLEW HARD throughout the night of April 23, 1853. Gusts raised dust off the wagon road at Fort Nephi, eighty miles south of Salt Lake. Red dirt also blew inside the canvas tents of the Nauvoo Legion company headed by Captain William Wall. The horses neighed. The soldiers coughed. But neither man nor beast could dislodge the fine-grained powder that caked their eyes, mouths, and noses. No one slept more than a few minutes at a time.[1]

Rumors of war blew even harder. The Ute shaman and slave trader Baptiste was camped nearby. He and his brothers, Wakara and Peteetneet, were on their way north to the fish festival at Timpanogos Lake. The next morning, Baptiste came down to the fort very agitated. He had heard from other Utes that Brigham Young had sent Wall to kill him and his brothers. The settlers told Baptiste that he had heard wrong. Still, they warned him to behave better and end his cattle-thieving depredations on the citizens of Nephi.[2]

Yet, Baptiste was right to fear that Young was on a war march. Young told his faithful that the legion's special military operation, which he assigned Wall to lead, was intended to stop Wakara from trafficking in Indian slaves once and for all. Baptiste knew that in such an operation, he, along with Wakara, would be targeted. After all, it was Baptiste who, in the fall of 1847, inaugurated the Ute-Mormon slave trade when he tortured his captives until Young family members relented and bought Sally (Pidash).

But righteous talk of ending Wakara's slaving was a fig leaf. The Mormon prophet's actual goal was to prevent Wakara from building an arsenal of weapons and ammunition, through trade in Indian slaves, which he could use to defend his people from violent Mormon aggression.[3]

While camped at Fort Nephi, Wall received updated orders from Young via a courier on horseback. Ready your company for war in days, not weeks, the Mormon prophet commanded. Young and his own entourage were thirty-five miles north at Provo, making their way south to personally rally the settlers for the coming fight.[4]

In some ways the war had already begun. Just days before, a stranger clad in buckskin calling himself Dr. Wallace Alonzo Clark Bowman showed up unbidden at Provo, demanding a private conversation with Young. Bowman was an Anglo from Abiquiú who had come north with New Mexican trading partners determined to restart the now outlawed slave trade. The Mormon prophet agreed to hear Bowman out. Bowman told Young that he had an arsenal of weapons, which he planned on using "to buy Indian children, and sell them for slaves." If Young tried to thwart his plans, Bowman claimed to have 400 New Mexicans and Utes on standby, ready to attack. Young did not find the boastful Bowman amusing. Soon after their meeting, Young silenced him permanently—first with arrest, then with a blade or a bullet, though the Mormons would blame Wakara for Bowman's apparent murder.[5]

According to Young, Bowman and his "horde of Mexicans" were bent on whipping up the Utes against the Mormons. But Bowman's threats also gave Young the excuse to speed up his preparations against Wakara. On April 25, Young ordered Wall to ascertain

Wakara's whereabouts and, if possible, take "him prisoner with those of his band who [were] determined to follow him." But if Wall found that Wakara's soldiers were strong enough in number to prevent the legion from making such an arrest, Young ordered Wall to send a runner north to inform the Mormon military brass that he needed more reinforcements.[6]

For Young there were many paths forward in his coming confrontation with Wakara. But he expected that all would lead to the same end: Wakara in the ground. Perhaps Wakara's end would come with a whimper, like that of Bowman and Wakara's fellow Ute Patsowet, who were arrested, then quietly killed. Perhaps Wakara's end would come from gun blasts or from a bout of coughing after smoking poisoned tobacco. Whatever the manner, Young was finally ready to dispatch his most formidable challenger to the mantle of the Great Basin's most powerful man.

IN AUGUST 2007, ARMED WITH SHOVELS AND A small earthmover, a crew of excavators broke through Utah topsoil. Their mission was to carve out a basement for the home of Kevin Creps in Nephi, a small village built out of a meadow along I-15, west of the southern Wasatch Front. With ease, the men removed surface fill, the same kind of silty dirt that William Wall's men and horses choked on when they camped near the same spot more than a century and a half before. The crew then dug past layers of hardened sand. The foreman shouted halt when they hit something unexpected: a set of cedar planks covering human remains.

The foreman called Creps to look at what they found. Creps called the police. The police called the medical examiners. The medical examiners inspected the bones. A jawbone with well-worn teeth got the examiners' attention, and they called the Utah state archaeologist. The excavation that followed unearthed a mass grave, with seven sets of remains, along with brass and glass buttons, copper hair pipe beads, a glass mirror, a leather buckle, a few scraps of cloth, and a fragment of a lead bullet.[7]

The comingled nature of the remains and objects suggested that the individuals were buried together, and in a rush. Further study of the seven crania, specifically the teeth, demonstrated that the remains were of Native Americans who were in good health before they died. Further testing revealed that the seven individuals were male, ranging in age from early teens to mid-thirties. All this evidence and the location of the mass grave—a quarter mile from where the fort at Nephi stood in the early 1850s—made clear that the excavation had unearthed a group of Native American men and boys who, according to the official record of the "Walker War," had attacked the Nephi settlers in October 1853 and been killed and buried by the settlers.

The narrators of the "Walker War" claim that from July 1853 to May 1854, Wakara led a series of bloody attacks against Mormon settlers and settlements, which led to the deaths of twelve Latter-day Saints and eight US government surveyors. Official settler counts of the Ute dead range from twenty-four to thirty-four, though these numbers are certainly low and don't include dozens of noncombatant Utes, Paiutes, and Goshutes killed. As the Utes and Mormons engaged in cycles of violence perpetuated by vengeance, the Mormons were forced back to their forts, abandoning outlying settlements, including around Provo, Manti, Parowan, Fillmore, and Nephi—all settlements that Wakara had either directly helped found or at least blessed a few years before. Mormon settlers also lost thousands of cattle and horses.[8]

The Mormon dead included William Reed, James Nelson, William Luke, and Thomas Clark. In late September, under orders from Isaac Morley, the four men left Manti leading a wagon team laden with wheat bound for Salt Lake City. In the early hours of October 1, while they camped at Fountain Green on the road between Manti and Salt Lake, a group of Utes ambushed and killed the four men.

The Fountain Green Four were supposedly killed to avenge a group of Utes massacred in Manti in late summer 1853. Those Utes had sought safety at the fort from the ongoing Ute-Mormon violence. But the settlers executed the men and boys and took the women and girls captive. The settlers also committed this massacre at Manti out of revenge, claiming that the Utes they killed had stolen food from another group of settlers.

On October 1, within hours after the massacre at Fountain Green, Isaac Morley and other Manti settlers recovered the bodies of the four men. They brought the remains to Nephi and prepared to carry out another round of vengeance at the next opportunity.

Such an opportunity came the next day. Mormon settlers recorded detailed descriptions of what they described as a "skirmish" at Nephi on October 2. According to Major George W. Bradley, the officer in charge at Nephi, armed Utes approached the fort. Bradley told them to lay down their arms. The Utes not only refused but also "showed fight." The militiamen at the fort claimed they had no choice but to shoot the males dead and take the women and children captive. Bradley's account became the narrative of record, archived in the Utah Territorial Militia Records and published first in the *Deseret News*, then republished in canonical accounts of the "Walker War" and other histories of what came to be known as the "Indian depredations" of early Mormon Utah.[9]

But other accounts, notably from settler women, told different stories of what happened at Fort Nephi in the first days of October 1853. Martha Heywood wrote in her journal that on October 1, Isaac Morley and other settlers from Manti arrived at Nephi, bringing with them the mutilated bodies of the wagon team. An eye for an eye was the mood of Morley and another settler leader, Anson Call, Heywood recalled. So when a group Natives came to the fort "looking for protection and bread with us," the settlers shot them down "without one minute's notice."[10]

To Heywood's account, we can add that of Adelia Hatton. At the end of September, Hatton and her family had stopped at the fort on their way north to Salt Lake to attend the church's semiannual General Conference. In her memoirs, Hatton recalls that Morley was so anxious to exact vengeance on any Indians, guilty or not, for the previous day's massacre at Fountain Green that he ordered seven male Natives "shot down like so many dogs, [then] picked up with pitchforks [and put] on a sleigh and hauled away." But unlike the official narrative, Hatton claimed that the massacred group of seven "had no hand in the murdering of our brethren" at Fountain Green.[11]

Hatton's account of Mormon violence against Utah Natives is particularly poignant. Just weeks before the massacre at Nephi, Natives had shot and killed her husband, William Hawthorne Hatton, while he stood guard over cattle at Fillmore. A few years later she married Heber C. Kimball, becoming one of the forty-three women the Mormon apostle would eventually wed. Hatton's record and that of Martha Heywood, which went unread beyond their own families until their memoirs were published in the twentieth century, functioned as minority reports to the official narrative written by settler men about the violence at Nephi in early October 1853.

Native oral histories have also insisted that it was Brigham Young's Mormons, not Wakara's Utes, who started the "Walker War" and committed the conflict's most atrocious acts. And so do the narrators buried in shallow graves at Nephi. "Bones make great witnesses," said famed forensic anthropologist Clyde Snow, who pioneered the examination of mass graves to uncover the histories of genocide. "They speak softly but they never forget and they never lie." Ronald Rood, who was in 2006 the assistant state archaeologist for Utah, led the examination of the remains of the seven individuals unearthed at Nephi to see what they might have to say.

Rood determined that the archaeological and forensic evidence, along with the written records from Hatton (Kimball) and Heywood, demonstrated that what happened on October 2, 1853, was no "skirmish," as Bradley had put it in his official narrative. Instead, it was "a cold-blooded execution." The four adult males were shot in the head at close range, with the settlers likely standing above their victims, whom they had forced to kneel before bullets ripped through their brains. The youngest of the seven, a boy between the ages of twelve and fourteen, had a gunshot wound through his right distal femur, from which he likely bled out. Premortem traumas to the victims' wrists suggested that they tried to cover their heads and faces as the settlers beat them before filling their bodies with lead.[12]

The tribe of origin of the Nephi Seven is less certain. Bradley described them as Utes from three different bands, the Willow Creek Band, the Sanpitch Band, and Kanosh's Pahvant Band. But other contemporaneous records suggest that they might not have been Ute at all. Soon after Young and Wakara agreed to end the cycles of violence at a peace conference in May 1854, George Bean met a group of Goshutes who refused to agree to live in peace until they were compensated for the murder of their kin massacred by settlers at Nephi in October 1853. Also, in a letter to Brigham Young, Goshute leader Tovashant inquired about relatives who he claimed were killed at Nephi in October 1853. For his study of the mass grave, Rood consulted Numic-language linguists who provided translations for the names of Tovashant's murdered kin: Upsavoa-pu (Hunchback), Tuso-qa-chi (Early Dawn), Nuu-as-gha-pu (Brave One), Aka-taa or Aka-tuachi (Red Shirt or Red Child), Tin-ta-dyes (Little Rock), Tacha-pu-chi (Little Summer), Paach'a-chi or Paa-ta'wa-chi (Bat or Water Man), and Naso-karu-ru (Sitting Depressed). The linguists suggested that these names were either Ute or Goshute in origin.[13]

Of course, whether the victims of the massacre at Nephi were Ute or Goshute mattered to their kin. But it did not seem to matter to settler leaders Morley, Call, and Bradley. They wanted to kill Indians, be they combatants or not. Perhaps Major Bradley's claim in his official narrative that the Nephi Seven were Ute and part of Wakara's war parties was a way to cover up the militia's overarching genocidal mission: to extinguish all Native claims to Utah lands by extinguishing the lives of Utah Natives. After they buried the bodies of their victims in a mass grave, this cover-up continued first in the nineteenth-century archive, in which the Mormons labeled themselves as avenging angels, and in the twentieth century on roadside memorials erected by the Daughters of Utah Pioneers to honor the four victims of the Fountain Green Massacre. No such memorial exists for the Nephi Seven.

The chance discovery of the mass grave gave voice to the voiceless, as Rood suggested in his study of the remains. What's more, these remains give voice to a history about what happened not just at Nephi but throughout the so-called Walker War.

Wakara was not blameless. He used violence or the threat of violence to steal horses, enslave Paiutes, kill rivals in his own band and other tribes, and coerce travelers to buy slaves and to pay tolls to cross his lands. But Wakara did not start the war that bears his name. Neither was Wakara directly involved in much of the war's prosecution, though he did use the war to renegotiate terms of trade and territorial control with the Mormons. Wakara did not want the settlers to abandon their homes and towns or leave their crops to wilt in the sun. For if their crops died, the Mormons would have to leave the area, and "there would be no cattle for him to take," he told the settlers in the fall of 1853. And if the Mormons left, there would be no more settlers to whom he could sell slaves and horses.[14]

Brigham Young wanted the war. And he waged the war he wanted. The "Walker War" was really Brigham's War. And Brigham's War was one war in a long line of Native-settler conflicts named after Native leaders to cover up settler aggression. This practice started with the first major "Indian war" in American history. Brigham Young was a direct descendant of a foot soldier in that conflict, the so-called King Philip's War.

Chapter 15

The Names of Wars

In December 1675, the colonial militia of Brigham Young's great-great-great-grandfather, Samuel Howe (1642–1713), trudged through the hard-packed snows of what is today Rhode Island, following a path made by their commanding officer, Captain Nathaniel Davenport, and their Mohegan and Pequot allies. The soldiers' thin-soled boots failed to keep the winter's bite away. They were also tired. The volunteers and conscripts, drawn from the United Colonies of Plymouth, Massachusetts, and Connecticut and totaling some 1,000 men, had spent the previous night in an open field, huddled together without a fire.

The sleepless militiamen marched toward the Great Swamp, near what is today Kingston, Rhode Island, at the center of which they found a palisaded fort that protected hundreds of Narragansett wigwams. The previous year, the Narragansetts had built the sanctuary for 4,000 mostly women and children who wanted to avoid the "war" between the settlers and Wampanoags led by Metacom, known to the settlers as Philip. In 1621, Metacom's father, Massasoit (Ousamequin), had provided starving English settlers with food, friendship, and permission to settle along the coastline of the Atlantic Ocean. Massasoit aided the settlers not only out of kindness. In the previous decades, disease and war with other Natives had devastated his people. So he agreed to a mutual-aid treaty with his new English neighbors. But the English aimed to turn the New World into New England and Natives into new Englishmen. Over the next half century, the English broke their treaty promises, pushing west into Wampanoag hunting and fishing grounds—felling trees and dirtying waterways to make room for English towns, livestock, and farms. The settlers also pushed Christianity west, creating villages of "praying Indians," Native converts whom the English believed were not ready to be integrated into their own towns.

After failed attempts at diplomacy, starting in 1675, Metacom and his allies began to push back. As the Utes would do almost two centuries later, the Wampanoags forced the settlers to retreat to their strongholds. They also killed dozens of settlers. The English framed this Native resistance to settler incursion as a war of aggression. "Philip, and the Indians . . . have sought to dispossess us of the Land which the Lord our God hath given us," wrote Puritan leader Increase Mather in the first published history of the war.[1]

To the south, the Narragansetts in Rhode Island tried to stay out of the fight. With the support of Roger Williams, they dispatched diplomats to Boston to sign a neutrality pledge. But the Massachusetts Council accused the Narragansetts of harboring and conspiring with Philip. They declared it necessary to launch a preemptive wintertime war against the Narragansetts before they could mount an offensive in the spring.[2]

Once they arrived at the swamp on December 19, Davenport and his troops expected to lay siege and make quick work of the fort and its inhabitants. But their gunshots failed to penetrate the walls of the Narragansett wigwams, which had been fortified with corn, catching settler bullets with a thud. When the Narragansett shooters found their own targets, killing seventy soldiers and wounding just as many, the colonial troops retreated. The next day, they attacked again, this time setting ablaze the fort and wigwams. Those Narragansetts who weren't burned alive became target practice for soldiers who picked them off as they ran from the inferno. Estimates of the dead range from 600 to 1,000 Narragansett and Wampanoag men, women, and children. Some survivors were captured and sold into slavery. Others were forced to beg for food from the people who had massacred their families and razed their homes.

Samuel Howe's commanding officer, Nathaniel Davenport, was among the English killed. Metacom survived. In fact, reports placed him away from the swamp, despite the English's claim to have attacked the Narragansetts because they were harboring him.[3]

For the first months of 1676, Metacom and his allies brought the fight closer to the population centers on the coast. One such center was Howe's hometown of Sudbury, twenty miles west of Boston. On April 21, 500 Wampanoag, Nipmuc, and Narragansett warriors shot at villagers and set structures ablaze. Howe's home and barn were destroyed. His brother was killed along with half of the fifty men who came to the village's defense.

Sudbury would be Metacom's last major victory. For the rest of the spring and summer of 1676, English forces massacred hundreds of Natives and captured hundreds more, shipping many out of New England as slaves. By July, under Captain Benjamin Church, soldiers began clearing Wampanoags out of Plymouth. They hunted Metacom to Mount Hope, in what is today Bristol, Rhode Island. There, a praying Indian named John Alderman killed Metacom, supposedly because Metacom had killed Alderman's brother.

Metacom's remains were mutilated. His hands were cut off and brought to Boston. His head was mounted on a pike in Plymouth. The rest of his body was quartered and "hanged up as a monument of revenging Justice," recalled Increase Mather. Metacom's wife,

Wootonekanuske, and their nine-year-old son were taken captive. Wootonekanuske died in September 1676. The son, whose name has been lost to history, was sold to Bermuda. Mather celebrated the capture of women and children, the killing of "Philip," and the massacre of the 3,000 to 4,000 New England Natives. He was especially pleased that English swords and famines had reduced the Narragansetts, who had been "the greatest body of Indians in New England," to less than 100 men—so few, Mather noted, that there was no one left to bury their dead. The Indians deserved such divine retribution, Mather and many of his contemporaries concluded, because they committed treason and blasphemy by failing to live up to the covenants they had made with the English and the English's God. Years later, Increase Mather's son, Cotton, who was the intellectual leader of the Salem Witch Trials, visited Plymouth to see Metacom's head still mounted on a spike more than two decades after his death. To commemorate his pilgrimage, the younger Mather wanted a souvenir. "So, [I] took off the Jaw from the Blasphemous exposed Skull of that Leviathan," Cotton wrote.[4]

The English did not come out of the war unscathed. Between 600 and 800 soldiers and civilians—close to one in ten of the colonists—lost their lives, making the war the deadliest conflict in American history on a per capita basis.

Still, the war had some winners, including Samuel Howe. He rebuilt his home and farm. With his friend and fellow King Philip's War veteran Samuel Gookin, Howe also bought hundreds of acres from nearby Natick Natives, then claimed thousands of acres of Natick land that they had no rights to. The Naticks took Howe and Gookin to court. A judge forced them to return some of the land. However, since Howe and Gookin had improved the land and used it to care for some "squaws" in their possession, a court allowed them to keep more than 1,500 acres. Howe's great-great-great-grandson, Brigham Young, would make similar arguments about "squaws" and land improvements when he lobbied the federal government to empower and pay him to take over Ute lands that Young's settlers squatted on in the 1850s.

Howe became a prominent landowner and local politician. When he regaled his children and grandchildren in his Sudbury home with stories about doing battle with Metacom's Native forces, Howe likely called it "the Warr with the Indians in New England," as Increase Mather did in 1676, or the "Narragansett War," as other late-seventeenth-century narrators did. But by the 1710s, when, as an old man, he held court over pints of cider at the Sudbury's local tavern, of which he was the proprietor, Howe might have started using the name by which the war had become known. In 1716, Thomas Church published his father Captain Benjamin Church's memoir, *Entertaining History of King Philip's War*, some forty years after the older Church led the company that captured and killed Metacom. That book was the first to call the war "King Philip's War."

"NAMING THE CONFLICT 'KING PHILIP'S WAR' CREATED AN impression of finality," historian Lisa Brooks (Missisquoi Abenaki) has written. The literal death of Philip and the public display of his severed head symbolized the death and removal of all Natives and the extermination of Native land claims in New England. This, even though many Narragansetts, Wampanoags, Naticks, and Nipmuc continued to live on or near their ancestral lands.[5]

Indeed, in the memory of Natives in New England, the war with "Philip" was not the last but the first in a long series of struggles with settlers, cycling between periods of violence and peace. Likewise, while the settlers misnamed their enemies "Indians," the Narragansetts and Wampanoags called themselves "the People" (*Alnôbak* in Abenaki), as the Utes did (*Nuche* in Numic) in Utah. And while the settlers called the land "New England," as did Wakara's Timpanogos (meaning "rocky") in Utah, Natives in what became America's Northeast named themselves after the land to which they belonged. The Nipmuc were from the "freshwater" interior; the Wampanoags were from Pocasset, "on the coast." And yet, in the settlers' written narratives, naming the war after "Philip" not only helped the settlers contain the story but also fixed the blame.[6]

In settler American narratives, the practice of naming conflicts after Native leaders or Native tribes—Pontiac's War, Tecumseh's War, the Black Hawk War, the Seminal Wars, the Comanche Wars—stuck. These names established a culture of covering up the violence—armed conflict, lawless and "legal" land seizures, enslavement, environmental degradation, and disease—that settlers wrought upon Natives. This violence was both literal and literary. American settlers killed noncombatant Natives in flesh and bone. But because they controlled the means of production of history—pens and paper, printing presses—settlers got to name Natives as the belligerents, casting them as "savages" who threatened blameless settlers, while the settlers portrayed themselves as righteous innocents. In such dramas, the settlers' own acts of savagery became not only just but holy.[7]

Samuel Howe's wealth and prestige, which he accumulated by killing Natives and cheating them out of their lands, followed his progeny through the generations. In 1785, Abigail (Nabby) Howe married John Young over the objections of her father, Phineas Howe Sr., who believed a union with a former indentured servant was beneath his high-born daughter. On June 1, 1801, on a small farmstead in Whittingham, Vermont, near the border with Massachusetts, Nabby gave birth to Brigham, the eighth of their eleven children.[8]

Fifty years later, Brigham Young followed the tradition of his great-great-great-grandfather as an Indian killer and Indian land usurper, all the while blaming Natives for the violence and loss of their own land. In July 1853, Young gathered his followers to the Tabernacle soon after the first round of Ute-Mormon violence broke out.

Young declared that he was innocent of starting the conflict—a lie, as he had sent Captain William Wall and his legionnaires to arrest Wakara (or worse) and rally the settlements to war. Young declared to the several hundred gathered in the adobe brick tabernacle on the southwest corner of Temple Square that it was Wakara's Utes, and Wakara in particular, "who [had] declared war on Utah."[9]

WAKARA ATTACKED THE MORMONS, YOUNG EXPLAINED, because the Mormons objected to his slaving predations, especially against the Paiutes. In the face of Wakara's slaving and open hostilities against the Mormons, Young feigned patience and friendship. "How many times have I been asked in the past week, what I intend to do with Walker. I say, 'let him alone,' severely. I have not made war on the Indians, nor am I calculating to do it. . . . Instead of being Walker's enemy, I have sent him a great pile of tobacco to smoke when he is lonely in the mountains. He is now at war with the only friends he has upon this earth, and I want him to have some tobacco to smoke" to remind him of this friendship.

Still, Young told the faithful to arm themselves. His own family history in New England and his own studies of "the Indian character" made clear to Young that "when the Indians are in war . . . [l]et every man, woman, and child, that can handle a butcher knife, be good for one Indian, and you are safe." Yet Young also explained that Wakara's attacks against the Mormons were part of a divinely ordained "mission." It wasn't the mission to change Indians into Lamanites, as Young himself once believed Wakara was chosen to do. Instead, it was to finally convince the Mormons to see the Indians as threats to Zion and to launch attacks—physical and emotional—against them. In this area, Young explained that in waging his "war" against the Saints, "Indian Walker . . . is doing with a chastening rod what I have failed to accomplish with soft words."[10]

Young wasn't alone in moving quickly to declare the conflict a "war" that Utah Natives had waged against the settlers. Earlier in July, Major George Bradley—who would, only a few months later, carry out the massacre of innocent Utes or Goshutes at Nephi—told Nauvoo Legion General Daniel Wells that "Walker had declared war with the white settlements." George A. Smith wrote from Parowan to Brigham Young, warning that Wakara was mustering the Utes for "war."[11]

Newspapers from coast to coast also began publishing vivid descriptions of "Utah Indians" at war, attacking innocent settlers tending to cattle or milling wood. A report in Sacramento's *Daily Union* described the origins of the new "Indian war" in Utah as a fish trade gone bad. The *Daily Union* concluded, "The history of this war will, however, be like all the others in which white men engage with Indians—the white wins and the red loses." In February 1854 the *Buffalo Commercial* reported that "Walker, the Utah Chief" had declared war on the Mormons to push back against their usurpation of Indian territory. Some Mormons, the paper reported, also wanted to go on the offensive and hunt down Wakara's head, for which they had asked Young to propose a price. By spring 1854, newspapers had dispatched with the general "Indian war" talk and settled on labeling it the "Walker War." "The Utah chief, Walker, was preparing to give the Mormons battle," reported Ohio's *Perrysburg Journal* on March 20. The Mormons had offered him a treaty, the paper reported, but Wakara's demands, including cash, a house as large as Brigham Young's, and "as many wives as their veritable governor," were too steep. On March 22, the *Chicago Tribune* reported that Wakara had sworn to conduct a war of "extermination" against the Mormons. This Walker "war" will not only cause the Mormons trouble, the *Tribune* predicted: "During the prevalences of Indian difficulties, the route to California across the plains will be one of much danger, especially to small parties of emigrants."[12]

"Indian difficulties" in the West weren't the only supposed dangers posed to emigrants crossing the continent. An increasing number of Americans worried that the growing Mormon presence—some called it a menace—in the Great Basin presented a threat to the realization of complete American continental dominance. By 1854, anti-Mormon politicians voiced concerns that the converts from England, Wales, and Scotland, who were pouring into Utah each year, placed under Young's command the largest and most zealous settler population in the West. They feared that Young could turn these converts out in voting booths or turn them into armies to fend off attempts from Washington to stop him from expanding his kingdom in the Great Basin.

Anti-Mormons believed that the threat that the Mormons posed to the American republic wasn't just political and military. It was moral. Benjamin G. Ferris spent the better part of a year in Utah as President Millard Fillmore's secretary of the Utah Territory. In his 1854 book *Utah and the Mormons*, one of the first in an emerging genre of exposés on the alleged depravity and dangers of Mormon culture, Ferris described how Young and other "high priest dignitaries of the church are exceedingly skillful in procuring young girls for wives." Still, Ferris wrote that despite their attempts at cultivating "Lamanites," with whom they could covenant and marry, "the Indians . . . [had] never blossomed at all under Mormon horticulture." "On the contrary," Ferris wrote in his book, published at the height of the 1853–1854 Mormon-Ute conflict, the Mormons were the aggressors. They "are now in open hostility with the Utahs, upon whose lands they have encroached; and Walker, or Wachor, the chief of this tribe, is their most deadly enemy, notwithstanding he has been purified by repeated baptisms."[13]

Still, against the rising tide of anti-Mormon sentiment and following the pattern established by his New England ancestors against Metacom, in the summer of 1853 Brigham Young framed the

"Walker War" as a fight between innocent settlers and bloodthirsty savages. As historian Richard White has famously noted, in this "inverted conquest" Euro-American conquerors retold the history of the American West so that they, and not the Natives, were the victims of unprovoked aggression. In this way, Young nationalized his local fight with the Utes. He claimed that he was battling Wakara to defend not only Mormon lives and lands but American ones too. He hoped that such claims would garner sympathy from the rest of America and support from the federal government to extinguish Ute land claims.[14]

Despite all the attention the "Walker War" got from newspapers across the country, Brigham's War against Wakara's Utes had begun long before the summer of 1853. Three years before, on a cold, snowy morning in Parley P. Pratt's cabin inside Salt Lake City's Old Fort, Young and his Mormon brethren made their first plans to "exterminate" the Utes and other Native peoples of Utah.

Chapter 16

Keep the Women, Kill the Men

On the night of January 30, 1850, Parley P. Pratt tried to sleep. But the winter chill made him toss and turn. He was also saddle sore. Just a few hours before, Pratt had returned to the Old Fort in Salt Lake City after he and a company of fifty men had spent the previous two months trekking more than 700 miles across Ute, Goshute, and Paiute lands to scout locations for future Mormon settlements.

Soon after daybreak, Pratt was roused from bed by heavy fists on wood. Pratt opened his cabin's front door. Brigham Young, his counselors Apostles Heber C. Kimball and Willard Richards, and other church leaders pushed their way inside. Pratt could sleep later. The brethren were anxious to hear what Pratt had found.

Pratt wiped the sleep from his eyes and wrapped a blanket around his shoulders. He then gave a lengthy report of his journey. He explained that after visiting the settlers at Manti—the first Mormon settlement outside the Wasatch Front, which Wakara had helped found the fall before—Pratt and his company traveled along Wakara's Old Spanish Trail. They descended from the rich grasslands of the Sanpete and Sevier Valleys to the deserts of southern Utah.

Pratt also reported that as they traveled south, they met Paiutes, who kept their distance, fearing that the men on horseback had come to take their women and children, as Wakara had done for more than a decade. Pratt explained that on their return trip to Salt Lake City, they erected a forty-foot-high liberty pole at the future site of Louisa (Parowan)—a place of great promise, which Pratt estimated could house 50,000 people. Further north, along the Pahvant Mountains, they crossed Chalk Creek, the future home of Fillmore, then passed the future sites of Payson and Nephi. In the Utah Valley they were forced to dismount and lead their horses through knee-deep snows. Starving and freezing, they reached Fort Utah (Provo), where they were able to reprovision and warm their frozen limbs before making the final push to Salt Lake.[1]

Soon after Pratt concluded his report, there was another knock on his door. It was Isaac Higbee, one of the founders of Fort Utah, with news of fresh troubles with the Utes, which threatened plans for growth that Pratt's expedition inspired. The Timpanogos were stealing the settlers' horses and killing their cattle, Higbee reported. Worse, they were shooting at the settlers and threatening to unleash their warriors to route the Mormons from the lake. Higbee informed the brethren that every male settler wished to take the fight to the Timpanogos and defend Fort Utah. After all, without the fort, Pratt and his men would have frozen to death before reaching Salt Lake.

"My voice is for war," Willard Richards proclaimed, with the hope to "exterminate them." Brigham Young agreed and put the motion to a vote. Every right hand shot up. But Pratt asked the Mormon war makers to draw distinctions between male and female Indians, as well as between adults and children. "I would take the women and children and clothe them and make them do what we want and don't let them prowl about." Young agreed to spare the women and children if they behaved themselves. But "we shall have no peace until the men are killed off." Soon after, the plan became a military mandate to raise a company of fifty men, outfitted with horses, arms, and rations for a twenty-day campaign. The directive was to stop "the operations of all hostile Indians and otherwise act, as the circumstances may require, exterminating such as do not separate themselves from their hostile clans, and sue for peace."[2]

With these orders—more than three years before the start of the so-called Walker War—Brigham's war of extermination of the Natives of Utah commenced.

ONE OF THE FIRST BATTLES IN THIS WAR of extermination—remembered later as the Battle at Fort Utah or the Fort Utah Massacre of February 1850—drove the Timpanogos from the lands and fisheries in and around Timpanogos (Utah) Lake. The battle literally and figuratively succeeded in cutting off the heads of the band's leadership, a vacuum that Wakara filled. Before they rotted in the hot sun inside Fort Utah, the heads of the dead Timpanogos leaders and warriors became spoils of war. In the twentieth century, the remains of the last of the Mormons' Ute foes, Antonga (Black Hawk), who as a young man sought shelter in Fort Utah during the massacre, would be displayed in a trophy case in the Church History Museum in Temple Square.

A few months after the campaign against the Timpanogos, during the spring fish festival of 1850, Young, Heber C. Kimball, Dimick Huntington, and other members of Young's war cabinet met Wakara and twenty Ute leaders, including Sowiette, Arapeen, and Antonga, at Wakara's camp in the Utah Valley. Through Huntington, Young told Wakara that he wished he hadn't been forced into killing the Timpanogos and wished not to do any more of it. Young hoped that Wakara would prove more amenable to Mormon presence on Ute lands. "We want to smoke the pipe of peace and be friends, and make an everlasting covenant" in trade and religion, Young told Wakara.

The Mormons also wanted to feed and clothe Wakara and his men, teach them how to raise grain and cattle, and send Ute children to school. Wakara agreed. "Mormons love us, we love them," the Ute leader proclaimed. Yet, while he welcomed the Mormons to "settle on" his land, he did not want them to "buy" it. He also expressed wariness about the expansion of the settlements on his sacred fishing grounds at Timpanogos Lake. Instead, he wanted the Mormons to focus their settlements in the Sanpete Valley.[3]

Despite Wakara's misgivings, Mormon sprawl around the lake went unabated. In April 1851, Young led a large caravan of foodstuffs and other goods on what would become an annual journey to the southern settlements. Apostle Wilford Woodruff recalled the stop at Provo, where the brethren dined on trout from Timpanogos Lake, then met Wakara at his camp near the lake. It was Woodruff's first time meeting the Ute leader, and he was unimpressed, describing him as an "ugly cunning chief." The next day, Woodruff and Nauvoo Legion Major General Daniel Wells toured a wheat field, which the year before had been the battlefield where Wells oversaw the massacre of the Timpanogos. Woodruff had missed that excitement—he was leading 200 church members across Nebraska—so Wells gave him an account of the battle, which Woodruff found quite interesting, Woodruff recalled in his journal. The battlegrounds of Brigham's War against the Utah's Natives had already been cultivated into tourist sites and farmlands.[4]

In June, Young opened a new front in his war against Utah Natives. He dispatched attachments of the Nauvoo Legion west of Salt Lake City to hunt Goshutes who had objected to Mormon expansion in their homelands. As was the case in the Utah Valley, in the Tooele Valley, overgrazing by Mormon cattle destroyed the water and grasses upon which the Goshutes had relied for generations. Starving, the Goshutes took Mormon cattle. In response, the Nauvoo Legion attacked Goshute camps, killing the men and tracking the women to another camp. Seeing the riders approach, the women retreated, leaving behind cookery, butchered cattle and horses, and a freshly dug well. The leader of the company, William McBride, reported to General Wells that his legionnaires unleashed scorched-earth warfare, burning all the cookery and food supplies. McBride requested that Wells send him another tool to flush out the remaining Goshutes. "We wish you without a moment's hesitation to send us about a pound of arsenic. We want to give the Indians' well a flavor. . . . A little strickenine [*sic*] would . . . serve instead of salt, to their too-fresh meat." Wells was pleased. In his reply, he encouraged McBride to continue to kill Goshute men and capture Goshute women and children. As for poisoning meat and water, Wells thought it a fine strategy. But alas, at the time he could not locate the requested seasoning materials.[5]

AFTER HIS ORDINATION AS A MORMON ELDER IN Salt Lake City in June 1851, Wakara headed south to Timpanogos Lake. Again, to the Nauvoo Legion leadership, Wakara expressed his displeasure at seeing further expansion on the Utes' hunting and fishing grounds as well as an expanded military presence at the lake. General Wells told Wakara to hold his tongue and stop his cattle stealing. The legionnaires were ready to treat him like they had other Timpanogos the year before and the Goshutes that same month. Wells cautioned, "[You] may [even] share the same fate as Pat-sow-ette," the Ute leader who, with Wakara's help, had recently been executed. Still, the general understood that conflict with Wakara's well-mounted cavalry was not the same as exterminating the horseless Goshutes or laying siege to Patsowet's Timpanogos. Wells did not want a quarrel. But he did expect Wakara to respect Mormon property and to make sure his men did the same. Wakara did not want a quarrel either. "I would be a fool to fight," he said. Still, Mormon fences and corrals notwithstanding, Wakara told the legionnaires that he would see his horses roam on the festival grounds and eat up the valley's grasses, as they had done for generations. And Young's ban notwithstanding, he would trade for guns and ammunition that he needed to hunt, raid, and defend his people.[6]

That summer, Wakara realized that he needed the help of outsiders to stop Mormon encroachment on his ancestral lands. In a meeting with the federal Indian agent Henry Day, Wakara and Sowiette explained that since their arrival in 1847, the Mormons had driven the Utes off their lands and stolen their game and fish. Sowiette begged Day to tell the "Great Father" in Washington to prove he was "powerful" by intervening on the Utes' behalf. "'American good! Mormon no good!,'" Sowiette told Day. "American friend. Mormon kill, steal." Later that same summer, when Young called on Washakie's Shoshones and Wakara and Sowiette's Utes to attend a pan-tribal peace meeting at Fort Laramie in Wyoming, Wakara and Sowiette sent their lieutenants but refused to go themselves. The Utes feared that the treaty talks were really "a trap set by the Mormons to kill them," Day wrote to his bosses back east. Soon after, Day returned to Washington, where he delivered the Utes' complaints about Brigham Young, then ex officio superintendent of Indian affairs. Indian agents accused Young of using federal funds to bribe Ute and Shoshone leaders to grant the Mormons' permission to seize larger swaths of their lands. Despite these warnings from governmental officials, Young remained unreprimanded and unrepentant. In fact, that fall of 1851, he announced plans to establish more settlements in the areas Pratt had scouted the year before. Young predicted that the Indian complaints (and Indian lives) would die out once the Saints, ensconced in settlements from Parowan in the south to Salt Lake City in the north, outnumbered the population of Utah Natives.[7]

Cut off from raiding in California, Wakara spent the winter of 1851–1852 with the Pimas, Hopis, and Navajos in Arizona. In April, after learning that Wakara was on his way to the fish festival, Young wrote him a letter, which he sent Dimick Huntington to deliver. Young told Wakara that upon his return he should prepare himself to find Utah changed even more, with more Mormon settlements and more regulations on Native trade with emigrants, Mexicans, and Mormons. Also, because he was worried that Indian agents were sowing discord between the settlers and Utah Natives, Young begged Wakara, "Remember we are your friends all the time. Don't believe what bad men say about us." As a sign of goodwill, Young promised Wakara more presents. "We mean to give friend Walker a suit of clothes when he comes to see us."[8]

But Wakara needed no convincing by Indian agents not to trust the Saints. And promises of new clothes were a poor salve for the pains that Mormon expansion caused to his way of life. No longer able to raid and trade on the Old Spanish Trail, Wakara relied even more on trade with the Americans who traveled through Utah on their way west, which Young's new regulations also aimed to stop. Even more frustrating was that the Mormons were preventing the Utes from fishing their sacred waters, while the settlers' own nets were constantly pulling in fish. Tensions rose further when, upon his arrival at Timpanogos Lake in May 1852, Wakara discovered that another wheat field had been planted on their festival grounds at the lake. Wakara expected payment for the use of these lands, payment that was not forthcoming.[9]

This unchecked and uncompensated growth made the Utes angry. They were angry because of the damage Mormon grazing cattle and their thirsty fields did to their hunting and fishing grounds. They were also angry because of the violence against their own bodies that followed when Utes and other Utah Natives made the most meager objections. In the spring of 1852, another Indian agent, Jacob Holeman, met with Sowiette in the Utah Valley, where the Utes' political leader described his peoples' "disapprobation to any settlement being made by the whites, and more particularly the Mormons," as Holeman wrote to his superiors in Washington. Holeman then described what by then had become a familiar and disconcerting pattern. First, the Mormons build a settlement on Ute lands with promises to compensate them through trade or direct payments in beef and grain. Next, the Utes demand payment. The Mormons refuse. The Utes then take what they believe is fair payment—horses or cattle from pens, wheat from wagons or fields. On paper and from their pulpits, the Mormons describe these "trivial" actions as an "'Indian war'" against the innocent and aggrieved settlers. But on the land, it's the Mormons who, "being better armed and equipped than the Indians," unleash "a most brutal butchery" against the Utes.[10]

In the spring of 1852, Young needed more time to gather soldiers before he could start a new "Indian war" against Wakara. In the meantime, he worked to keep a lid on the violence. He talked up peace between the settlers and Wakara and between long-warring Native tribes. In September 1852, Young hosted a peace parley in the lower room of the State House between the Shoshones and the Utes. (It was also at this meeting when artist William Warner Major painted portraits of Wakara [see Warner's painting on page 4], Arapeen, and leading Shoshones). Young called on Wakara and Sowiette and the Shoshone leaders to say whether their tribes had made peace with each other. Wakara and the rest of the Ute delegation and Shoshone leader Washakie all raised their right hands to indicate yes. Through Dimick Huntington, Young also asked the tribal leaders whether they were happy with the Mormons settling on their lands. Wakara and Sowiette said *ashante*, while the Shoshone leaders demurred since the lands the Mormons had settled on were (mostly) not theirs. Wakara passed the peace pipe. And Young handed out presents—more clothes and Mormon beef—to the leaders. Conspicuously absent from the meeting were representatives from the Ute bands who had most opposed Mormon settlement, including those from Timpanogos Lake. They had all been killed in the massacres of February 1850.[11]

At the end of 1852, Young celebrated the fact that, instead of war, peace had broken out between the settlers and their "tawny neighbors," a fact that Young tied to the fact that there were some 30,000 Mormons in Utah, with more to come. Still, Mormons were readying themselves for war, with their well-armed military numbering more than 2,000. (The US Army at the time was no bigger than 11,000 regulars.) Young encouraged all militiamen and civilians alike to keep "powder on hand, for such emergencies as might occur in wild, Indian country."[12]

Emergencies began soon after the new year when, during a raid, Wakara's band murdered Paiute men and captured women and children near Fort Harmony. At Fillmore, unknown Natives stole gun powder from one settler and stabbed another. Young counseled the settlers to hold their fire for now, so as not to put more Mormon lives and property at risk. Yet, by spring instructions were sent to all settlements to prepare for war. The time had come when "ignorant savages [were] liable to be incited to rob, plunder, and kill for the most trivial reasons," General Wells wrote to one militia leader. During the last week of April, Young dispatched William Wall and his men to march from Fillmore to Parowan and rouse settlers to fight and, if the opportunity presented itself, to arrest Wakara. According to Baptiste, who rushed to Nephi when Wakara, Baptiste, and his other brothers heard of the orders, they understood them as a command not just to capture but to kill the Ute leaders.[13]

The Nauvoo Legion's tour of the southern settlements had the desired effect of growing the appetite for war among the settlers and Utes alike. The fear of war also moved the Paiutes to join the Mormons and aid in their efforts to fort up. "Many have gone to live with the whites; some are learning trades, others farming," Dimick Huntington reported during a visit to Fort Harmony in southern Utah. "They can cut and set pickets as well as whites."[14]

For his part, in late April Wakara knew that Young would likely use as a pretense to start a war the reports from Parowan that he had leveled guns against the Mormon posse that tried to stop his trade in slaves with a group of emigrants. Hoping to prevent bloodshed, Wakara rushed north. On April 30, Wakara reached Manti, where he spoke with Isaac Morley, the man with whom he had founded the settlement three years before. Wakara claimed that he had tried to stop the conflict south of Parowan so as not to create tensions between the Utes and his Mormon brethren. Instead of trading in human flesh, which so upset the Mormons, Wakara also told Morley he had brought north animal skins to trade. As a sign of that friendship, Morley reported, Wakara smoked the tobacco that Young had recently sent him. Writing back to Wakara, Young claimed that he was relieved to hear that the Ute leader was of a peacemaking disposition. And Young invited Wakara to Salt Lake, where he could expect to receive more presents from the prophet in exchange for his skins.[15]

Yet, despite his private messages of friendship to Wakara, the next day Young told the Mormon public that he did not, in fact, expect Wakara to heed his warnings. And thus war—and a war of extinction—was inevitable. "We can scarcely read of one colony founded among the aborigines in the first settling of this country," Young proclaimed at the Tabernacle in Temple Square, "wherein the tomahawk of wild Indians did not drink the blood of whole families." Just as Young's ancestors had in New England, and just as the founders of what would become the national parks did in the late nineteenth and early twentieth centuries, Young justified mass killings and displacement of Utah's Native Americans as part of making the wilderness safe for White pilgrims and pioneers who wanted to seek shelter in America's wild places. As for Wakara in particular, Young declared him untrustworthy: "I shall live a long while before I can believe that an Indian is my friend, when it would be to his advantage to be my enemy."[16]

After participating in the fish festival, in early July, Wakara and his brothers Ammon and Peteetneet accepted Young's invitation to come to Salt Lake City. They set up their camp in the foothills above Temple Square. With Nauvoo Legion troops drilling in the warm summer air nearby, Wakara visited Young in his office and told the Mormon prophet that he meant peace.[17]

Still, the meeting did not go well. Brigham Young did not believe Wakara, or chose not to. All Wakara's peace talk was further proof of his "hypocrisy," wrote Mormon clerk Thomas Bullock about the meeting. Within a week, following a new proclamation from Young calling for actions to suppress "Indian hostilities unhappily existing in [the Utah Valley]," General Wells commanded the creation of a minutemen unit to be sent into battle at a moment's notice. Young and the rest of the Mormon religious and military leadership had finally lost all faith that Mormons and Natives could live in harmony in Utah—if they ever had such faith in the first place.[18]

By then, Wakara and his fellow Ute leaders had also lost faith in the Mormons. After the failed peace meeting in Temple Square, and before they left to go south to Timpanogos Lake for the fish festival, Wakara and Sowiette met with their longtime acquaintance, Mexican fur trader M. S. Martenas. They did so at the request of Indian agent Jacob Holeman, who wanted a written record of the Ute leaders' views on the settlers' presence in their homelands. In Spanish, Wakara recounted how the Mormons had initially pledged friendship and goodwill. But when they grew in numbers, they expanded into the Utes' hunting and fishing grounds, driving them from their homes, dirtying their waters, and killing their game. Even the Utes' dead did not go unmolested. As the Mormons built their new homes, they tore up the graves of their ancestors, Wakara explained. Martenas also interviewed Sowiette. The Ute civil leader told him that the settlers' actions had demonstrated that Natives and settlers couldn't share the land. "The whites want every thing, and will give the Indians nothing," Sowiette declared.[19]

THE 1853 FISH FESTIVAL WAS OVERSHADOWED BY A "war" that would come to bear Wakara's anglicized name. But it was Brigham Young who provoked the conflict—one of many in Brigham's War against Utah Natives that he inaugurated in 1850. The Mormons made repeated promises, in writing and directly to Wakara's face, that they would not "throw him" away. They would not drive Wakara and his people off their lands. They would not hinder Wakara's access to his sacred fishing grounds. They would not prevent Wakara from moving freely among the settlements; nor would they stop him from trading horses and Paiutes. But the Mormons broke these promises. They fought to circumscribe Wakara's travels and seize control of Ute land and water.

Fittingly for a confrontation that targeted the Fish Eater Wakara, this next battle of Brigham's War began with a fight over fish.

In mid-July 1853, after his visit to Salt Lake, Wakara and his band camped at Spring Creek, near today's Springville. There, they fished for chubs, trout, and suckers returning to Timpanogos Lake from their spawning runs. They also traded fish with local settlers for the bread and grains on which the Utes increasingly relied. On July 15, a Ute woman visited Elizabeth and James Ivie, who had recently built a cabin near Wakara's camp. The Ute woman offered five large trout and received four pounds of flour in return. But soon after, the Ute woman and her husband, Shower-o-cats, whom Wakara later called his cousin, returned to the Ivies' home. James Ivie claimed that Shower-o-cats, enraged by how little flour his wife got for the fish, started a fight. The result left Shower-o-cats near death.[20]

The day after the fight, settler James McClellan sent an urgent message to Brigham Young informing him about "the scrape" with the Utes over the fish. McClellan also reported that Arapeen told him that if Shower-o-cats died, then “Ivie’s blood must atone for it.” Young wrote back immediately. Though his army was mustered, he did not want this incident to spark violence. He counseled Arapeen and Wakara to remain at peace. But Shower-o-cats died. And violence broke out. On July 18, Utes shot guards at Nephi, Payson, and Manti, killing one. At Summit Creek, Utes forced settler families from their homes. Utes also stole 200 head of cattle in the Sanpete Valley.[21]

Young might not have been ready. But following this outbreak of violence, he decided to launch his war on Wakara. Young drafted “special orders,” commanding Colonel Peter Conover to lead a campaign of legionnaires against the Utes “until Walker the chief of the Indians is executed. To him, when found, you will show no quarter.” It seems that Young thought better of trying to kill Wakara right away. In a later draft of the orders, Conover was instructed to “pursue and capture Walker,” but the command to execute him was crossed out.[22]

Still, Wakara was not out of danger. Later that month, Young sent Wakara his most ominous letter, along with his “peace” offering of tobacco, which General Wells delivered to him. “You are a fool for fighting your best friends,” Young bellowed. “Everybody else would kill you if they could get a chance.” Anticipating Wakara’s worry that Young might himself take a chance at killing him, Young concluded, “If you are afraid of the tobacco which I send you, you can let some of your prisoners try it first and then you will know that it is good.”[23]

On the last day of July, Young addressed the Saints gathered at the Tabernacle. He announced that a full-blown “war” had broken out. And Young held Wakara responsible. “I have been teased and teased by men who will come to me and say, ‘Just give me twenty-five, fifty, or a hundred men, and I will go and fetch you Walker’s head.’” Young claimed that he did not want Wakara’s head. Or at least not yet. Still, Young believed Wakara’s days, and the days of all the Utes, were numbered. Young proclaimed that the Saints would exterminate those Natives who tried to stop them from fulfilling their divine mandate of colonizing the four corners of Utah and making it their promised land in the Intermountain West. But ironically, Young said it was Wakara's practice of stealing women and children from the Paiutes that was having the effect of "extinguish[ing] the [Indian] race."[24]

Narrators of the "Walker War" would later claim that Wakara started the war out of anger over the Mormons' efforts to stop this slave trade. But at the outbreak of the war, both Wakara and Young made clear that the conflict was as much about control over land as it was about slavery. And in that coming war, Young told his followers not to fear. The multiyear campaign to curtail Wakara's trade in horse and slaves and to prevent him from moving freely across lands he had long dominated meant that Wakara was "hemmed in," Young declared. "He dare not go into California again. Dare he go east to the Snakes? No. Dare he go north? No, for they would rejoice to kill him. Here he is, penned up in a small compass, surrounded by his enemies; and now the Elders of Israel long to eat up, as it were, him and his little band."[25]

THE MORMON ELDERS OF ISRAEL BEGAN TO EAT up Wakara's Utes right away. One settler wrote in his journal that by mid-July, Mormon missionaries who weren't fishing for converts overseas were "appointed missions to the Lamanites with muskets, yawgers, & good rifles as their mouth pieces." For the next two weeks, the Nauvoo Legion, comprising a few hundred men and boys from the Utah and Sanpete Valley settlements, secured Payson and Manti, then followed the Utes into the surrounding woods and mountains where they engaged in sporadic gun battles. By the end of the month, the body count on the settler side was one dead and a handful wounded, including at least one friendly-fire injury. For the Utes, at least fifteen were killed, with an unknown number wounded. More violence occurred in August, when Utes stole cattle, burned down mills, and killed settlers. A wagon team was attacked on its way to Salt Lake City with lumber for the construction of fortifications. In late September, south of Spanish Fork, Utes killed Mormon settlers and at least one California-bound migrant. They also stole Mormon cattle and wheat. In response legionnaires attacked a Ute camp in the Goshen Valley, starting a fire fight that resulted in at least four dead Utes and the rest of the camp seeking shelter in nearby canyons.[26]

While legionnaires patrolled the mountains between the Salt Lake and Utah Valleys with special orders to "route" Indians they came across from their hiding places, martial law was declared on the home front. Settlers in outlying areas were ordered to pack food and hay into wagons, wrangle horses and cattle, and abandon homes, farms, and fields for shelter in nearby forts. There, they were put to work raising stockyards to house livestock and hold grain. They also began to erect wooden and earthen walls around the strongholds. Such "forting up" was ordered from Ogden in the north to Parowan in the south. Young and his military leaders hoped that this forting up would become more than a temporary response to Indian aggression. The Mormon prophet envisioned a network of fortified towns linked together by Mormon roads and bridges. Such a system would allow the Saints to defend themselves against all enemies, Native or otherwise.[27]

Not all settlers responded well to calls to fort up. At Nephi, one settler refused to leave his farm, preferring to stand guard at home. As punishment, the settler had three horses confiscated. Further south at the Mormon mining outpost of Cedar City, a dozen settlers brandished guns and swore that they'd kill their own cattle before they let the brethren confiscate them. Major John D. Lee reported that some settlers at Harmony threatened mutiny. Those who refused Young's orders to fort up were "wicked apostate[s]," Lee declared, whose blood he would shed himself if they didn't behave as their prophet commanded. Even some militiamen failed to follow Young's orders. Throughout the summer and fall of 1853, dozens were court-martialed for offenses ranging from sleeping while on guard to disobeying orders.[28]

In contrast, the Paiutes in the region seemed happy with the war preparations. "I apprehend but little danger from the native Piedes; they are not disposed to be friendly with Walker at all," Lee reported in September. "They say that his promises are too easily broken to be of much force: & his friendship cost[s] the sacrifice of their wives & children; to be carried off & used by them, or traded off to the Spaniards as slaves."[29]

Young also worked to convince the rest of America that it was Wakara who had declared war on the Mormons. Despite the Mormons' gifts and kindness to him, "Indian Walker and his band" were waging a war of unprovoked aggression against the settlers, Young wrote to the Secretary of Indian Affairs George W. Manypenny in late September 1853. Young made exaggerated claims that the Utes had attacked settlers' bodies, burned down the territory's infrastructure, and stolen thousands of their cattle and horses. Like savage animals, Wakara and his men continued "prowling around the weaker settlements, watching [for] their opportunity to kill defenseless and unarmed persons." The Mormons thus had no choice but to organize defenses, husband crops and cattle for the coming winter, tear down houses, and put up militarized forts. These "exceedingly expensive" efforts, Young explained to Manypenny, weren't done just to protect the Mormons but also to make the West safe for all Americans. Young hoped that sooner rather than later, the federal government would repay the Mormons for their expenses in blood and treasure.[30]

Despite Young's claims that Wakara was responsible for the war, during the first months of the conflict, Wakara was often hundreds of miles away from the violence, a fact that Young knew either from the start or soon after. In the last week of July, George A. Smith and Heber C. Kimball marched south toward Fillmore with a company of soldiers to deliver Young's "peace" letter and tobacco to Wakara, or to arrest him, if they could locate him. Along the way, they met a member of Kanosh's Pahvant Band, who told them that Wakara was not behind any of the recent Ute attacks and had taken refuge from the fighting with New Mexican traders in southern Utah. In August, from Utes visiting Fort Nephi, George A. Smith learned that it was another Ute, Wy-o-nah, not Wakara, who called for attacks against settlers to avenge the murder of Shower-o-cats. In September, John D. Lee reported from Cedar City that Wakara had gone further south to Navajo country.[31]

Wakara might not have started the war, but by early fall he may have been willing to enter it in full force. Lee learned from "two squaws" who had escaped Wakara's camp that Wakara had sent his brother Ammon to trade with the New Mexicans for gun powder. Lee reported that Wakara also hoped to enlist New Mexicans and Navajos in an attack on the southern settlements when winter set in. But other records suggest that even after all the killings of the Utes in the summer and early fall of 1853, Wakara did not want the violence to continue. US Marshal Joseph Heywood wrote to Brigham Young that a group of Utes visited Fort Nephi in mid-September in search of food and shelter. The Utes informed the settlers that Wakara was not in the south as Lee had reported. Instead, Wakara and his lodges had gone to the Uintah Valley in northeastern Utah. The visitors spoke of a divide within Wakara's family; Wakara hoped to make peace, but Arapeen wanted to fight. In exchange for work, the settlers offered to clothe and feed the starving Utes. But the Utes left as quickly as they came, afraid that the Mormons would coerce them into the fort, then kill them.[32]

Of course, the Ute visitors to Nephi were not without cause for worry. At the fort in Manti on September 13, a group of Ute men who had agreed to lay down their arms, smoke a peace pipe, and accept protection and food in exchange for work were soon after "taken down the street and shot," wrote Azariah Smith in his journal. The settlers, led by Manti leader Isaac Morley, justified the killings by accusing the Utes of stealing from other settlers and acting as spies on behalf of belligerent Utes. The settlers then buried the massacred Utes "in one hole[,] for [a] grave it could not be called," recalled settler Andrew Siler. Soon after, the massacred Utes' possessions and children were auctioned off. Morley offered three bushels of wheat for a young girl. But Morley was outbid by William Black, who offered sixteen bushels.[33]

On October 1, Isaac Morley and other Manti settlers brought the mutilated bodies of the wagon team at Fountain Green—later testimony recalled that the settlers' tongues had also been cut out—to Nephi, where more plans for vengeance were born. When a group of Utes or Goshutes arrived at the fort the next day, these plans were executed. The official report of the "skirmish at Nephi" claimed that the settlers believed that these Natives were responsible for the killing of the wagon team. But, as Adelia Hatton (Kimball) recalled, in reality, "the brethren were so exasperated" by the murder of the wagon train that Morley "ordered them shot down without even considering whether they were the guilty ones or not." Like the victims of the massacre at Manti, the Nephi Seven were then buried in one large hole, where they would remain until their chance discovery when the Crepses dug out their new basement in 2006.[34]

More violence marked the rest of October. While gathering wood in the canyon above the grist mill near Manti, John Warner and William Mills were shot, killed, and stripped of their clothes. Oxen were stolen, as was the wheat from the mill. A few weeks later, at the settlement at Santaquin just south of Payson, a few dozen Natives of unknown tribal origin attacked settlers in their gardens as they gathered potatoes. One was killed and scalped, and the Natives stole the settlers' cattle. Soon after, militiamen were dispatched to track down the perpetrators. When the soldiers found a Native camp, a firefight ensued. The Natives fled, and the militiamen helped themselves to buckskins and bows and arrows that the Natives left behind. It wasn't clear if the camp belonged to the Natives responsible for the violence at Santaquin, but that didn't matter to the soldiers. They celebrated their victory by covering their faces in war paint and dancing around the sacked camp.[35]

IN BRIGHAM'S WAR AGAINST WAKARA, THE MOST FAMOUS victim was neither Ute nor Mormon, but American: Captain John W. Gunnison of the US Army Corps of Topographical Engineers. And Gunnison's death most likely had little to do with the conflict between Young and Wakara.

In 1850, as part of Howard Stansbury's topographical expedition, Gunnison explored and surveyed the Salt Lake Valley and befriended Mormon pioneers. In 1852, Gunnison helped introduce the region and its new inhabitants to the rest of the country when he published a book about his experiences with the Mormons and Utah's Natives, including Wakara. In the fall of 1853, Gunnison was back in Utah, leading a survey team mapping potential routes for the coming transcontinental railroad. On October 25, Gunnison made camp near a stand of willow trees, forty-five miles northwest of Fillmore, then a hoped-for hub for the railroad. At daybreak on October 26, Gunnison and his men were ambushed by some sixty Pahvant Utes who sought to avenge the killing of one of their own by a California-bound group of emigrants not associated with Gunnison's expedition. A few of Gunnison's men escaped, mounted their horses, and raced back to locate other members of their party in hopes of gathering reinforcements. But when Gunnison's men returned, they found their comrades dead, their naked bodies riddled with arrows, and the camp's survey books and equipment gone.[36]

The next day, Gunnison's men galloped to Fillmore to alert the Mormon authorities of what had transpired. Distraught that his people had committed such an act of violence, Kanosh retrieved the surveyors' equipment, animals, and guns from the Pahvants who had attacked Gunnison. A company of settlers rushed to the massacre site but found wolves had gotten there first. They buried the remains they could find near the Sevier River. As for Gunnison, nothing remained but a femur and some hair. They buried the bone at Fillmore. Brigham Young mailed the hair to Gunnison's widow.[37]

Initially Wakara was blamed for the massacre, though he was hundreds of miles away at the time of the attack. Later, anti-Mormons in the federal government, as well as Gunnison's widow, claimed that Young had ordered Kanosh's Pahvants to instigate the ambush to forestall the arrival of the railroad. But in his report, Gunnison's second in command, Edward Beckwith, rejected that notion. In fact, Beckwith reported that Kanosh, along with a dozen other Pahvants, came back to Fillmore to make further amends. Kanosh explained that a group of young men had committed the act without his permission. In March 1855, an all-Mormon jury convicted six Pahvants of manslaughter, not murder. There were extenuating circumstances, the jury concluded, as the massacre had occurred during the "Walker War" and emigrants bound for California had killed one of the Pahvants' own.[38]

In the fall of 1853, the Utes did not burn grass on their way to California to promote growth for their return the next spring. But some Utes did burn settler buildings, including a sawmill near Manti and houses at Summit Creek, which had been abandoned as the Mormons forted up. The burnings didn't solve the Utes' most pressing problem: hunger. Some stole cattle from Provo. Others streamed into Mormon strongholds begging for food.

Young took the cooldown in the season of violence to take stock of the war and to continue to blame Wakara for it. "During the past

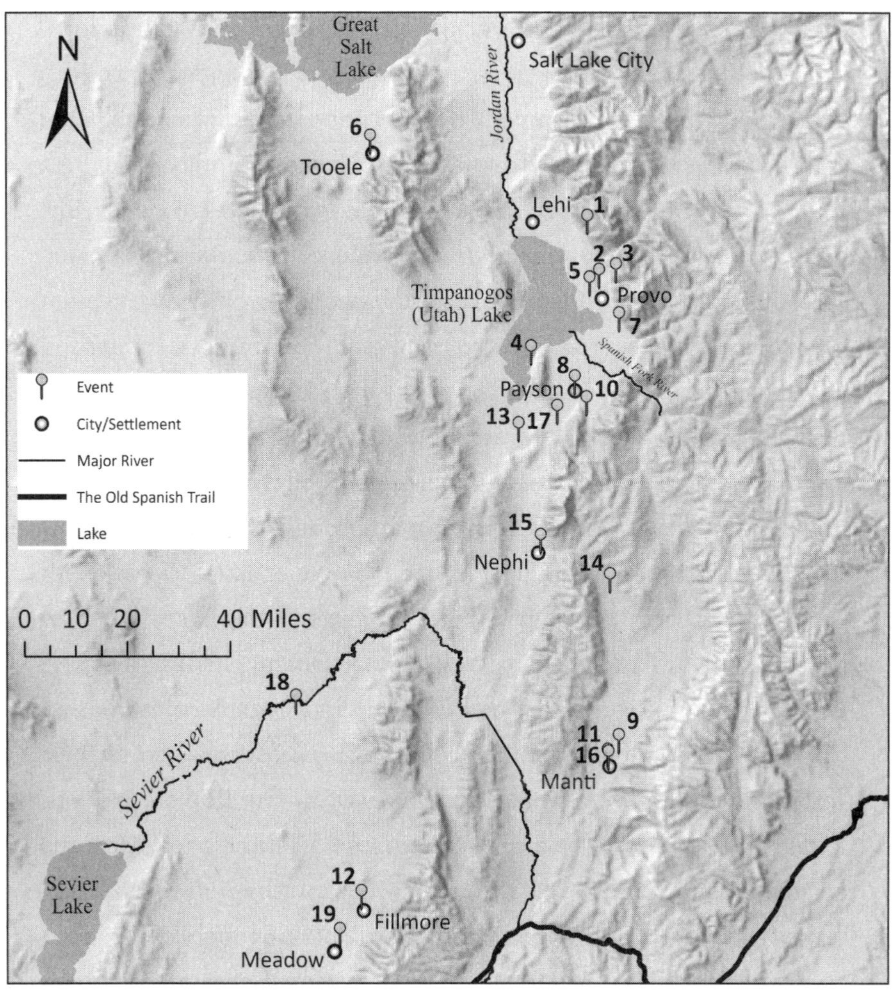

1. Battle Creek Massacre, March 1849. Four to seven Timpanogos men and boys killed; one boy, perhaps Antonga (Blackhawk) captured.
2. Fort Utah Massacre, February 8–10, 1850. Twenty to forty Timpanogos men, women, and children killed or died due to measles and exposure. One Mormon soldier killed.
3. At least ten Timpanogos captured, killed, or died from exposure and disease in Rock Canyon, including band leader Old Elk, February 11–12, 1850.
4. Table Point Massacre, February 13–14, 1850. Twenty to thirty Timpanogos men and boys killed; twenty to thirty women and children captured.
5. At least thirty heads of dead Timpanogos displayed at Fort Utah, Spring 1850.
6. Mormon militia attacked Goshute villages in Toole Valley, April–June 1851. Approximately ten men and boys killed; five to ten women and children taken captive.
7. Shower-o-cats murdered near Payson, July 17, 1853.
8. Utes killed Alexander Keel at Payson, July 18, 1853.
9. Mormon militia killed at least seven Utes north of Manti, mid-July 1853.
10. Mormon militia killed at least six Utes in Peteetneet (Payson) Canyon, mid-July 1853.
11. Mormon settlers killed at least six Utes in Manti, September 13, 1853.
12. Utes killed William Hatton in Fillmore, September 13, 1853.
13. After Utes attacked settlers, Mormon militia attacked Ute camp in Goshen Valley, killing at least four, September 25–26, 1853.
14. Utes killed four-man Mormon wagon in Fountain Green, October 1, 1853.
15. Mormon militia massacred Goshutes or Utes at Nephi. Seven men and boys dead; one woman captured/enslaved, October 2, 1853.
16. Unknown Natives killed John Warner and William Mills near Manti, October 4, 1853.
17. Utes killed Fernee L. Tindrell at Summit (Santaquin), Mormon Militia attacked and sacked Ute camp, October 14–16, 1853.
18. Gunnison Massacre, October 26, 1853. Eight American surveyors killed by Pahvant Utes.
19. Wakara died near Meadow, Utah, January 29, 1855.

Sites of Young's Wars Against Utah Natives, 1849–1855. (Map by Wenjie Wang) season the Indian Walker & his band have caused us some trouble," wrote Young in a letter to Edward Martin, a missionary in Glasgow, Scotland. Young counted nine dead Mormons, several wounded, and the loss of hundreds of cattle and horses. Nineteen Indians had died. Still, Young believed the fight had a salutary effect. The various Mormon settlements had unified in their hatred of a common enemy and a common purpose to fort up. As for the Natives, Young learned that the conflict had caused Wakara's band to split up, with some hiding out with kin along the Yampa River in northwestern Colorado and Wakara and his lodges wintering among the Navajos.[39]

Young hoped to sow further divisions among the Utes by offering peace to some Ute leaders while furthering his war efforts against Wakara. In early December, Young penned a letter to Sowiette. Young wanted to meet the Ute political leader in person, but "for some reason [you] keep away" from the settlements, wrote the Mormon prophet. Of course, Young knew why Sowiette kept his distance: He rightfully feared for his life. Still, Young claimed that he wanted the season of killing to end. If peace could be established, Young promised Sowiette, he would induce his people to give the Utes food, clothing, and weapons. But these would not be gifts. The Utes would have to trade their valuable skins for the White men's goods. Young told Sowiette that the Utes needed to "quit begging, for we all have to work for what we have."[40]

Just as he was dispatching peace letters to Sowiette, Young dispatched his representative in Washington, John Bernhisel, to leverage his war against Wakara to secure federal funds to extinguish "Indian title of the lands" in the territory. Young gave Bernhisel more talking points to share with his political contacts. Because of Mormon industry in the Great Basin, flourishing cities and settlements had sprung up where previously there had been nothing more than "Indian wigwams." They had turned Wakara's "trail of the Indians" to California into a "great highway to the Pacific," dotted with trading posts for emigrants bound for the West Coast. Bernhisel asked Secretary of Indian Affairs George Manypenny to lobby the US Congress to repay the Mormons for the fortune they had spent fighting Wakara and moving settlers and supplies out of harm's way. They also wanted the government to authorize the Mormons to deal with the Utes directly by removing them to reservation-like "Indian farms" that the Mormons would run. On these farms, the relocated Natives would finally be trained to work for their bread.[41]

Sowiette did not respond to Young's request for a parley. Nor did the federal government give Young the green light or the money to extinguish the Utes once and for all. Still, by the beginning of 1854, Young had gotten what he wanted: the Utes forced to rely on him, not Wakara. Manti settler Albert Smith described how two Ute men approached the fort, declaring that they were "very ticubu [hungry]" and wanted to be friends. The settlers told the two ambassadors to fetch the rest of their people hiding among the ceders above Manti, promising that they would feed and protect them. An untold number of Utes came to the fort, where they feasted on bread and meat and smoked a peace pipe. According to Smith, "That ended the Indian war." Young also believed that the war was ending, due in part to starvation and cold and in part to the growing rifts among the Utes, with their ranks blocked from reuniting by winter snows.[42]

BUT THE WAR WASN'T OVER. OR NOT OFFICIALLY. In the first months of 1854, Wakara and his lodges moved north, setting up camp on the Sevier River. Once again, it was Wakara who sought to make peace and to set the record straight. In March, as the ice cracked on the Sevier Valley creeks, a delegation of Wakara's Utes invited Isaac Morley to come to camp and have a talk. Morley did not go. In his place, he sent James T. Allred, a Ute-speaking veteran of the Mormon Battalion whose family had founded another Sanpete Valley settlement. Allred also brought with him a letter from Morley, which Allred read and translated to Wakara. Wakara was pleased with what he heard, explaining that "Father Morley was a good man and he had always treated him well." Wakara then took the letter and pressed it against his chest. Wakara further explained that Allred's coming was the "fulfillment of a dream which he had some time ago." After praying for several minutes, Wakara bade Allred to sit with him on the spring's dewy grass to listen to (and write down) Wakara's version of Brigham's War against the Utes.[43]

Wakara explained that when the Mormons first came to Utah, they massacred the Timpanogos, including "some of his friends." Those killings "did not make him mad, but some of his men became very mad and wanted to fight." Still, Wakara convinced the Utes to remain friendly toward the Mormons. Despite his efforts toward peace, the Mormons had started the war the previous July, when James Ivie killed his cousin Shower-o-cats following the "affray" over the fish and flour. Wakara said that Shower-o-cats's death "made him a little mad." Wakara admitted to killing a settler at Payson and stealing some property. But that was enough to avenge Shower-o-cats's murder. Still, Wakara explained to Allred, two things bothered him. First was that the Mormons accused him of being "a liar" by breaking promises of peace. Wakara insisted that such accusations were false. He explained that while he could not stop his men from stealing the settlers' cattle, horses, and grains, he had convinced them not to target settlers' lives. Second, and more important, Wakara was upset that the Mormons had "taken his land and fishing places." Wakara told Allred that he wanted compensation for this unjust land seizure in the form of guns, ammunition, and blankets. And he wanted to restart their trade in horses.[44]

A few days later, Brigham Young wrote back to Wakara and dispatched Huntington and Indian agent Edward Bedell, who had replaced Jacob Holeman, to bring the letter to the Ute leader.

The peace emissaries met Wakara and seventy-five of his warriors near Fillmore on the last day of March. Bedell and Huntington sat with Wakara outside in a round in the warming spring air, with local Mormon leaders and eighty Utes in attendance. Huntington read the letter's contents, in which, notably, the Mormon prophet returned to addressing Wakara with the honorific of "Captain" not "Indian," as Young had done in his anti-Wakara public statements during the war.

Young wanted Wakara to know that he'd "never been mad" with him nor called him "a liar," Huntington declared aloud, switching between Ute and English for the mix of settlers and Natives in attendance. (That Young had never called Wakara a liar, of course, was a lie. Since their first encounter, Young had frequently accused Wakara of deceit.) Still, Huntington explained that Young accepted Wakara's version of events—that despite his best efforts, Wakara could not always constrain his men from carrying out depredations. Huntington then explained that like the Ute leader, Young too had dreamed about a reconciliation between himself and Wakara in which they again became "brothers" and "good friends." To make that dream a reality, through Huntington Young requested Wakara's presence for the church-wide General Conference in April in Salt Lake. He even invited Wakara to address the Mormons from the dais of the Tabernacle in Temple Square, where Huntington would interpret what Wakara said. Young also encouraged Wakara to stop his wanderings and become a farmer and rancher. The future was bleak for the Native way of life in Settler America. "Have you never heard how the Indians have always been used up when they warred with the whites?"[45]

After Huntington finished reading and translating, Wakara stood up. Once again, he told the Indian interpreter emphatically that he had not started the war and had done everything he could to prevent it. Then, Indian agent Bedell stood up and declared that, while that might be true, it was also too late. A report had been sent to

Washington, which, based on Brigham Young's account, blamed Wakara for the Gunnison massacre. "The people and also the Great Father were justly indignant that such a terrible cold-blooded murder should be committed upon men in the service of the United States," the Indian agent said. And the Great Father would want his own revenge. Bedell and Huntington again pressed Wakara to sell "his land to the general government" to make way for more settlers and the railroad. And again, Wakara demurred. He preferred not to sell as long as he could live in peace with the Whites, "which he was anxious to do."[46]

Wakara did not make it to Salt Lake that April. Instead, at the General Conference, Young spoke on Wakara's behalf to the faithful gathered at the Tabernacle. Young changed his tune about Wakara and the Walker War. "I tell this congregation and the world that 'Indian Walker,' as he is called, has not been at the foundation of the difficulties we have had." Wakara was not completely innocent. He had grown angry and threatened to tear down the settlements, Young explained. But he was not in favor of killing the Whites. Instead, Young laid blame for the war at the feet of a few bad Indians and settlers. Some Indians thirsted for the blood of the Indian children they enslaved as well as the settlers they targeted. Some settlers acted just as badly as their racial inferiors, gambling, racing horses, and trading Indian children with them. Still, Young believed that the Mormons had the Utes where they wanted them, weakened and dependent on the settlers. "They came pretty nigh starving to death last winter; and they now see, if they are driven from these valleys in winter, they must perish; therefore they now want to make good peace."[47]

After the General Conference, Young sent south a group of Mormon missionaries, including the one-armed, Numic-speaking George Bean, to restart outreach to the Paiutes and Utes. In early May, Bean met Wakara at Corn Creek, near Fillmore, where again he urged Wakara to go north and speak with Young about peace. No, Wakara told Bean. He was busy sowing wheat on his twenty-acre farm next to Kanosh's land, which had been set aside for him earlier in the year. Instead, Wakara expected Young to travel to him and bring presents of oxen, flour, guns, and whiskey. Wakara also laid out demands for a permanent peace, including resumption of trade in Indian slaves. In anticipation of this, Wakara had sent his brother Ammon to procure a new crop of Paiute children to sell to the Mormons or to the New Mexicans. But Wakara recognized that his land was still his most valuable commodity. When Bean asked again about selling the land outright, Wakara refused. Instead, Wakara proposed a twenty-year lease, which he expected to be paid in cash, cows, and horses.[48]

Young obliged Wakara's demand to come to him. "If the mountain will not come to Mahomet, Mahomet must go to the mountain," Young reportedly quipped. In early May, Young left Salt Lake City to meet Wakara for their peace parley at Wakara's camp at Chicken Creek, about fourteen miles south of Nephi. Accompanying Young, along with nearly 100 wagons weighed down with blankets, clothing, and guns, were fifty mounted militiamen, a cadre of church brethren, and the daguerreotypist and portrait artist for John C. Frémont's last Rocky Mountain expedition, Solomon Nunes Carvalho. Young had invited Carvalho to participate in the peace brigade and, if the occasion presented itself, to paint portraits of Wakara and other leading Utes.[49]

For Carvalho, a Sephardic Jew from South Carolina, the journey to Utah's southern settlements was a return of sorts. The winter before, he had almost died of exposure and starvation when members of Frémont's party were caught in snowstorms crossing Utah's mountains. After fording the Green River in south-central Utah—following Wakara's Old Spanish Trail and guided part way by Ammon—the men, reduced to walking skeletons, shuffled into Parowan. At first, Parowan residents mistook Carvalho for an Indian, with his long hair, unwashed face, torn clothes, and emaciated frame. While

Frémont and most of his men recovered and pressed on to California, Carvalho remained too weak to continue and was transferred to Salt Lake. There he recovered and befriended Brigham Young, of whose famed Beehive House, where Sally toiled in the kitchen, he made a daguerreotype.[50]

On May 9, Young and the cavalcade reached Nephi. Just a few hundred yards away from where massacred Goshutes or Utes were buried in an unmarked grave, the prophet detailed the expenses that the Mormons had incurred to fight the "Walker War," the cost of which Young estimated to be close to $500,000. Still, Young believed that the blood spilled and treasure spent would eventually pay off. Young declared that Utah would soon gain its autonomy as a state, freed from federal government overlords. And the few Indians who survived would "be a white & delightsome people." Young mentioned one such Lamanite, a "good squaw in my house," almost certainly a reference to Sally.[51]

The next day, the cavalcade reached Wakara's camp, which was guarded by dozens of mounted warriors. Carvalho followed Young and the rest of the brethren into Wakara's lodge, where they found fifteen Ute leaders, including Ammon, Washear (Squash Head), Peteetneet, Arapeen, Sanpitch, Tabby, and Kanosh. Seated in the center on a buffalo skin and wrapped in his signature blanket, Wakara did not rise. The Ute leader was in a sour mood. Still, he offered Young his hand and motioned for him to take a seat next to him.

With Dimick Huntington again serving as interpreter, the Mormon prophet explained that he hoped "the calumet of peace would be smoked, and no more cause given on either side for a continuation of ill-feeling," recalled Carvalho. But ill feelings did remain. One Ute leader rose, declaring he would never lay down his rifle and tomahawk against the "Americats" and "Mormons" who had broken their promises, time and time again, to be friends. Another leader rose. Through tears, he explained that settlers had murdered his son and

"Portrait of Wakara; Later Chief of the Utah Indians, 1854." Painting by Solomon Nunes Carvalho. (Courtesy of the Gilcrease Museum, Tulsa, Oklahoma)

wife. Still others rose to call for peace. Wakara remained quiet. He told Young that he needed to convene with the Great Spirit before he was ready to negotiate. The first meeting ended after the pipe was passed. Wakara retired to his bed. Young ordered flour delivered to Wakara's tent.[52]

At 4 p.m. Wakara awoke in an improved mood. He told the Mormons that they could build settlements on his lands. In exchange, Wakara again asked for "a Mormon wife." That night, Young ordered an ox slaughtered, and the whole camp dined on fresh beef. After they ate, Carvalho finished sketches of Wakara and Kanosh that he had begun during the council earlier that day.

With the sun setting behind the Wasatch Mountains, Carvalho had to rely on firelight, which danced across the leaders' faces, to capture details with his brush.[53]

The next day, the council gathered again in Wakara's lodge. Before peace was established, Wakara had grievances of his own to share. Wakara was angry that he had been blamed for the war. And he was particularly upset that he had been accused of killing Gunnison, given that he was hundreds of miles away when the American captain was slain. Still, Wakara revealed what he heard from the "Great Spirit; Great Spirit say—'Make peace.'" Young was relieved to hear this, telling Wakara and the other Utes that he loved them like a father. And like a father he would give them food and clothing. But Young's love was conditional. The Utes had to stop killing settlers. Wakara agreed and promised, "If Indian kill white man again, Wakara make Indian howl."[54]

Before the peace pipe was passed again, Young handed Wakara another gift. As Wakara had requested, Young had composed a new letter of recommendation allowing Wakara to pass unmolested through the Mormon settlements where he'd offer his skins and horses for trade. When Young stepped out of Wakara's tent into the May sunshine, Wakara stepped out with him. "We now understand each other," Wakara told the Mormon leader. From now on, the settlers could sow their wheat and corn without fear of anyone coming to kill them, and both Wakara's people and the Mormons could travel the road "clear without any blood on it." Save, perhaps, for the blood of Indian slaves. Before the Mormon company broke camp, Young purchased two toddlers from Wakara. The children were so thin, recalled Carvalho, that they were nothing more than "living skeletons" reduced to digging in the dirt for grassnuts.[55]

Wakara joined Young and the Mormon cavalcade on their southern tour. He and thirty mounted warriors served as bodyguards against any potential Indian attacks. Still, when they reached

Parowan, Young again told Wakara, "[The] war is over." The reason, Young implied, had less to do with Mormon violence and more to do with Mormon cultivation. Within four years of its founding, Parowan had become a model settler community of 100 houses laid out in the Mormon plat, with an elaborate irrigation system to water flower and vegetable gardens, and with a 400-acre field just outside town where the settlers grew corn and wheat. "Wakara had long considered himself President Young's equal," wrote Parowan's clerk, James H. Martineau, about the visit. In broken English and sign language, Wakara would hold "up his forefinger and say 'Brigham: Great Chief!' Then placing his other forefinger beside the first [he] would say, 'Me Walker! Me big chief all same as Brigham!'" But from the Mormons' perspective, their claim that they had done more in four years to cultivate southern Utah than Wakara's Utes had done in a thousand showed Young's superiority. The Saints knew how to better use both Utah's land and its people. Many of the tidy homes in Parowan were ornamented not only with bright flower gardens but also with "one or more Pah-Utah children," observed the western explorer Gwinn Harris Heap.[56]

Though he told Wakara that he hoped to make no more war, Young told his followers to act as if war would last forever. At Parowan, Young praised the settlers for how they had handled the "Lamanites" during the "Walker War." Still, Young urged Parowan's men to construct a twelve-foot-tall earthen wall around the fort, post nightly guards, and train watchdogs, lest "1000 Indians could get in and the first you would know they would be at your doors."[57]

In early June, settlers began raising walls around their towns. But according to Wakara, walls and fences did not, in fact, make good neighbors. The Ute leader rushed to Nephi, where he told George Bean that the fortifications must be taken down. Wakara refused to stand outside, like "a dog or a slave," begging for something to eat.[58]

This confrontation over the wall at Nephi caused another set of "rumors & reports" that Wakara was preparing for war. Yet, unlike those of the previous summer, these rumors were true. In June at Wakara's camp near Nephi, George Bean, along with the infamous Mormon bodyguard Porter Rockwell, delivered another letter from Young to Wakara, which Bean read and interpreted. Young chastised Wakara for threatening the settlers over their plans to wall up their cities. Such fortifications, Young wrote, were good for Wakara too, as he could seek refuge within them when his enemies attacked. Young also reminded Wakara that he was now reliant on the Mormons for food. "The game in the mountains is scarce, you told me so. There is not a hundredth part as much as there was a few years ago, when you were young."

Wakara was disgusted by the implication that he was now Young's vassal, requiring his protection and food. He told Bean that he had fought many enemies before the Mormons arrived and that he would not hide behind walls like a coward. Wakara snatched Young's letter from Bean's hand, ripped it up, and trampled on it, then ordered fifty men to surround Bean and Rockwell. Ute warriors, including Baptiste and Tintic, taunted the two Mormons. Wakara's kin recounted their bloody deeds from the summer before and snapped their bowstrings, which made a "not very pleasant music to us," Bean recalled. Bean picked up Young's letter and told the Ute leader that he would let the prophet know how Wakara received his counsel. Bean's old friend Washear (Squash Head) pleaded with Wakara and Bean to cool down. Bean and Rockwell slipped away and drove back to Nephi.[59]

That afternoon, Wakara sought out Bean to tell him that his anger had passed. He even invited Bean to join the Utes in Sanpete County for a trading season. Bean agreed. Bean and his party spent five days with Wakara's Utes at Fort Ephraim, exchanging Mormon guns for Wakara's captives. To justify participation in the slave trade, Bean offered the familiar refrain: "[We] were obliged to take eight little Indians (Slaves), rather than have them butchered by the cruel Utes." Still, Wakara and other Ute leaders expressed frustration that the Mormons stopped them from trading in New Mexico. Wakara demanded payment—this time in gold—for the use of his lands. And he once again demanded a Mormon "squaw," like the women his Native trading partners gave him.[60]

From the Mormons' point of view, this episode of Wakara ripping up and trampling on Young's letter, threatening war, and demanding tribute in gold and Mormon women signaled that they would need to deal with Wakara once and for all. One settler who witnessed Young's confrontation with Bean over the fortifications wrote in his journal in June 1854, "Brother Walker's end is fast approaching."[61]

Wakara and his Utes might have been the ones making threats, but other tribes did the killing. On August 8 at Pole Canyon west of Utah Lake, to avenge the massacre of their own at Nephi in October 1853, Goshutes killed the teenage sons of the bishop of Cedar Fort, Allen Weeks. George Bean, who was then serving as the Utah territory's deputy marshal, oversaw the hangings of two men, Longhair and Antelope, who were convicted of the killings. Bean recalled that fulfilling this duty was difficult but necessary, as "the Indians had to get the idea of right and wrong established in their minds." In September, Shoshones took revenge for Wakara's massacre in Wyoming four years earlier, killing a handful of Utes camped in Provo. After failing to track down the Shoshone assailants, Ute warriors, including Black Hawk (Antonga), demanded that the Mormons turn over a Shoshone woman whom they were harboring at Fort Utah. When the Mormons refused, the Utes threatened to lay siege to the fort and declared that Wakara would soon arrive with reinforcements.[62]

Wakara did make plans to go north, but not to make war. In October, Wakara sent a runner to Young asking for help to secure peace with the Shoshones and requesting more cattle and whiskey. Wakara also wanted to know what Young's current feelings were toward him, hoping that a peace might endure among the Mormons, Americans, and Natives.[63]

But a multiparty peace parley would have to wait for the next spring. The cold began to set in. Wakara and his main lodges went south to Parowan. On November 8, Wakara arrived in town with fifty men and women, 120 horses, and a few dozen oxen, cows, sheep, and goats. The settlers took note of the size of the train and of Wakara's friendly disposition. He would not make trouble for them, Parowan leader John Steele wrote to George A. Smith. But he would likely raid and trade for Paiutes.[64]

Just before Wakara's arrival in October, Steele met with a Paiute "captain," to whom he gave a suit of clothes and words of advice: Stop trading away women and children to slavers like Wakara, "or pretty soon . . . there would be no Piedes." Steele didn't oppose Paiutes trading their young ones to the Mormons. In fact, Steele brought a group of Mormon-purchased Paiute children with him to his meeting with the Paiute captain, including a young girl who belonged to George A. Smith. The captain recognized the girl as his niece. Her father had been "a great captain" himself but perished from a cause his brother did not specify. Perhaps he died of measles brought west by the Mormons and forty-niners or due to bad water or lack of grains and game, which the settlers and Wakara had destroyed in the previous decades. Perhaps he died doing battle with Wakara. Steele recalled that the old captain was "pleased" to see his niece. But how pleased he was to see one of his kin being raised in a settler household, we will never know.[65]

The next month, the Mormons continued buying Paiute children. At John D. Lee's Fort Harmony mission, Jacob Hamblin exchanged a gun, a blanket, and some ammunition for a six-year-old boy and sent him to Parowan to see if the Mormons "might make him useful." Hamblin and a group of missionaries then traveled to the Santa Clara River on Wakara's Old Spanish Trail. Their arrival was met with alarm. The Paiutes thought that Hamblin was Wakara coming to raid. The Paiutes were relieved when Hamblin explained that he had come to protect them from Wakara. Over the next weeks, Hamblin erected a cabin out of the area's plentiful cottonwood timber. Hamblin also received a visit from Wakara's brother Sanpitch, who, as the Paiutes expected, led an expedition to buy Paiute children. Sanpitch was not happy to see Hamblin building permanent structures in Wakara's slaving fields. But Sanpitch was appeased when, a few days later, Hamblin facilitated the purchase of three girls, no older than ten or eleven, in exchange for a few guns and some beads. "The girls' father and mother cried to see them go," Hamblin wrote in his journal, "but they had nothing to eat and it would be better for the children [to go] than to stay and starve." The Leaders of Zion needed to do more, Hamblin concluded, "to ameliorate the condition of this miserable people" and protect them from slavers like Wakara.[66]

SOON MORE WOULD BE DONE. IN LATE NOVEMBER, Wakara set up his winter camp near Parowan. Just as he had at the start of the "Walker War," Young sent Wakara two plugs of tobacco. In a letter that accompanied the gift, Young also bid Wakara early holiday greetings and wished that Wakara "may be enabled to live comfortably thro' the winter." Young also pledged, "You will hear from me before next Spring."[67]

That winter, David Lewis served as Young's envoy to Wakara. Lewis frequently rode the seven miles southwest of Parowan to Wakara's camp. During these meetings, Wakara explained that he was worried that the brethren at Parowan were again spreading rumors that he was preparing for war. Wakara implored Lewis to tell Young that he meant to keep the peace, so that "all might lay down and sleep good, and none need to stand guard or be afraid."[68]

During his visits with Lewis, Wakara also made plans for the spring. He asked Lewis if he would accompany him on a trading expedition to the Navajos. He also asked that Jacob Hamblin bring his brother Sanpitch with him when he visited the Paiutes so that Sanpitch could procure more captives. It was at one these meetings that Wakara gave Lewis the "papoose," which Wakara instructed Lewis to bring to Young, in hopes that the gift would be reciprocated with a good gun, a coat, a vest, and a white blanket.[69]

Wakara told Lewis that he expected to travel north in the new year. And he put in another order to Young. Wakara wanted ten good rifles, along with powder, lead, and caps, and enough cattle to last him until he went to the Navajos. He also wanted Young to send a "large American colt," which he'd use as a stud for his mares. All these things, Wakara told Lewis, should be sent to his farm at Corn Creek just south of Fillmore.[70]

As planned, in late January 1855, Wakara traveled north. And as planned, on January 28 he met Lewis on the road south of Fillmore, where Lewis delivered to him another letter of greeting from Brigham Young.

Wakara died the next day.

Part VI

Wakara's Skull

CHAPTER 17

"The Graves of Their Fathers"

IN EARLY FEBRUARY 1855, Arapeen and eight other Utes mounted their horses at Wakara's camp near Corn Creek for a four-day ride to Sanpete Valley. The weather was warm and clear, unlike the previous week, when two feet of snow blanketed central Utah's mountains and valleys. The melting snowpack muddied the road, leaving the riders and horses caked in dirt and sweat when they trotted into Manti.

John Lowry Jr. jogged out to greet Arapeen. The two men had known each other since 1850, when Lowry was part of Parley P. Pratt's first southern expedition—an expedition that Arapeen and Wakara briefly joined. In Ute, Arapeen explained to Lowry, a skilled Indian translator, that he had a message from Wakara. The twenty-six-year-old Lowry was surprised at this news. A few days before, Ute runners dispatched from Corn Creek had told the Manti settlers that Wakara had died suddenly at the end of January. The runners also reported that Arapeen's first duty as Wakara's successor was to oversee his brother's burial, which included the throat slitting of two Paiute children and two of Wakara's "squaws," whose bodies were laid next to Wakara's in his massive stone crypt.

Arapeen dismounted, wiping mud from his face. Lowry and other settlers gathered around him. Arapeen explained that Wakara had appeared to him in a vision and told his brother to go to Manti, deliver to its leaders a message, and have that message written down on paper so "that the Mormons might all hear it."[1]

In this vision, which Arapeen narrated while Lowry translated, Wakara told Arapeen not to blame the Mormons for his passing. He had "died a natural death." Wakara also told Arapeen to continue his brother's work of creating a lasting peace between the Mormons and the Utes, based on sharing the land and its bounties. This message of peace came not just from Wakara but also from God, Arapeen explained. The Lord told Wakara that "the land, the timber, and water, and horses, cattle &c was the Lord's and did not belong to the Indians nor the Mormons." And it was now up to Arapeen to prevent Utes from stealing the Mormons' property. If they did, Arapeen was "to put a ball & chain on them and . . . to whip them." But the Lord also forbade spilling "blood on the land."[2]

The Lord also had demands for the Mormons. It was good for the Mormons not to trade guns to the Utes, for some were "bad." But it was also good to help the Utes "raise wheat and to travel the road in small companies in peace." Heed my words to work with the Utes, the Lord told the Mormons through Wakara (and Arapeen). For "if the Mormons throwed away the Lords words," then the Lord would remove his blessing from the Saints. On the other hand, if the Mormons and the Utes remained "at peace he would come and live on the earth and not go back." This part of the vision had come to Wakara, Arapeen explained, in the form of "three personages [whose] garments were as white as snow and as brilliant as the sun." After all, just like Brigham Young, in life and even after death Wakara was a prophet to whom the Father, Son, and Holy Spirit spoke.[3]

John Lowry might have been a seasoned translator of Ute. But his "transcription" of Arapeen's vision of Wakara sounds more

Mormon than Ute—more like what the Mormons hoped Arapeen (and Wakara and the Lord) would say, not what they might have actually said. Arapeen's plea for peace and insistence not to "throw away" the Utes fit with (the living) Wakara's final message and actions. But also present in the transcription are specific Mormon theologies of the godhead ("three personages" cloaked in white garments), blood atonement ("spill[ing of] blood on the land"), and prophecies ("this is the lord's talk not mine"). Also present are out-of-place calls not to arm the Utes, when both Wakara and Arapeen had insisted that they be permitted to trade for guns to defend themselves and to raid Paiutes.[4]

Finally, the insistence in Arapeen's vision that Wakara died of natural causes is, to borrow from Shakespeare, a protest too much—indicating that the rumors of poisoning were prevalent enough that the Mormons felt compelled to dispel them. On this vital point, Lowry's transcription of Arapeen's vision contradicts other written reports of Arapeen's disposition toward the Mormons in early February 1855. Other settlers who encountered him in the days after Wakara's death recalled that, instead of bringing a message of peace to Manti, as Lowry's transcription maintained, Arapeen blamed the Mormons for Wakara's death and declared that the settlers would not sleep peacefully until a Mormon "captain" of similar stature was sacrificed to atone for Wakara's killing.[5]

After hearing that Wakara's brother demanded restitution in blood, Young dashed off a letter to Arapeen professing his own grief at the passing of "Captain Walker," his friend and longtime trading partner. But Young told Arapeen that he was wrong to blame the Mormons for Wakara's death and thus wrong to expect the Mormons to pay restitution for the Utes' loss. "Nobody killed Walker," Young wrote to Arapeen. "He took sick and died, just as people frequently do." Or Wakara died as punishment for the Utes' depredations during the previous season of bloodshed. Or Wakara died to atone for the killing of "Gunnison and his party . . . for you know that no person was ever taken and killed on account of that atrocious deed."[6]

Whatever the cause of death, Young insisted, he had nothing to do with it. This, even though Young joked about placing a bounty on Wakara's head. This, even though Young himself hinted that the tobacco he sent Wakara after the outbreak of Ute-Mormon hostilities in July 1853 might be poisoned. And this, even though years later a Mormon missionary turned dissident also hinted that Young had poisoned Wakara, as "he died very suddenly by devouring, as is supposed, an innocent bowl of bread and milk." Fairly or not, Brigham Young and the Mormons would frequently be accused of poisoning Native and settler adversaries for the next several decades.[7]

Soon after Wakara's death, other Utes voiced skepticism about the accuracy of the Mormons' written archives of what the Utes had said, as well as the Mormons' dedication to the faithful narration of the history between the Utes and the Mormons. In the summer of 1855, during another meeting at the bowery in Provo, Ute leaders complained about the expanding farms and ranches around Timpanogos (Utah) Lake, which prevented them from accessing their fish festival grounds and waters. Highforehead (Tow-om-bu-gah) accused the Mormons of exaggerating the damage to life and property the Utes had caused the previous year. He also accused them of twisting what the Utes said to settlers into written records to serve the settlers' purposes. They "pretend to understand . . . [our] language when they understand but a few words," Highforehead declared, "and owing to this many of them are apt to convey a wrong idea respecting the Indians, and they may influence the [White] people against" the Utes.[8]

Though he was illiterate, Wakara too understood that in the settler world, words written on the page carried more weight than words spoken in the air. At the peace parley in May 1854, Wakara asked for and received another letter of recommendation from Young, which Wakara showed settlers to let them know that he and the Mormons

"Walker's Writing," 1851. (Courtesy of the Church Archives, the Church of Jesus Christ of Latter-day Saints)

were at peace. And Wakara took to his grave the final letter that Young wrote to him, which David Lewis delivered the day before his death. Years before, in 1851, wanting to get around unreliable translators and scribes, Wakara also tried his own hand at writing a letter to Young. On the thick, yellow-tinted paper that the Mormons in Utah preferred because of its durability, Wakara wrote a set of looping lines, some of which resemble *W*'s. The paper was then folded into eighths, so that it became its own envelope. Wakara then wrote another set of lines, some of which resemble *Y*'s, where the address was typically written.[9]

Though it's illegible, the letter says a great deal. Perhaps it represents Wakara's attempt to narrate his understanding of Ute-Mormon relations since the settlers' arrival in 1847. "When they first commenced the settlement of Salt Lake Valley," Wakara told the New Mexican trader M. S. Martenas just before the outbreak of the "Walker War," the Mormons had been kind and promised "many comforts, and lasting friendship." But once the Mormons' numbers grew, they began to drive the Utes "from place to place. Settlements have been made on all their hunting grounds in the valleys, and the graves of their fathers have been torn up by the whites."[10]

AFTER WAKARA'S DEATH, THE MORMONS CONTINUED TO TEAR up the graves of the Utes' fathers and mothers and to remake Utah in the form of their Old and New England agrarian homelands. Especially around the Utes' fishing grounds at Timpanogos (Utah) Lake, the Mormons "improved and fenced in" the land, turning the Utes' grasslands and fish festival grounds into fields for row crops and hay to feed their beef, explained Indian agent George W. Armstrong in his report in the summer of 1855. Beyond the Utah Valley, from the Wasatch Front to Parowan, the Mormons also tried to "improve" Utah Natives, molding them into images of themselves as farmers and ranchers. Soon after Wakara's death, Brigham Young convinced the federal government to help him establish "Indian farms" that served as proto-reservations where, under the tutelage of the Saints, Utes received training in the art of cultivation. Among the largest was the Spanish Fork Indian Farm near Wakara's birthplace, a twenty-square-mile reserve south of Provo that Brigham Young created for the Utes displaced around Utah Lake.[11]

But improvements were in the eye of the beholder, Highforehead told Young at the July 1855 meeting in Provo. While the Mormons claimed that they were making the desert bloom like a rose, Highforehead claimed that it was the Mormons who had made Utah Valley a desert. Their irrigation ditches dirtied the water and dried up the ground, making it so "hard" that they could not eat the plants and animals that once flourished in the valley. At that meeting, when the Mormons again asked the surviving Ute leadership to sell their land and move onto the Indian farms, Highforehead rejected that idea as an impossibility. The Utes could not simply move to other lands. "We love the land where our fathers and mothers have died, and we cannot bear the thought of selling it."[12]

More Ute fathers, mothers, and children died on Ute homelands in the years that followed. Over the winter of 1855–1856, starving Utes killed and ate Mormon cattle that had been grazing on the Utes' traditional hunting grounds around Utah Lake. In February 1856, after a peace parley over the stolen beef turned violent, settlers reportedly shot Wakara's brother Baptiste, resulting in a wound that eventually killed him. A week later, George Bean's longtime friend Washear (Squash Head) was arrested on suspicion of murder and stealing cattle and horses. Imprisoned in a Springville jail cell, Washear died after his throat was cut from ear to ear (the Mormons claimed that he committed suicide to avoid the hangman's noose). In spring 1856, a "war" named for Wakara's close kin Tintic, which began when Tintic stole some cattle, sheep, and horses from Utah Valley settlements, led to the deaths of more of Wakara's kin, along with two settlers. When Tintic died in March 1859, his band held the largest funeral since Wakara's, including the sacrifice of eight horses.[13]

Other kin died as the Utes' various "earths" became increasingly inhospitable to Ute life. To build more homes and fences, more timber was felled in Upper Earth mountain canyons, polluting downstream rivers and damaging fisheries in Lower Earth. The Mormons also introduced invasive plants to Middle Earth pastures, pushing out native grasses that fed the game that the Utes hunted when they weren't fishing. To the annoyance of the Mormons and federal Indian agents, the Utes did not embrace the Indian farms. Some lent a hand from time to time, but for the most part, they viewed the fruits that the farms produced as supplemental to their seasonal hunting, fishing, and foraging, the harvests of which grew smaller and smaller each season.

As a result, the Utes grew hungrier. Reports circulated that, in order to feed their families, some women and girls were forced to trade sex to settlers and soldiers for food rations and cash. That trade, along with already rampant smallpox, measles, and tuberculosis, led to outbreaks of venereal diseases, which rendered many Ute men and women infertile. In 1858, Wakara's brother and fellow slave trader Peteetneet killed six women at Spanish Fork because he believed they carried syphilis. In January 1860, five years after Wakara died, a settler in Sanpete Valley reported that Wakara's successor, Arapeen, was also sick and not expected to recover. "The aborigines in this part of the Territory seem to be wasting away very fast," the settler wrote, "and the band, which under Walker, their former chief, was the terror of the surrounding tribes and Lower California and New Mexico, has dwindled down to a mere handful of warriors." Arapeen died that December at the Utes' winter camp near Fish Lake and was buried with four slain horses and five head of cattle. Peteetneet died a year later in Cedar Valley near the Utes' old slaving grounds along the Old Spanish Trail. According to news reports, following Peteetneet's own wishes that no horses be sacrificed, his wife was bludgeoned to death with an ax as part of his funeral.[14]

The next year, Young sent an expedition to the Uintah Basin in eastern Utah to scout for settlement expansion. Instead of the rumored rich meadows and grasslands, in the basin the party found "one vast contiguity of waste," Young's scouts reported back, "measurably valueless, excepting for nomadic purposes, hunting grounds for Indians." In other words, a perfect place to relocate the dwindling Utes from their homelands in central Utah. The Mormons petitioned the federal government to establish a reservation in the Uintah Basin, which President Abraham Lincoln did by executive order in 1861. In 1865 Congress passed a law formalizing the reservation with the explicit purpose of "extinguish[ing] the Indian title to the lands of Utah suitable for agriculture and mineral purposes."[15]

IN JUNE 1865, WAKARA'S THEN-AGED KIN SOWIETTE, TABIONA (Tabby), Sanpitch, and Kanosh, along with several hundred of their followers, gathered at the Spanish Fork Indian Farm. Unlike the pan-tribal

Nuche fish festivals, which had taken place for the previous 500 years on the lush fields around Timpanogos (Utah) Lake, this gathering was far from festive. The Utes were once again starving and sick, and their leaders were filled with fear and anger.

During the previous winter, measles and smallpox had again killed untold numbers of Utes. A lodge in the Sanpete Valley, which was particularly hard hit, accused nearby Mormon settlers of deploying poison and witchcraft against them. In early April, Arapeen's son, Jake Arapeen, and Wakara's kin Antonga (Black Hawk) came to Manti demanding restitution. When the settlers refused, Jake Arapeen allegedly drew his bow and arrow. John Lowry Jr., then serving as an interpreter for the US government, responded by grabbing Jake Arapeen by the hair and beating him. Soon after, to avenge the personal afront and to retaliate against decades of Mormon incursion into their lands and genocide against their people, Jake Arapeen and Antonga called on the Utes to rise up against the settlers.[16]

In an attempt to nip the growing Ute uprising in the bud, newly appointed Superintendent of Indian Affairs for the Utah Territory Orsamus H. Irish summoned Ute leaders to meet him in Spanish Fork. Irish's task was to carry out the wishes of Congress, which had called for a permanent solution to the "Indian problem" in Utah. Washington also hoped that removing the Utes would be a step toward solving the "Mormon problem"—the political and cultural stranglehold the Latter-day Saints had over the Great Basin. Non-Mormon politicians feared that the Mormons and the Natives might become allies in a conflict with the federal government, which hoped to displace both Natives and Mormons from the region with the expected flood of non-Mormons into the West that would follow the completion of the transcontinental railroad. During the summer of 1857, after President James Buchanan accused Brigham Young of interfering with the federal government's jurisdiction over the Utah Territory, including over Indian policy, the Mormons prepared to go to war with the United States. They stockpiled grain and cattle and made plans to torch their settlements and hide in the mountains if the US Army marched on Utah. The Mormons even spread rumors that the Americans might try to kill off Utah Natives by poisoning their water supplies. At Mountain Meadows in southwestern Utah on September 11, 1857, Mormon militiamen from local settlements, including Major John D. Lee, and aided by a number of Paiutes, massacred some 100 members of an emigrant wagon train bound for California. The victims' bodies were buried in shallow graves. Seventeen children, "too young to tell tales," as Nauvoo Legion major and massacre leader John H. Higbee infamously declared, were spared. They, along with their murdered parents' worldly possessions, were distributed to local Mormon families.[17]

Still, in June 1865, Indian agent Irish believed it wise to include the Mormons in the negotiations with the Utes. The US government and the Mormons shared the short-term goal of forcing Natives onto reservations. As such, to the treaty negotiations, Irish invited Brigham Young, Indian interpreters George Bean and Dimick Huntington, and a cadre of church leaders who had for decades traded with Sowiette, Kanosh, and Tabby.[18]

Young and Irish arrived at Spanish Fork with armed escorts, which alarmed the Utes. Young and Irish assured them that military forces would not attend the council and did not intend to attack. Still, the show of force made manifest the alternative approach the settlers could take if the Utes resisted what Irish and Young saw as the inevitable removal of the Utes from their homelands.[19]

Once gathered, the starving Utes were fed bread, but no beef, which they desperately wanted. After they ate under the thatched-roof bowery, the Ute leaders sat on the ground in a circle and listened to Irish and Young. Their message was that the only way to end the unacceptable settler-Native conflicts was to separate settlers and Natives once and for all. And such conflicts were again on the rise. In central Utah, Utes had attacked stagecoaches and mail lines, killing emigrants and Mormon settlers. To the north, in southern Idaho's Cache Valley, on January 29, 1863, eight years to the day after Wakara's death, at the behest of Mormon settlers in the region, US Army troops slaughtered a group of Shoshones camped in a bend on the Bear River (*Boa Ogoi*, or "Big River," in Shoshone). The massacre left some 350 Shoshone men, women, and children dead, perhaps the largest massacre of Native Americans in US history. Just before the June 1865 council got underway, Antonga had attacked more settlements in southern Utah, lending more urgency to reaching an agreement.[20]

Through the Mormon translators, Irish read the text of the treaty. In sum, the US government required the Utes to cede their land claims in the Utah and Sanpete Valleys and to relocate to the Uintah Valley Reservation. In exchange, the government promised to give them annual annuities of cash, totaling about 62.5 cents per acre for the land they would cede, as well as clothing, cooking goods, and materials to build and furnish homes, schools, and farms. After translating the treaty's contents, Dimick Huntington offered what amounted to a basic lesson in the tenets of Manifest Destiny. "The Great Spirit in Heaven, who controls you and me and the Great Father in Washington, . . . has put it into the hearts of white men to come here and open farms and build houses." The Great Spirit and the American government "extend the same privilege to you," the Ute leaders. Just not here, Huntington implied, on the rich lands of the Utes' forefathers, but in the Uintahs, an area that the Mormons declared a wasteland fit only for nomadic Indians.[21]

No, the Ute leaders said, we do not want to leave. This is a bad deal, Kanosh explained. Whatever the government offers—money, clothing, even cash—will soon be used up while the Utes' land would last forever. Let us stay on the lands of our forefathers, Kanosh pleaded. After all, Kanosh's people at Corn Creek had proven they could live in peace with their White neighbors at Fillmore.[22]

Ute Leaders. Carte de visite, Savage & Ottinger (1865). Seated from left to right: Tabby (Tabiona), Sowiette, Kanosh, and Sanpitch. (Courtesy of the Church Archives, the Church of Jesus Christ of Latter-day Saints)

Through Huntington's translations, Young begged the Ute leaders to understand. It was no longer possible for Natives and settlers to live together. "If you do not sell your land to the Government, they will take it," with force if necessary. The Mormon prophet promised the Utes that they could still, on occasion, have the "privilege" to return to their ancestral lands in the Utah and Sanpete Valleys to "fish, hunt, pick berries, dig roots."[23]

At the end of the three-day council, all but one of the Ute leaders signed the treaty with their *X*'s. Ten days later, the lone holdout, Sanpitch, signed the treaty in Brigham Young's offices in Temple Square. Afterward, Sanpitch, Kanosh, and a few other Ute men visited the studio of photographer Charles Savage and his then partner, Martin Ottinger, where the leaders sat together for a portrait. To commemorate the signing of the peace treaty, and to display the Utes' "curious looking faces" for other Salt Lake City residents to see, Savage and Ottinger placed a print of their photograph on display in their studio showroom.[24]

Those who opposed the treaty, including Sanpitch's son Antonga, had history on their side. Representatives of the US government were already notorious for failing to uphold treaties that they had drawn up. Preoccupied with Reconstruction in the South and the assassination of President Lincoln, Congress never ratified the treaty and never delivered the promised annuities and supplies.

Despite breaking their promises, federal officials and the Mormons expected the Utes to leave the land of their fathers and mothers. Most Utes were slow to relocate. Others refused altogether. In 1866, Antonga's Utes conducted sporadic attacks on settlers and their livestock. In turn, the Mormons massacred more Utes, including Sanpitch, whom they shot to death, along with others, at Birch Canyon on the west side of the Sanpete Valley. The mountain range where Sanpitch was killed now bears his name. On April 21, ten days after slaying Sanpitch, Mormon settlers who had established a settlement on the Sevier River at one of Wakara's favorite watering holes in modern-day Circleville, Utah, took advantage of the Mormon-Ute conflict to rid themselves of their Paiute neighbors. Claiming that Paiutes had killed one of their own, settlers at Circleville captured thirty Paiutes of the Koosharem

Band, including Wakara family members who had joined the band after Wakara's death, and imprisoned them in a church. According to Ammon, Wakara's son, the settlers slit the throats of the women and children and shot some of the men when they attempted to escape. In all, at least twenty-four Paiutes were killed. The youngest children were placed in Mormon homes.[25]

In the months after the Circleville massacre, more blood of Wakara's kin and the kin of Wakara's Native enemies was spilled on the land of their forefathers. In June 1866, Antonga led an attack against the Mormon settlement at Scipio, twenty-five miles north of Fillmore, killing the leader of the settlement and stealing hundreds of cattle and dozens of horses. Days after the attack, members of the Nauvoo Legion tracked Antonga and his men to the Sevier River, where they shot Antonga in the stomach, inflicting a wound from which he never fully recovered. The next summer, Antonga traveled to the Uintah Reservation. There, he sued for peace and agreed to encourage the remaining Utes to move to the Uintah Basin. Before he died in 1870, with the blessing of Brigham Young and accompanied by a Mormon guard, Antonga traveled throughout the Mormon colonies explaining that he had fought to defend his people's land and asked the settlers to forgive him for bringing violence to Utah.[26]

Over the next decade, most of the surviving Utes made their way to the reservation where former Western Ute band affiliations—the Sanpitches, the Timpanogos, the Pahvants, the Seuvarits, and the Uintahs—began to dissolve into a pan-Ute identity. This identity was formed in large part in the crucible of collective hunger and anger due to the US failure to provide the promised money, rations, and equipment. Still, these newly formed "Uintah Utes" did not give up their claims to their ancestral lands. Many saw their resettlement as a temporary diaspora from the places that defined them as peoples.

In the spring of 1872, Tabby and Kanosh led some Utes off the Uintah Reservation and to Fountain Green, with its sacred hot springs, twenty-five miles north of Manti in the Sanpete Valley. There, over the spring and summer, more than 2,000 Utes from Utah and Colorado, as well as clans of Navajos (Diné), participated in a Ghost Dance. This new dance—which emerged from a combination of Native beliefs about the connections between land and ancestors and Christian beliefs about the coming millennium—had begun among the Paiutes of Nevada, then swept through Native communities in the Southwest and the Great Plains. The Ghost Dance prophets proclaimed that if enough Natives purified themselves by returning to Native food ways and Native religion and then performed the Ghost Dance ceremony, the dancers would break open the earth to form a portal. Through this portal, deceased human and animal relatives killed by settler invasion would return, while "the whites would be swallowed up" in the portal, explained one of the Ghost Dance Paiute prophets.[27]

Sanpete settlers saw the gathering as a threat to their settlements. They pledged to kill as many Natives as it took to finally establish peace. That year, settlers also sent falsified reports of "Indian depredations" to Washington, hoping once again to enlist federal troops in their efforts to cleanse Utah of Native Americans. But once again, the federal government did not respond to the Mormons' pleas to help them secure the land they believed was theirs by divine mandate. (Two decades later, the US government would respond to another Ghost Dance gathering at Wounded Knee on the Pine Ridge reservation, resulting in more than 250 dead Lakota.)[28]

The 1872 Ghost Dance failed to cause the earth to swallow the Whites. No matter, Tabby told the Indian agents. Since the Spanish Fork Treaty was never ratified, the land still belonged to the Utes. "The white man was only occupying" their ancestral lands, Tabby declared. The Indian agents warned that if the Utes did not return to the reservation on their own, the soldiers would force them back at the ends of bayonets. Fine, replied Tabby and other Ute leaders. They "would rather be killed by the soldiers here by their dead friends who were buried here, than to go to the reservation and starve to death." But after making more promises to provide food and cash, the agents convinced Tabby to return to the reservation. By the end of the 1870s, most Western Utes would join Tabby in the Uintah Basin, forming settlements including White Rock, Neola, and Tabiona, named after Tabby.[29]

Still, not all relocated to the reservation. Even after the settlers founded Kanosh City in 1866 on Kanosh's ancestral lands, Kanosh did not leave. He moved his mixed Paiute and Ute community—a remnant of which today is the Kanosh Band of Paiutes—closer to Walker's Mountain, where Wakara was buried and where Kanosh would soon bury his brother and son. Kanosh did so, as he explained during the Spanish Fork Treaty negotiations, because he and his people "wanted to live around the graves of their fathers."[30]

In 1872, during the same summer as the Ghost Dance at Fountain Green, which Kanosh and other Utes believed would help raise their fathers and sons, brothers and sisters, from their graves, the graves of the Utes' relatives were indeed opened. But the ancestors were not brought back to life. Instead, Wakara's skull and those of the six other ancestors buried with or near him on Walker's Mountain were boxed up and sent to Washington, DC.

IN THE SUMMER OF 2018, AFTER VISITING THE Territorial Statehouse State Park Museum in Fillmore, I headed south on I-15. As I drove, I looked out the driver's side window to see the massive talus field that is "Walker's Mountain" (the Cow), where Wakara was buried in 1855, then unburied in 1872.

I was on my way to the Fish Lake Lodge to meet Kanosh Band elders Rick and Rena Pikyavit to talk to them about Wakara's life and legacy and the looting of his grave. As I drove, I might have been retracing the path that Arapeen and his warriors took soon after Wakara's death on their way to deliver Arapeen's vision of Wakara to the settlers at

Manti. As those riders might have done on long-forgotten Ute paths, I followed the spine of the Pahvant Mountains south, then took a sharp left on what is today I-70 through Clear Creek Canyon.

About twenty miles up the canyon, I made an impromptu stop at the Fremont Indian State Park and Museum. The park's origins were also impromptu. When workers widened the canyon to make way for I-70 in the 1980s, they unearthed the remnants of a large village of the Fremont Indians. Fremont (from John C. Frémont) is the name ascribed to the people who populated the Great Basin before the Numic ancestors of the Utes and Paiutes arrived around 1300 CE. Today, outside the museum, visitors can come almost face-to-face with massive walls of intricate petroglyphs and pictographs, which the Fremont Indians etched and painted on the soft stone over generations. Inside the museum, visitors can inspect pottery, baskets, and arrowheads pulled from the long-gone village. For much of the past two decades, visitors have also been treated to lessons in traditional grain grinding and bread baking led by Rena Pikyavit, who worked as a ranger's aide at the park. Or they might have watched Rick and Rena's son Nathaniel throw an atlatl, which the Fremont Indians used to hunt game.

Because of its focus on "ancient" Indian history, I did not expect to find much from Wakara's time at the Fremont Indian State Park and Museum. Still, tucked along a side wall and next to the large pithouse display, I found a large glass box. Inside were thirty-one funerary goods, including bowls, knife handles, horse tack, a horseshoe, and a Belgian-made double-barrel pistol. "The artifacts appear to come from the site of Chief Walkara's (Chief Walker's) burial site outside Kanosh, Utah," a sign on the display read.

The Fremont Indian museum display contained no bones. Still, it reminded me of the display of Wakara's nephew Antonga's skeleton, which for decades had been exhibited at the Church History Museum in Temple Square. Like viewers of the Black Hawk display, visitors to the Fremont Indian museum were invited to leer at the remains of the deceased and defeated Ute leader and celebrate how settlers had vanquished him, then vanished his people from the American landscape. Such vanishing included literally tearing open Wakara's grave and taking objects—objects that the thieves might have seen as "souvenirs" but are as sacred to Wakara's descendants as physical remains.

I knew that the 1872 grave robbers were after the skulls in Wakara's grave. So, if these funerary goods were in fact from Wakara's burial site, then they were the fruits of a different grave-robbing event.

Surprised to find such funerary goods presented to the public, let alone those that were supposedly taken from Wakara's grave, I inquired at the museum's front desk about their provenance. A ranger running the register told me that she didn't know much, only that they were "donated" by an archaeologist some years ago. I left my card, hoping she might put me in touch with someone who might know more.

On my way to Fish Lake to meet Rick and Rena, I passed through the town of Richfield. There, I stopped by the Fishlake National Forest Service headquarters, where I collected a copy of the archaeological survey that Robert Leonard, the longtime archaeologist for the Fishlake National Forest, conducted of Wakara's grave in September 1984. The survey of Walker's Mountain became the informational source for the Wakara placards that Leonard helped erect outside the Territorial Statehouse State Park Museum at Fillmore. Based on the "extent of vandalism" to the burial ground that he found during that survey, Leonard recommended that Walker's Mountain be patrolled by Forest Service personnel to prevent further looting.

Ironically, it was Forest Service personnel who became looters. This act of looting would soon add to the body count associated with Wakara's grave.

Chapter 18

Crania Americana

On January 29, 1855, James Duncan and John King, two Mormon settlers from Fillmore, started the day looking for lost cattle in the foothills of the Pahvant Mountains. King, the eighteen-year-old son of one of Fillmore's founders, Thomas King, and Duncan, a twenty-seven-year-old Scottish-born convert, suspected that hungry Utes had stolen the cattle from nearby corrals. The likely culprits, the two thought, were Wakara's band, who had just a few days before set up camp at Corn Creek.[1]

Soon after they began trotting their horses through the oaks that lined the foothills, Duncan and King heard mourning songs wafting toward them from below. The settlers dismounted, grabbed their horses by the reins, and took cover in a grove of trees.

Like the rest of the settlers in the region, that morning the two young men had learned of Wakara's death when Ute runners rushed through town shouting the news—and shouting warnings that the Utes blamed the Mormons for Wakara's demise. Still, they decided to follow Wakara's funeral party as it weaved up the canyon to the Utes' burial ground. Reaching the talus field, the two settlers stayed out of sight but close enough to watch the Utes provision Wakara's crypt with horses, hunting equipment, and "the Chief's two squaws, and two small children," Duncan recalled. Though they claimed to have been horrified to see a boy placed inside the tomb "still alive and pleading for help," Duncan and King decided not to rescue him. They feared doing so would renew violence with Wakara's Utes.[2]

The boy, tied up inside Wakara's tomb, could not be spared. But the Mormons hoped that he, along with the women and young children whose throats had been cut, would be the last to endure such a fate. This must stop, Brigham Young wrote to Arapeen soon after he learned of the ritual killings. Such spilling of blood was "a wrong idea and one that you must get rid of and then teach your people better," he reprimanded. Young's chastisement dripped with irony. During the decade before (and for decades after), Young was credibly accused of spilling the blood of many Native and settler Americans in acts of ritual retribution.[3]

What's more, Young and the other Mormons misunderstood the ritual. They said it occurred so that Wakara would not be alone in "the happy hunting grounds" on the other side of the veil. But Wakara's funeral was not just about preserving his life in the land beyond. It was also about renewing the Utes' claim to the land of their fathers and preserving their way of life in this plane of existence.

From this misunderstanding emerge two competing creation stories of America: one from Wakara's Utes; another from the settlers who claimed Ute land as their own based on religion, law, and, later, science. Wakara's Utes believed that one important way that the *Nuche* laid claim to their lands, given to them at the beginning of time, was by burying their ancestors in their lands. From the arrival of the Spanish conquistadors in New Spain to the arrival of the English settlers in New England, from American presidents to Supreme Court justices to archaeologists working for the Smithsonian, settlers have made their claims to American land in part by digging up Native remains in order to break the bond between Native people and their lands.

THE FIRST CREATION STORY IS ABOUT BONES—ABOUT how the bones of ancestors lay claim to lands for the sake of the ancestors' living descendants. The Ute tellers of this story—including Wakara's direct descendant and Ute historian Clifford Duncan—say that, at the beginning of time, there were no people on the earth. Creator God (*Sünawav*) cut up sticks and placed them in a bag until the bag was full. When *Sünawav* was away, his brother, Coyote, whose curiosity often got him into trouble, opened the bag. Out flowed many people, scattering in every direction. When *Sünawav* returned, he was angry to see what his brother had done, for *Sünawav* had planned to distribute the people equally across the land.

Sünawav named the few people left in the bag "the People" (the *Nuche*, or Utes). He declared that the lands of what would become Utah and Colorado, as well as the animals and plants, water and air of those lands, would be entrusted to the *Nuche*. *Sünawav* told Coyote that it would be the Utes' responsibility to safeguard the land, so that there would always be plenty of fish and deer, berries, roots, and water. These resources were also to be shared with newcomers to the land, so long as newcomers respected the special relationship between the *Nuche* and the land. Wakara himself frequently expressed willingness to share, but not sell, Ute lands. So did his brother and successor, Arapeen, who soon after Wakara's death declared, "The land, the timber, and the water and horses, cattle—all was the Lord's," and the Lord intended that these resources would benefit all. Because *Sünawav* created the Utes and the land, when the Utes died, they were to be buried in the land, renewing the Utes' claim to the land for another generation. It was the task of the ancestors to protect these claims when living Utes traveled seasonally away from the graves; it was the task of living Utes to protect the graves of the ancestors from those who would disrupt them.[4]

The second creation story is also about bones—about how the bones of the Utes' ancestors and those of other Indigenous peoples of what became known as the Americas were torn from their graves. This grave robbing served, in part, to justify the removal of the ancestors' living descendants from the land to make way for newcomers and to create America itself.

This story, as told by Pope Alexander VI starting in 1493, was that God declared that explorers from European Christian nations who "discovered" lands could take these lands as their own. And the Europeans took these lands with violence, deceit, disease, and slavery. They often did so on behalf of religion, namely, the Catholic Church. The *Requerimiento* of 1513, which the Spanish conquistadors read aloud upon arrival on the shores of "discovered" lands throughout the Americas, informed the lands' inhabitants that the king and queen of Spain were henceforth the rulers of these lands and the Indigenous people were vassals to the Spanish Crown. As such, they were required to acknowledge the superiority of the Crown and the Crown's Catholic faith. If the Indigenous people refused, then "we shall powerfully enter into your country, and shall make war against you," the *Requerimiento* declared. And "we shall take you and your wives and your children, and shall make slaves of them." Whether Indigenous peoples accepted these dictates or not, the conquistadors followed through on their threats. They plundered lands and possessions. They slaughtered many of the living and enslaved others. They also refused to let the ancestors rest. In search of gold and silver, they dug up graves, leaving skulls and bones scattered all over the ground, reported archaeologists centuries later.[5]

To the north, in founding what they called New England, Puritan settlers conducted themselves toward both living and dead Indigenous peoples much like their sectarian enemies, the Catholics. This, despite their claims that in order to Christianize and civilize the New World's Indigenous inhabitants, the Puritans had brought with them a purified church of Christ and not the "Whore of Babylon," the Catholic Church, or its redheaded stepsister, the Church of England.

One of the founding acts of the Pilgrims at Plymouth was Indian grave robbing. In December 1620, less than a month after they dropped anchor off the coast of the peninsula that they named Cape Cod, two settlers went in search of Wampanoags with whom, according to what became, in the nineteenth century, the most popular creation story of America, they would share a great Thanksgiving feast. (According to the myth, both Pilgrims and Natives contributed to this meal. In reality, that first winter, the Wampanoags saved the settlers from starvation—a decision that, 400 years later, many Wampanoags regret.) The settlers followed a path that they hoped would lead them to a Wampanoag village where they could procure food. Or if that failed, they hoped to find a cache of Indian wheat and corn, like the one that they had unearthed the day before. "It was God's good providence," the starving settlers explained, "that we found this corn, for else we know not how we should have done."[6]

The settlers failed to find more Wampanoag food. They also failed to find any living Wampanoags. But they did find dead ones. A gravesite that they located impressed them—long and deep, covered by boards. Even after they realized the grave did not contain food, the settlers decided to dig it up, revealing an even more elaborate construction of crisscross boards, under which they found finely crafted bowls, dishes, and trays. The settlers also found two bundles. Tearing into the first, they found the bones of a man who had died recently enough that his skull still bore flesh and hair. Ripping into the second bundle, they found the remains of a small child encircled by beads. The settlers claimed that they reburied the bones, but they didn't leave empty-handed. "We brought sundry of the prettiest things away with us." The hungry settlers continued to dig. But apparently God's providence had left them, as they failed to find any more food.[7]

More than three centuries after the pope first green-lit the Spanish Crown's seizure of Native American lands, lives, and property by invoking God's will—a sentiment echoed by the Spaniards' colonizing rivals, the English—this second American creation story combined religion with law. In 1823, the US Supreme Court in Washington, DC, found that the "Discovery Doctrine" had been transferred from the European empires to the United States. In *Johnson v. McIntosh*, Chief Justice John Marshall explained the unanimous finding of the court: The "Indians" merely occupied the lands of the New World. They did not own them. And like the monarchs of the Old World, the prelates and presidents of the United States told the Indians that they should be grateful to exchange their "unlimited independence" for the gifts of "civilization and Christianity." Associate Justice Joseph Story later explained the ruling this way: Because they were not Christians, but "infidels, heathens, and savages," the "Indians were not allowed to possess the prerogatives belonging to absolute, sovereign and independent nations." According to Story, the evidence for their savagery was how the Indians used—or failed to use—the land. "The territory over which they wandered, and which they used for their temporary and fugitive purposes, was, in respect to Christians, deemed, as if it were inhabited only by brute animals." This is why unearthing Native American remains was such an important, and insidious, project of the American colonial enterprise. Care for the dead—so that they could one day rise again at the millennium—signified for many founders of the American nation the height of civilization. Proper treatment of the bodies of the deceased separated the savage "brute" from the Christian. Removal of the evidence of Native Americans' care for their dead erased evidence of "civilized" Native Americans and thus their claims to American lands.[8]

In the decades during and after the birth of the United States, the creation story of the removal of "Indian" bones to make way for "Americans" changed. And herein a third creation story emerged, one that moves from religion and law to science—notably the science of archaeology. Thomas Jefferson, the great polymath, author of the

Declaration of Independence, founder of the University of Virginia, and father of several of his own enslaved people, was also an Indian grave robber.

As he described in *Notes on the State of Virginia* (1785), Jefferson excavated Indian burial mounds near his estate, Monticello. Jefferson estimated that one mound he dug up might have been the resting place of thousands. (It's most likely that Jefferson did not do much of the digging himself; his enslaved people did). The future third US president insisted that these mounds were not repositories of ancient civilizations, as others had claimed. Instead, when the "Aboriginal Indians," as he called them, "settled in a town, the first person who died was placed erect, and earth put around him, to cover and support him; . . . when another dies, a narrow passage was dug to the first, the second reclined against him, and the cover of earth replaced, and so on." What's more, Jefferson had personally observed the mound in active use. He watched a party of Indians—scholars later identified them as members of the Monacan Nation—who, passing through the region, went directly to the mounds "without any instructions or enquiry." None were needed. Just as Kanosh knew who was buried where on Walker's Mountain in Utah, the Monacans knew who was buried where at their nation's cemetery. Jefferson noted that after performing sorrowful observances, the party left the mound, restarting their journey. Without realizing it, in his description of the Monacans' relationship to their mounds, Jefferson echoed *Süna-wav*'s description of the relationship between Utes and their lands: The lands and the people, both living and dead, make each other through their relationship with each other.[9]

Jefferson suggested that he excavated the mounds to preserve "Aboriginal" Virginia's patrimony. The mounds that he had not excavated, which had recently been "cleared of their trees and put under cultivation, [were] much reduced in their height, and spread in width, by the plough, and [would] probably disappear in time."

But what Jefferson claimed were well-intentioned acts of preservation, so that the Monacan remains would not fall victim to the English-cum-American plow, others would call acts of ghastly plunder. Jefferson displayed some of the skeletal fruits of his diggings at his plantation home and sent others to museums, where they were studied to justify Jefferson's and most other Founding Fathers' views on the inherent supremacy of White settlers.[10]

Because of these excavations, the long list of Jefferson's offspring—the American nation, public universities, a multiracial family—for a long time also included American archaeology. More recently, some have questioned this creation story, because, as Edward R. Adams (Choctaw) has observed, "archeology, much like any other science, implies observance of objective fact and adherence to scientific truth." But perhaps Jefferson does deserve such acclaim. After all, "science," and especially the science of archaeology, like theologies of Christian supremacy and Anglo-American law before it, is an ideology. To create the American nation, these ideologies were developed and then deployed not to just serve objective truth but to advance the agenda of White settler American supremacy and Native American displacement.[11]

In the nineteenth century, this third creation story of removing Native remains as part of a race-based scientific ideology became an intentional rather than incidental part of the project of Manifest Destiny. Removal of Native American bones provided the explicit justification for the removal of living Native Americans. For without the graves of their ancestors present in the land, settlers believed that the living descendants lost their claims to their homelands. For this project, American archaeological interest in Native American remains narrowed to skulls of the long buried and the recently deceased.

During the so-called Seminole Wars in the 1830s, which the US government waged to remove that last Native American nation west of the Mississippi who resisted removal, doctors were often on hand at battlefields to care for wounded soldiers. They were also there to collect dead Seminoles' heads as souvenirs and objects of study. For example, Dr. Eugene Abadie collected at least nine Seminole skulls between 1837 and 1838, including from warriors killed in battle as well as noncombatants and children as young as three who likely died of pneumonia, tuberculosis, or dysentery. After boxing them up, Abadie sent the skulls to his friend and colleague Dr. Samuel Morton, a founder and professor of anatomy at the Pennsylvania Medical College. The two doctors had met in Philadelphia—the city to which the French-born Abadie emigrated and where Morton was born in 1799 and raised among Pennsylvania's Quaker elite. Both men attended the University of Pennsylvania for their medical degrees, Morton completing his at the age of twenty-one.[12]

Soon after they arrived at his offices in Philadelphia, Morton cracked open the wooden shipping crates and separated the skulls from their wrappings. He cleaned the crania, boiling a few to remove bits of skin and hair clinging to bone, and then painted them with varnish. After these preparations, Morton began studying the crania to uncover what origins of humanity they might reveal. He picked up a skull with one hand, perhaps sticking his fingers inside the eye sockets, then turned it round and round. With a pencil in the other hand, he wrote in his ledger book what he saw, noting sex, approximate age, and evidence of trauma from violence, disease, or malnutrition. He also gave each of the skulls an identifier. To do so, Morton put down his pencil and picked up a pen, scrawling numbers on the skulls' foreheads in India ink. In doing so, he added them to his massive collection of human crania that ran into the hundreds—almost certainly the largest in the world at the time—and grew weekly as dozens of collaborators sent him skulls from their travels across the

Americas, and later around the world. Sometimes Morton's collectors gathered skulls by chance, when warfare or plague led to massive Native die-offs. Other times, they conducted adrenaline-producing skull-hunting expeditions that put their own lives and limbs in danger, as would be the case for the collector who dug up Wakara's skull decades later.[13]

Abadie had sent a fine set of Seminole skulls, Morton said to himself. But only one, No. 707, warranted closer study. Morton took thirteen measurements, including the longitudinal diameter, the length of the intermastoid arch, the volumes of the anterior chambers, and the angle of the face. Morton had standardized these measurements so that he could compare skulls across time, space, and, most importantly, race.[14]

The next year, Morton published the measurements of his collection of hundreds of Indian skulls in *Crania Americana: A Comparative View of the Skulls of Various Aboriginal Nations of North and South America*. In this pioneering work of physical anthropology and ethnology, which also contained detailed illustrations of skulls, including that of Seminole No. 707, Morton contended that his comparative study of crania demonstrated the empirical fact of human difference among races. Morton's argument was a radical departure from previous religious and scientific understandings of the varieties of humankind. Well into the nineteenth century, theologians and scientists agreed that all human races descended from one human family. Morton rejected this theory of monogenesis and instead argued for the polygenesis of humanity: The various human races were created at different points in time and at different places across the world, Morton contended. Each race was given immutable characteristics. Morton believed that the human skull was stable across generations, immune to environmental and cultural factors that might lead to changes in other parts of the body. As such, "craniology," Morton claimed, allowed scientists to study for the first time in an empirical fashion the differences in the races and how those differences related to each race's specific aptitudes for intelligence, culture, and self-government.

For his taxonomy and hierarchy of humanity, Morton was interested in, but did not rely on, the skulls' bumps, ridges, and valleys, which phrenologists of the era contended were associated with mental traits. Instead, Morton decided that since it was obvious that the larger the brain, the smarter the human, he settled on cranial volume as the single most important measurement to compare across the races. Cranial volume was also ostensibly simple to measure. Into the hundreds of skulls in the "cranial library" that he amassed over the 1830s, Morton poured mercury, the handling of which in the same era rendered hatters "mad" and might have contributed to Morton's infamously gloomy mood. Later, he found that BB-sized buckshot pellets caused less mess while allowing him to estimate the volume of a skull down to the cubic inch.[15]

Morton found that the "Caucasian" race, which he said came from Europe, northern India, and northern Africa, had the biggest brains. The fifty-two Caucasian skulls he had in his library averaged eighty-seven cubic inches. The "American" race, of which he had 147 examples—gathered from the mounds of Peru to the mounds of Wisconsin and from ancient tombs and recent battlefields in Mexico, Florida, and the longitudes in between—averaged eighty-two cubic inches. The "Ethiopian" race, which for Morton meant peoples from sub-Saharan Africa, southern India, Oceana, and Australia, were the smallest. Based on the twenty-nine skulls in his collection, these crania averaged seventy-eight cubic inches.[16]

Morton's findings stamped the veneer of science on what popes, kings and queens, conquistadors and Pilgrims, Supreme Court justices and US presidents already claimed to know. The "Negro is joyous, flexible, and indolent," Morton concluded. While their brains were the feeblest, incapable of advancing when exposed to education, the

Negros' bodies were strong and ready for work, if they were properly tasked by a superior race. The brains of the Caucasians, in particular those of "the English, or Anglo-Saxons," were the font of civilization and progress, enabling them to spread their "colonies widely over Asia, Africa, and America." For Morton, it was also no surprise that when the Anglo-Saxons brought advanced ideas and learning to the "American Family" of Indians (Native Americans), they found fallow soil. "Their proximity, for more than two centuries, to European institutions, has made scarcely any appreciable change in their mode of thinking or their manner of life." Morton, who compiled *Crania Americana* during the height of the forced exile of the "Five Civilized Tribes," including the Cherokees and the Seminoles west of the Mississippi River, argued that the separation of the Native and White American races was inevitable and warranted. And yet, even during this period of forced removal, Morton acknowledged the connection between graves and claims to the land in Native American life. "The Indians have an extraordinary veneration for their dead, which sometimes induces them, on removing from one section of the country to another, to disinter the remains of their deceased relatives, and bear them to the new home of the tribe."[17]

Morton's conclusions buttressed the anti-Black and anti-Indian policies of many politicians and scientists in the 1840s and 1850s. After his death in 1851, the *Charleston Medical Journal* celebrated Morton's legacy for upholding the proto-Confederate worldview. "We of the South should consider him as our benefactor, for aiding most materially in giving the negro his true position as an inferior race." As Morton protégé Josiah Nott, director of the Confederate General Army Hospital in Mobile, Alabama, during the Civil War, wrote in a tribute to his mentor, "It is as clear as the sun at noon-day, the last of these Red men will be numbered with the dead. . . . To one who has lived among American Indians, it is in vain to talk of civilizing them. You might as well attempt to change the nature of the buffalo."[18]

CIRCULAR NO. 2 OF THE SURGEON GENERAL'S OFFICE, dated April 4, 1867, included a call for army medical officers to collect crania of American Indians, along with specimens of Indian weapons, dress, implements, diet, and medicines. These officers, many of whom were attached to army units fighting the so-called Indian Wars in the West and Great Plains, were instructed to send their collections to the Army Medical Museum (AMM) in Washington, DC, along with explanatory notes of the items' provenance. Morton's collection had been a vital start. But it wasn't big enough, the craniologists who came after him concluded. AMM needed many more skulls to calculate statistically relevant averages of the nation's principal tribes. And Morton's dabbling in phrenology, which the new generation of ethnologists ridiculed as pseudo-science, was embarrassing.[19]

AMM was founded in 1862 at the height of the Civil War, the conflict that produced the most dead and maimed bodies in the history of the nation. The museum's original mandate was to collect examples of battlefield pathology. The hope was that through careful study of these specimens, army doctors could provide better outcomes for the injured. In its first year of existence, the museum gathered 988 skeletal remains. Curators noted the pathologies on body parts from head to toe, with femur bullet wounds found in nearly half the collection's specimens. Army surgeons also began sending to AMM crania collected from battlefields, including Gettysburg, where some 51,000 Union and Confederate soldiers died over a three-day period in early July 1863.[20]

The museum made few advancements in surgery for living soldiers and ultimately evolved into a museum of dead Indians. After the Civil War, the US Army also evolved, turning its attention to forcing tribes throughout the West off their ancestral lands and onto reservations.

By the fall of 1867, doctors attached to the army in the American West were sending a steady stream of crania back to Washington, frequently sourced from graves of recently deceased Natives. To prepare the skulls for shipment, the doctors often boiled off their flesh, sometimes in full view of Native kin still grieving the loss of their loved ones. Assistant surgeon William Henry Forwood, who would later become the surgeon general of the United States, procured and sent back to Washington at least two Cheyenne crania from victims of the Sand Creek Massacre. (Three years before, the 3rd Colorado Cavalry had attacked a Cheyenne village in southeastern Colorado, killing at least 150 Cheyennes and Arapahos.) Another assistant surgeon, James P. Kimball, sent three crania that he took from the site of a battle between the Blackfeet and Crows in Montana. In a letter to Dr. George Otis, who was AMM's curator from 1864 until his death in 1881, Kimball explained that the skulls were those of the Blackfeet; "the Crows being the victors, carried away their dead leaving the bodies of their enemies upon the field." In September 1868, the Surgeon General's Office reported that since the initial call had gone out little more than a year before, AMM had collected forty-seven Indian crania from over a dozen tribes.[21]

Over the next decade, from an expanding network of skull collectors, the museum amassed thousands more skulls, gathered fresh from battlefields and massacre sites and unearthed from cemeteries and ossuaries. Some of these grave-robbing surgeons were particularly prolific. While stationed at Fort Randall in South Dakota in the late 1860s, George P. Hachenberg, who had earned his dental degree from New York University, gathered fifteen Sioux skulls, one Winnebago skull, and seven Ponca skulls. To procure one of the skulls, Hachenberg had climbed a scaffold where a dead Sioux had been placed by his kin. The good dentist then snatched his prize before the deceased's family could stop him. In early 1869, after army soldiers and local settlers slaughtered a peaceful Pawnee trading party in central Kansas, surgeon E. B. Fryer cut the heads off the victims, then sent those skulls, along with twenty others from the

Cheyenne, Caddo, Wichita, and Osage tribes, back to AMM. On October 3, 1873, at Fort Klamath, Oregon, Major Henry McElderry, an army surgeon well versed in battlefield amputation, cut the heads off four Modoc Indians who had been executed by hanging hours before, after having been convicted by a jury of army officers of war crimes against the United States during the so-called Modoc War. The Army Medical Museum also relied on the marketplace to fill out its collection, paying $3 to $5 for complete skulls, including those from Europe and South America, which it needed to make comparisons to Native American skulls. This market grew competitive as other museums, including Harvard's Peabody Museum, New York's American Museum of Natural History, and Chicago's Field Museum, worked to expand their own collections of Native crania.[22]

On occasion, the market was upended when collectors stumbled upon a "Big Bonanza," as Dr. Henry Yarrow, then an assistant surgent in the US Army, described the cache of remains that his expedition unearthed in the Channel Islands near Santa Barbara in 1875. Yarrow claimed that the burial ground contained several tons of human remains, including burials ornamented with whale bones, beads, and shells packaged in ornate jars. In other trenches, the dead appeared to have been buried en masse, likely due to a massive die-off caused by another bonanza: the gold rush of the early 1850s, which led to the deaths of thousands of California Natives in a few short years. Yarrow learned from mission records that in 1823, there were 900 Indians, most likely Chumash, in the area. He also learned from a local settler that the only survivor of the area's Native community was an "old crone [who] for many years continued to visit this spot annually to mourn the departed greatness of her people." By 1875, the woman had died, leaving no one but ethnographers like Yarrow, he insinuated, to tell the story of her people. The Channel Islands expedition yielded 459 skulls, split between AMM and Harvard's Peabody Museum, which jointly financed the operation.[23]

In the 1860s and 1870s, shipments from collectors like Hachenberg, Fryer, and Yarrow packed AMM's shelves with skulls of American Indians. Still, a few non-Native specimens were also added to the collection. In 1869, the museum received the remains of eight African Americans from Vicksburg, Mississippi, including the skull of a four-year-old boy. The museum curators prized skulls of young children. Their fragile nature meant that they were hard to come by, and they were valuable because they froze in time the early stages of human development. Dr. Bennett Clements, a veteran of both the Civil War and the Indian Wars, delivered to the museum a portion of the skull of a twelve-year-old victim of the Mountain Meadows Massacre. The museum also received a skull that, at least according to one account in AMM's records, belonged to the first soldier killed at the Battle of Little Bighorn in 1876. These "Negro" and "White" crania led the museum to create "Negros" and "Whites" sections for its skulls on the museum's shelves and in its catalogs, which it began publishing in the 1870s.[24]

Collecting skulls was the first step. Next, in their laboratories, AMM's curators devised a system to catalog and study these diverse crania. As did Morton, the museum's craniologists assigned each skull a number, most often based on the order of its arrival. The skulls that Yarrow delivered to the museum from the Channel Islands expedition ran consecutively from 1,446 to 1,545, with these numbers inscribed on the skulls in ink. The museum's craniologists also noted the sex, age, and provenance, if known. Using calipers, they took basic measurements like length, height, and total circumference of the crania.[25]

While they followed Morton's blueprint, AMM's craniologists evolved away from his methods for measuring cranial elements, believing that they were too susceptible to human error. To reduce discrepancies introduced by shaking hands holding tape measures, the museum's craniologists experimented with photography. AMM

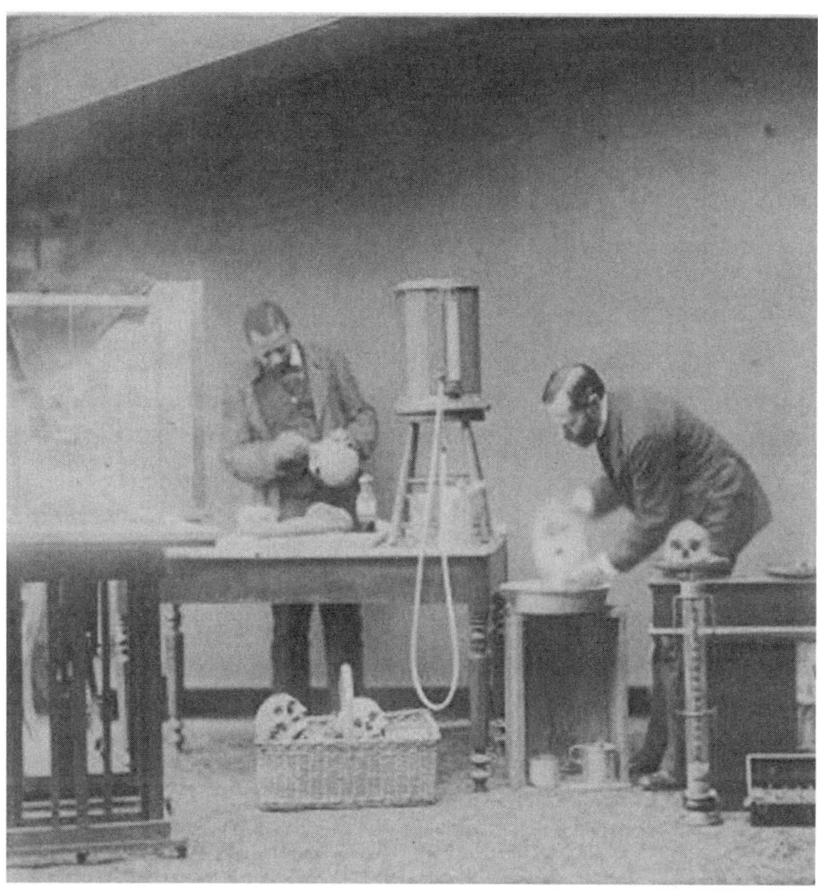

“Ascertaining Capacity of Cranial Cavity by Means of Water,” Army Medical Museum (1884). (Courtesy of the Miriam and Ira D. Wallach Division of Art, Prints and Photographs: Photography Collection, New York Public Library)

took “composite images,” created when one single negative was exposed multiple times to a series of skulls. Such images captured all but instantly, and froze on film, what the museum’s curators believed were the maximum variations within Indian tribes. Nevertheless, cranial volume remained the central point of interest. In the 1880s, water replaced buckshot for “cubing skulls” since craniologists could not force through “muscular exertion” more water into a skull, as they could with compactable materials like buckshot. These advances in Morton’s techniques only reinforced his conclusion that the "American" Indian race was on a much lower rung in the hierarchy of humanity than settler Americans.[26]

The final step was to bring these findings, and the specimens themselves, to the public. On April 16, 1867, the American Medical Museum moved to Ford's Theatre in downtown Washington, DC. The theater had been shuttered almost exactly two years before following the assassination of President Abraham Lincoln. "What nobler monument could the nation erect to [Lincoln's] memory than this sombre treasure-house to the study of disease and injury, mutilation and death," wrote Dr. Joseph Woodward soon after the museum's reopening. Woodward spoke from experience. He was one of the surgeons who performed the autopsy on Lincoln's brain after it had been destroyed by John Wilkes Booth's bullet. Over the next few years, the museum became one of Washington's most popular tourist attractions. Tens of thousands of visitors inspected Civil War specimens of dismembered limbs in glass cabinets. The display of Booth's brain, heart, and vertebra was also popular. The skulls of Native Americans were displayed in floor-to-ceiling cabinets. Morton's own cabinet of dead Indians was revived when the Academy of Natural Sciences in Philadelphia purchased it and opened it to the public, free of charge, Tuesdays and Saturdays. Such displays allowed East Coast Americans who flocked to these museums, and others like them, including the Peabody at Harvard and the American Museum of Natural History in New York City, to participate vicariously in the conquest of the American West.[27]

THE LEADERS OF THE ARMY MEDICAL MUSEUM NEEDED lots of skulls to find their averages and make their claims about the inferiority of the Indian brain. But they also wanted special skulls from famous deceased Indians. By 1880, in AMM's catalog of close to 2,000 cranial specimens, only 9 had names attached to them.

There was "'Vendovi,' chief of one of the Fiji Islands," who was purported to be a cannibal. There was "'Hee-taw,' sub-chief of [the] Bannock tribe." There was "'Weak Eyes,' one of Two Kettles' band" (a Lakota band). There was "'Shota,' chief of [the] Ogallallas." There was "'Walk-a-bed,'" who was purported to be an Arapaho medicine man. There was "'Cunning Jim,' a Cheyenne chief." There were two named Comanches: One was "'Eath-Ath,' Red, 'Qua-ha,' Day"; the other was "'Tooh-Parrah,' Black Bear," whose skull came to the museum with the skull of his wife, who was not named.[28]

And there was "'Wah-ker,' a celebrated chief" of the Utes. Like Black Bear's, Wakara's skull did not come to AMM alone. Henry Yarrow sent six other skulls to Washington after he collected them from or near Wakara's grave in central Utah, in late summer 1872.[29]

Chapter 19

"Please Say Nothing About the Crania"

HENRY YARROW AND HENRY Henshaw had only been out on Utah Lake for an hour on a summer day in 1872. But the floor of their borrowed boat was already full of Bonneville trout. The most recently caught flopped at their feet, trying in vain to catch her breath. The high Utah sun glinted off her bright silver sides and stung Yarrow and Henshaw's eyes, as did the sweat that poured from their brows.

Yarrow and Henshaw were not fishermen. The twenty-two-year-old Henshaw was an aspiring naturalist from Cambridge, Massachusetts, who would go on to help found the National Geographic Society. Ten years older than his assistant, Yarrow was also a naturalist—later he'd become the first curator of herpetology at the Smithsonian's National Museum of Natural History—and a doctor. He earned his medical degree at the University of Pennsylvania in his native Philadelphia, then served as a surgeon for the 5th Pennsylvania Cavalry in the Civil War. Still, that summer day on Utah Lake, the trout were so plentiful and, it seems, so eager to bite that even novices like Yarrow and Henshaw caught fish with ease. The men's forearms ached from wrestling the trout, which averaged four pounds, into the boat.

Henry Crécy Yarrow (1840–1949). Undated photograph. In the 1870s, Yarrow became one of the American Medical Museum's most prolific skull collectors. (From University Historical Materials Collection, Series 1, Box 4, Folder 35, RG0031. Special Collections Research Center, George Washington University Libraries, Washington, DC)

Yarrow and Henshaw decided to make one more cast before calling it quits. They baited a large steel hook with a minnow and tossed it into the lake. Within seconds the line of piano wire went taut. Yarrow grabbed the wire. Hand over hand, with Henshaw's assistance, Yarrow pulled the fish out of the lake's cool, dark depths. Once they got it close enough to the boat, they used a net to scoop the trout out of the water, then dumped it on the bottom of the boat, where it joined its glassy-eyed kin. That's enough, Yarrow said to Henshaw. The younger man grabbed the oars and rowed toward the mouth of the Provo River and the docks of the Danish-born Mormon convert

Peter Madsen, the proprietor of the largest commercial fishing outfit on Utah Lake, from whom they had borrowed the boat.

Back on land, Yarrow and Henshaw unloaded their catch. Yarrow estimated it weighed thirty to forty pounds in total. Yarrow cut open the belly of one large trout. Out spilled finger-length minnows and grasshoppers. Madsen helped the men clean the rest of the fish. As they worked, the Mormon remarked that the trout did not disdain eating snakes and frogs.

After they were done, Yarrow, Henshaw, and Madsen sat on the dock. With notebook in hand, Yarrow peppered Madsen with questions about the trout, the other native fish of Utah Lake, and the history of settler fishing. Though he had enjoyed his morning on the water, Yarrow had not gone fishing for sport. He was in Utah as the surgeon and naturalist for George Wheeler's survey of the United States west of the 100th meridian. Part military, part scientific expedition, starting in 1869, Wheeler and his men spent a decade mapping and collecting natural and ethnological specimens of the American Southwest before that last wild part of America disappeared following the expected victories over the Indians, the influx of settlers after the Civil War, and the completion of the transcontinental railroad. The "wedding of the rails" had taken place three years before just north of the Great Salt Lake.

As were many visitors to the lake before him, Yarrow was struck by its beauty and its great fisheries, about which he published the first scientific study for the US Fish Commission. But even by 1872, the fisheries were in decline. Madsen told Yarrow that the fishermen's hauls shrank each year due to unsustainable fishing practices and the growing number of settlers' insatiable appetite for fish. Yarrow warned that the trout and other native species would be extinct in just a few years unless fishing practices were regulated.[1]

That summer, Yarrow, with the help of Henshaw, collected specimens of fish, native plants, birds, and insects from the Utah Valley, under the assumption that they too would go extinct due to settler sprawl and the introduction of invasive species. The Native peoples of the lake—Wakara's Timpanogos Fish Eaters—were already gone. Most had been killed by massacres, measles, and starvation in the 1850s. By the 1860s, the few that remained mixed with other bands when they were sequestered onto the reservation in the arid Uintah Valley. Still, Yarrow did not leave the West without human specimens of Natives who had once called Utah (Timpanogos) Lake the center of their world. Later that summer, after a tour through the deserts of Nevada, the expedition was back in central Utah. Near Fillmore, Yarrow went searching for the grave "of Wah-ker, a celebrated chief, who for a long time was a scourge to the people of New Mexico, California, and Utah," Yarrow later wrote.[2]

Raised and educated in Dr. Samuel Morton's Philadelphia, Yarrow long harbored a fascination with crania and the secrets they contained. And as a good army man, he wanted to answer the call to collect Indian skulls for the collection of the Army Medical Museum (AMM). During his stays in Salt Lake City and Provo, Yarrow heard stories about Wakara from people who knew him, including Brigham Young and Dimick Huntington. He also heard the story of Wakara's lavish and deadly funeral. Yarrow knew he could make a name for himself, or at least impress his colleagues back at the museum, by securing the skull of such an infamous Indian.

Yarrow could not get to the gravesite on his own. The tomb's location—chosen for maximum concealment at the bottom of a rockslide on an almost unscalable mountain—made locating it without a guide impossible. Yarrow hired such a guide, most likely a Mormon settler from Fillmore or Kanosh, to escort him. This guide likely took Yarrow on horseback up the same switchback path that Wakara's death party had taken seventeen years before. The journey was not easy. It took Yarrow, his guide, and three soldiers who provided military escort to the survey several hours to plod their way up the canyon and across the mountainside to the talus field. Once they arrived, Yarrow's guide pointed out the cairns of boulders that covered dozens of graves, which had multiplied in the last few years. The guide then led them to the largest of the crypts. The skull collectors got to work. With the help of the soldiers, Yarrow lugged boulders off Wakara's grave, exposing a lattice of mountain aspens, which they tossed aside. Yarrow then climbed into the vault, which he noted "was lined with skins, the corpse placed therein, with weapons, ornaments, etc." Yarrow did not have much interest in these objects. He was hunting for skulls. After riffling through the grave, Yarrow located the skull that he believed belonged to Wakara, along with others, including that of a boy who, Yarrow wrote, "tradition states . . . was buried alive at this place."[3]

Yarrow and his party did not tarry long. Their guide warned them that there were Natives in the area—notably Kanosh's band—who would object to their pilfering the remains of their relations. Still, Yarrow was proud of his work. "I am glad to be able to tell you I have procured some 'Ute' crania," Yarrow wrote in a September 15 letter to AMM curator Dr. George Otis in Washington soon after he left Walker's Mountain, "among others that of Wah-ker the celebrated chief who instigated the war of .65." In his haste, Yarrow conflated Wakara with his kin "Black Hawk" (Antonga), who led the "war" against Mormon settlers in 1865 when Antonga and his allies refused to relocate to the Uintah Reservation. While Yarrow had managed to collect the skulls without interference from local Natives, he and his party were not out of danger. They would continue south to St. George for the rest of the fall, hoping to collect other skulls along the way. They'd return to Salt Lake by early winter. For this reason, Yarrow concluded, "Please say nothing about the Crania outside of the office as I would not wish it to appear in any paper, having to pass through the same tribe a month or so later."[4]

The skulls came east with Yarrow when he returned to Washington after the conclusion of the expedition's 1872 collection season.

AMM received the skulls in two boxes. In the transmittal letter to Otis that accompanied the skulls, Yarrow explained that one box contained Wakara's skull and part of his skeleton, along with a "Paiute Indian said to have been buried alive with him." In another box were the crania of five other Utes from the same location.[5]

In AMM's laboratories, the crania were unboxed. A curator pulled the larger skull from Box No. 1. Inside the skull, the curator found a paper tag, written in Yarrow's hand, indicating that the skull belonged to "Wah-ker Ute Chief." The curator wrote "966" in black ink on the skull's forehead, then wrote the same number in the museum's ledger book. The curator also wrote into the ledger a brief biography of Wakara, which Yarrow had provided, explaining that 966 came from "a celebrated Ute Chief, long the terror of the people of Utah, New Mexico, and California. This chief was born about the year 1815 on Spanish Fork River Utah and died at Dry Creek Utah in 1858. Several horses and two prisoners were killed and buried with him." Again, Yarrow's biography was slightly off. Wakara died in 1855, not 1858. More importantly to Yarrow, in the ledger the curator credited him with collecting such a unique specimen. The crania and the skeletal remains inside the box seem to have been separated at this point, since only the skull was cataloged.[6]

The unboxing continued. The curator pulled the small "calvaria" (top part of the skull) from Box No. 1, then wrote "967" on its forehead and wrote in the ledger, "Portion of the right and left parietals and occipital bones found near the grave of Wakher." The curator then opened the second box, again scrawled AMM numbers onto the specimens—968, 969, 970, 971, 972—and added details provided by Yarrow into the ledger book. The curator appreciated the specimens that Yarrow had collected from and near Wakara's grave. All but one were intact enough that their cubic volumes were measured. A decade later, two of the skulls that Yarrow collected from central Utah were pulled from the shelves. They and four others were photographed to create a composite image of "Pah Utes." How these skulls were selected seems mysterious, even random. Two were from Walker's Mountain. Another came from Fort Cameron, Utah. But the rest came not from the Ute homelands of Utah and Colorado but from Nevada and Oregon.[7]

Yarrow became arguably AMM's most celebrated skull collector. Otis credited him with gathering 100 skulls: 7 from Utah, 93 from California. Yarrow agreed with AMM's director George Otis that the skulls of Native Americans revealed innate intellectual inferiority when compared to those of White settler Americans. Yet Yarrow also believed that even Whites could learn something about the human condition by studying living Native cultures, not just dead Indians' crania. In 1880, Yarrow published *The Introduction to the Study of Mortuary Customs Among the North Americans*, a compilation of observations of Native funerary rites—from cremation and embalming to water graves—that Yarrow gathered from AMM's network of skull collectors. Yarrow, along with one of his biggest boosters, John Wesley Powell, who was then the director of the U.S. Geological Survey, argued that by studying these diverse death rituals, anthropologists and ethnologists could locate the origins of human culture. "For the same longing to solve the mysteries of life and death," Powell wrote in an introduction to Yarrow's study, "the same yearning for a future life, the same awe of powers more than human, exist alike in the mind of the savage and the sage."[8]

According to Yarrow, Wakara's grave was typical of the Utes' cave, cairn, and rock burials. Yet the grave's location and size—composed of a "large enough [set of boulders] to have marked the last resting place of an elephant"—made it noteworthy. It was also surrounded by hundreds of horse bones. From his network of skull collectors and from his own observations, Yarrow also reported that such rock burials were common among the Utes' Numic kin, including the Paiutes and Shoshones. In late summer 1872, while he and the Wheeler Survey explored western Utah near the Nevada border, Yarrow bribed a Goshute guide to take him to a hard-to-reach cave where the Goshute had himself buried deceased tribal members. From a physician at an Indian agency in Oklahoma, Yarrow learned that, as did the Utes for Wakara, Comanches buried dead leaders in rock and cave graves, dressing the deceased in their favorite clothing, outfitting the graves with weapons, food, and tobacco, and sacrificing horses, which they left near the tombs.[9]

By the time Yarrow published his first mortuary study in 1880, AMM had collected thousands of skulls, which its curators had numbered, examined, and shelved in their laboratories or placed on display on the museum floor in the former Ford's Theatre. Two events during the rest of the 1880s marked a sea change at AMM. First, Dr. George Otis, who turned the museum into the world's center of comparative racial anatomy, died in 1881. His successors returned AMM to its original purpose as a museum of medicine, focused on collecting, studying, and displaying specimens of human pathology. Body parts torn apart by bullets or cannon blasts again found their place of central importance for the edification of medical students and the titillation of museum guests. AMM also expanded its holdings in presidential assassinations. Parts of President James A. Garfield's spine, severed by his assassin Charles J. Guiteau's bullet in 1881, joined fragments of Abraham Lincoln's skull. The spleen of Guiteau joined the brain, heart, and vertebra of John Wilkes Booth.[10]

The second change occurred on the killing fields of the American West. The appetite for collecting Native skulls, and for finding in their cavities further proof of Indian incapacity for participation in the White American republic, waned as the Natives died from disease and warfare or were forced onto reservations. Indian removal seemed inevitable. Instead, as Thomas Jefferson argued a century before, archaeologists claimed that the need to collect Native remains, stories, and artifacts was increasingly about safeguarding (Native)

American patrimony, before it was razed by settler farms, cities, and railroads. Still, these national treasures would be preserved not on Native land but in settler museums.

Or more precisely, in one museum: the Smithsonian. After languishing on AMM's shelves for the better part of two decades, in 1898, the more than 3,700 sets of skeletal remains in AMM's collection were transferred to the Smithsonian's National Museum, today known as the National Museum of Natural History (NMNH), where each was given a new number and stored in another set of shelves and cabinets. Again, the focus was on Indian skulls. Only a small portion of the 2,206 skulls and skull fragments transferred to the National Museum were of European, Asian, or African origin. Most had been looted from Native American graves, unearthed from sites of massive die-offs, picked off the battlefields, or severed from the corpses of Natives executed for purported crimes against the United States.[11]

IN JUNE OF 1902, AS THEY ATTEMPTED TO return to their ancestral lands from which they had been exiled, 150 Yaqui Indians were massacred by Mexican troops in Sonora, Mexico. Three weeks later, Aleš Hrdlička, a Czech-born medical doctor turned anthropologist who was conducting fieldwork among the Yaquis, traveled to the massacre site. There he found the remains of sixty-four Yaquis, including many women and children, piled in heaps. Hrdlička hacked off the heads of the dead with a machete and boiled the skulls to remove flesh. He then shipped twelve skulls to the Museum of Natural History in New York, which had sponsored his expedition. Still, as he wrote dryly in his published report, "most of the skulls, whether from a peculiar effect of the Mauser cartridges or from the closeness of the range, were so shattered as to be of no use." Perhaps to soften the disappointment of his benefactors, Hrdlička included a "papoose" board to which a massacred infant had been strapped. He threw away the baby's body.[12]

Two years later, Hrdlička became the founder of the Smithsonian's Department of Physical Anthropology. At his invitation, skulls continued to flow into the museum's collection. Anthropologists who lived with and studied Native tribes with the professed goal of preserving Native culture and language dug up ancestors of their living subjects and forwarded them to Hrdlička. Choosing to build their collections on regional histories, smaller American museums also turned over their bone collections to the Smithsonian, as well as to larger natural history museums in Philadelphia, Chicago, and New York.[13]

In the 1910s, in order to gather human remains from every "race," Hrdlička himself crisscrossed the globe. He ransacked European graves and took casts of skulls in the continent's natural history museums. In Siberia, Hrdlička faced resistance from officials in Saint Petersburg, who were suspicious of foreigners looking to collect relics for transport abroad. But Hrdlička insisted that he was not an "antiquities" hunter. He only wanted to take measurements of the living and collect skeletal material of the dead, the value of which was not financial but scientific. In the Andes of Peru, Hrdlička collected hundreds of pre-Columbian crania, hoping to understand what diseases plagued the Peruvians before contact with the Spanish.[14]

The outbreak of World War I prevented other planned expeditions to Australia and Africa, which Hrdlička believed necessary to make his collection global in scope. Despite these limitations, the Smithsonian's *The Story of Man Through the Ages* opened to great fanfare in 1915 on the Pan-California Exposition's massive grounds in San Diego's Balboa Park. During its two-year run, several million visitors wandered through *The Story of Man Through the Ages*'s hall. In one room, they heard lectures on human evolution, learning that each race (according to Hrdlička, there were three: "White," "Black," and "Yellow-Brown") had evolved from its own ancestors. In another room, visitors puzzled over a series of busts dramatizing the evolution of each race and examined some 200 contemporary "racial portraits" from around the world. In a final room, visitors marveled over hundreds of skulls laid out in flat-top glass cases, including crania Hrdlička had brought back from Peru. When the exposition closed in 1917, about half the remains were shipped to Washington, while the other half stayed in San Diego as part of the permanent collection of the "Museum of Man."[15]

Hrdlička was not done collecting bones. For the next thirty years, he personally led expeditions or oversaw them from the National Museum of Natural History. Alaskan bones became his obsession. He believed they contained evidence of the link between Native Americans and their Asian ancestors. In his frequent trips to Kodiak Island and Larsen Bay, he dug up the remains of more than 1,000 Alaska Natives. Local Alutiiq, to whom he paid ten cents per bone collected, nicknamed Hrdlička "the bone doctor."[16]

Hrdlička and his bone doctor network also collected some 280 brains. Forty-eight came from Black people from the Washington, DC, area, including from fetuses and children who died in local hospitals that served the city's almshouse. Hrdlička performed most of the autopsies, including that of Moses Boone, a twenty-one-month-old who died at Children's Hospital in DC. The Army Medical Museum also sent Hrdlička more than twenty brains. Most of the rest of the brains came from Indigenous people and other people of color. Hrdlička's now debunked study of these brains concluded that brains of Whites were the most developed, those of Asians and Native Americans were in the middle, and the brains of Africans and African Americans were the least developed.[17]

Hrdlička's studies of skulls, bones, and brains won him admirers at the highest levels of American politics. During the Pan-California Exposition, former President Theodore Roosevelt wrote to Hrdlička to quiz him about his theories on the origins of people in the Americas. To determine apportionment of reservation lands, in

1915 the Justice Department tasked Hrdlička with identifying "full-blooded" Chippewas on the White Earth Reservation in Minnesota. In the 1920s, Hrdlička served on the advisory board of the American Eugenics Society, which advocated for the forced sterilization of the mentally and physically handicapped, as well as of certain non-White and immigrant populations. In the years before the outbreak of World War II, Hrdlička corresponded with Franklin Roosevelt about the growing aggression of the Japanese in the Pacific. In 1933, Hrdlička explained to then President-Elect Roosevelt that he believed that Japanese belligerence came from the fact that they were, as a people, "utterly egotistic, tricky and ruthless." He predicted that the Japanese Empire would fight to drive out of Asia all but its own, "particularly the white man."[18]

When Hrdlička died in 1943, the Smithsonian had amassed more than 30,700 body parts. *The New York Times* eulogized Hrdlička as the greatest "student of man," whose study of human remains unlocked long-held secrets of the origins of the human races. But before his death and in the decades after, criticism of Hrdlička's methods and conclusions grew from within anthropology and outside it. Many found fault with his obsession with collecting masses of remains without careful attention to provenance. More importantly, more anthropologists, led by Franz Boas, rejected the conceit that scientists could draw a straight line between physical anatomy and innate abilities. Instead, the anthropologist's mandate became to document and understand cultures, not races. The fact that Hrdlička's findings in physical anthropology had been embraced by the Axis powers also made clear that Hrdlička's brand of "scientific" racism was not only unscientific and unpalatable but dangerous.[19]

Still, Hrdlička's legacy and that of his skull-collecting predecessors, including Morton, Otis, and Yarrow, continued to dominate the face that the Smithsonian's National Museum of Natural History presented to the world. In the mid-twentieth century, the museum's skull collection was repurposed to tell a story not of the distinctions between the human races in various corners of the globe but of the exponential growth of the human race across the planet. In 1965, the Smithsonian opened its Hall of Physical Anthropology, in which the most prominent display was a "Skull Wall" of 160 specimens of Hrdlička's ancient Peruvian crania. The display was laid out like a mushroom cloud to demonstrate how the human population had exploded since the beginning of the Common Era. Three skulls at the bottom represented the 300 million people believed to be alive in 1 CE. At the top, 106 skulls represented the 3.5 billion people alive in 1965, at the height of the "Space Age." A *Washington Post* reporter asked Dale Stewart, director of the National Museum of Natural History and a mentee of Hrdlička, why they chose to use Peruvian skulls for the display. "Because we had so many of them," Stewart replied.[20]

During the same period, the Civil Rights movement in the United States and anticolonial movements around the globe renewed scrutiny of how race science had buttressed slavery, colonization, and genocide. Indigenous communities organized to call out the cavalier misuse and abuse of their ancestors' remains and the stereotypical presentation of Native American history in American museums. They demanded the restoration of their ancestors' remains and an end to the continued unearthing of their ancestors. Native groups found many museums, and the anthropologists and archaeologists who ran them, reluctant to part with their collections. Subscribing to a version of Manifest Destiny's most pernicious myth—that it had succeeded in eliminating living Natives—museum curators believed themselves to be the true protectors and narrators of Native history. For example, in 1971, archaeologists led a student group on a six-week excavation of a precolonial Indian village in southwestern Minnesota. The group was confused and angered when members of the American Indian Movement (AIM) seized shovels, buried trenches the students had dug, and burned their excavation notes. Some of the would-be archaeologists declared that they had lost respect for Native Americans because AIM had destroyed the group's work and disrespected their preservation efforts. "None of the whites could understand that they were not helping living Indians preserve their culture by digging up the remains of a village that had existed in the 1500s," wrote Vine Deloria Jr. about the incident. The attitude of the White archaeologists and their students "was that they were the true spiritual descendants of the original Indians and that the contemporary Indians were foreigners who had no right to complain about their activities."[21]

During this period, Native Americans who objected to the "study" and public display of Native remains also waged campaigns of protests, picketing, and political lobbying. In 1987, the Larsen Bay Tribal Council passed a resolution that called on the Smithsonian to repatriate their ancestors whom Hrdlička had stolen in the 1930s. Over the next few years, the council's efforts forced the museum to return the remains of about 1,000 ancestors. The Larsen Bay community's work catalyzed the passage of two landmark federal laws, the Native American Graves Protection and Repatriation Act (NAGPRA) and the National Museum of the American Indian Act (NMAIA). Together, the two laws required the Smithsonian's National Museum of Natural History and museums across the country to inventory their collections and, in consultation with Indigenous communities, work to repatriate remains from Native American, Alaska Native, and Native Hawaiian peoples to their lineal or tribal descendants. NAGPRA also made it a criminal offense to traffic in Native American remains and funerary objects, punishable for the first offense with up to twelve months' imprisonment and a $100,000 fine. NMAIA established a national museum as "a living memorial to the Native Americans and their traditions," which opened its doors on the National Mall in 2004.[22]

Some lamented that the Smithsonian was being forced to return its collection of Native remains. In a biography of Hrdlička published in 1994, archeologist Stephen Loring and anthropologist Miroslav Prokopec wrote that Hrdlička had "salvaged [the remains] from the ravages of time, the indiscriminate disturbances of vandals, and environmental perturbations." But the new repatriation laws meant that "this unassailable scientific monument to one man's collecting zeal is under attack. Changing political and social mores have invaded the previously sacrosanct halls of the academy." The Skull Wall came down in the 1980s, but the 160 Peruvian skulls that made up the wall were not repatriated. NMAIA and NAGPRA do not require American museums to inventory remains taken from outside the United States. Instead, those skulls rejoined the more than 4,000 skeletal units from Peru that remain in the Smithsonian's holdings.[23]

OVER THE PAST DECADE, THE SKULLS STOLEN FROM Walker's Mountain have, once again, been unboxed—this time, in the repatriation office at NMNH. And once again, they have been subjected to study.

The seven skulls represent less than .01 percent of the Smithsonian's holdings in human remains. (The Smithsonian has not confirmed how big the collection actually is, likely because it doesn't know itself. Some estimates place the range of individual sets of body parts between 10,000 and 35,000.) The vast majority lack provenance—another legacy of the Hrdlička era—making the museum's legal mandate to sort through, and if possible return, these body parts to their descendants difficult, if not often impossible. Still, the law requires the museum to start somewhere. The museum's repatriation office has prioritized remains with individual names associated with them. As such, because they had a name associated with them in the NMNH's accession catalog—"Wah-ker"—the seven skulls that Yarrow took from Utah in 1872 received special attention.

David Hollinger, a tribal liaison officer at NMNH, has been thinking about these skulls ever since he was hired at the museum in the early 2000s. Since then, in fits and starts, Hollinger has reached out to tribal contacts in the Great Basin to inform them of the remains in the museum's possession. In 2017, Hollinger and his colleagues started a formal "cultural affiliation" study of the skulls—a study required to determine to which tribes the remains should be made available for repatriation.[24]

Hollinger and his colleagues started with Wakara's skull—or so they thought. In his 1873 transmittal letter to AMM curator George Otis, Yarrow wrote that the remains in one box included the "cranium and part of skeleton of Wah-ker." A century and a half later, NMNH curators examined the skull, noting that "966," which had been scrawled on the frontal bone, was crossed out, and a Smithsonian accession number "P225085 Ute [male symbol] /Utah" had been written on the skull in black ink. They also found bright orange paint spots situated across the skull—marks used to line it up when it was photographed to make AMM's composite image for the "Pah Utes." The skull's relative robustness and bone fusion suggested that it belonged to a male about thirty to forty years old at death. All this fit living descriptions of Wakara. When he and Nauvoo Legion General Daniel Wells measured the Ute leader in 1852, the Mormon clerk Thomas Bullock wrote that Wakara was about thirty-five, meaning that he was about thirty-eight when he died in January 1855. What didn't fit were the teeth. When he transferred the remains to AMM, Yarrow drew Otis's attention to the fact that the skull's wisdom teeth were unerupted. Yet the curators found no evidence of such unerupted teeth in the skull. The curators did find another mandible in the group that matched Yarrow's description, from a child no older than fifteen years old. Since Yarrow had found this child's remains and the remains of P225085 in the same grave, Yarrow likely mistook that child's mandible for Wakara's.

Hollinger and colleagues had another candidate for Wakara's skull, P225086 (AMM970). The skull came with the cranium intact but no mandible. It was also from a male and had the same pattern of reddish-orange paint from when it too sat before AMM's camera in the 1880s to make the composite image. This skull was slightly older than P225085. The cranium, among other indicators, had signs of arthritis and dental disease associated with aging. Critically, the curators noted the presence of green staining around the base of the skull, likely from a copper alloy. These remains were the only ones in the set from Wakara's grave that had likely been in contact with brass objects. In his first published report on mortuary customs, Yarrow wrote that when he dug up the remains, the skull he thought belonged to Wakara had been buried with ornamental metal objects. Wakara's name also translated to "yellow" or "brass."

In 2018, Smithsonian curators again photographed the two skulls. This time, however, the purpose was not to compare them to other Ute skulls or to skulls from other "races." Instead, the goal was to see if the curators could further determine which belonged to Wakara.

To do so, Hollinger and colleagues turned to the National Center for Missing and Exploited Children (NCMEC), experts at using twenty-first-century technologies to match images with cranial remains. NCMEC digitally reconstructed the skulls, then superimposed on them the portrait that Solomon Carvalho had painted of the leader eight months before he died (see Carvalho's painting on page 307). They found that P225085, the skull Yarrow associated with Wakara, was an acceptable match, though the mandible in the portrait was found to be too thin compared to the reconstructed image. P225086 matched even more closely than the other skull, with the eye sockets lining up with the eyes in Carvalho's painting. But without a mandible to compare chins, the curators concluded that the facial superimpositions meant that either skull could have been Wakara's.

And yet a cultural affiliation is only half done in bone. The other half is done in paper—using contemporaneous written materials and, to a lesser extent, oral narratives that can connect the dead's remains to living descendants and tribal nations. In consultation with cultural preservation officers from the Ute and Paiute tribes, the curators traced Wakara's affiliation with the Timpanogos and how, after Wakara's death, most of the surviving Timpanogos merged with the Utes on the Uintah Reservation in northeastern Utah. Yet Kanosh's Pahvants stayed on their ancestral lands, just below the Ute cemetery where Wakara and other Utes, including Kanosh's own kin, were buried. Intermarrying with Paiutes, the Kanosh Band took it as their duty to look after Wakara and all the ancestors buried on Walker's Mountain. In the end, Hollinger and colleagues concluded that the evidence connects both skulls to the Ute Indian Tribe of Utah and the Paiute Indian Tribe of Utah. By statute, lineal descendants of Wakara could make first claims to the remains. But if no such descendants emerged, the repatriation office recommended that the remains be repatriated jointly to the tribes.

Five other sets of remains that Yarrow collected from or near Wakara's grave needed to be studied. The curators found that each had been subjected to the same cataloging pattern, with an AMM number printed in ink, most often on the forehead. That number was then crossed out, and a Smithsonian number was written onto the bone in ink or graphite.

The study and conclusions regarding four of the remains were straightforward. One was a partial cranium of a young child, two to four years of age, too small to determine the sex. The skull bones appeared to have been bleached white by the sun. Another was from a slightly older child, ranging from three to five years old. These remains were ivory in color, with some brown and black stains and evidence of plant root etching and soil staining, along with some insect debris trapped in the base of the cranium. The curators determined that a third set of remains, a complete cranium and mandible, belonged to a woman between twenty-four and thirty-five years of age, with some evidence that she had suffered from disease or malnutrition as a child. A set of beads from the 1800s, which had been observed with the remains a decade prior, had gone missing. The fourth set of remains was from a slightly older female, thirty to forty years of age. Her cheek and nasal bones showed signs of trauma from blunt force, but the breaks had healed before her death. The curators suggested that the two adult females could have been the women variously reported as slaves, wives, and "squaws" who were killed as part of Wakara's funeral. They also suggested that the remains of the slightly older child could have belonged to a little girl, variously reported as a child or a slave, who was sacrificed to join Wakara in his crypt. Yet the fact that the remains of the smaller child had been exposed to the elements and not protected in a cairn grave meant that they might have come from the graves of other Ute kin buried near Wakara.

The final set of remains were those of a teenager. Based on dental formation and fusion of the cranium, Hollinger and colleagues determined that the child was between twelve and fifteen years of age at death. Growth at the chin resulting from secondary-sex characteristics suggested that it was likely male. They found tissue and soil on the right side of the back of the skull, suggesting that the skull was resting on dirt after death. They also found evidence of rodent gnawing around the eye sockets and jawbone.

The thorniest issue that Hollinger and colleagues had to work through was this teenager's purported status as a Paiute slave buried alive with Wakara. Among the hundreds of cultural affiliations that the NMNH has completed, these remains "pose an unusual, possibly unique, challenge for interpreting cultural affiliation," Hollinger wrote in the final report. The evidence was clear that the child was named a Paiute ("Piede") and a "slave" or "prisoner" in eyewitness accounts of the burial written soon after Wakara's death. The evidence was also clear that Wakara's band had long raided and traded Paiutes. It is possible that this child was among the Paiute children whom Wakara purchased while he was in southern Utah near Parowan in late 1854 in the months before his death. There was also the precedent that Wakara's people sacrificed Paiutes to accompany dead Utes in their graves. But it is also known that some of Wakara's Paiute prisoners became tribal kin through adoption or marriage. Even if reports that claimed the child was Paiute were accurate, Wakara might have seen the child—and the child might have seen himself—as a member of Wakara's band.

But American law, more than Native custom, posed a problem. When he was sacrificed in January 1855 as part of Wakara's funeral, the child became "human remains" culturally affiliated with one tribe and a "funerary object" of another—a possibility that the drafters of the NAGPRA repatriation legislation never foresaw. Still, in consultation with elders from both tribes, Hollinger and colleagues concluded that these unique remains and the other six individuals associated with Wakara's grave should "be made available for repatriation jointly to the Ute Indian Tribe and the Paiute Indian Tribe of Utah."

Yarrow and his grave-robbing colleagues did not just unearth Wakara's grave. In 1874, when Kanosh made his visit to Walker's Mountain, he discovered—to his horror—that the graves of his brother Shot and son Stambo had also been destroyed.

Kanosh's account opens another possibility for the origins of this set of skulls. Yarrow's Box No. 1, which he said contained the skulls of Wakara and the Paiute slave buried alive to watch over the grave, might have contained the remains of Shot and Stambo. The age of the older skull matches the age of Shot. The age of the teenager matches the age of Stambo. Likewise, Box No. 2 might have been from Wakara's grave, including the skull of Wakara, the "squaws," and children or "slaves" sacrificed to join the Ute leader in the world beyond.

Yarrow wasn't the last grave robber to make the arduous trek to Walker's Mountain. Many have been drawn by the lurid spectacle of Wakara's death rites. In 1946, as research for a never-published book on Wakara, historian of the American West Charles Kelly asked Joe Pikyavit, a longtime leader of the Kanosh Band, to take him to Wakara's grave. Kelly wanted to photograph the gravesite "of the only great chief the Utahs ever had." Joe Pikyavit, the grandfather of Rick Pikyavit, agreed to help Kelly, but only on the condition that Kelly promised not to disturb the graves. Kelly agreed and Pikyavit guided him and his friend Frank Beckwith, a newspaperman and amateur photographer from Millard County, Utah, to Walker's Mountain. On the climb up the mountain, Pikyavit warned the two other men not to expect to find much. As Kelly put in a magazine article about the visit to the gravesite, "White ghouls had removed everything—bones, clothing, rifles and all the other goods buried with the chief." After the exhausting, hours-long climb, the three men reached Wakara's grave. As predicted, all that was left was a large hole. Wakara's grave had been picked so clean that "we did not find even a loose bead." Kelly, Beckwith, and Pikyavit explored some of the rest of Walker's Mountain and found several other burial sites. As promised, Kelly and Beckwith left them alone.[25]

In the decades that followed, despite the challenges of reaching the gravesite, dozens of parties likely visited Wakara's grave. A handful were documented. Richard S. Van Wagoner, a prolific historian of early Mormonism, and Steven C. Walker, a Harvard-educated professor of English at Brigham Young University (BYU), made the trek in 1979. The US Forest Service also made several visits to the gravesite as part of cultural resource inventories of the lands it manages. One set of visits would become revelatory. They would also become deadly.

IN SEPTEMBER 1984, ALMOST EXACTLY 112 YEARS AFTER Yarrow's grave-robbing visit, Robert Leonard, the archaeologist for the Fishlake

Forest Service, which manages the land upon which the gravesite sits, conducted a survey of Wakara's grave.

In the cool morning light at the small town just below Walker's Mountain, Leonard and three of his Forest Service colleagues saddled up their horses and spent all morning climbing up the mountain. Around noon they crossed a creek, pausing briefly to water their horses in the mountain stream and wipe sweat from their faces. They then weaved through the thick forest. Emerging into the hot, early-fall sun, they scrambled over the talus field to arrive at Wakara's grave.[26]

Leonard was confident that this was the right place. It matched the photos that Kelly's excursion partner, Frank Beckwith, had taken of the grave in 1946. As had Kelly and Beckwith during their visit four decades before, Leonard and his party noted the oblong "burial pits" and what remained of the wooden poles that formed the roofs of the vaults, Leonard wrote in the report he later turned in to the Forest Service. Leonard estimated that around Wakara's own vault seven graves had been disturbed. Another three had not. The vaults were oriented north-south and northwest-southeast. Leonard and other members of his party then jumped into the open vaults, which were as deep as 1.5 meters, 1 meter wide, and 1.5 meters long. Inside the vaults, Leonard and his party observed no burial goods. They did find what they believed was a horse scapula, which they collected and sent to BYU for verification.

Daylight was fading, and the horses were whinnying, ready for fresh hay back at the horse trailer. The trip up had taken longer than expected, and the trip down in the dark would be dangerous for both horses and riders. So Leonard and his party decided not to inspect the burial ground further up the field. Before they left, Leonard snapped a few pictures of his party standing inside Wakara's vault. Leonard then passed the camera to another party member and got back in the vault. He smiled at the lens. He then stepped out of the vault, sat down on a nearby rock, and drew a rough sketch of the cemetery and vaults surrounding Wakara's grave.

And yet, curiosity bit Leonard. Just before the party departed, Leonard scampered higher onto the rockslide. For a few minutes, he scanned the field. As had other visitors to Walker's Mountain before him, he saw bones everywhere—out in the open, on the surface, perhaps exposed by erosion and time, and partially hidden in crevices and rocks. Wakara's grave had been completely plundered of grave goods. But up here, Leonard saw other human-made objects that had been buried with the deceased. A whistle from down the mountain snapped Leonard back to attention. The rest of the party had already mounted their horses.

In the conclusion of his report, Leonard recommended that the "historic Ute burial ground . . . should be avoided by all project activity[,] in that the site is religiously significant to contemporary groups of Utes and Paiutes." He also recommended that more "cultural resources surveys should be conducted in the future to ascertain the extent of the burials on the higher talus slopes." Leonard sent a copy of the report to the Paiute tribal headquarters in Cedar City "in hopes that they will cooperate in some type of effort designed to protect this area from further vandalism." Soon after, Leonard made public these findings, along with a vivid description of the history of Wakara's life and death, in the series of placards that he helped erect outside the Territorial Statehouse State Park Museum in Fillmore.

Leonard took it upon himself to conduct the resource studies he recommended. He returned to Wakara's grave at least twice. Leonard did not leave empty-handed. On a cold, cloudy fall day in November 2014, Leonard climbed down into Wakara's vault along with three other adventure seekers. "One of the guys was turning over rocks," Leonard told me, and discovered a bone about four centimeters long and one centimeter wide. Leonard pocketed the bone. Leonard said that later analysis showed that it was a human toe bone.

Echoing Yarrow's plea, "please say nothing about the crania," Leonard expressed worry that some people might become upset if they learned that he had taken human remains from the gravesite.

Leonard allegedly took other objects home, either from Wakara's vault or, more likely, from other vaults, which in 1984 he had noticed were full of grave goods but had not had time to explore. These objects included horse tack, a copper bracelet, a Belgian-made pistol, and jingle cones that Wakara's Utes used to decorate their horses. These items ended up on display at the Fremont Indian State Park and Museum, where they were described as "appear[ing] to come from the site of Chief Walkara's (Chief Walker's) burial."

Despite his concerns that his activities at Wakara's gravesite might not be well received, Leonard did not believe he had done anything wrong when he took these objects and the toe bone from Walker's Mountain. To the contrary, like generations of archaeologists and anthropologists before him, Leonard believed he was protecting Native history, not destroying it. When living and breathing Native Americans objected to his actions, including Rick and Rena Pikyavit, Leonard told me that their objections showed that Natives couldn't understand the value of such preservation efforts. In 2019, he became irate when Rena, who then worked as a ranger aide at the Fremont museum, succeeded in getting the funerary items removed from display. He saw that action as connected to deep-seated, generations-old antipathy to Wakara. "She is Navajo and Rick is Paiute. Wakara preyed on both groups," he told me. But in our many conversations, Rena expressed nothing but admiration for Wakara. She described her efforts to remove the funerary items—which she considers just as sacred as human remains—from public view as protecting Wakara and her own people from further harm.

Over the next two years, Leonard worked to complete his magnum opus: a comprehensive study of the "Fish Lake Cutoff" of the Old Spanish Trail. Weaving together firsthand accounts, historical narratives, and archaeological digs, including some he collaborated on with the Pikyavits, Leonard showed that Wakara's Utes and other trail travelers had taken this more direct route across central Utah. For his scholarship, Leonard won several professional accolades, including being twice named the National Park Service Intermountain Region Archaeologist of the Year and winning the Outstanding National Interpreter of the Year Award. In October 2020, he self-published a book of his findings on the Old Spanish Trail.[27]

At the same time, Leonard's health began to fail. Years earlier he had been diagnosed with Parkinson's. His behavior became erratic, even violent. After he retired from the Forest Service in 2017, a confrontation at the service office in Richfield, where he worked for four decades, led to his being banned. Not long afterward, Leonard was also banned from the Fremont Indian State Park and Museum after accosting Rena Pikyavit about her work to have Wakara's grave materials removed. That banishment, Leonard told me, hurt dearly. After all, he had spent "thirty-five years building and funding and cultivating a partnership between the [Fremont Indian] park and the Forest Service."

It only got worse for Leonard. Not long after, an investigation was launched to determine whether he had broken laws associated with the looting of Wakara's grave. In March 2021, Leonard died suddenly. Some of Leonard's associates heard that the cause of death was suicide.

Conclusion

Wakara's Return

What Remains of Wakara's Fish

In the summer of 2023, Forrest Cuch and I pulled over on Lakeview Parkway in Provo, Utah, and stepped out of an air-conditioned car into the heat and sun. We each shaded our eyes with one hand and waved with the other to Hilary Hungerford, a geographer at Utah Valley University. Hungerford walked toward us, holding fast to the hand of her young daughter as traffic buzzed by.

We met Hungerford, a member of the Utah Lake Authority Board, which oversees the restoration of Utah Lake, to talk about the present and future of Utah's waterways. We stood on a bridge above the largest of Utah Lake's tributaries, the Provo River, near where Wakara's Timpanogos held their fish festival for generations. Looking to the west, where the river flows into the lake, we shouted to hear each other over the rumbling of three earthmovers carving trenches into 260 acres of soil.

In the past few years, water in Utah has been in the news, and not for good reasons. Due to the population explosion along the Wasatch Front sucking up groundwater and due to rising temperatures wrought by climate change, the water levels of the Great Salt

Lake have plummeted. The lake is increasingly not a lake at all but a massive salt flat. Scientists predict that without mitigation efforts, within a decade the Salt Lake Valley, now home to 1.5 million people, will become unlivable. Windstorms will whip up lethal clouds of toxins from the increasingly exposed lake bed. These toxins—produced by the region's massive mining interests, then deposited into the lake—will poison the air, making humans and animals sick, or worse.[1]

The desertification of the Great Salt Lake—which some have called an impending "environmental nuclear bomb"—has garnered the world's attention. Yet, here in Provo, some good news has developed that has gone less reported. Lake Restoration Solutions (LRS), the company that wanted to build multi-billion-dollar, Dubai-inspired islands in the lake, failed in their bid—and failed spectacularly, filing for bankruptcy in 2022 following loud and sustained public backlash. Ironically, the biggest creditor in the company's bankruptcy filing was Ben Abbott, the Brigham Young University (BYU) professor who became the face of the opposition to the island proposal, whom the company had sued for defamation. Abbott countersued. LRS owed Abbott close to $400,000 for his time and expenses fighting the failed project.[2]

"Instead of making man-made islands," Hungerford explained to Forrest and me that summer day as her daughter tossed stones from the bridge into the gurgling river below, "those earthmovers are trying to recreate the natural, braided river that once was the mouth of the Provo." This three-decade effort to restore Utah Lake—the ancestral home waters of the fish that defined Wakara's band of fish-eating Timpanogos—shows that a different future in Utah's waterways than an ecological end-time is possible. And this future is, in some ways, a return to the past.

In 1855, a few months after Wakara's passing, Arapeen, Tabby, Tintic, Washear (Squash Head), and their Ute bands arrived at the mouth of the Provo River. There, they found their sacred fish festival grounds replaced by hundreds of acres of Mormon wheat, corn, and potatoes. The fields were also surrounded by fences, which the Utes promptly tore down before pitching their lodges. The Utes' horses and cattle snacked on the few tender leaves spared by an apocalyptic infestation of Rocky Mountain locusts that had decimated the Mormons' crops.

The crop failure was so severe that the Mormon farmers were forced to fish. They squatted along the river. At some points during the summer, the settlers fished day and night, preserving their hauls in salt and distributing them to feed settlements along the Wasatch Front. Were it not for Wakara's fisheries, which his band had carefully managed for hundreds of years, the Mormon settlers would have likely starved to death or been forced to abandon their settlements.[3]

The Mormons' overfishing with nets meant that the Utes' usual fishing with baskets and bows and arrows failed to yield enough fish to sustain them. This angered the Utes. In June, George A. Smith and Dimick Huntington brokered a deal, which for a time prevented a reopening of hostilities. With a 300-foot-long net, the Mormons hauled in some 1,000 suckers from the Provo River, a catch that they gave to the Utes in exchange for removing their horses and cattle from the cultivated fields. The Utes packed as much fish as they could and left.[4]

The 1855 fish festival was the last to take place at Utah Lake. The next spawning season, the Utes moved the festival to the Spanish Fork River. In 1865, the Spanish Fork Treaty initiated the Utes' removal from central Utah to the Uintah Valley Reservation. When anthropologist Nan Smith visited the Utes there in 1936 and 1937, Wakara's grandson, John Duncan (Ungatowinorokant), told her that the Utes had returned to their homelands during spawning seasons until the 1920s, when Indian agents forbade their pilgrimages. With the Timpanogos cut off from their homelands, centuries-old knowledge of sustainable fishing at Timpanogos (Utah) Lake died off with the last of the band's elders. John Duncan died in 1941. His sister Karoomp Kate Red Cap Long Hair died in 1938.[5]

With the Fish Eaters gone, Mormon settlers destroyed the lake's fisheries because they did not know how to manage them or the land and waters on which the fish depended. At a July 1855 Mormon-Ute gathering at Provo to settle disputes over fishing access, Ute leader Highforehead described the lush forests that used to grow next to Utah Valley streams. But deforestation and irrigation had drained the valley of its water. That same summer, Wilford Woodruff acknowledged how these changes to land and waters affected the fauna in the Ute homeland. "Before the whites came, there was plenty of fish and antelope, plenty of game of almost every description," noted the future church president. "But now the whites have killed off these things, and there is scarcely anything left for the poor natives to live upon." The Mormons' 1855 fishing frenzy continued through that fall and winter and into the next spring. "If I were a prophet," explained Utah Valley Mormon leader James C. Snow at another church meeting in April 1856 to negotiate fishing access among the Saints, "I would say there will be no fish in 5 years."[6]

In 1856, Peter Madsen established the first fishing company at the mouth of the Provo River. Commercial fishing expanded throughout the next two decades to help feed the settler population in Utah, which had more than doubled between 1860 and 1870 to over 85,000. After the arrival of the railroad, demand for Utah Lake's fish increased further as the fish were shipped by railcar to other booming settlements in California, Denver, and Chicago.

At the same time, water diversion for farming around the lake put the already stressed fisheries in greater peril. In the spring, suckers and trout that weren't caught in the nets at the mouth of the Provo River swam upriver to spawn. A few weeks later, millions of small fry swimming down the river ended up not in the lake but in farmers' fields as temporary dams diverted the river onto farmlands to irrigate crops. The water changed too: the cold and clear snowmelt turned warm and brown due to farming and industry runoff. The City of Provo corralled the once multifingered Provo River into one channel, leading to further turbidity and habitat destruction. Woolen mills, sawmills, and, later, wastewater treatment plants sprang up along the lakeshore. By the early twentieth century, the lake was habitable only for the most robust of invasive species, like carp, which the settlers introduced to the lake in the 1880s. Of the thirteen native fish species in Utah Lake before Mormon settlement, only the June sucker, along with a tiny number of Utah suckers and Utah chubs, remained.

That the June sucker survived even in such tiny numbers was a good sign. The June sucker was one of the most cherished fish of Wakara's Utes, likely because they knew that its health indicates the overall health of the lake. As Ben Abbott, the BYU fish biologist, has told me, a healthy June sucker population supports a chain of other species, including mollusks that filter the water, promoting the flourishing of plants and animals in water and on land. In the 1980s, when the June Sucker Recovery Implementation Program (JSRIP) began, an estimated 500 adult suckers swam in Utah Lake. Over the last four decades, through trial and error, JSRP has supported the June sucker population by combining local knowledge systems and cutting-edge laboratory science. And as the June sucker population has rebounded, other animals, including migratory birds, waterfowl, and birds of prey, have also returned to the lake. Hungerford, Abbott, and other lake advocates hope that through the JSRP and the associated Provo Delta River Restoration Project the suckers will again spawn in the river as they did for thousands of years. Abbott explained that instead of forcing nature to bend to humans' will, as his own Mormon settler ancestors did, June sucker advocates are "working with nature" as Wakara's ancestors learned to do over centuries. According to Mary

Reconstructed Provo River Delta. Aerial view looking southeast at the Provo (Timpanogos) River in December 2024 as it flows through the reconstructed delta into Utah (Timpanogos) Lake. The line of trees to the right of the delta marks the river's former channel. (Courtesy of Utah by Air)

Meyer, the CEO of the Timpanogos Nation who claims descent from Wakara's brother Arapeen, as a result "the lake is healing itself."

To be sure, it's happening in fits and starts. But such collaborations among Natives and settlers at Utah Lake suggest that history is not linear. Settlers thought that removal of the Timpanogos' fish was permanent. But the diaspora of the fish, as well as the destruction of the ecosystem of relations they were a part of, has proven to be not final but seasonal—though that season has certainly been a long one.

The Fish Eaters are not gone, either. To be sure, they are not currently present on their ancestral lands and waters around Utah (Timpanogos) Lake. Yet, despite the efforts of settlers and settler governments, Wakara's Utes are still here, in Utah. And like their ancestor Wakara, the Utes are *here*: fully American *and* fully Native.

Wakara's descendants on the Uintah and Ouray Reservation participate in perhaps the most defining of American industries: fossil fuel extraction. The Ute Indian Tribe of Utah runs some of the most profitable oil and gas companies of any tribal nation in the United States, pulling tens of thousands of barrels of Uintah Basin "black wax crude" from the ground each week. And like most Native American communities, the Utes have demonstrated their patriotism as members of the US military. From the muddy trenches in Belgium during World War I to the deserts of Iraq, the Utes have sent hundreds of young men and women to fight and die in American wars. In fact, the most prominent structure on the reservation is a monument honoring Ute veterans. Opened on Veterans Day 2013, the memorial is built in the shape of the sacred medicine wheel. Five stone towers, representing the five military branches, lean together to hold up a cauldron, which is lit when a tribal veteran dies or during national holidays. On the columns, names of veterans are engraved for each service branch. The Utes "did their DUTY," the monument's main plaque reads, "even in times when they were not considered citizens of the country. . . . They served without hesitation and with distinction because they understood the need to defend one's own land, and they understood fundamental concepts of fighting for life, liberty, property, and the pursuit of happiness."

On their reservation, Wakara's descendants have also created new ways of being Native, or, more specifically, being *Nuche*. They have bonded themselves to the lands and waters of the Uintah Basin and to the plants and animals living there. The reservation's dance grounds, where they host the Bear Dance to inaugurate spring and conduct powwows in early July to celebrate America's birthday, have become their new sacred center. In the mountains to the north, tribal members hunt plentiful elk and deer. After a kill, "hunters make offerings in gratitude for animals who have given their lives to feed the people," Forrest Cuch recently wrote in his book that synthesizes Christian and Ute theologies, *A Native Way of Giving*. On the basin's plains the tribe raises a large bison herd, whose meat is distributed to tribal members. In the foothills of the Uintah Mountains, the tribe has also opened a fish hatchery to stock the lakes and ponds on the reservation and to reintroduce native trout to the Utes' ancestral waterways.[7]

The restoration of native fish to the waters in which they once swam and from which Wakara's Utes fed themselves can be seen as part of the broader "rematriation" movement. In its modern iteration, rematriation began with the return of sacred seeds to the Indigenous lands where they once flourished and fed humans and other animals. In what Shiloh Maples (Ojibwe and Odawa) calls "relation foodways," Indigenous seed keepers share with each other sacred seeds. They also teach each other how to plant, care for, and consume the fruits of these seeds. Likewise, Ute and other Great Basin Native peoples, along with partners in Utah's major universities, see the restoration of fish on and off the reservation lands as rematriation: a homecoming for animals, plants, and humans, the end of a long season of diaspora.[8]

What Remains of Wakara's Horses

Forrest and I left Hilary Hungerford and headed north along the lakeshore. Passing through streets of suburban sprawl, we pulled onto a dirt road, with a golf course to our left and a ten-foot chain-link fence to our right. On the other side of the fence, we watched a dozen cattle graze on massive stands of invasive phragmites.

The cows stand on a pilot plot for Walkara Way, a conservation project started by Jacob Holdaway on land first settled by his ancestors in the village of Vineyard. Before his great-great-great-grandfather Shadrach Holdaway came to the lake in 1849, the "parks," as Parley P. Pratt once described them, along the northeastern shore were lush grasslands that fed deer, antelope, and herds of Wakara's horses. Small streams braided the land with clear runoff from the mountains to the east. At the shore's edge, wetlands served as a seasonal home for ducks, geese, and other migratory birds. Wakara's Utes fished and swam from sandy beaches. Today, phragmites suck up the water, creating an ideal habitat for disease-carrying mosquitos and rendering much of the lake inhospitable to waterfowl, unswimmable for fish, and inaccessible to humans.

"It wasn't this bad when I was a kid," Holdaway told me as the jovial forty-something took me on a tour of the plot the summer before. When he was in grade school, after milking cows alongside his father and grandfather, Holdaway spent hours exploring his family's land and imagining what it was like before the settlers arrived. "In school, I read something about Wakara and did some research on him," Holdaway told me. Then, on his family's land near the lake's shore, "I built wickiups and spent nights, playing like I was him." But in the decades since, as dairy farmers have gone bankrupt and sold off the herds that kept the phragmites down, the overgrowth has gotten so bad, Holdaway told me, "We can't even see the lake that's less than a half a mile that way. And my kids can't play on the land because we're worried that they'll get bit by mosquitos and contract West Nile."

In 2018, Holdaway launched the Walkara Way project to restore the lakeshore to its parklike ecology and beauty. By convincing other private landowners to provide land easements, Holdaway's vision is to create a 1,000-acre nature preserve where locals can hunt and fish, as Wakara's Utes did for generations. Replanted trees will remove excess dirt from the water and provide habitat for birds and insects to feed the fish. Artificial beaver dams will recreate wetlands. Raised nests will provide homes for raptors to survey the wetlands and fields. A cultural center, which Holdaway tentatively calls the Wickiup, will tell the story of Wakara's Timpanogos people. Eventually a 100-mile bike trail will encircle the entire Utah Lake.

"The whole vision starts with hoofed animals," which, Holdaway explained, once served as the natural cleaning agents, vacuuming up vegetation and keeping the land open and the water flowing. But the deer and elk that Wakara's Utes hunted, which were decimated by the arrival of Holdaway's ancestors, are not coming back anytime soon. So Holdaway's plan is to have cows eat up the phragmites. It seems that the cows are effective. In just three months, Holdaway told me, the thirty cows he borrowed from a local rancher devoured most of the phragmites on his fifty-acre pilot plot.

The herds of horses that used to run, eat, and mate on the eastern shore of Utah Lake are also gone from the Timpanogos homelands. After Wakara's death in 1855, his heir and brother, Arapeen, struggled to keep the band together. He could no longer raid horses in California, and he could no longer purchase or steal Paiute women and children, as the Mormons moved to "adopt" them as fast as they could. He could not gather his people at the fish festival grounds in the spring to hunt and fish. And increasingly, within Wakara's own homelands, Arapeen and other Utes' movements were blocked physically by walls, forts, and fences. They were also blocked legally by settler land claims.

In the summer of 1856, Dimick Huntington led a convoy up and down the Mormon Road, delivering warnings and promises to Arapeen and other surviving Ute leaders. "Walker's death has been a good thing," Huntington proclaimed. Utah's Natives needed to settle down and become farmers, or they would "go like Walker did," Huntington threatened. Forget Wakara's horses and horse-raiding culture, he told the Native leaders. In his conversations with Utes, Goshutes, and Shoshones, the Mormon interpreter pointed to Kanosh as the model to emulate. "He has ten oxen, 2 yoke of cows, 5 horse wagons and harness. He has given up hunting. He has got a good adobe house and is living like white folks. He is the first chief that has made any law among them. He whips for stealing."[9]

Yet, in the following years, most Utes did not follow Kanosh's example. Arapeen and others refused to settle down on the farms that the Mormons and the federal Indian agents established in central

Utah. They believed they would die if they gave up their horseback, seasonal travels for sedentary farming. And they were right. The Indian farms mostly failed due to harsh winters, droughts, and poor governmental support. And most of the Utes who stayed yearlong on the farms experienced disease and starvation, not to mention abuse from their White caretakers.

When they were forced into exile on the Uintah Reservation, Wakara's Utes took their horses and horse culture with them. So did their Ute (*Núuchiu*) kin from Colorado, who in the 1870s were forced off their own homelands and moved onto reservations on the western slope of the Rockies. There, the Colorado Utes continued to raise, train, and race horses—and gamble on the outcomes. This angered White River Indian agent Nathan Meeker, who believed gambling immoral and horse racing a waste of time. Meeker seized the Utes' horses and plowed up their racetrack. In late September 1879, a group of Colorado Utes attacked members of the 9th Cavalry, whom Meeker had called in for support, leading to the death of twenty-three Utes and seventeen US soldiers. The Colorado Utes also set fire to the agency building, killing Meeker, eight of his employees, and two civilians. After a lengthy investigation, Congress passed a declaration that forced the White River and Tabeguache (Uncompahgre) Utes to join their Utah kin on what would become the Uintah and Ouray Reservation.[10]

And yet Ute horse culture persisted. Even after federal Indian agents continued to pressure them to give up equestrianism for farming and ranching—including forcibly disbanding the tribe's herds—the Utes continued to leave the reservation to hunt the dwindling number of bison and other game in Utah, Colorado, and Wyoming into the 1920s. As they had during Wakara's time, horses remained status symbols and signs of cultural power.[11]

Even today, when livestock and mineral extraction have become the two leading industries on the reservation, many Utes continue to keep horses. "We use . . . [our horses] for a lot of things. Use them to herd cows, ranching," explained Sapianaze Larose, who raises and rides horses in the Uintah Basin and teaches his children to do the same. The Ute connection with horses "goes back to the old people," explained Sherwood Cuch, longtime Ute Indian Tribe cattle manager and world champion bareback rodeo rider. "[Our Ute ancestors] were undefeated in their war times because of the horse. . . . [W]hen elders passed away, they used to sacrifice their best saddle horses for them." Champion barrel racer Lara Jean Arrowchis-Ivie has been riding horses since she was a little girl. "My dad and my grandfather always taught me," she said, "if you take care of your horse, it'll take care of you."[12]

On his ranch just north of Roosevelt, Utah, Wakara's descendant Forrest Cuch and his own small herd do "horse medicine," a traditional form of Indigenous equine therapy, wherein specially trained (and selected) horses, whom the Utes consider spiritual kin, interact with individuals suffering from physical and emotional traumas. "Horses can sense the pain of people," Cuch explained. "They are deeply spiritual beings. They can see and smell demons and push them out." Horse medicine, like sweat lodge ceremonies, "cleanses us, revitalizes us, and gives us strength and power," Cuch continued. "The horse today is as important as it was during the North American conquest and before that. Those of us who were part of horse culture need to revitalize that part of us because it will make us strong."

The Utes and their horses remain a symbol of both Native resistance to settler colonialism and Ute Americanness. Over the July 4 weekend in 2016, a thirteen-foot bronze statue of a Ute warrior sitting astride a horse was added to the Ute veterans' memorial. The massive statue was paid for out of a settlement that the tribe won in a right-of-way suit, which netted tens of millions of dollars. "The battleground [for Native sovereignty] in the twentieth and twenty-first centuries is the court system," explained Ronald Wopsock, then head of the Ute Indian Tribe of Utah Business Committee, the governing body of the Ute Indian Tribe of Utah.[13]

Forrest Cuch and his horses. Forrest Cuch (Ute Indian Tribe of Utah) chats with his horses, with whom he performs "horse medicine" to help Utes and settlers alike deal with trauma and other illnesses. (Photo by the author)

Statue of Ute warrior at the Ute Veterans Memorial, Fort Duchesne, Utah. (Photo by the author)

Wakara's horsemen are still here, in the American West. So are Wakara's horses. In fact, in some of the dozens of horse paddocks next to homes on the reservation are descendants of the Spanish colonial horses that Wakara stole from California in the 1840s. Perhaps a handful are direct descendants of the horses that the Utes brought with them when they were forced to leave central Utah in the 1860s. Others have been adopted at events held each spring at the Wild Horse and Burro facility in Delta, Utah, when the Bureau of Land Management puts members of the Sulphur herd up for adoption.

The Utes aren't the only Americans who feel called to reintroduce these historic horses to wider parts of the Southwest that they and their riders once dominated. Naomi Wilson and her husband, Stephen Shultz, have adopted Sulphur horses, which they ride around Moab, Utah, as part of the Canyonlands Back Country Horsemen. Shultz, the president of the group, calls the horses "genetic treasures"—the last surviving herd directly related to the horses reintroduced by the conquistadors in the 1500s. "When I look at these horses, I see history running through their veins with every beat of their heart." Shultz and other champions of these horses, including the Haydens from Baker, Utah, continue to work against the government's efforts to cull the herd. The protectors of the Sulphur herd also lobby for a future in which these horses are celebrated as historically important, as well as cherished for their work and companionship.[14]

Perhaps as they did during Wakara's time, one day these horses will also run along the shores of Utah (Timpanogos) Lake on Walkara Way, keeping down the phragmites and clearing the land so that fish, fowl, and humans can also return.

What Remains of Wakara's Slaves (and Kin)

Wakara came to her in a dream while she slept in her home in suburban Minnesota, Fernetta Lerwick recently explained.

The Ute leader appeared to Lerwick in the 2000s, shortly after a DNA test revealed that her father was the issue of an affair between her grandmother and an unknown man. The affair had not been spoken about for decades. "I now know why the family reunions of my childhood were so awkward!" Lerwick continued. A member of the Church of Jesus Christ of Latter-day Saints, Lerwick had long been interested in genealogy and family history. But the revelation of a long-covered-up branch of her family tree sent Lerwick down a path, now more than twenty years in the making, to discover more about her biological grandfather and his extended family.

Through DNA testing combined with genealogical records, Lerwick soon learned that this grandfather was part Ute and likely a direct descendant of Wakara by his daughter Nellie (Nelley) Wadze. This revelation led her to locate other living Wakara descendants. One of the hundreds of distant relatives Lerwick has found is Michelle Bradley Wesley (Eastern Band of Cherokee). A descendant of Wakara's son Arkansas, Bradley Wesley is also a genealogist. Together, she and Lerwick have constructed a multigenerational family tree of the Northern Utes, which, among other things, helps correct the historical record about their ancestors, as well as other Native children who were "adopted" into Mormon homes.

Lerwick's great-great-grandmother Nellie/Waddie was nine years old and living with her adoptive family, the Leitheads, in the Sanpete Valley when her biological father Wakara died in January 1855. Up the road in Provo in the summer of that same year, Mormon families were ordered to submit to the Utah County Court written terms of indenture for the "Indian children held in servitude" in their households. In July, Susanna Ewing came to court with an infant Ute girl she called Fransina, whom Susanna had acquired from her father, a Ute whom the settlers called Tommy. Susanna took in the sickly child, washed and fed her, and anointed her with consecrated oil. Smitten with her tiny charge, Susanna wrote to Brigham Young to lean on Tommy to relinquish his claim to his daughter. The girl's mother had already died, and Tommy was also sick. But some of Tommy's Ute relatives wanted the child back. Still, Young convinced the Utes to let Susanna keep her. On the morning of July 23, 1855, after she had delivered the required terms of indenture to the court, "the little babe [was] bound over to me according to the law," Susanna happily reported to Brigham Young.[15]

"It is our duty, brethren and sisters," proclaimed Mormon apostle Ezra T. Benson at a church conference in Provo that same month, to integrate these adopted, then indentured Indian children into Mormon homes. Instead of leaving them to wander across the land, the Saints were to "teach them to till the earth, and earn their bread by the sweat of their brows." (The irony was lost on Benson and others that the Mormons would not have survived that summer of drought and starvation were it not for the fish that Wakara's Utes had managed for half a millennium.) Nevertheless, Benson insisted that the work of civilizing Indians out of existence began with the smallest of Utah Natives. Describing two children he had recently purchased for fifty pounds of flour, Benson said, "I have a little Indian boy and girl, and certainly it is repugnant to my feelings to have to put up with their dirty practices." But Benson pressed on valiantly, knowing that "we shall be rewarded for all we do for this lost and fallen race."[16]

Not all adoptions were spurred by a Mormon version of the supposedly noble "White man's burden." After Wakara's death, Mormons continued to purchase Native children who performed the vital labor of building Zion. They did so as domestics, plural wives, and intermediaries to other Native tribes the Mormons missionized. For example, in 1857, federal Indian agent George Armstrong cited just one of many instances in which Mormons were putting the "red children of the mountains" to good use. In the Santa Clara Valley, Armstrong reported that Jacob Hamblin taught the two Paiute boys whom he had recently purchased to shepherd sheep, and one of Hamblin's wives instructed two Paiute girls, Eliza and Ellen, in how to milk cows and spin the wool that the boys collected. Indirectly or directly, Hamblin's wife also taught the girls how to be plural wives to her husband. In the early 1860s, Hamblin brought Eliza, his Indian daughter turned wife, with him on a missionary campaign to the Hopis.[17]

In the years after Wakara's death, the amount of time Native children spent in their adoptive parents' homes often ended well before the term of indenture. Santa Clara settler Samuel Knight adopted a Native girl they named "Jane" in 1865 because his wife's health was failing and the Knights needed help caring for their children. After Samuel's wife died and he remarried, his new wife, Laura, did not want Jane around and sent her to work in the homes of settlers in St. George. Some Native children ran away. Nellie, a Paiute girl whom the Judds of Parowan had purchased, ran back to the Paiutes after one of her siblings warned her that "the food of the white folks would kill the Indians if they eat it." The Indian boy raised by Ezra T. Benson also ran away after his adoptive father died. In 1863, when Jacob Hamblin traveled to the Endowment House in Salt Lake City, he expected to be sealed not only to Eliza but also to Ellen, another of his Indian children. But Ellen refused. And soon after, Eliza ran away from her Mormon father/husband, returning to the Shivwits Band and marrying a Paiute man.[18]

Still, after Wakara's death, Native children's time in settler Mormon homes was cut short most often because they died of disease. In December 1855, missionary to the Indians Thomas Brown reported that he traded rifles and ammunition for five Paiute children, but three died of an unknown illness. Z. N. Baxter gave a young Paiute boy, "Omer," to Fort Nephi founder Joseph Heywood, the husband of Martha Heywood, who witnessed the massacre of the seven Goshutes or Utes at Nephi in October 1853. Heywood family history claims that they brought Omer with them when they moved south to John D. Lee's Fort Harmony. There, Omer served in the territorial military and helped construct fortifications against Indian raiders. The Heywoods remember Omer fondly as a "white-Indian." His White side came from his work on behalf of the settlers; his Indian side from his prowess at busting broncos. But Omer died at the age of twenty-one of tuberculosis. In 1860, Susanna Ewing was still in Provo, making ends meet as a seamstress. But census records indicate that she was childless and widowed. Her husband Samuel had died of an illness that had plagued him for years. And Fransina, who would have been no more than five, had also disappeared. Perhaps Fransina had also succumbed to illness. Or perhaps the indentured Ute child had, along with Samuel Ewing's other property, been divided up among the settlers in Provo when Samuel died in 1856.[19]

Still, some Native children survived and assimilated into their adoptive families' households. As early as 1856, Kanosh began to ask Brigham Young to give Sally—the first enslaved Native purchased by the Mormons—to him as a wife. Yet Sally managed to resist Kanosh's advances by making herself indispensable to Young as a servant and cook in his many households. Only in June 1877, just a few months before Young's death and little more than a year before her own, did Sally finally marry Kanosh and relocate to his farm near Walker's Mountain. While Eliza ran away from her father/husband Jacob Hamblin, some marriages between Native women and White Mormon men were long enough to be fruitful. In 1859, Hamblin's missionary companion Ira Hatch married Sarah "Maraboots" a few years after her father, a Navajo leader, had given his teenage daughter to Hatch. The couple produced at least five children before she died at the age of thirty, soon after giving birth to a daughter who died in infancy. According to Hatch family genealogists, today there are hundreds of living descendants of the union.[20]

Sarah and Ira's descendants are rare in that they have worked to remember their Native matriarch, writing books that champion her life and sharing stories of Sarah at family gatherings. In contrast, the offspring of other couplings between Native women and White Mormon men worked hard to forget their Native mothers. In 1860, already married to three women, Dudley Leavitt initially refused to marry Janet, a teenage Navajo girl whom settlers in Parowan had purchased from slavers a few years before. But Apostle George A. Smith convinced him that it was his duty to take her, promising that their offspring would be, like the children produced with his other wives, "white and delightsome." Janet and Dudley Leavitt eventually had eleven children. At least six produced their own large families. One of Leavitt's granddaughters by one of his other wives, Thirza, was the famed Mormon historian Juanita Brooks, who also served as the family historian. Brooks recalled that Janet and Dudley's children insisted "they were not Indians, but whites, the sons and daughters of Dudley Leavitt." When an agent from the Carlisle Indian boarding school came to the Leavitts' home in St. George to offer the children scholarships, Brooks recalled, "How insulted they were! They were white. . . . They preferred to pay their own way to white institutions rather than to go free to an Indian school."[21]

It was rarer for Native men to marry White Mormon women. During the so-called Walker War, George A. Smith, the same apostle who leaned on Dudley Leavitt to take Janet as his fourth wife, joked that he could "close the war forthwith . . . if any lady wishes to be Mrs. Walker." No White Mormon women volunteered. However, Emilia Hicks married the Ute-born Zenos Hill after Brigham Young told the would-be couple that "all their children would be fair and not have brown skin of the Indians," recalled their daughter Emma Hill Hanson. The Hills of Ephraim had traded two cows for Zenos soon after his birth in 1855. They then raised their adopted son "as a white child," Zenos told a newspaper reporter years later, sending him to school, including three terms at BYU. In return, as a teenager in the late 1860s, Zenos put his Indian "instincts" to use when the Mormon settlers fought against his Ute kin Black Hawk (Antonga). "I thought it my duty to do my part on the side of the whites," Zenos recalled. "One time I stole 30 head of Indians' horses singlehanded." By 1880, Zenos had married Emilia, an English convert, and the couple were raising two "half-Indian" children in Fountain Green. Emilia would give birth to at least another nine children. As Brigham Young had promised, most were counted as "white," at least on their death certificates. Today, according to Hill family genealogists, the couple likely has hundreds of direct descendants living in the Sanpete and Salt Lake Valleys of Utah. Many know nothing of their Ute lineage.[22]

The history of buying Indian children in order to free them from Indian slavers like Wakara, and from their own Indian natures, helped disappear Native children and their progeny into the White Settler American West. That work continued well into the late twentieth century with the Mormons' Indian Student Placement Program, through which Native children were sent off their reservations to live with adopted families and attend school in majority-White Mormon communities. And, until recently, America's focus on defining slavery along the axes of Black and White, North and South, helped disappear a more expansive version of slavery that encompassed the entire nation. But in the last two decades there has been a movement to resurface the history of Indian slavery in award-winning books and in the popular press, uncovering both the horrors of the Indian slave trade and the resilience of the enslaved and their descendants. Such work has brought to the fore a new understanding that, just as the South was shaped by African chattel slavery, the American West was shaped by Indian slavery, as practiced in their own ways by Natives and settlers.[23]

Perhaps the most important researchers into Indian slavery are working not on university campuses but in home offices and at dining room tables across the nation. Ironically, descendants of enslaved and/or adopted patriarchs and matriarchs are unearthing their family trees' often complicated roots and unexpected offshoots using the tools developed by the Church of Jesus Christ of Latter-day Saints. "I'm a member of the Church and that is where my interest in genealogy began," explains the most public Wakara genealogist, Fernetta Lerwick, a descendant of Nellie Wadze Justet. "My work on my Utah Tribe ancestors didn't begin until some family members, which included some over the veil, began to prompt me to really dig into Nellie's blood family."[24]

Lerwick's efforts, along with those of other Wakara family members who also conduct genealogical research, have allowed Wakara's descendants to trace their family extending out from Wakara's many wives and children—and to see how Indian slavery shaped various branches of these knotty family trees. Most of the children that Wakara's daughter Nellie had with her Italian-born husband, Daniel Justet, built large families in southern Utah and lived as White Latter-day Saints. Hundreds of their descendants are now spread across the country. After her father's death, another of Wakara's daughters, Peaweeds, joined the Paiutes, perhaps because her mother was Paiute by birth. Peaweeds married John Kanosh, who as a child was a gift from Wakara to the Pahvant leader Kanosh. Peaweeds and John Kanosh had five children and became members of the Koosharem Band of Paiutes. They were also kin of Rick Pikyavit of the Kanosh Band. Wakara's son Kanab Arkansas married a Ute woman and moved to the Uintah Reservation. Their grandson Philip Arkansas Sr. married into an Eastern Cherokee family in North Carolina, of which dozens of his descendants, including Wakara family genealogist Michelle Bradley Wesley, are enrolled members. On the Ute reservation, another of Wakara's daughters, Marie Panakare, and her husband, Jim Duncan, had seven children, including Karoomp Kate Red Cap Long Hair and John Duncan (Ungatowinorokant), whom Nan Smith interviewed in the 1930s during her fieldwork among the Northern Utes. One of John Duncan's great-grandsons was Clifford

Duncan, the beloved tribal historian. And another is Luke Duncan, the former chairman of the Business Committee of the Ute Indian Tribe of Utah.

The current chairman of the business committee, Julius Murray III, is also a direct descendant of Wakara. On one branch of his family tree, he is the great-great-great-great-great-grandson of Marie Panakare. On another branch, he is the great-great-great-great-great-grandson of Rachel Wanzits Murray. Some family historians claim that the Allred family adopted Rachel after her Ute family of origin was slaughtered during the Fort Utah Massacre. Yet Wakara genealogists assert (and DNA strongly suggests) that Rachel was in fact Wakara's daughter, whom he traded or gave to the Allred family as an infant when they were among the first settlers in the Sanpete Valley. Whatever her origin, Rachel married John Bates Murray, with whom she eventually moved to the Ute reservation. There, the couple became the matriarch and patriarch of the Murray family, which now spans seven generations and counts hundreds of members.

Today Wakara's descendants, some of whom he placed in Mormon homes to forge bonds of kinship and trade with the settlers, and the descendants of people he captured, some of whom married Wakara's own children, likely number in the thousands. They can be found in more than a dozen states. They are members of at least five federally recognized tribal nations. A family reunion of Wakara's kin would rival in size a reunion of the descendants of almost any of the Mormon pioneers with whom Wakara traded, raided, and warred. Perhaps as more of Wakara's kin rediscover their connections to their famous Ute forefather, as well as to their long-forgotten Paiute and Ute foremothers, one day soon such a reunion will take place. Perhaps such a reunion, another form of rematriation, will occur on their ancestral lands, in the shadow of Walker's Mountain. Or perhaps it will occur on the shores of their ancestral waters of Utah (Timpanogos) Lake at Walkara Way. There, Wakara's descendants could once again fish and ride horses during the day and swap stories of their forefathers and foremothers around campfires at night.

What Remains of Brigham's Wars

Cars and trucks zoomed by on State Street in the summer of 2023 as Forrest Cuch and I stood in front of the "Walker War" monument in Payson, Utah, a small city in the Utah Valley, where the "war" supposedly began. The sign reads,

> "You are a fool for fighting your best friends, for we are the best and the only friends that you have in the world" wrote Brigham Young to the Ute Indian Chief Walkara in 1853, after the latter had engaged the settlers of Utah in their first major Indian war.
>
> Angered because the whites had put an end to the Indian slave trade in the territory and had encroached upon their lands, the redmen found a pretext for beginning hostilities at Springville, July 17, 1853, when an Indian, while beating his squaw, was killed by a white man. The following day, Alexander Keele, a guard at Payson, was shot by Indians and the war was on. The policy of the white defenders was one of vigilant watch and limited offensive warfare. However before Governor Brigham Young led a peace mission into Walkara's camp in May 1854 that ended the conflict, 20 whites had been killed including the U.S. Government surveyor Captain John W. Gunnison, who was massacred with 7 of his men near the present site of Hinckley, Utah.

"With friends like Brigham, Walker didn't need enemies!" Forrest quipped. Erected in the 1970s by the Utah Highway Department, the monument is the most visible public history lesson on the

Ute-Mormon wars of the 1850s. Over the din of eighteen-wheelers passing by, Forrest and I discussed how this history lesson is full of half-truths and outright lies.

The lesson names Wakara as the aggressor, when history shows it was Young who started the war against the Utes. And he did so long before and long after the "Walker War." The lesson claims that the Whites ended the slave trade, when history shows that they worked to take it over from Wakara and other slavers through the legal facade of adoption and indenture. The lesson also praises Young as the author of peace, when in fact, throughout the conflict, Wakara petitioned the Mormon prophet to end hostilities. And finally, the lesson is also full of omissions. Apparently the scores of Utes, Paiutes, and Goshutes who died during the conflict were not worthy of being numbered in the war's body count.

Perhaps the most glaring omission is the careful editing of the quote from Brigham Young that opens the history lesson. It comes from the letter that Young sent to Wakara in July 1853. In it, Young implied that Wakara might have cause to worry that the tobacco the Mormon prophet sent him along with the letter was poisoned. "If you are afraid of the Tobacco . . . you can let some of your prisoners try it first and then you will know that it is good."

Later that same day, Forrest and I sat in a diner in Richfield, Utah, with Rena Pikyavit to talk about the latest we had learned about Robert Leonard's alleged grave robbing on Walker's Mountain. We also told her about our stop in Payson to visit the "Walker War" monument. "I grew up in Payson!" Rena told us. "All that talk of Walker as the one who started the war. All that 'redmen' talk as if they were the evil ones. How the Whites treated Walker and his people—starting the war, taking the lands and children—that was the evil!"

Rena's comments about the daily horror of passing by the "Walker War" monument reminded me of the trauma that Waziyatawin Angela Wilson (Dakota) highlighted in her work on the forced removal and massacre of her ancestors in Minnesota in 1862 and of how historical narratives, including those embodied in monuments celebrating Indian wars, spark trauma anew. "Every Dakota person since [1862] has had to be assaulted on a near daily basis with a celebration of these leaders responsible for the 'ethnic cleansing' of our people from Minnesota," Wilson has written. "This would be comparable to Jewish people living in a state in which there existed counties, streets, numerous statues, paintings, schools, parks all created in the honor of Hitler or Eichmann and bearing their names."[25]

Utah roadways are also dotted with a handful of memorials to the White victims of the "Walker War." On a dusty road along the often dried-up Sevier River, a rock obelisk pokes out of the sagebrush, marking the spot where John Gunnison and his men were killed by Pahvant Utes on October 26, 1853. Over in Sanpete County, in Fountain Green's city park, the Daughters of Utah Pioneers erected a memorial to the Fountain Green Massacre, where on October 1, 1853, Utes ambushed the wagon train piloted by William Reed, James Nelson, William Luke, and Thomas Clark.

There is no memorial to the Nephi Seven, the Goshutes or Utes whom the settlers at Nephi massacred to avenge their slain brethren—a massacre that the settlers covered up with their official reports blaming the Natives for their own deaths. Instead, the bodies of the Nephi Seven were dumped in a mass grave, only to be unearthed in 2006 during an excavation for the foundation of a new home. That home stands today, a three-bedroom, two-bathroom suburban ranch, with an attached garage, shaded by a century-old willow tree. The owner of the home told a newspaper reporter in jest that he was glad to have the remains removed, so they would not haunt his family. Still, he also said that he wished that the remains would be returned to their tribal descendants. So did Forrest Cuch, who in 2006 was the executive director of the Division of Indian Affairs in Utah. But after almost two decades, the Nephi Seven remain, along with hundreds of other ancestors, boxed up and all but forgotten in a state warehouse in the Salt Lake Valley.[26]

Well before they raised monuments and memorials along Utah's highways, center streets, and city parks, beginning in the second half of the nineteenth century, Mormons staged celebratory reenactments of Utah's "Indian Wars." On Pioneer Day in 1878, 3,000 people gathered in Provo's Union Square to watch "a representation of an Indian attack on [the] Pioneer Fort," reported the *Deseret News*. Mormon boys and men dressed as Indians "encircled [the fort] on their horses, and with war [w]hoops and yells, laying over the necks of their horses, firing their guns and shooting arrows at full speed, mingled with fierce shouts of the brave defenders, silenced occasionally by the roar of the cannon of the fort." The production brought blood to the faces of all in attendance, but especially to the "old residents" who witnessed the wars firsthand. The crowd jumped to their feet with cheers of relief and righteous triumph when "the rear guard [of the militia came] to the rescue. The Indians defeated, [the] wounded cared for, [and the] treaty made."[27]

Reenactments of Utah's Indian Wars became immensely popular in Provo, serving as the centerpiece of Pioneer Day celebrations between 1890 and 1930. During the day, younger Mormons dressed as Indians and adorned their faces with war paint, then reenacted violence against innocent settlers. Actual veterans of the conflict donned their old Nauvoo Legion uniforms, perhaps tighter fitting after so many years, to repel the attacks. At night around campfires, elderly legionnaires regaled younger generations with tales of the horrors and glories of doing battle with Indian foes. Veterans of the "Walker War" had their own annual gatherings in social halls along Utah Lake, during which they danced, sang songs, and gave speeches about facing off with early Mormon Utah's greatest Indian adversary. A poem by "Walker War" veteran George McKenzie, which dramatized the fish fight between James Ivie, Shower-o-cats, and the Ute "squaw" that the Mormons claimed started the war, was frequently recited. These gatherings also had a practical goal: to petition the government to award "Walker War" veterans the pensions they had sought since the outbreak of the war in 1853. Starting in 1909, the few surviving veterans of the war were awarded monthly pensions of $20.[28]

Ute born and Mormon raised, Zenos Hill was himself a veteran of the Utah Indian Wars, fighting alongside settlers against Black Hawk (Antonga). Decades later, when he gathered with his fellow veterans, Hill wore the medals and ribbons that signified his status as a Black Hawk War veteran. But because he was "red-skinned in the true sense that the words apply to Indians," wrote a reporter for the *Spanish Fork Press* who interviewed Hill in 1937, he also wore an Indian headdress when he played Black Hawk, which he did for at least three decades at annual reenactments. In 1938, at the age of eighty-five, Hill died at his home in Fountain Green, preceded by his wife, who had died six months before. The couple was survived by seven children, nineteen grandchildren, and fifteen great-grandchildren.[29]

Yet the dominant narrative—that Wakara and his Ute kin were responsible for the bloodshed of the wars that bear their names—has recently come under new scrutiny. Reevaluations of Mormon-Native conflicts have brought public attention to the truths that Utah Native communities have long known: that settlers often killed innocent Natives out of fear or bloodlust.

On April 22, 2016, settlers and Natives came together in Circleville, where more than thirty Paiutes were massacred 150 years before, supposedly out of revenge. Members of the Koosharem Band, represented by the cultural resource manager of the Paiute Indian Tribe, Dorena Martineau, alongside Richard E. Turley Jr., then assistant church historian for the Church of Jesus Christ of Latter-day Saints, whose own ancestor participated in the massacre, dedicated a seven-foot-tall granite monument "to the memory of the Koosharem Band

Dedication of the Circleville Massacre Memorial, April 22, 2016. In April 1866, 150 years before, Mormon settlers captured and then massacred around thirty southern Paiute men, women, and children, including Wakara's descendants who had joined the Koosharem Band after Wakara's death. (Courtesy of Utah Historical Quarterly)

of the Paiute Indian Tribe of Utah, massacred by local Mormon settlers, April 22–24, 1866, during Utah's Black Hawk War (1865–1872)," as one side of the monument reads. On the other side etched in stone is the "Paiute Oral Tradition [of the] Circleville Massacre . . . as told by Jimmy Timmican, Koosharem Band (~1895–1972) who heard this story from Walker Ammon (~1854–1920), son of Chief Walker (~1815–1855)."[30]

The stone of the Circleville monument did not emerge out of the earth on its own. It was erected because the Paiutes, including Wakara's kin who joined the tribe after his death, kept the story alive. It also stands today because settlers like Turley and Susan Weeks, the author of the most detailed book on the massacre and whose ancestor James T. Allred also participated in it, spoke as much of the truth of history as they could. "I do not know all the reasons why my ancestor and other men did what they did a hundred and fifty years ago, but I am deeply sorry for it," Turley said at the dedication. Dorena Martineau agreed with Turley's sentiment. "My hope is that by facing the past, difficult though it can sometimes be, and learning from it, we can build a better future." And yet Martineau also acknowledged that this bloody past affects the present and future. The slaughter of these thirty Paiutes in 1866 felled family trees that in the 150 years since would have sprouted dozens of new branches. "Today, the Paiute [Indian] Tribe of Utah has a total of 918 members," Martineau proclaimed. "There are only five bands left, out of the many that there used to be, but we're still hanging in there!"[31]

There is no memorial to the largest of the massacres of Native Americans in Utah—the Fort Utah Massacre of Wakara's Timpanogos Band in February 1850—in part because there is no federally or state recognized Timpanogos Band to demand one. Most of the surviving Timpanogos moved to the Uintah Reservation in the 1860s. Disconnected from their homelands and the memories therein, they became part of the Ute Indian Tribe of Utah.[32]

Still, one recent change to the landscape of the Utah Valley relates to the massacre and reflects a reimagining of the public narrative of the region. In 2022, the US Board of Geographic Names approved the renaming of "Squaw Peak," which towers above Provo. The decision came after Native Americans, including many Native BYU students, spent years advocating to change the peak's name. Members of the name-change committee found the origin story for the peak's name—that after the Fort Utah Massacre in 1850, Old Elk's wife jumped or fell from the summit to avoid capture by Mormon scouts—suspect. What's more, they argued that "squaw" was a racial epithet, used for centuries by White settlers to turn Indigenous women into objects of derision, curiosity, and desire. In 2022, after consultation with the Ute Indian Tribe, on whose ancestral lands it resides, the peak was renamed *Kyhv*, or "mountain" in Ute.[33]

Kyhv Peak was not the only geographical landmark to shed the name "squaw." In 2022, under the leadership of US Interior Secretary Deb Haaland (Laguna Pueblo), the first Native American to hold a cabinet-level position, the US Geological Survey removed the epithet from hundreds of mountains, bodies of water, canyons, and roads. These places were renamed with descriptive terms, like Artists Fingers for the sandstone rock formation in western Colorado that resembles curled fingers, or Indigenous names, like Tukuhnikivatz Spring ("the place where the sun shines longest") in eastern Utah.

These changes mark the culmination of a long season of reimagining the American landscape, decentering settler dominance and violence, and recentering Native presence, greatness, and sacrifice, including sacrifices made in wars fought for America. Scholar Delores Mondragón (Chickasaw) has described the act of renaming "Squaw Peak" near Phoenix, Arizona, after Army Specialist Lori Ann Piestewa (Hopi) as a part of this current era of rematriation. Piestewa was killed in Iraq on March 23, 2003, becoming the first female soldier killed in action in the Iraq War and the only known Native American female US soldier to die in combat. "In having the peak renamed Piestewa, Lori redefined the land and therefore the people," Mondragón has written. "Lori continues to provide healing and to help others, by standing in 'the Hopi Way' and reminding us of the epistemic violence that haunted Indigenous people, especially women, for so long."[34]

Wakara's Return

Wakara's skull and the six other ancestors stolen from Walker's Mountain in 1872 sit in boxes in a Smithsonian warehouse in the Washington, DC, area. So do tens of thousands of other Native American ancestors yet to be repatriated.

There are two major hurdles to repatriating the skulls stolen from Walker's Mountain. The first is the fact that the skulls likely belong to both Paiute and Ute ancestors, which means the Paiute and Ute tribes would have to cooperate on repatriation. This is a less significant hurdle because of the long-standing relationships that the tribes have built over the last 100 years. The second, bigger hurdle is the fact that Wakara's gravesite currently sits on US Forest Service land.

Despite these complexities, many of Wakara's lineal and spiritual descendants with whom I have consulted make clear that they want Wakara's remains, and the remains of the other ancestors, returned.

And yet, for these descendants, simply "repatriating" the remains is not sufficient—for practical, legal, and spiritual reasons. Practically speaking, returning the remains to Walker's Mountain (the Cow) yet again places them in danger of grave robbing as Forest Service land is open to the public. Legally speaking, repatriating the remains is impossible since the legal definition of repatriation "involves a 'return of prisoners of war to their home country,'" as former executive director of the Indigenous Law Institute Steven Newcomb has written. It bears repeating: Walker's Mountain no longer sits in Wakara's home country. It is no longer Walker's Mountain. It is the Cow. That (home)land, along with most American land, is "'held captive' by the United States." Finally, spiritually speaking, returning Wakara's remains, and those of the other ancestors, to their living descendants without also returning to them their homelands does not address the trauma of turning ancestors into artifacts, whose removal served to break the very bond between the *Nuche* and the land that *Sünawav* bound together at the beginning of time.[35]

Since repatriation is insufficient, one approach is to rematriate Wakara's remains and those of the other ancestors. Rematriation, after all, seeks to restore the sacred relationship of a people and their ancestral lands in ways that center the spiritual well-being and health of all members of the ecosystem of relations that comprise a homeland. Some of Wakara's ancestors have suggested that, if and when Wakara is returned to the Cow, perhaps the Cow could be restored to the stewardship of the Kanosh Band of Paiutes, comanaged with the Ute Indian Tribe. And the Cow could be renamed "Wakara's Mountain." Comanagement could also break the colonial-built walls among the tribes. Before and for some time after the arrival of the settlers, who brought to Utah fixed ideas about race and ethnicity, tribal identities were fluid among the Numic Ute, Paiute, and Shoshone peoples. Individuals and families often changed their associations within tribal bands and even moved between tribes. To be sure, distinct tribal identities and cultures are of vital importance, beauty, and power. But rematriation restores to the tribes their own agency to determine these boundaries, without interference from the settler state.

A case in point is Kanosh, the founding father of the Kanosh Band, who created a joint Ute and Paiute community in the 1860s. He refused to move to the Uintah Reservation so that he could stay on the lands where his (Ute and Paiute) kin were buried. Kanosh said as much at the Spanish Fork Treaty in 1865. His people "did not want to sell their land and go away. . . . They wanted to live around the graves of their fathers."[36]

A FEW SUMMERS AGO, FORREST CUCH AND I drove over a series of bumpy dirt roads in his white pickup. We were on our way to visit the Ute fish hatchery, nestled in the foothills of the towering Uintah Mountains. As we drove, with country music crooning out of the truck's speakers, Forrest pointed to oil derricks, pumping up and down in the midday heat, extracting from the earth the substance that is the lifeblood of the American "progress"-driven economy. Fossil fuels, including the Uintah Basin's black wax crude, have lifted billions of people around the globe out of poverty and are the main source of our global climate's impending doom. Today, most of these derricks in the basin sit on private land once held in trust by the Utes, which Forrest believes should still belong to the tribe. Forrest says the Utes are better stewards of the land, even if they decide to pump out the oil. "People like to say, 'Indians are always getting in the way of progress.' Well, perhaps that's our purpose!"

It is here, at this intersection of Native and settler imaginations, that this book emerged. This book is a work of historical reimagining of Forrest's great-great-great-great-grandfather Wakara and what remains of him—and what remains of his fish and horses, his slaves and his kin, and the often, but not always, violent relationships he had with settlers. This reimagining refutes Manifest Destiny, a notion of history as linear progress, erasing Native history and presence from the American landscape. Instead, this book demonstrates that the Native America that Wakara defended, and the Settler America Wakara helped build, are not gone. They're both still here with us, a part of our shared history. This book further argues that Native and settler, human and nonhuman actors are part of an ongoing *process of history*—organized around places, relationships, and cycles of time.

This historical reimagining leads to a suite of other reimaginings.

There are political reimaginings. The work of dividing people into categories of race, tribe, and nation, so that people are pitted against each other, is a tool of tyrants. Waking up to see that these political categories are both constructed and experienced as very real can help forge new political communities who can work together to form a more just, sustainable, and equitable America.

There are also practical reimaginings. Settler Americans like me, and like many of you, are waking up to the fact that our ways of "progress" have produced unprecedented wealth for a few and apocalyptic consequences for most. Scientists predict that in less than a decade, the Salt Lake Valley might become unlivable due to toxins contained in the Great Salt Lake sediment. The toxin of most concern, ironically, is arsenic, the poison that the Mormon militias wanted to use to "discipline" Wakara's Utes and other Utah Natives in the 1850s when they objected to the Mormon settlers' destruction of and incursion onto their lands. Some believe Brigham Young might have laced with arsenic the tobacco he sent to Wakara just before the Ute leader's death.

Still, parts of Settler America are also waking up to how our notion of progress has made America inhospitable—not only for many Native Americans but for settlers too. Coalitions of scientists, environmentalists, landowners, fishermen, state leaders from both political parties, and Native Americans are coming together to "bring back to life" the long-left-for-dead Utah Lake, as Mary Meyer, CEO of the Timpanogos Nation, has explained to me. Similar coalitions are also reimagining an Indigenous future for the Great Salt Lake. Instead of doing what the settlers did, imposing their will on a place they did not understand, new efforts work with nature by combining the best of Western science with Indigenous methods of resource management—like those that Wakara's Timpanogos practiced for generations at Timpanogos (Utah) Lake.

These political and practical reimaginings might foster a moral reimagining too. We must consider how settler Americans' identities, as well as their—or our—ownership of American lands, were often made possible by the displacement and genocide of Native Americans. And then, we must ask the (literally) $100 trillion question: What does a moral and impactful reparation of the damage caused by this theft of Indigenous lands, wealth, and history look like?

Settler Americans like me, and like many of you, might balk at the idea of giving back the lands that we own collectively as federal, state, and local governments, as corporations, as nonprofits, as churches. And then there are the lands that we own privately, some of which have been in our families for generations and are, for many of us, the main storehouses of our generational wealth. Instead of perpetuating an idea of scarcity, which lies at the heart of the settler imagination, a moral reimagining of the relationship between Settler and Native America could lead to an embrace of the idea of abundance and generosity, more "we than me," as Forrest Cuch has put it.

Returning land back isn't giving land away. Instead, it is a process of rematriation through which all of us—settlers and Natives alike—understand ourselves as sacred stewards, not extractive owners, of the lands that give us all life. So that, after many generations have passed, when we are all ancestors, our descendants can proclaim, "We are still here."

Acknowledgments

A comprehensive description of the many institutions, communities, and individuals who have assisted in the research and writing of this book would take up another whole book itself. So here I focus on those who have had the greatest impact in bringing *Wakara's America* to fruition.

Let me start with the financial and research support. A National Endowment for the Humanities Public Scholars Fellowship for 2022–2023 funded a year away from my other university duties, during which I did the bulk of the writing for this book. I also received support from the Phillips Fund for Native American Research of the American Philosophical Society, the Charles Redd Center of Brigham Young University (BYU), and the University of Nebraska–Lincoln (UNL) College of Arts and Sciences' Impact Grant and Layman Seed Grant. UNL's UCARE program funded multiple years of undergraduate research assistant fellowships for two exceptional young scholars, Abby O'Brien and Chelsea Hanway (Northern Arapaho), who helped me gather and organize thousands of pages of archival materials. UNL funds also helped me engage Ashlyn Stewart, one of the brightest students I've ever worked with, to create the first interactive map of Wakara's movements, which allowed us to visualize the West he helped shape. In summer 2022, I was a fellow at

BYU's Maxwell Center for Religious Scholarship, where I presented early portions of the book. Special thanks go to Spencer Fluhman, Philip Barlow, and Rosalynde F. Welch for their support. I was a member of the 2020–2023 Young Scholars in American Religion cohort, mentored by Penny Edgell and Jonathan Walton, during which we navigated Covid-19, a coup, births, deaths, publications, tenure, job moves, losses, and gains. I'm so lucky to count Tazeen Ali, Philipp Gollner, Darrius Hills, Courtney Irby, Emily Johnson, Alyssa Maldonado-Estrada, Samuel Perry, Ansley Quiros, and Leslie Ribovich as lifelong colleagues. In summer 2024, I was a member of the Association for Public Religion and Intellectual Life (APRIL) colloquium, directed by S. B. Rodríguez-Plate and Brook Wilensky-Lanford, where I presented a portion of the book.

Dozens of UNL colleagues have read various parts of the book. I thank my colleagues in the Ethnic Studies program, directed by Joy Castro, and the Nineteenth-Century Studies program, headed by Peter Capuano and Jeannette Eileen Jones, for hosting work-in-progress discussions of the book. Thanks to Timothy Cook, Katrina Jagodinsky, Laura Muñoz, James Garza, Angel Hinzo, Matt Cohen, Melissa Homestead, Kenneth Price, Laura White, and Tom Gannon. Special thanks to William Thomas and Margaret Jacobs for their mentorship and friendship, as well as to Kristi Montooth, who models reading and writing across the disciplines. My colleague Wenjie Wang designed the beautifully detailed maps in this book. I reserve my biggest Husker thanks to Kelsy Burke, who has been there from the beginning to the end of this project.

Dozens more colleagues beyond Lincoln have contributed to making this book much better. I especially thank Thomas Murphy and Jana Reiss, who provided the best reading and criticism of early drafts of this book. Much of my thinking on Wakara's fish-eating Utes comes from the work of and conversations with Jared Farmer. David Holland, Laurel Ulrich, Sally Gordon, R. Marie Griffith, and

Paul Harvey have served as mentors and friends for going on two decades. Gregory Smoak, Hilary Hungerford, Jacob Holdaway, Ben Abbott, Sarah Klain, and Mary Meyer (Timpanogos Nation) helped me think through the intersections of land, fish, and fish management in the past, present, and future. Darren Parry (Northwestern Band of the Shoshone Nation) and his work at *Boa Ogoi* (Bear River) model how Indigenous-led Land Back efforts bring people, history, and fish back to their homelands and home waters. Kathryn Renton, William Taylor, Carlton Shield Chief Gover (Pawnee), Isaac Hart, Ron Roubidoux, Reva Maria S. ShieldChief (Pawnee), and Kat and Robert Hayden opened my eyes to the role that horses have played in American history. Sheri Wysong and LeRoy Johnson helped me think through Wakara's influence on the Old Spanish Trail. Brian Cannon, Erika Bsumek, Linford Fisher, Jeffrey Ostler, Virginia Kerns, and Estevan Gael-Galvez helped me suss out the intricacies of Indian slavery in the Great Basin. Thanks to Corey Smallcanyon (Diné), Christopher Jones, and Amy Thiriot for introducing me to the best practices of DNA-based genealogical research. Special thanks go to Ariel Munyer (Certified Genealogist) for her great work verifying genealogical claims made in this book. Ronald Rood, Ryan Wimmer, Lisa Brooks (Missisquoi Abenaki), Barbara Jones Brown, and Jenny Pulsipher worked with me to puzzle out the history of settler-Native "wars." Ann Fabian, Eric Hollinger, and Elizabeth Nagengast-Stevens were especially helpful in placing the grave robbing of Wakara and other ancestors in the context of the Great Basin and broader American history.

Just before his death, Will Bagley and I had several hours-long conversations about Wakara and his relationship with Brigham Young. We also exchanged archival materials and shared our interpretations of these materials. Those conversations greatly informed this book. Robert Leonard's impact on this book, and Wakara's legacy writ large, is a complicated one. May his memory be a blessing.

Thanks to Woody Johnson and Carl Camp for sharing photos of the Territorial Statehouse State Park Museum before recent updates to its "Indian" displays. And thanks to Rev. Michael Carney and St. Elizabeth's Episcopal Church at Whiterocks for welcoming me into their community.

Of course, I also thank the editorial staff at Basic Books, led by Brian Distelberg. Alex Cullina provided the most direct and impactful readings and critiques of the many drafts of this book. Alex's insightful eye has made this book so much better, as I'm sure it will for dozens of books in the future. Thanks to the design, copyediting, and production mavens at Basic Books, Annie Chatham, Jen Kelland, and Emmily O'Connor, for piloting this book the last few miles.

Wakara's America could not have been written without the input and friendship of the many tribal, spiritual, and lineal descendants of Wakara. Thanks especially to Rena and Rick Pikyavit (Kanosh Band of Paiutes) for our many conversations and shared meals. Great thanks to Fernetta Lerwick and Michelle Bradley Wesley (Eastern Cherokee) for their incredible genealogical research. Thanks to Larry Cesspooch (Ute Indian Tribe of Utah) for his lessons on how to think "in Ute" about history and its connection to the present and future. Thanks to members of the Ute Indian Tribe of Utah Business Committee, especially its chairman, Julius Murray, for allowing me to present my research on Wakara's remains to them. I also thank LaTosha Mayo (Paiute Indian Tribe of Utah), a Wakara descendant, and Autumn Gillard (Paiute Indian Tribe of Utah) for their engagement, which allowed me to ensure that Paiute perspectives were accurately presented in this book. I reserve the highest thanks for the Cuch family, including Marilyn and Cameron, and Forrest, first and last, for his years of friendship and mentorship.

When I make my frequent visits to Utah, I always stay with my dear friend Buddy Tangalos, with whom I've crisscrossed the state, paddled rapids, scrambled over boulders, and skied "hors-piste" in search of Wakara's trail. He has heard me talk more about Wakara than anyone. Buddy is my Utah family. I thank my original family, Duke and Janice Mueller, Lizzy Perry and Steven Hatfield, and my Auntie Marti Mueller, for their support through the years.

As always, home is where Zora, Sophie, and Anna are.

I have already benefited personally and professionally (and spiritually) from this work. To end the cycle of extractive research in our profession and begin to reciprocate that benefit, I have already donated and will donate going forward personal proceeds generated from this book to Wakara descendants, namely, to the Ute Indian Tribe of Utah's Higher Education Fund, Seven Generations, the David Arapene Cuch Scholarship Fund at the University of Utah Law School, and the Paiute Indian Tribe of Utah's higher education scholarships.

Notes

Source Abbreviations

BYP Brigham Young Papers, CR 1234, Church History Library, the Church of Jesus Christ of Latter-day Saints, Salt Lake City.

BL Bancroft Library, Special Collections, University of California–Berkeley, Berkeley.

CHL Church History Library, the Church of Jesus Christ of Latter-day Saints, Salt Lake City.

DN Deseret News, Salt Lake City, June 15, 1850–present.

JD Journal Discourses by Brigham Young, His Two Counsellors, the Twelve Apostles and Others, vols. 1–26 (Liverpool and London: various publishers, 1854–1886).

JH Journal History of the Church, CR 100 137, Church History Library, the Church of Jesus Christ of Latter-day Saints, Salt Lake City.

GASJ George A. Smith Journal, MS 17190, Church History Library, the Church of Jesus Christ of Latter-day Saints, Salt Lake City.

GCM General Church Minutes, CR 100 318, Church History Library, the Church of Jesus Christ of Latter-day Saints, Salt Lake City.

HBLL Tom Perry Special Collections, Harold B. Lee Library, Brigham Young University, Provo, UT.

HOCHD Historian's Office Collected Historical Documents, CR 100 397, Church History Library, the Church of Jesus Christ of Latter-day Saints, Salt Lake City.

ML Marriott Library Special Collections, University of Utah, Salt Lake City.

MS Latter-day Saints' Millennial Star: (Manchester) May 1840–March 1842; (Liverpool) April 1842–March 3, 1932; (London) March 10, 1932–December 1970.

RMMP Max Perry Mueller, *Race and the Making of the Mormon People* (Chapel Hill: University of North Carolina Press, 2017).

TWWET Will Bagley, ed., *The Whites Want Every Thing: Indian-Mormon Relations, 1847–1877* (Norman: Arthur H. Clark Company, 2019).

UTMR Utah Territorial Militia Records, 1849–1877, FamilySearch, https://www.familysearch.org/en/search/collection/1462415.

WHK Nauvoo Legion (Utah) Papers, 1853 July-August, Southern Military Department, William H. Kimball Detachment, MS 17208, Church History Library, the Church of Jesus Christ of Latter-day Saints, Salt Lake City.

Introduction: Wakara's Remains

1. Because of the looting of this gravesite and the history of looting Native American graves writ large, in consultation with Ute and Paiute tribal members and Wakara family members, I have changed some identifying details of the burial site. Federal and state laws make it a criminal offense to disturb or remove human remains and grave goods from public lands without proper consultation with and permission from affiliated tribes.

2. Reuben McBride to Dimick Huntington, August 18, 1874, BYP.

3. Thomas Callister to Young, August 18, 1874, BYP. In the body of his letter, Callister affirms that the remains of Kanosh's kin were stolen. But he claims that Wakara's remains were not disturbed. Yet, in a postscript, Callister writes that through further investigation—likely a conversation with McBride, who went to the gravesite with Kanosh—he learned that Wakara's remains were also likely removed.

4. Reuben McBride to Dimick Huntington, August 18, 1874, BYP.

5. On the dynamism of war and diplomacy of equestrian Native empires like Wakara's, see Pekka Hämäläinen, *Indigenous Continent: The Epic Contest for North America* (New York: Liveright Publishing, 2022), 385–457. On Native

nations' sovereignty and survival, see Kathleen DuVal, *Native Nations: A Millennium in North America* (New York: Random House, 2024).

6. Reuben McBride to Dimick Huntington, August 18, 1874, BYP.

7. For model scholarship that focuses on Native presence in and vital influence on America's past, present, and future, see Ned Blackhawk, *The Rediscovery of America: Native Peoples and the Unmaking of U.S. History* (New Haven, CT: Yale University Press, 2024).

8. Renée L. Bergland, *The National Uncanny: Indian Ghosts and American Subjects* (Hanover, NH: Dartmouth College Press, 2015), 28–29, 85.

9. Vine Deloria Jr., *God Is Red: A Native View of Religion* (Golden, CO: Fulcrum Publishing, 2003), 62; J. Kēhaulani Kauanui, "'A Structure, Not an Event': Settler Colonialism and Enduring Indigeneity," *Lateral: Journal of the Cultural Studies Association* 5, no. 1 (2016).

10. Deloria, *God Is Red*, 62.

11. In further conversations, after we built mutual trust, they have acknowledged that his remains were stolen.

12. Forrest S. Cuch and Michael Carney, *A Native Way of Giving* (New York: Morehouse Publishing, 2021), 8–9. Thanks to Autumn Gillard for helping me conceptualize the idea of "ecosystems of relations."

13. *RMMP*, 181–211.

14. As Robin Wall Kimmerer (Potawatomi) writes, "Time is not a river running inexorably to the sea, but the sea itself—its tides that appear and disappear, the fog that rises to become rain in a different river. All things that were will come again." Robin Wall Kimmerer, *Braiding Sweetgrass: Indigenous Wisdom, Scientific Knowledge and the Teachings of Plants* (Minneapolis: Milkweed Editions, 2013), 206–207. On "blood quantum" and the Northern Utes, see R. Warren Metcalf, *Termination's Legacy: The Discarded Indians of Utah* (Lincoln: University of Nebraska Press, 2002), 133–136.

15. Steven Newcomb, "Perspectives: Healing, Restoration, and Rematriation," *News & Notes: American Indian Ritual Object Repatriation Foundation* 2, no. 1 (1995): 3.

16. Margaret Kovach, *Indigenous Methodologies: Characteristics, Conversations, and Contexts* (Toronto: University of Toronto Press, 2021), 1–9.

17. For model scholarship that implicates settler history in the genocide and cultural erasure of Indigenous peoples, in order to move toward reconciliation of settlers and Native Americans in the present and future, see Margaret Jacobs, *After One Hundred Winters: In Search of Reconciliation on America's Stolen Lands* (Princeton, NJ: Princeton University Press, 2021).

18. Robin Wall Kimmerer describes the most generous and constructive model of "becoming Indigenous to a place." Kimmerer, *Braiding Sweetgrass*, 9, 205–215.

Chapter 1: Wakara's Last Days

1. Paul Bailey might have been the first to call Wakara "the greatest horse thief in history," but during his lifetime, Wakara's horse raiding was already legendary. Paul Bailey, *Walkara, Hawk of the Mountains* (Los Angeles: Westernlore Press, 1954), 13. Ned Blackhawk describes how Pegleg Smith connected himself to Wakara in order to buttress his own reputation. Ned Blackhawk, *Violence over the Land: Indians and Empires in the Early American West* (Cambridge, MA: Harvard University Press, 2006), 139–140.

2. *TWWET*, 326–330; Brown to Young, December 22, 1854, in Thomas Brown, *Journal of the Southern Indian Mission: Diary of Thomas D. Brown*, ed. Juanita Brooks (Logan: Utah State University Press, 1972), 103–105. Wakara called, among others, Sanpitch, Arapeen, Peteetneet, and Baptiste his "brothers." In Ute and some other Native cultures, close kin of the same gender, including those who would be called "cousins" today, were called "brothers" and "sisters" if they were raised together.

3. John C. Frémont, *Report of the Exploring Expedition to the Rocky Mountains in the Year 1842* (Washington, DC: Gales and Seaton, Printers, 1845), 272; David Lewis, "Death of Indian Walker," *DN*, February 8, 1855.

4. Joanna Brooks, *Mormonism and White Supremacy: American Religion and the Problem of Racial Innocence* (New York: Oxford University Press, 2020), 41–43.

5. David Lewis to Young, January 9, 1855, BYP; Brown, *Journal of the Southern Indian Mission*, 105.

6. Lewis, "Death of Indian Walker."

7. Gwinn Heap and E. F. Beale, *Central Route to the Pacific, from the Valley of the Mississippi to California* (Philadelphia: Lippincott, Grambo & Company, 1854), 93.

8. Adelia Kimball, *Memoirs of Adelia Almira Wilcox: One of the Plural Wives of Heber C. Kimball*, ed. Stanley Kimball (New York: Stanley Kimball, 1956), 228. On the letter Young sent to Wakara with the implicit reference to poison, see Young to Captain Wacher, July 25, 1853, UTMR.

9. Solomon Nunes Carvalho, *Incidents of Travel and Adventure in the Far West* (New York: Derby & Jackson, 1857), 189–191.

10. Brigham Young, "The Lamanites," December 3, 1854, *JD*, 2:143; minutes of meeting with Walker, GCM, May 11–12, 1854; Wilford Woodruff, *Wilford Woodruff's Journal, 1833–1898: Typescript*, ed. Scott C. Kenney (Salt Lake City: Signature Books, 1983), 4:272–274.

11. Carvalho, *Incidents*, 194.

12. Lewis, "Death of Indian Walker."

13. Ibid.

14. On the seasonal activities associated with "Lower Earth," "Middle Earth," and "Upper Earth," see Virginia McConnell Simmons, *The Ute Indians of Utah, Colorado, and New Mexico* (Boulder: University Press of Colorado, 2000), 9.

15. Dimick Huntington, "Trip to Manti," *DN*, February 22, 1855.

16. Henry C. Yarrow, *Introduction to the Study of Mortuary Customs Among the North American Indians* (Washington, DC: Smithsonian Institution, Bureau of Ethnology, 1880), 48–49.

17. Lewis, "Death of Indian Walker"; "News from Great Salt Lake," *Los Angeles Star*, March 31, 1855; "Death of Indian Walker," *Southern Californian*, April 4, 1855. See, among dozens of other reports on Wakara's death that reached the East Coast by May 1855, "By Telegraph, from California," *Pittsburgh Gazette*, May 4, 1855; "By Magnetic Telegraph," *Baltimore Sun*, May 3, 1855; "California News," *Swanton Journal*, May 4, 1855; "Scraps & Facts," *Yorkville Enquirer*, May 10, 1855. On suspicions that Wakara was poisoned, see "News from Great Salt Lake," *Los Angeles Star*, March 31, 1855; "A 'High Old' Indian," *Green-Mountain Freeman*, June 21, 1855. See also *TWWET*, 239–240, 337–340.

Chapter 2: A Pilgrimage into the Wilderness

1. Edward Johnson, *Wonder-Working Providence of Sions Saviour in New England*, ed. J. Franklin Jameson (New York: Charles Scribner's Sons, 1910), 23.

2. Ibid., 116–117.

3. Ibid., 210–211.

4. Sarah Shear et al., "Manifesting Destiny: Re/presentations of Indigenous Peoples in K-12 U.S. History Standards," *Theory and Research in Social Education* 43, no. 1 (2015): 68–101.

5. David Treuer, "Return the National Parks to the Tribes," *The Atlantic*, May 2021.

6. Hermann Hagedorn, *Roosevelt in the Bad Lands* (New York: Houghton Mifflin, 1921), 355; Robert H. Keller and Michael F. Turek, *American Indians and National Parks* (Tucson: University of Arizona Press, 1999), xiii.

7. Richard Stoffle et al., "Ethnographic Overview and Assessment for Arches National Park" (Bureau of Applied Research in Anthropology, School of Anthropology University of Arizona, June 3, 2016), 189–191.

8. For a Ute retelling of the "Posey War," see the "100 Years of Silence" project at https://100yearsofsilence.com/home.

9. "Bones of Black Hawk Indian Warrior Now on Exhibition [at] L.D.S. Museum," *DN*, September 20, 1919.

10. See Proclamation No. 1875, Herbert Hoover, *Herbert Hoover: Proclamations and Executive Orders* (Washington, DC: US Government Printing Office, 1974), 1:12–13; Mark David Spence, *Dispossessing the Wilderness: Indian Removal and the Making of the National Parks* (New York: Oxford University Press, 2000), 4.

11. Stoffle et al., "Ethnographic Overview and Assessment for Arches National Park," 188–189.

Chapter 3: Pioneer Days

1. Bullock, proceedings of July 24, 1849, GCM; *JH*, July 24, 1849.

2. Brigham Young, "The Holy Ghost Necessary in Preaching," August 17, 1856, *JD*, 4:32.

3. Bullock, proceedings of July 24, 1849, GCM; *JH*, July 24, 1849.

4. *JH*, July 24, 1849.

5. Thomas Kane, *The Mormons* (Philadelphia: King and Baird, 1850), 80.

6. *RMMP*, 35–39.

7. Parley P. Pratt, "To President Orson Pratt," September 6, 1848, printed in *MS*, January 15, 1849; Bullock, June 14, 1849, GCM.

8. Bullock, June 14, 1849, GCM; minutes about Indians, February 28, 1850, BYP.

9. Bullock, proceedings of July 24, 1849, GCM.

10. On Wakara's supposed racial transfiguration, see Bullock, meeting at the Bowery, May 19, 1850, GCM.

11. "Utah's Pioneer Day," *DN*, July 25, 1890.

12. Bullock, council meeting with Jim Bridger, June 28, 1847, GCM.

13. Willard Richards and George Smith to Orson Pratt, July 21, 1847, MS 1490, CHL.

14. Jared Farmer, *On Zion's Mount: Mormons, Indians, and the American Landscape* (Cambridge, MA: Harvard University Press, 2008), 88–89.

15. "Utah's Pioneer Day."

Chapter 4: Fillmore

1. Richard Payne, "A History of Utah's Territorial Capitol Building at Fillmore, 1851–1969" (master's thesis, Brigham Young University, Provo, UT, 1971), 3–42, 79–81.

2. In the fall of 2022, Kanosh Band elders successfully petitioned for the removal of the Indian display. They are currently working with museum curators to create a new display of Native history and life at the museum.

3. On Mary's murder, see "Correspondence," *DN*, August 11, 1869.

4. Marriage of Indian Kanosh to Kahkeputz (or Sally), June 8, 1877, Marriage Certificates, CHL; Thomas Callister, telegram, June 13, 1877, BYP.

5. Edward Leo Lyman, "Chief Kanosh: Champion of Peace and Forbearance," *Journal of Mormon History* 35, no. 1 (2009): 178n69; LaVan Martineau, *The Southern Paiutes: Legends, Lore, Language, and Lineage* (Las Vegas: KC Publications, 1992), 283.

6. Michael M. Ames, *Cannibal Tours and Glass Boxes* (Vancouver: University of British Columbia Press, 2014), 3.

7. M. Y. Brave Heart and L. M. DeBruyn, "The American Indian Holocaust: Healing Historical Unresolved Grief," *American Indian and Alaska Native Mental Health Research: Journal of the National Center* 8, no. 2 (1998): 56–78.

8. Lyman, "Chief Kanosh," 191–195.

9. "The Talk," *DN*, June 14, 1865; notes of Kanosh's interview, December 17, 1872, Kane Family Papers, HBLL.

10. See May 31 and June 12, 1876, Baptisms for the Dead, in George W. Hill Collection, MS 8172, CHL.

Chapter 5: The Name of a Lake

1. Stephen Van Hoak, "Waccara's Utes: Native American Equestrian Adaptations in the Eastern Great Basin, 1776–1876" (MA thesis, University of Nevada, Las Vegas, 1998), 53–63.

2. Anne Smith, *Ethnography of the Northern Utes* (Santa Fe: Museum of New Mexico Press, 1974), 61–63.

3. Smith, *Ethnography*, 221–222.

4. Daniel Jones, *Forty Years Among the Indians* (Salt Lake City: Juvenile Instructor Office, 1890), 41.

5. Deanna Strohm, Phaedra Budy, and Todd Crowl, "Matching Watershed and Otolith Chemistry to Establish Natal Origin of an Endangered Desert Lake Sucker," *Transactions of the American Fisheries Society* 146, no. 4 (May 22, 2017): 732–743.

6. This description of Native Americans is not to be confused with what Shepard Krech has described as the "ecological Indian"—the mythic, noble figure who lived in harmony with nature until the White man destroyed both him and his natural environment. Instead, I follow Robin Wall Kimmerer's description of indigeneity: the deeply spiritual and scientific process that, through the generational wisdom of human and nonhuman ancestors, along with their own knowledge of a place developed through trial and error, peoples become "naturalized" or "Indigenous" to a place. Shepard Krech, *The Ecological Indian: Myth and History* (New York: W. W. Norton & Company, 2000); Kimmerer, *Braiding Sweetgrass*, 128, 205–215.

7. On the history of this reorientation of Utah Valley away from the lake and toward the mountains, see Farmer, *On Zion's Mount*.

8. Jon Benson, "Working Together to Save Utah Lake," *Salt Lake Tribune*, March 24, 2022, https://www.sltrib.com/sponsored/2022/03/22/working-together-save; Benjamin Abbott et al., "Utah Lake Islands," Brigham Young University, December 29, 2021, https:/pws.byu.edu/utahlakeislands. LRS removed the proposal to use Rotenone in its application to the US Army Corp of Engineers.

9. Morenne Benoît, "Dredging Up the Past," *DN*, August 8, 2022, https://www.deseret.com/2022/8/8/23061534/dredging-up-the-past. For LRS's proposal, see Lake Restoration Solutions, Inc., "Utah Lake Restoration Project Proposal," Utah Division of Forestry, Fire and State Lands, January 2018, https://ffsl.utah.gov/wp-content/uploads/UtahLakeRestorationProject-DigitalRedacted-011718-1.pdf.

10. Benoît, "Dredging Up the Past."

Chapter 6: Spawning Season

1. Timothy Modde and Neal Muirhead, "Spawning Chronology and Larval Emergence of June Sucker (*Chasmistes liorus*)," *Great Basin Naturalist* 54, no. 4 (1994): 366–370. On Ute fishing techniques and practices, see Smith, *Ethnography*, 61–63.

2. George Bean, *Autobiography of George Washington Bean*, ed. Flora Diana Bean Horne (Salt Lake City: Utah Printing Co., 1945), 51.

3. Ibid., 47; Edward Tullidge, "History of Provo City," *Tullidge's Quarterly Magazine* 3 (1883): 234.

4. Bean, *Autobiography*, 52–53; Parley P. Pratt, "Correspondence from America," letter dated July 8, 1849, *MS*.

5. Richard E. Fike et al., *A Nineteenth Century Ute Burial from Northeast Utah* (Salt Lake City: Bureau of Land Management, 1984), 91.

6. Charles Oviatt, "Chronology of Lake Bonneville, 30,000 to 10,000 Yr B.P.," *Quaternary Science Reviews* 110 (2015): 166–171; Mark Milligan and H. McDonald, "Shorelines and Vertebrate Fauna of Pleistocene Lake Bonneville, Utah, Idaho, and Nevada," *Geology of the Intermountain West* 4 (2017): 181–214.

7. Richard Heckmann, Charles Thompson, and David White, "Fishes of Utah Lake," *Great Basin Naturalist Memoirs*, no. 5 (1981): 107–127.

8. Steven Simms, *Ancient Peoples of the Great Basin and the Colorado Plateau* (Walnut Creek, CA: Left Coast Press, 2008), 27–37, 244–257; Joel Janetski, "Wetlands in Utah Valley Prehistory," in *Wetland Adaptations in the Great Basin* (Provo, UT: Brigham Young University, 1990), 233–257.

9. Farmer, *On Zion's Mount*, 25–26, 70–76; Silvestre Vélez de Escalante, *The Domínguez-Escalante Journal: Their Expedition Through Colorado, Utah, Arizona, and New Mexico in 1776*, ed. Ted J. Warner, trans. Fray Angelico Chavez (Salt Lake City: University of Utah Press, 1995), 63, 68; Gregory Smoak, *Ghost Dances and Identity* (Berkeley: University of California Press, 2008), 19.

10. Farmer, *On Zion's Mount*, 25–26; Pekka Hämäläinen, *The Comanche Empire* (New Haven, CT: Yale University Press, 2009), 24. On bands and their malleability, see "Field Notebooks," 1936–1937, Anne M. Smith Papers, ML.

11. Joshua Reid, *The Sea Is My Country: The Maritime World of the Makahs* (New Haven, CT: Yale University Press, 2015), 4. Ethnologist Anne (Nan) Smith interviewed Wakara's grandchildren when she visited the Uintah and Ouray Reservation in the 1930s. "Field Notebooks"; Smith, *Ethnography*, 61–64; Bean, *Autobiography*, 51.

12. "Field Notebooks"; Smith, *Ethnography*, 48–61.

13. Rosemary Sucec, *Fulfilling Destinies, Sustaining Lives: The Landscape of the Waterpocket Fold* (Washington, DC: National Park Service, US Department of the Interior, 2006), 326; Smith, *Ethnography*, 62.

14. William Atlas et al., "Ancient Fish Weir Technology for Modern Stewardship: Lessons from Community-Based Salmon Monitoring," *Ecosystem Health*

and Sustainability 3, no. 6 (2017); Jesse Morin et al., "Indigenous Sex-Selective Salmon Harvesting Demonstrates Pre-contact Marine Resource Management in Burrard Inlet, British Columbia, Canada," *Scientific Reports* 11, no. 1 (2021).

15. Thanks to Joel Janetski for helping me think through the Timpanogos' preference for chubs and suckers.

16. Escalante, *Journal*, 64.

17. Bernardo de Miera y Pacheco, "Miera's Report," *Utah Historical Quarterly* 11, nos. 1–4 (1943): 115–116.

18. Le Roy Hafen and Ann Hafen, *The Old Spanish Trail* (Lincoln: University of Nebraska Press, 1993), 120; Frémont, *Report*, 273–274.

19. Parley P. Pratt, letter to Orson Pratt and the Saints in Great Britain, *MS*, September 5, 1848.

Chapter 7: Too Much Fishing

1. Bullock, minutes of a meeting with Walker, May 14, 1849, BYP; Young to Walker, May 14, 1849, BYP.

2. *JH*, April 17, 1849; D. Robert Carter, *Founding Fort Utah* (Provo, Utah: Provo City Corporation, 2003), 99.

3. Young to Isaac Higbee, April 18, 1849, BYP.

4. Dimick Huntington to Young, April 19, 1849, BYP.

5. Bullock, minutes of a meeting with Walker, May 14, 1849, BYP; Young to Walker, May 14, 1849, BYP.

6. On Wakara laying in Huntington's arms, Bullock, minutes of a meeting with Walker, May 14, 1849, BYP.

7. Ibid. On the Battle Creek Massacre, see *TWWET*, 96–103.

8. Bullock, minutes of a meeting with Walker, May 14, 1849, BYP; Young to Walker, May 14, 1849, BYP.

9. On Wakara's recollection of his life story, which he told to Huntington, see James Piercy, *Route from Liverpool to the Great Salt Lake Valley* (Liverpool: Franklin D. Richards, 1855), 104–105; Dimick Huntington, *Vocabulary of the Utah and Sho-Sho-Ne or Snake Dialects, with Indian Legends and Traditions* (Salt Lake City: Salt Lake Herald Office, 1872), 27–28.

10. Wakara's recollection about when the horse first arrived at Timpanogos Lake might have been faulty. As I discuss in Part III, ten years before Wakara's birth another Spanish explorer, Manuel Maestas, was dispatched to the lake to recover stolen horses.

11. Huntington, *Vocabulary*, 27–28.

12. Dimick Huntington to Young, May 18, 1849; Young to Dimick Huntington, May 19, 1849, BYP.

13. Parley P. Pratt, "Correspondence from America," letter dated July 8, 1849, *MS.*

14. James Bean, statement, June 12, 1854, HOCHD; Carter, *Founding Fort Utah*, 114–115.

15. Bean, *Autobiography*, 56–61.

16. Alexander Williams to Young, January 7, 1850, BYP; Young to the Brethren in Utah Valley, January 8, 1850, BYP; James Bean, statement, June 12, 1854, HOCHD.

17. Young to the Brethren in Utah Valley, January 8, 1850, BYP.

18. Bullock, council meeting for January 31, 1850, GCM; Special Order Nos. 1, 3, January 31, 1850, UTMR.

19. George Howland to Daniel Wells, February 9, 1850, UTMR; Carter, *Founding Fort Utah*, 172–173.

20. George Howland to Daniel Wells, February 9, 1850, UTMR.

21. *TWWET*, 145–147.

22. Daniel Wells, "Daniel H. Wells' Narrative," *Utah Historical Quarterly* 6 (1933): 126; John Gunnison, *The Mormons* (Philadelphia: Lippincott, Grambo & Company, 1852), 146–147.

23. Abner Blackburn, *Frontiersman: Abner Blackburn's Narrative*, ed. Will Bagley (Salt Lake City: University of Utah Press, 1992), 170–171; Carter, *Founding Fort Utah*, 222–224.

24. Carter, *Founding Fort Utah*, 220–222.

25. Farmer, *On Zion's Mount*, 73–76; Wells, "Wells' Narrative," 126; *TWWET*, 151–152.

26. Minutes about Indians, February 28, 1850, BYP; Carter, *Founding Fort Utah*, 234.

27. Isaac Morley to Young, February 20, March 15, 1850, BYP; minutes about Indians, February 28, 1850, BYP. For names of Utes baptized, see list of Indians baptized, July 7, 1850, BYP.

28. Isaac Morley to Young, April 21, 1850, BYP.

29. *TWWET*, 162–163.

30. Isaac Morley to Young, April 21, 1850, BYP.

31. John Wilson to Thomas Ewing, August 22, 1849; *Annual Report of the Commissioner of Indian Affairs* (Washington, DC: Government Printing Office, 1850), 67.

32. Carter, *Founding Fort Utah*, 238–239.

33. D. Robert Carter, "Fish and the Famine of 1855–56," *Journal of Mormon History* 27, no. 2 (2001): 92–124.

34. Isaac Morley to Young, April 17, 1850, BYP; meeting with Utes, May 22, 1850, BYP.

35. Meeting with Utes, May 22, 1850, BYP.

36. See May 1850 entries in William Harwell, ed., *Manuscript History of Brigham Young, 1847–1850* (Salt Lake City: Collier's Publishing, 1997), 295.

37. Ibid.

38. Andrew Jackson's Second Annual Message to Congress, December 6, 1830; First Presidency to John Bernhisel, November 20, 1850, BYP.

Chapter 8: Horse Wars

1. George Harwood Phillips, *Chiefs and Challengers: Indian Resistance and Cooperation in Southern California* (Norman: University of Oklahoma Press, 2014), 74–84, 93.

2. George Beattie and Helen Beattie, *Heritage of the Valley, San Bernardino's First Century* (Pasadena, CA: San Pasqual Press, 1939), 65–66.

3. James Sandos, *Converting California: Indians and Franciscans in the Missions* (New Haven, CT: Yale University Press, 2008), 8, 1–14.

4. Benjamin Madley, *An American Genocide: The United States and the California Indian Catastrophe* (New Haven, CT: Yale University Press, 2016), 35–36, 3.

5. José del Carmen Lugo, "Life of a Rancher," *Historical Society of Southern California Quarterly* 32, no. 3 (1950): 231–232; George Brewerton, "A Ride with Kit Carson," *Harper's New Monthly Magazine*, June 1, 1853.

6. Beattie and Beattie, *Heritage*, 66. On other threats that the *Californios* or U.S soldiers would kill Wakara, see *JH*, March 4, 1851.

7. Cristina Luís et al., "Iberian Origins of New World Horse Breeds," *Journal of Heredity* 97, no. 2 (2006): 107–113.

8. Kathleen Hayden, "Perspectives from the Field: Wild Horses Are Cultural Resources," *Environmental Practice* 18, no. 3 (September 2016): 232.

9. Peter Mitchell, *Horse Nations: The Worldwide Impact of the Horse on Indigenous Societies Post-1492* (New York: Oxford University Press, 2015), 76–80.

10. Jordan Curnutt, *Animals and the Law* (Santa Barbara, CA: ABC-CLIO, 2001), 141–145.

11. "Wild Horse and Burro Program," Bureau of Land Management, 2022, https://www.blm.gov/sites/default/files/docs/2022-01/BLM_WHB_Infographic_FY21_FINAL.pdf.

12. Dave Philipps, "Success Spoils a U.S. Program to Round Up Wild Horses," *New York Times*, October 14, 2016; Wayne Pacelle, "Feds Must Dismiss Unhinged Advice on Wild Horses," *A Humane World* (blog), September 13, 2016, https://blog.humanesociety.org/2016/09/advisory-board-recommends-euthanasia-45000-wild-horses.html; Madeleine Pickens, "Response to BLMs Report to Congress," Saving America's Mustangs, n.d., http://savingamericasmustangs.org/wp-content/uploads/2018/05/Response-to-BLMs-Report-to-Congress.pdf; Kathleen Hayden, "American Wild Horses Set On Path to Extinction?," *All-Creatures.org* (blog), October 14, 2019, https://www.all-creatures.org/articles2/mdi-wild-horses-extinction.html.

13. "Sulphur Herd Management Area," Bureau of Land Management, 2025, https://www.blm.gov/programs/wild-horse-and-burro/herd-management/herd-management-areas/utah/sulphur.

14. Hayden, "Perspectives from the Field," 232–233.

15. Fernanda Santos, "On Fate of Wild Horses, Stars and Indians Spar," *New York Times*, August 11, 2013; Leland Grass, "Horses Are Sacred," Animal Welfare Institute, fall 2013, https://awionline.org/awi-quarterly/2013-fall/horses-are-sacred-view-nohooka-dine.

16. "Sponsor a Horse," Return to Freedom, https://returntofreedom.org/donate1/sponsor-a-horse/.

17. Mitchell, *Horse Nations*, 85.

18. Hayden, "Perspectives from the Field," 233; "Manes & Trails: Original Horses of Ramona," *Ramona Sentinel*, June 28, 2012, https://www.sandiegouniontribune.com/ramona-sentinel/sdrsmanes-trails-original-horses-of-ramona-2012jun28-story.html; Coyote Canyon Heritage Herd, "In 2003 the Anza Borrego Desert State parks absconded . . . ," Facebook, March 7, 2022, https://www.facebook.com/permalink.php?story_fbid=pfbioiodeNvjh8JwGZqeCbt555g2R5d9moxAfB6UmFXHdPY9Zh1swouvkz9KSx4359kkSl&id=208957562491269.

19. Ariele Johannson, "Wild Horses in Ramona: The Coyote Canyon Heritage Herd," *East County Magazine*, January 15, 2013, https://www.eastcountymagazine.org/wild-horses-ramona-coyote-canyon-heritage-herd.

20. "Manes & Trails."

Chapter 9: We've Always Had the Horse

1. Laura M. Holson, "An Ancient Horse Is Unearthed in a Utah Backyard," *New York Times*, May 3, 2018.

2. William Taylor et al., "Interdisciplinary Analysis of the Lehi Horse," *American Antiquity* 86, no. 3 (July 2021): 465–485.

3. Ludovic Orlando et al., "Recalibrating *Equus* Evolution Using the Genome Sequence of an Early Middle Pleistocene Horse," *Nature* 499, no. 7456 (2013): 74–78.

4. David W. Anthony, *The Horse, the Wheel, and Language: How Bronze-Age Riders from the Eurasian Steppes Shaped the Modern World* (Princeton, NJ: Princeton University Press, 2007).

5. Per Cornell and Adam Andersson, "The Past, Ethnic Purity, and the Foundations of Nazi Ideology: Archaeology at War," *Journal of Archaeological Research*, January 9, 2025.

6. Adolf Hitler, *Mein Kampf* (New York: Reynal and Hitchcock, 1941), 404–405; Bettina Arnold, "The Past as Propaganda: How Hitler's Archaeologists Distorted European Prehistory to Justify Racist and Territorial Goals," *Archaeology* 45, no. 4 (August 1992): 30–37.

7. David W. Anthony et al., "The Origins of Horseback Riding," *Antiquity* 65, no. 246 (March 1991): 22–38.

8. Pablo Librado et al., "The Origins and Spread of Domestic Horses from the Western Eurasian Steppes," *Nature* 598, no. 7882 (October 2021): 634–640.

9. Robert Denhardt, *The Horse of the Americas* (Norman: University of Oklahoma Press, 1975), 36–38; Luis Rivera, *A Violent Evangelism: The Political and Religious Conquest of the Americas* (Louisville, KY: Westminster John Knox Press, 1992), 98–99.

10. J. Edward De Steiguer, *Wild Horses of the West: History and Politics of America's Mustangs* (Tucson: University of Arizona Press, 2011), 58–59; Heather Pringle, "How Europeans Brought Sickness to the New World," *Science*, June 4, 2015, https://www.science.org/content/article/how-europeans-brought-sickness-new-world.

11. Steiguer, *Wild Horses of the West*, 33, 57–61.

12. Ibid., 60–62.

13. Ibid., 62.

14. Victor Hanson, *Carnage and Culture: Landmark Battles in the Rise to Western Power* (New York: Knopf, 2007), 180–216; Steiguer, *Wild Horses of the West*, 63–65.

15. Ramón A. Gutiérrez, *When Jesus Came, the Corn Mothers Went Away: Marriage, Sexuality, and Power in New Mexico, 1500–1846* (Stanford, CA: Stanford University Press, 1991), 49–50.

16. Ned Blackhawk, "The Displacement of Violence: Ute Diplomacy and the Making of New Mexico's Eighteenth-Century Northern Borderlands," *Ethnohistory* 54, no. 4 (2007): 730–732.

17. Charles Hackett, *Revolt of the Pueblo Indians of New Mexico and Otermín's Attempted Reconquest, 1680–1682*, ed. George Hammond, trans. Charmion Clair Shelby (Albuquerque: University of New Mexico Press, 1970), 2:246–251; 1:120; Gutiérrez, *When Jesus Came*, 133–135.

18. Gutiérrez, *When Jesus Came*, 143–175.

19. Hämäläinen, *Indigenous Continent*, 189.

20. Yvette Running Horse Collin, "The Relationship Between the Indigenous Peoples of the Americas and the Horse: Deconstructing a Eurocentric Myth" (PhD diss., University of Alaska Fairbanks, 2017).

21. William Taylor et al., "Early Dispersal of Domestic Horses into the Great Plains and Northern Rockies," *Science* 379, no. 6639 (March 31, 2023): 1316–1323. See also Andrew Curry, "Horse Nations," *Science*, March 30, 2023, https://www.science.org/content/article/horse-nations-animal-began-transforming-native-american-life-startlingly-early.

22. Blackhawk, *Violence*, 30, 19–20; Simmons, *The Ute Indians*, 29, 9.

23. Mitchell, *Horse Nations*, 195; Frances Swadesh, *Los Primeros Pobladores: Hispanic Americans of the Ute Frontier* (South Bend, IN: University of Notre Dame Press, 1974), 32–33; Blackhawk, "The Displacement of Violence," 734–737; Hämäläinen, *The Comanche Empire*, 88–89.

24. Escalante, *Journal*, 63–73.

25. Fred Conetah, *A History of the Northern Ute People* (Salt Lake City: Uintah-Ouray Tribe, 1982), 28.

26. Farmer, *On Zion's Mount*, 28.

27. Escalante, *Journal*, 70–71; de Miera y Pacheco, "Miera's Report," 115; Joseph J. Hill, "Spanish and Mexican Exploration and Trade Northwest from New Mexico into the Great Basin, 1765–1853," *Utah Historical Quarterly* 3, no. 1 (1930): 16–17.

28. Hill, "Spanish and Mexican Exploration," 18–19; Jedediah Smith, *The Southwest Expedition of Jedediah Smith*, ed. George R. Brooks (Lincoln: University of Nebraska Press, 1989), 41–42; Clifford Trafzer, *A Chemehuevi Song: The Resilience of a Southern Paiute Tribe* (Seattle: University of Washington Press, 2015), 17.

Chapter 10: Land Pirate

1. *JH*, March 4, 1851; Robert Cleland, *The Cattle on a Thousand Hills: Southern California, 1850–1870* (San Marino, CA: Huntington Library, 1941), 92–93.

2. *JH*, March 4, 1851. See also Beattie and Beattie, *Heritage*, 65–66.

3. March 3–10, 1851, GASJ.

4. Jones, *Forty Years*, 41; Huntington, *Vocabulary*, title page.

5. Beattie and Beattie, *Heritage*, 37–38, 45. The *Californios* named Wakara's diverse raiding parties *los Chaguanosos*, perhaps after the Sabuagana Utes, from what is today Colorado, who counted Wakara's Timpanogos Utes as kin. Blackhawk, *Violence*, 139–140.

6. Blackhawk, *Violence*, 139–140.

7. Beattie and Beattie, *Heritage*, 65–66; George Beattie, "San Bernardino Valley Before the Americans Came," *California Historical Society Quarterly* 12, no. 2 (1933): 111–112; Natale Zappia, *Traders and Raiders: The Indigenous World of the Colorado Basin, 1540–1859* (Chapel Hill: University of North Carolina Press, 2014), 105.

8. Beattie and Beattie, *Heritage*, 65.

9. Horace Bell, *Reminiscences of a Ranger* (Los Angeles: Yarnell, Caystile & Mathes, Printers, 1881), 283; Juan Caballería y Collell, *History of San Bernardino Valley* (San Bernardino, CA: Times-Press, 1902), 102–104.

10. Van Hoak, "Waccara's Utes," 59–60.

11. Brewerton, "Ride," 315–326.

12. Elliott West, *The Way to the West: Essays on the Central Plains* (Albuquerque: University of New Mexico Press, 1995), 20–22, 72–74. On the Utes' controlled burns along the Old Spanish Trail, see Charles Preuss, *Exploring with Frémont*, ed. Erwin G. Gudde (Norman: University of Oklahoma Press, 1958), 87.

13. William Manly, *Death Valley in '49*, ed. LeRoy Johnson and Jean Johnson (Berkeley, CA: Heyday Books, Santa Clara University, 2001), 55–61, 78, 180; Smith, *Ethnography*, 247–252; Bean, *Autobiography*, 98.

14. Van Hoak, "Waccara's Utes," 66–67.

15. Will Bagley, *So Rugged and Mountainous: Blazing the Trails to Oregon and California, 1812–1848* (Norman: University of Oklahoma Press, 2010), 188; Hampton Sides, *Blood and Thunder* (New York: Anchor, 2007), 66, 77–78.

16. Frémont, *Report*, 272; Preuss, *Exploring with Frémont*, 132–133.

17. Frémont, *Report*, 273–274; Alexander Baugh, "John C. Frémont's 1843–44 Western Expedition and Its Influence on Mormon Settlement in Utah," in *Far Away in the West: Reflections on the Mormon Pioneer Trail*, ed. Scott C. Esplin et al. (Salt Lake City: Deseret Book, 2015), 23–55.

18. "Weight Size, etc. of Indians," August 2, 1852, BYP.

19. Brewerton, "Ride," 323–326; Vernon Lunt and Rachel Petty Hunt, *Life of Henry Lunt* (n.p.: n.p., 1944), 124–125, 143.

20. Brewerton, "Ride," 323–326; Frémont, *Report*, 272; Kane, *The Mormons*, 72–73.

21. Brewerton, "Ride," 323–326; Heap and Beale, *Central Route*, 92.

22. For roles within the band, see Adelia Sidwell, "History of South Sanpete," 10–11, ML.

23. Theodore Talbot, *The Journals of Theodore Talbot*, ed. Charles H. Carey (Portland, OR: Metropolitan Press, 1931), 41–42.

24. Osborne Russell, *Journal of a Trapper* (Boise, ID: Syms-York Company, 1921), 121–122; Parley P. Pratt, letter to Orson Pratt and the Saints in Great Britain, *MS*, September 5, 1848; Karen Lupo, "The Historical Occurrence and Demise of Bison in Northern Utah," *Utah Historical Quarterly* 64, no. 2 (1996): 168–180.

25. Natale Zappia, "Revolutions in the Grass," *Environmental History* 21, no. 1 (2016): 30–53; George Bean to Young, May 1, 1854, BYP; Juanita Brooks, "Indian Relations on the Mormon Frontier," *Utah Historical Quarterly* 12, nos. 1–2 (1944): 3.

26. Farmer, *On Zion's Mount*, 24–25.

27. Escalante, *Journal*, 64–66.

28. Conetah, *A History*, 28.

29. Hafen and Hafen, *Old Spanish Trail*, 271; Jones, *Forty Years*, 49–50.

30. Frémont, *Report*, 276.

31. Phillips, *Chiefs and Challengers*, 94–96.

32. Leonard Pitt, *Decline of the Californios* (Berkeley: University of California Press, 1998), 132, 151–152.

33. Phillips, *Chiefs and Challengers*, 95; Beattie and Beattie, *Heritage*, 84–88.

34. Norma Ricketts, *The Mormon Battalion* (Boulder: University Press of Colorado, 1997), 148–149.

35. *TWWET*, 87–90, 116–118.

36. *TWWET*, 120–121; Carter, *Founding Fort Utah*, 123, 135–137.

37. George A. Smith, letter of recommendation to Captains Walker and Peteetneet, Louisa [Parowan], March 20, 1851, HOCHD; Ordination of Ute leaders, June 5, 1851, GCM.

38. Daniel Wells to Peter Conover, June 30, 1851, UTMR; George A. Smith, letter to the editor, *DN*, November 29, 1851.

39. D. Robert Carter, *From Fort to Village* (Provo, Utah: Provo City Corporation, 2008), 100–101.

40. Isaac Higbee to Young, May 26, 1852, BYP; Young to Isaac Higbee, May 28, 1852, BYP.

Chapter 11: "The Saddest-Looking Piece of Humanity"

1. For the most comprehensive study of Pidash/Sally's life, including her tribe of origin and her torture, see Virginia Kerns, *Sally in Three Worlds: An Indian Captive in the House of Brigham Young* (Salt Lake City: University of Utah Press, 2021), 32–34, 78.

2. James Little, "Biography of Lorenzo Young," *Utah Historical Quarterly* 14, nos. 1–4 (January 1, 1946): 104–105.

3. John R. Young, *Memoirs of John R. Young* (Salt Lake City: Deseret News, 1920), 62.

4. Ibid. See also Kerns, *Sally in Three Worlds*, 35–42.

5. Brigham Young testimony, *U.S. v. Pedro León et al.*, January 15, 1852, Enslavement in Territorial Utah Documents Collection, ML, https://collections.lib.utah.edu/ark:/87278/s6q77b60.

6. See "Sally, Indian," in entry for "Brigham Young," "U.S. Census, 1860," FamilySearch, https://www.familysearch.org/ark:/61903/3:1:33SQ-GBSF-98WG?view=index. On Sally's life as a servant, see Kerns, *Sally in Three Worlds*, esp. 120–153.

7. *RMMP*, 186–188.

8. Thomas Murphy has argued that Baptiste's use of firebrands on Pidash was not torture at all but the cauterization or treatment of wounds, a well-established form of Indigenous medicine. Thomas Murphy, "Views from Turtle Island: Settler Colonialism and Indigenous Mormon Entanglements," in *The Palgrave Handbook of Global Mormonism*, ed. R. Gordon Shepherd, A. Gary Shepherd, and Ryan T. Cragun (Cham, Switzerland: Springer International Publishing, 2020), 751–779.

9. Brooks, "Indian Relations on the Mormon Frontier," 39.

10. "Funeral of a Lamanite," *DN*, December 18, 1878.

11. Gary Tom and Ronald Holt, "The Paiute Tribe of Utah," in *A History of Utah's American Indians*, ed. Forrest S. Cuch (Salt Lake City: Utah Division of Indian Affairs and the Utah Division of State History, 2000), 123–166.

12. On the Kanosh Band, see Ronald Holt, *Beneath These Red Cliffs: An Ethnohistory of the Utah Paiutes* (Albuquerque: University of New Mexico Press, 1992), 43–44.

13. Andrés Reséndez, *The Other Slavery: The Uncovered Story of Indian Enslavement in America* (Boston: Houghton Mifflin Harcourt, 2016), 1.

14. Andrés Reséndez, "Perspective: The Other Slavery," Smithsonian, https://americanindian.si.edu/sites/1/files/pdf/seminars-symposia/the-other-slavery-perspective.pdf; Reséndez, *The Other Slavery*, 5.

15. James F. Brooks, *Captives and Cousins: Slavery, Kinship, and Community in the Southwest Borderlands* (Chapel Hill: University of North Carolina Press, 2002).

16. See, among others, the entry for "Grandma Peaweeds" in the 1920 census of the "Pahvant Indians . . . living at Koosharem, Utah," and that of her daughter, also named Peaweeds. "U.S. Indian Census Rolls, 1920," FamilySearch, https://www.familysearch.org/ark:/61903/3:1:3QS7-89W8-SVPS?view=index. In other censuses, the daughter Peaweeds (also known as "Buitch" and "Anna") is listed as Ute or Pahvant. See also the description of the Arapeen family as leaders of the Koosharem Band in "Mrs. Arapene's Christmas Dance," *Southern Censor*, January 1, 1897.

17. On works that have misidentified Kanosh as a Paiute, see Martha Knack, *Boundaries Between* (Lincoln: University of Nebraska Press, 2004), 61; *RMMP*, 172–173; Blackhawk, *Violence*, 235–236.

18. December 26–27, 1850, GASJ.

Chapter 12: "Gold and Silver and the Richest Treasure"

1. Francisco Atanasio Domínguez, *The Missions of New Mexico, 1776*, ed. Eleanor B. Adams and Fray Angelico Chavez (Albuquerque: University of New Mexico Press, 1956), 252.

2. Lesley Poling-Kempes, *Valley of Shining Stone: The Story of Abiquiú* (Tucson: University of Arizona Press, 1997), 64–66.

3. Domínguez, *The Missions of New Mexico*, 252. For a description and discussion of the "month of slaves," see Sondra Jones, *The Trial of Don Pedro León Luján* (Salt Lake City: University of Utah Press, 2000), 27; S. Lyman Tyler, "Before Escalante: An Early History of the Yuta Indians and the Area North of New Mexico" (PhD diss., University of Utah, 1951), 98–100; Blackhawk, "The Displacement of Violence," 741–742.

4. Reséndez, *The Other Slavery*, 172–173.

5. Patricia Seed, *Ceremonies of Possession in Europe's Conquest of the New World, 1492–1640* (Cambridge: Cambridge University Press, 1995), 69–73.

6. Reséndez, *The Other Slavery*, 61–64.

7. Brooks, *Captives and Cousins*, 24–25.

8. Reséndez, *The Other Slavery*, 135.

9. Ibid., 116–119, 100–103.

10. Gutiérrez, *When Jesus Came*, 135–136; Reséndez, *The Other Slavery*, 167–171.

11. Blackhawk, *Violence*, 77–78.

12. James F. Brooks, "'We Betray Our Own Nation': Indian Slavery and Multi-ethnic Communities in the Southwest Borderlands," in *Indian Slavery in Colonial America*, ed. Alan Gallay (Lincoln: University of Nebraska Press, 2009), 324–325.

13. Reséndez, *The Other Slavery*, 179–180; Charles Wilson Hackett, *Historical Documents Relating to New Mexico* (Washington, DC: Carnegie Institution of Washington, 1937), 487.

14. Domínguez, *The Missions of New Mexico*, 252; Blackhawk, *Violence*, 47.

15. Russell Magnaghi, "Plains Indians in New Mexico: The Genízaro Experience," *Great Plains Quarterly* 10, no. 2 (Spring 1990), 88.

16. Gutiérrez, *When Jesus Came*, 174, 171.

17. On Abiquiú and the Ute–New Mexican slave trade, see Blackhawk, *Violence*, 71–80, 107.

18. Ibid., 75–76.

19. Ibid.

20. Madley, *An American Genocide*, 27.

21. Ibid., 26; Sandos, *Converting California*, 49–50.

22. Steven W. Hackel, *Junípero Serra: California's Founding Father* (New York: Hill and Wang 2013), 201.

23. Blackhawk, *Violence*, 90–97.

24. Ibid., 112; Hafen and Hafen, *Old Spanish Trail*, 85.

25. Gutiérrez, *When Jesus Came*, 171–172; Michael González, *This Small City Will Be a Mexican Paradise: Exploring the Origins of Mexican Culture in Los Angeles, 1821–1846* (Albuquerque: University of New Mexico Press, 2005), 124–134.

26. Thomas Farnham, *Travels in the Great Western Prairies* (New York: Wiley & Putnam, 1843), 107–108; Jones, *Forty Years*, 50.

27. Blackhawk, *Violence*, 72–73, 137–139; Jones, *Trial*, 97.

28. William Snow, "Utah Indians and Spanish Slave Trade," *Utah Historical Quarterly* 2, no. 3 (July 1929): 70.

29. Jones, *Forty Years*, 50.

30. William Palmer, "Pahute Indian Government and Laws," *Utah Historical Quarterly* 2, no. 2 (April 1929): 40.

31. December 1854, Jacob Hamblin Journal, MS 1951, CHL.

Chapter 13: "A New Feature in the Traffic of Human Beings"

1. Parley P. Pratt to Wives and Children, December 8, 1849, Pratt Family Papers, MS 14392, CHL.

2. *TWWET*, 126.

3. Ibid., 126–127.

4. Ibid.

5. Minutes about Indians, February 28, 1850, BYP; Isaac Morley to Young and Council, March 15, 1850; Presidency to Isaac Morley, March 24, 1850, BYP.

6. Young to Isaac Morley, April 4, 1850, BYP.

7. Presidency to Isaac Morley, March 24, 1850, BYP.

8. Richard Morley, "The Life and Contributions of Isaac Morley" (MA thesis, Brigham Young University, 1965), 158–160.

9. On Waddie/Nellie's origins, see Michael K. Bennion, "Captivity, Adoption, Marriage and Identity: Native American Children in Mormon Homes, 1847–1900" (MA thesis, University of Nevada, Las Vegas, 2012), 82–84. Local legends and family history claim Mountain Fawn was either Wakara's daughter or his sister. Pat Wilde, "Mountain Fawn," *Herald Journal*, August 18, 2020, https://www.hjnews.com/bear_laker/mountain-fawn/article_5fc0a110-e179-11ea-a2ed-33100b0e5557f.html.

10. Isaac Morley, "Confidential" to Young, April 13, 1850, BYP.

11. *TWWET*, 67; George A. Smith, "The Indian War," October 7, *JD*, 1:197.

12. Young to Daniel Wells, February 14, 1850, UTMR; George Montgomery to Commissioner of Indian Affairs, July 26, 1850, letters received by the Office of Indian Affairs, Utah Superintendency, 1849–1880, HBLL.

13. Winter 1850, Autobiographical Sketch and Journal, Joel Hills Johnson Papers, MS 1546, CHL; Young to Joel Johnson, June 12, 1854, BYP; February 21, 1855, Autobiographical Sketch and Journal, Joel Hills Johnson Papers.

14. John Jones, letter to the editor of the *DN*, July 1, 1850, *DN* Editor's Files, MS 2054, CHL; "Indian Fight," *DN*, July 12, 1850; Adelia B. Sidwell,

"Reminiscences of the Early Days of Manti," *Utah Historical Quarterly* 6, nos. 1–4 (1933): 117–118; list of Indians baptized July 7, 1850, BYP.

15. Bennion, "Captivity, Adoption, Marriage and Identity," 85; George Brimhall, Autobiography of George Brimhall (transcription), 20–21, The Huntington Digital Library, https://hdl.huntington.org/digital/collection/p16003coll15/id/100; March 3–11, 1851, GASJ.

16. Juanita Brooks, "Indian Relations on the Mormon Frontier," *Utah Historical Quarterly* 12, nos. 1–2 (1944): 6.

17. Zerubbabel Snow to Secretary of the Interior, March 9, 1852, letters received by the Office of Indian Affairs, Utah Superintendency, 1849–1880, HBLL; Bennion, "Captivity, Adoption, Marriage and Identity," 153; George A. Smith, letter of recommendation to Captains Walker and Peteetneet, Louisa [Parowan], March 20, 1851, HOCHD.

18. Snow to Secretary of the Interior.

19. Joseph Sanchez, *Explorers, Traders, and Slavers: Forging the Old Spanish Trail, 1678–1850* (Salt Lake City: University of Utah Press, 1997), 173n307; Poling-Kempes, *Valley of Shining Stone*, 72–73.

20. Thomas Williams, ledger book, 1850–1852, MS 8199, CHL; Solomon Kimball, "Our Pioneer Boys," *The Improvement Era* 11 (1908): 735–776; Marva Pedersen, *Crozier Kimball: His Life and Work* (West Bountiful, UT: Carr Printing, 1995), 2–3.

21. Jones, *Trial*, 66.

22. Ibid., 58; John Greiner to Luke Lea, May 19, 1852, in *Official Correspondence of James S. Calhoun While Indian Agent at Santa Fe and Superintendent of Indian Affairs in New Mexico*, ed. Annie Heloise Abel (Washington, DC: Government Printing Office, 1915), 536–537.

23. Brigham Young testimony, *U.S. v. Pedro León et al.*, January 15, 1852, Enslavement in Territorial Utah Documents Collection, ML, https://collections.lib.utah.edu/ark:/87278/s6q77b60.

24. Ibid.

25. Jones, *Trial*, 86–92, 95.

26. Thomas Bullock, Young's scribe and secretary, read the speech on Young's behalf, perhaps because the prophet was too exhausted from his day dealing with Indian attacks, arranging marriages, and arbitrating land disputes. *Journals of the House of Representatives, Council, and Joint Sessions of the First Annual and Special Sessions of the Legislative Assembly of the Territory of Utah* (Great Salt Lake City: Brigham H. Young, 1852), 108.

27. *Journals of the House of Representatives*, 108; Amy Tanner Thiriot, *Slavery in Zion* (Salt Lake City: University of Utah Press, 2022), 13, 98–99, 18.

28. *Journals of the House of Representatives*, 109.

29. *Acts, Resolutions and Memorials Passed at the Annual Sessions of the Legislative Assembly of the Territory of Utah* (Salt Lake City: Brigham H. Young, 1852), 91–94.

30. Knack, *Boundaries Between*, 57; Snow to Secretary of the Interior.

31. "A Child's Memory of How Sarah Joined the Benson Family," FamilySearch, https://www.familysearch.org/en/memories/memory/107973134?cid=mem_copy; Thomas Benson, indenture of Sarah, October 1, 1853, Iron County, Utah, Enslavement in Territorial Utah Documents Collection, ML, https://collections.lib.utah.edu/ark:/87278/s6nzbgtr. See also Brian Cannon, "'To Buy Up the Lamanite Children as Fast as They Could,'" *Journal of Mormon History* 44, no. 2 (2018): 7.

32. Corey Smallcanyon, "Contested Space: Navajos and Hopi in the Colonization of Tuba City" (MA thesis, Brigham Young University, 2010), 27–28; Todd Compton, "Civilizing the Ragged Edge," *Journal of Mormon History* 33, no. 2 (2007): 174–182.

33. Cannon, "'To Buy Up,'" 2–4n2.

34. Jones, *Trial*, 109; Cannon, "'To Buy Up,'" 19; for Sarah Benson's literacy, see entries for the Harrop family in Parowan, Utah Territory, "U.S. Census, 1870," FamilySearch, https://www.familysearch.org/ark:/61903/1:1:MNCT-45J?lang=en; Elizabeth Kane, *Twelve Mormon Homes Visited in Succession on a Journey Through Utah to Arizona* (Philadelphia: William Wood, 1874), 73; Notes of Kanosh's interview, December 17, 1872, Kane Family Papers, HBLL.

35. Brooks, "Indian Relations on the Mormon Frontier," 6.

36. Apache County, Arizona, "U.S. Census, 1880," FamilySearch, https://familysearch.org/ark:/61903/3:1:33SQ-GYY1-95YV?cc=1417683&wc=X4S5-7M9%3A1589394954%2C1589397960%2C1589397741%2C1589394807; Maricopa County, Arizona, "U.S. Census, 1910," Family Search, https://www.familysearch.org/ark:/61903/3:1:33SQ-GRJM-44R?view=index&action=view; World War I draft registration card for Carlyle Sweat, Maricopa, Arizona, FamilySearch, https://www.familysearch.org/ark:/61903/1:1:KZVW-JVD.

37. For example, see Deborah Elison (née Justet), "U.S. Census, 1880," Escalante, Utah, FamilySearch, https://www.familysearch.org/ark:/61903

/1:1:MNSJ-YC8?lang=en; "U.S. Census, 1910," Garfield, Utah, FamilySearch, https://www.familysearch.org/ark:/61903/1:1:M5X3-Y1K?lang=en.

38. Letter from John D. Lee to Willard Richards, March 13, 1852, published in *DN*, April 17, 1852; *Los Angeles Star*, May 22, 1852.

39. Young to Captain Walker, April 9, 1852, BYP.

40. Jones, *Forty Years*, 53.

41. "Weight Size, etc. of Indians," August 2, 1852, BYP; *TWWET*, 219.

42. *TWWET*, 219–222.

43. Woodruff, *Journal*, September 23, 1854, 4:289.

44. "Indian Rumors," *Los Angeles Star*, December 25, 1852.

45. Letter from John D. Lee to Willard Richards, February 5, 1853, published in *DN*, March 19, 1853.

46. Ibid.

47. William Wall to editor, *DN*, May 31, 1853. On promises made to Paiutes to fend off attacks from Wakara, see entries for December 1854 in Jacob Hamblin Journal, MS 1951, CHL. On the executive order from Young, see William Wall to editor, *DN*, May 31, 1853.

48. John Steele to Young, April 10, 1853, BYP.

49. William Wall to editor, *DN*, May 31, 1853.

50. Brigham Young, "Indian Difficulties—Walker," *JD*, May 8, 1853, 1:108.

Chapter 14: A Massacre at Nephi

1. Report of Captain William Wall, April 24, 1853, UTMR.

2. Ibid.

3. Ibid.

4. "Orders to Capture Chief Walker if Possible," Young to William Wall, April 25, 1853, UTMR.

5. May 8, 1853, in Richard Van Wagoner, ed., *The Complete Discourses of Brigham Young* (Salt Lake City: Smith-Pettit Foundation, 2009), 2:665–667; *TWWET*, 225.

6. "Orders to Capture Chief Walker if Possible," Young to William Wall, April 25, 1853, UTMR.

7. Ronald Rood, "The Archaeology of a Mass Grave from Nephi, Utah and One Event of the Walker War, Utah Territory. Excavations at 42JB1470, Nephi, Utah," in *The Materiality of Troubled Pasts*, ed. Anna Zalewska, John Scott, and Grzegorz Kiarszys (Warsaw, Poland: Department of Archaeology, Szczecin University, 2017), 149–154. See also Jeremiah Stettler, "Skeletons Found in

Nephi May Reveal Details of 1853 Massacre," *Salt Lake Tribune*, September 15, 2006.

8. For the best study of the Walker War, see Ryan Wimmer, "The Walker War Reconsidered" (MA thesis, Brigham Young University, 2010).

9. George Bradley to Daniel H. Wells, October 2, 1853, UTMR; "Indian Difficulties," *DN*, October 15, 1853; Peter Gottfredson, *Indian Depredations in Utah* (Salt Lake City: Skelton Publishing CO, 1919), 74–75.

10. Martha Heywood, *Not by Bread Alone: The Journal of Martha Spence Haywood*, ed. Juanita Brooks (Salt Lake City: Utah State Historical Society, 1978), 97.

11. Kimball, *Memoirs*, 228.

12. Rood, "The Archaeology of a Mass Grave," 149–154.

13. Ibid. See also *TWWET*, 273.

14. Heap and Beale, *Central Route*, 91–92.

Chapter 15: The Names of Wars

1. Increase Mather, *A Brief History of the War with the Indians in New-England* (London: Printed for Richard Chiswell, 1676), postscript, 8.

2. "To Our Brethren and Friends, the Inhabitants of the Colony of Massachusetts," December 7, 1675, in John Easton et al., *Narratives of the Indian Wars, 1675–1699* (New York: C. Scribner's Sons, 1913), 62–63.

3. Mather, *Brief History*, 20; George Bodge, *Soldiers in King Philip's War* (Boston: Printed for the author, 1891), 121–122.

4. Mather, *Brief History*, 47, 49; Jill Lepore, *The Name of War: King Philip's War and the Origins of American Identity* (New York: Vintage, 1999), 174–175.

5. Lisa Brooks, *Our Beloved Kin: A New History of King Philip's War* (New Haven, CT: Yale University Press), 8.

6. Ibid., 8–9.

7. Lepore, *The Name of War*, xv–xviii.

8. John Turner, *Brigham Young: Pioneer Prophet* (Cambridge, MA: Belknap Press of Harvard University Press, 2012), 7–8.

9. Brigham Young, "Indian Hostilities," July 31, 1853, *JD*, 1:168.

10. Ibid.

11. George Bradley to Daniel Wells, July 19, 1853, UTMR; George A. Smith to Young, July 22, 1853, UTMR; *JH*, July 25, 1853.

12. See, among others, "Origin of the Indian War," *Sacramento Daily Union*, November 5, 1853; "Speaking of Walker, the Utah Chief," *Buffalo Commercial*, February 3, 1854; "Arrivals from Salt Lake City—the Walker War—Indians

Fighting and Starving," *Perrysburg Journal* (Ohio), March 20,1854; "An Indian War," *Chicago Tribune*, March 22, 1854.

13. Benjamin Ferris, *Utah and the Mormons* (New York: Harper and Brothers, 1854), 255, 204.

14. Richard White, "Frederick Jackson Turner and Buffalo Bill," in *The Frontier in American Culture*, ed. James R. Grossman (Berkeley: University of California Press, 1994), 7–65.

Chapter 16: Keep the Women, Kill the Men

1. Bullock, council meeting for January 31, 1850, GCM.

2. Ibid.; Special Order Nos. 1, 3, January 31, 1850, UTMR.

3. Bullock, minutes of a meeting with Utes, May 22, 1850, BYP.

4. Woodruff, *Journal*, April 25, 26, 1851, 4:20.

5. William McBride to Daniel Wells, June 24, 1851, UTMR; *TWWET*, 182.

6. Daniel Wells to Peter Conover, June 30, 1851, UTMR; Peter Conover to Daniel Wells, July 2, 1851, UTMR.

7. Henry Day to Luke Lea, January 2, 1852, in James Buchanan, *The Utah Expedition: Message from the President of the United States* (Washington, DC: House of Representatives, 1858), 131–132; *JH*, October 23, 1851; *JH*, October 24, 1851.

8. Young to Captain Walker, April 9, 1852, BYP.

9. Carter, *From Fort to Village*, 100–101; Isaac Higbee to Young, May 26, 1852, BYP; Young to Higbee, May 28, 1852, BYP.

10. Jacob Holeman to Luke Lea, April 29, 1852, in Buchanan, *The Utah Expedition*, 144–145.

11. Thomas Ellerbeck, Ute/Shoshone minutes, September 4, 1852, BYP; "Governor's Message," *DN*, December 25, 1852.

12. "Governor's Message," *DN*, December 25, 1852.

13. Young to Fillmore, January 16, 1853, BYP; "Millard County," *DN*, February 19, 1853; John D. Lee to Willard Richards, February 5, 1853, published in *DN*, March 19, 1853; Daniel Wells to Phineas Wright, April 25, 1853, UTMR; "Orders to Capture Chief Walker if Possible," Young to William Wall, April 25, 1853, UTMR; Wall, report, April 24, 1853, UTMR.

14. Dimick Huntington, letter to editor, *DN*, May 28, 1853.

15. Isaac Morley to Young, April 30, 1853, BYP; Young to Isaac Morley, May 7, 1853, BYP.

16. Young, "Indian Difficulties—Walker," *JD*, May 8, 1853, 1:105–106.

17. Bullock, Historical Department Office Journal, July 2, 1853, CR 100 1, CHL.

18. Ibid.; Daniel Wells to Jedediah Grant, July 10, 1853, UTMR.

19. Wakara interview with M. S. Martenas, July 6, 1853, Jacob Holeman Papers, MS 2178, CHL.

20. Wimmer, "The Walker War Reconsidered," 96–98.

21. James McClellan to Young, July 16, 1853, BYP. On the outbreak of violence, see Wimmer, "The Walker War Reconsidered," 108–111.

22. See drafts of Special Orders Nos. 1–4 July 19, 1853, BYP; "Col. Conover will take all possible measures to pursue and Capture Walker the chief of the Utahs and prosecuting the campaign until he is executed": Daniel Wells and James Ferguson, Special Orders No. 1, July 19, 1853, UTMR. See also *TWWET*, 239.

23. Young to Captain Wacher, July 25, 1853, UTMR.

24. Young, "Indian Hostilities," 168–170.

25. Ibid., 170.

26. Andrew Love, diary, July 16, 1853, MS 1675, CHL; Wimmer, "The Walker War Reconsidered," 113–116; *TWWET*, 262–263.

27. Special Orders No. 13, August 16, 1853, UTMR; *TWWET*, 257; William Wells to Henry Standage, August 31, 1853, UTMR.

28. George Bradley to Daniel Wells, July 19, 1853, UTMR; William Kimball to Daniel Wells, August 7, 1853, WHK; Smith to Heber C. Kimball, August 8, 1853, WHK; John D. Lee to Young, September 24, 1853, BYP. See also Wimmer, "The Walker War Reconsidered," 128.

29. John D. Lee to Young, September 24, 1853, BYP.

30. Young to George Manypenny, September 30, 1853, BYP.

31. George A. Smith to Daniel Wells, July 27, 1853, UTMR; George A. Smith to Daniel Wells, August 21,1853, UTMR; John D. Lee to Young, September 24, 1853, BYP.

32. Joseph Heywood to Young, September 22, 1853, UTMR.

33. Azariah Smith, Journals, September 14, 1853, MS 1834, CHL; Andrew Siler to Young, November 13, 1853, BYP.

34. Nelson Higgins to Daniel Wells, October 5, 1853, UTMR; Kimball, *Memoirs*, 228; "Indian Difficulties," *DN*, October 15, 1853.

35. Nelson Higgins to Daniel Wells, October 5, 1853, UTMR; Wimmer, "The Walker War Reconsidered," 145–147.

36. Report of E. G. Beckwith, in *Report of the Secretary of War Communicating the Several Pacific Railroad Explorations* (Washington, DC: A. O. P. Nicholson, 1855), 79–83. See also *TWWET*, 279–280.

37. Anson Call, statement, November 1853, BYP; Young to Mrs. Gunnison, November 30, 1853, BYP.

38. George A. Smith to Young, November 14, 1853, BYP; George A. Smith to Willard Richards, November 14, 1853, BYP; *JH*, November 13, 1853; report of Beckwith, in *Report of the Secretary of War*, 84.

39. Young to Edward Martin, November 30, 1853, BYP.

40. Young to Sowiette et al., December 3, 1853, BYP.

41. John Bernhisel to George Manypenny, December 23, 1853, found in John Bernhisel to Young, February 13, 1854, BYP; Young to John Bernhisel, December 28, 1853, BYP.

42. Albert Smith, Reminiscences and Journals, MS 1835, CHL; Young to Orson Pratt, January 31, 1854, BYP.

43. Carvalho, *Incidents*, 195; James T. Allred to Nelson Higgins, March 16, 1854, UTMR.

44. Allred to Higgins, March 16, 1854, UTMR.

45. Young to Captain Wackor, March 24, 1854, BYP; *TWWET*, 302–304.

46. *TWWET*, 303–304.

47. Young, "Proper Treatment of the Indians," April 6, 1854, *JD*, 6:327–329.

48. Thomas Brown, diary, April 25–26, 1854, MS 386, CHL; George Bean to Young, May 1, 1854, BYP.

49. Carvalho, *Incidents*, 189, 180–181.

50. Ibid., 105–107, 136–142.

51. Young to Elias Blackburn, May 8, 1854, BYP; Bullock, meeting at Nephi, May 10, 1854, GCM.

52. Carvalho, *Incidents*, 190–191.

53. *TWWET*, 313.

54. Carvalho, *Incidents*, 192–193.

55. Woodruff, *Journal*, May 12, 1854, 4:273–274; Carvalho, *Incidents*, 193–194.

56. James Martineau, Iron County Mission Historical Record, January 1855, LR 6778 25, CHL; Heap and Beale, *Central Route*, 91; see also *RMMP*, 158.

57. Bullock, council in Parowan, May 17, GCM.

58. Bean, *Autobiography*, 96; Andrew Love, diary, June 3, 1854, MS 1675, CHL.

59. Young to Captain Walker, June 13, 1854, BYP; Bean, *Autobiography*, 98; see also Andrew Love, diary, June 17, 1854, MS 1675, CHL.

60. Bean, *Autobiography*, 100; *TWWET*, 322–323.

61. Andrew Love, diary, June 17, 1854, MS 1675, CHL.

62. Bean, *Autobiography*, 106; Alexander Williams to Young, September 22, 1854, BYP; Woodruff, *Journal*, September 23, 1854, 4:144, 289; George Bean to Young, September 24, 1854, BYP.

63. James McClellan to Young, October 10, 1854, BYP.

64. *TWWET*, 327.

65. Letter from John Steele to George A. Smith, November 7, 1854, published in *DN*, November 30, 1854.

66. See December 1854 entries in Hamblin, Journals and Letters, MS 1951, CHL.

67. Young to Walker, November 22, 1854, BYP.

68. David Lewis to Young, January 9, 1855, BYP.

69. Ibid.

70. Ibid.

Chapter 17: "The Graves of Their Fathers"

1. Visions of Arapeen, February 4, 1855, BYP.

2. Ibid.

3. Ibid.

4. Latter-day Saints might interpret "the three personages" as a reference to the Book of Mormon's "Three Nephites."

5. William Maxwell to Young, February 2, 1855, BYP.

6. William Maxwell to Young, February 2, 1855, BYP; Young to Arrowpine (Arapeen), February 3, 1855, BYP.

7. *TWWET*, 338. On Mormons poisoning Native Americans, see Will Bagley, *Blood of the Prophets: Brigham Young and the Massacre at Mountain Meadows* (Norman: University of Oklahoma Press, 2002), 92, 105–111.

8. Remarks of Highforehead (Tow-om-bu-gah), July 15, 1855, Historian's Office Reports of Speeches, CR 100 317, CHL.

9. Woodruff, *Journal*, May 12, 1854, 4:273–274; Walker's Writing, 1851, BYP; *RMMP*, 204–211.

10. Walker's interview with Martenas, July 6, 1853, Jacob Holeman Papers, MS 2178, CHL.

11. George W. Armstrong to Brigham Young, June 30, 1855, *Annual Report of the Commissioner of the Office of Indian Affairs* (Washington, DC: A. O. P. Nicholson, 1855), 202.

12. Remarks of Highforehead (Tow-om-bu-gah), July 15, 1855, Historian's Office Reports of Speeches, CR 100 317, CHL.

13. George Peacock, on behalf of Arrowpine (Arapeen) to Young, February 27, 29, 1856, BYP; "Disturbance with the Indians," *DN*, March 5, 1856; "Letter from Manti," *DN*, April 6, 1856; Ronald Walker, "The Tintic War of 1856," *Journal of Mormon History* 42, no. 3 (2016): 35–68.

14. On sex trade among the Utes, see *TWWET*, 457. On the spread of venereal diseases among the Utes, see George A. Smith to Thomas Stenhouse, July 2, 1858, George A. Smith Papers, MS 1322, CHL. On the deaths of Arapeen and Peteetneet, see "Later from San Pete County," *DN*, February 2, 1860; "Death of the Great Chief," *The Mountaineer*, December 15, 1860; "Death of Chief Peteetneet," *DN*, January 1, 1862.

15. "Uinta Not What Was Represented," *DN*, September 25, 1861; *TWWET*, 487–488.

16. John Peterson, *Utah's Black Hawk War* (Salt Lake City: University of Utah Press, 1999), 16–17.

17. Ronald Walker, Richard Turley, and Glen Leonard, *Massacre at Mountain Meadows* (New York: Oxford University Press, 2008), 187. In the years directly after the massacre, Young blamed the Paiutes. In 1877, John D. Lee, who claimed he was just following orders from Mormon leadership, was convicted of murder and executed by firing squad at the site of the massacre. Beginning in the 1980s, the dominant narrative shifted from blaming the Paiutes to blaming the Mormons, including Young's anti-American, apocalyptic rhetoric. See, among many other studies of the massacre, Bagley, *Blood of the Prophets*.

18. Clifford Duncan, "The Northern Utes of Utah," in *A History of Utah's American Indians*, ed. Forrest S. Cuch (Salt Lake City: Utah State Division of Indian Affairs, distributed by Utah State University Press, 2000), 189–194.

19. E. L. Sloan, letter to the editor, *DN*, June 7, 1865; Spanish Fork Treaty, Bureau of Indian Affairs, Unratified Treaties File, ML.

20. George Bean to Young, May 26, 1965, BYP; Darren Parry, *The Bear River Massacre* (Salt Lake City: By Common Consent Press, 2019).

21. Spanish Fork Treaty.

22. Ibid.

23. Ibid.; Orsamus Irish to Commissioner of Indian Affairs, June 7, 1865, Letters Received, Record Group 75, National Archives.

24. "Indians in the City," *DN*, June 21, 1865.

25. Peterson, *Utah's Black Hawk War*, 240; Richard Turley, Dorena Martineau, and Jedediah Rogers, "Circleville Massacre Memorial Dedication," *Utah Historical Quarterly* 84, no. 3 (2016): 263–268.

26. Peterson, *Utah's Black Hawk War*, 267–270, 345–347, 352–356.

27. Duncan, "The Northern Utes of Utah," 193–194; Smoak, *Ghost Dances and Identity*, 119–120.

28. William Pace to Daniel Wells, including letter from George Halliday, August 30, 1872, William B. Pace Collection, MS 10411, CHL.

29. *TWWET*, 508–509.

30. "The Talk," *DN*, June 14, 1865.

Chapter 18: Crania Americana

1. Ann Fabian's canonical book, *The Skull Collectors*, also has a chapter titled "Crania Americana" after Dr. Samuel Morton's infamous book.

2. Tony Cowley, *The Early History of Meadow, Utah and Its People* (n.p.: Tony G. Cowley, 1997), 7–9.

3. Young to Arrowpine (Arapeen), February 3, 1855, BYP; Bagley, *Blood of the Prophets*, 50–52; Turner, *Brigham Young*, 259–262.

4. For the Northern Utes' creation story, see Clifford Duncan, *Weenoocheeyoo Peesaduehnee Yak: Anup: Stories of Our Ancestors* (Salt Lake City: Uintah-Ouray Ute Tribe, 1974), 7; Conetah, *A History*, 2. For explanations of how the Utes envisioned sharing the land and its resources with newcomers, see Visions of Arapeen, February 4, 1855, BYP; Walker's interview with Martenas, July 6, 1853, Jacob Holeman Papers, MS 2178, CHL.

5. Steven T. Newcomb, *Pagans in the Promised Land: Decoding the Doctrine of Christian Discovery* (Wheat Ridge, CO: Fulcrum Publishing, 2008), 32–36; Max Uhle, *Pachacamac* (Philadelphia: University Museum of Archaeology and Anthropology, University of Pennsylvania, 1991), 95.

6. Dwight B. Heath, *Mourt's Relation: A Journal of the Pilgrims at Plymouth* (Bedford, MA: Applewood Books, 1986), 26.

7. Ibid., 27–28.

8. "Johnson & Graham's Lessee v. McIntosh, 21 U.S. 543 (1823)," Justia Law, accessed July 18, 2022, https://supreme.justia.com/cases/federal/us/21/543; Joseph Story, *Commentaries on the Constitution of the United States* (Boston: Little, Brown and Co., 1858), 101. In his essay on the importance of repatriation of Native Hawaiian remains to reassert Hawaiians' claims to their own lands, Edward Halealoha Ayau cites the axiom most often attributed to Lord Gladstone,

"Show me the manner in which a nation cares for its dead and I will measure with mathematical exactness, the tender mercy of its people, their respect for the law of the land and their loyalty to high ideals." Edward Halealoha Ayau, "Restoring the Ancestral Foundation of Native Hawaiians: Implementation of the Native American Graves Protection and Repatriation Act," *Arizona State Law Journal* 24, no. 1 (1992): 215.

9. Thomas Jefferson, *Notes on the State of Virginia* (Philadelphia: Prichard and Hall, 1787), 103–107.

10. Ibid., 106.

11. Edward Adams, "Thomas Jefferson: Derailing the Native American Future," *Minnesota Journal of Law & Inequality*, November 23, 2021, https://lawandinequality.org/2021/11/23thomas-jefferson-derailing-the-native-american-future-2.

12. Pamela L. Geller, "Building Nation, Becoming Object: The Bio-politics of the Samuel G. Morton Crania Collection," *Historical Archaeology* 54, no. 1 (2020): 59–60.

13. For Abadie's Seminole skulls, see James Aitken Meigs, *Catalogue of Human Crania* (Philadelphia: Merrihew & Thompson, 1857), 67; Emily S. Renschler and Janet Monge, "The Samuel George Morton Cranial Collection: Historical Significance and New Research," *Expedition Magazine* 50, no. 3 (2008): 30–38.

14. Abadie to Morton, February 3, 1838, Samuel George Morton Papers, American Philosophical Society, Philadelphia, PA; Samuel George Morton, *Crania Americana* (Philadelphia: J. Dobson, Chestnut Street, 1839), 168.

15. David Thomas, *Skull Wars* (New York: Basic Books, 2001), 40; Ann Fabian, *The Skull Collectors* (Chicago: University of Chicago Press, 2010), 15.

16. Morton, *Crania Americana*, 260–261.

17. Ibid., 7, 17, 81–82.

18. Thomas, *Skull Wars*, 42–43.

19. Robert Henry, *The Armed Forces Institute of Pathology* (Washington, DC: Office of the Surgeon General, Department of the Army, 1964), 57–59.

20. Samuel Redman, *Bone Rooms* (Cambridge, MA: Harvard University Press, 2016), 28.

21. Redman, *Bone Rooms*, 29–31; Fabian, *Collectors*, 177.

22. Fabian, *Collectors*, 186–188; Thomas, *Skull Wars*, 57–58; Robert McNally, *The Modoc War: A Story of Genocide at the Dawn of America's Gilded Age* (Lincoln: University of Nebraska Press, 2017), 333–334.

23. The figure of 900 already represented a tiny portion of the presettler arrival population. In 1824 the Chumash led a revolt against forced labor

and captivity, which, along with disease, had decimated their population. See Henry Yarrow, "Report on the Operation of a Special Party for Making Ethnological Researches in the Vicinity of Santa Barbara, Cal.," in *Reports upon Archaeological and Ethnological Collections from Vicinity of Santa Barbara*, ed. Frederic Ward Putnam et al. (Washington, DC: US Government Printing Office, 1879), 40–43.

24. Fabian, *Collectors*, 177, 184; George Otis, *List of the Specimens in the Anatomical Section of the United States Army Medical Museum* (Washington, DC: Army Medical Museum, 1880), 142–155.

25. Otis, *Specimens*, iv, 75–80.

26. Fabian, *Collectors*, 191–195. On Otis's conclusions, see Daniel Smith Lamb, *A History of the United States Army Medical Museum, 1862–1917* (Washington, DC: s.n., 1917), 56A.

27. Fabian, *Collectors*, 175–177; Renschler and Monge, "The Samuel George Morton Cranial Collection."

28. Fabian, *Collectors*, 177.

29. Otis, *Specimens*, 51.

Chapter 19: "Please Say Nothing About the Crania"

1. Henry Yarrow, "On the Speckled Trout of Utah," in *Report of the U.S. Fish Commission 1872 and 1873* (Washington, DC: Government Printing Office, 1874), 2:363–368; Frederick Brown, "Itineraries of the Wheeler Survey Naturalists: Henry Wetherbee Henshaw," *Journal of the Lepidopterists' Society* 20 (1966): 71–82.

2. Henry Yarrow, "Report upon Natural History Collections," in *Progress-Report upon the Geographical and Geological Explorations and Surveys West of the One Hundredth Meridian in 1872*, ed. George Wheeler (Washington, DC: Government Printing Office, 1874), 55.

3. Yarrow, *Introduction*, 48–49.

4. Yarrow to Crane, National Anthropological Archives, Box 6, Army Medical Museum. See Eric R. Hollinger, Christopher J. Dudar, and Meridith Luze, "Inventory and Assessment of Human Remains Potentially Associated with Chief Wakara in the Collections of the National Museum of Natural History, Smithsonian Institution" (Washington, DC: Repatriation Office, Department of Anthropology, Smithsonian Institution, 2020), 12–13.

5. Hollinger, Dudar, and Luze, "Inventory and Assessment," 13.

6. Ibid.,16.

7. Ibid., 22; Otis, *Specimens*, 50–52.

8. Yarrow, *Introduction*, iii; John Wesley Powell, *Annual Report of the Bureau of American Ethnology to the Secretary of the Smithsonian Institution* (Washington, DC: US Government Printing Office, 1881), xxvi–xxvii.

9. Yarrow, *Introduction*, 48–49, 29–30; Henry Yarrow, *A Further Contribution to the Study of the Mortuary Customs of the North American Indians* (Washington, DC: Smithsonian Institution, Bureau of Ethnology, 1881), 142–143.

10. Lamb, *A History*, 152–153.

11. Redman, *Bone Rooms*, 34, 53.

12. Aleš Hrdlička, "Notes on the Indians of Sonora, Mexico," *American Anthropologist* 6, no. 1 (1904): 66.

13. Redman, *Bone Rooms*, 110–112.

14. Ibid., 166–171.

15. Ibid., 172–180.

16. Nicole Dungca, Claire Healy, and Andrew Ba Tran, "The Smithsonian's 'Bone Doctor' Scavenged Thousands of Body Parts," *Washington Post*, August 15, 2023, https://www.washingtonpost.com/history/interactive/2023/ales-hrdlicka-smithsonian-brains-racism.

17. Nicole Dungca and Claire Healy, "Smithsonian Targeted D.C.'s Vulnerable to Build Brain Collection," *Washington Post*, December 14, 2023, https://www.washingtonpost.com/history/interactive/2023/smithsonian-museum-washington-dc-brains-collection.

18. Dungca, Healy, and Tran, "'Bone Doctor'"; Redman, *Bone Rooms*, 244–245.

19. "Student of Man," *New York Times*, September 7, 1943; Redman, *Bone Rooms*, 223.

20. Christopher Heaney, *Empires of the Dead: Inca Mummies and the Peruvian Ancestors of American Anthropology* (New York: Oxford University Press, 2023), 1–2.

21. Deloria, *God Is Red*, 10–11.

22. Resolution by Larsen Bay Tribal Council, in *Native American Museum Claims Commission Act: Hearing Before the Select Committee on Indian Affairs, United States Senate* (Washington, DC: US Government Printing Office, 1989), 365–366.

23. Stephen Loring and Miroslav Prokopec, "A Most Peculiar Man: The Life and Times of Aleš Hrdlička," in *Reckoning with the Dead: The Larsen Bay Repatriation and the Smithsonian Institution*, ed. Tamara L. Bray and Thomas W. Killion (Washington, DC: Smithsonian Institution Press, 1994), 27; Christopher Heaney, "Skull Walls," *American Historical Review* 127, no. 3 (2022): 1071–1101.

24. Unless otherwise noted, the following analysis is based on Hollinger, Dudar, and Luze, "Inventory and Assessment of Human Remains Potentially Associated with Chief Wakara in the Collections of the National Museum of Natural History, Smithsonian Institution."

25. Note again: I have changed some identifying features of the gravesite and its location so as to dissuade further grave robbing. Charles Kelly, "We Found the Grave of the Utah Chief," *Desert Magazine* 9 (1946): 17–19.

26. The following is based on my conversations with Leonard and my study of his 1984 survey report. Robert Leonard, "Chief Walker's Grave—a Resurvey (1984)" (unpublished report on file, Utah State Historical Society, Salt Lake City).

27. Robert W. Leonard Jr., *A Trail of Many Tales: The Discovery of the Fish Lake Cutoff Along the Old Spanish Trail* (Parker, CO: Outskirts Press, 2020).

Conclusion: Wakara's Return

1. Christopher Flavelle and Bryan Tarnowski, "As the Great Salt Lake Dries Up, Utah Faces an 'Environmental Nuclear Bomb,'" *New York Times*, June 7, 2022, https://www.nytimes.com/2022/06/07/climate/salt-lake-city-climate-disaster.html.

2. Leia Larsen, "Utah Lake Dredging CEO Paid Himself Thousands Before Stiffing Scientist, Attorneys and Consultants," *Salt Lake Tribune*, August 4, 2023, https://www.sltrib.com/news/environment/2023/08/04bankruptcy-hearing-reveals-utah.

3. Farmer, *On Zion's Mount*, 88–89.

4. D. Robert Carter, *Troubled Times* (Provo, UT: Provo City Corporation, 2016), 23–45.

5. Smith, "Field Notebooks"; Smith, *Ethnography*, iii–iv.

6. Remarks of Highforehead (Tow-om-bu-gah), July 15, 1855; Wilford Woodruff, "Preaching the Gospel to, and Helping the Lamanites," July 15, 1855, *JD*, 9:227; Carter, "Fish and the Famine of 1855–56," 115.

7. Cuch and Carney, *A Native Way of Giving*, 21. For the most comprehensive study of Ute resistance, resilience, and adaptation, see Sondra G. Jones, *Being and Becoming Ute: The Story of an American Indian People* (Salt Lake City: University of Utah Press, 2019).

8. Robin Gray, "Rematriation: Ts'msyen Law, Rights of Relationality, and Protocols of Return," *Native American and Indigenous Studies* 9, no. 1 (2022): 1–27.

9. Dimick Huntington to the Church Historian, September 1, 1856, HOCHD.

10. On the "Meeker Affair," see Peter Decker, *The Utes Must Go: American Expansion and Removal of a People* (Golden: CO, Fulcrum Publishing, 2004), 173–194.

11. David Rich Lewis, *Neither Wolf nor Dog* (New York: Oxford University Press, 1994), 50–51, 66.

12. Larry Cesspooch, "KOOVAH NOOCHEW Ute Horse People," video uploaded to YouTube by Through Native Eyes Productions, June 8, 2018, https://www.youtube.com/watch?v=ePyocgp-Hao.

13. Willow Becker, "Ute Tribe Unveils $245-Thousand-Dollar Veteran Memorial Statue," *Uintah Basin Standard/Vernal Express*, July 1, 2016.

14. Justin Higginbottom, "Among Utah's Wild Horses Roam a 'Genetic Treasure,'" Aspen Public Radio, October 3, 2022, https://www.aspenpublicradio.org/environment/2022-10-03/among-utahs-wild-horses-roam-a-genetic-treasure.

15. Susanna Ewing to Brigham Young, May 28, July 23, 1855, CHL.

16. Ezra Taft Benson, "Time for All Things," July 13, 1855, *JD*, 3:64.

17. George Armstrong to Office of Indian Agency, June 30, 1857, *Report of the Commissioner of Indian Affairs, 1857* (Washington, DC: William A. Harris, 1858), 309; Compton, "Civilizing the Ragged Edge," 174–181.

18. Mary Minerva Dart Judd, biographical sketch, HBLL; Brooks, "Indian Relations on the Mormon Frontier," 33; Compton, "Civilizing the Ragged Edge," 181.

19. Thomas Brown, diary, December 23, 1855, MS 386, CHL. On Omer Heywood, see Manetta Prince Henrie and Anna Prince Redd, *Life History of William and Louisa E. Lee Prince* (Provo, UT: Self-Published, 1956), 105–106. On the Ewings, see Carter, *Troubled Times*, 36–37; Susanna Ewing, in Provo, Utah, "U.S. Census, 1860," FamilySearch, https://www.familysearch.org/ark:/61903/1:1:MH2W-4V2?lang=en.

20. Richard Ira Elkins, *A Person of Worth: The Story of Sarah Maraboots Dyson Hatch* (Salt Lake City: Specialty Press, 1987).

21. Brooks, "Indian Relations on the Mormon Frontier," 39.

22. George A. Smith, "The Indian War," October 7, 1853, *JD*, 1:198. On Zen Hill, see "Indian Who Fought on Side of White Men at Encampment," *Spanish Fork Press*, August 12, 1937. The census takers didn't know what to do with Hill and his offspring. In 1900, they were listed as Black. In 1910, they were listed as Indian and White. See entries for the Hills in Sanpete Country, Utah,

"U.S. Census, 1900," FamilySearch, https://www.familysearch .org/ark:/61903/1:1 :MMR5-SM2, and Sanpete Country, Utah, "U.S. Census, 1910," FamilySearch, https://www.familysearch.org/ark:/61903/1:1:M5X4-WQH.

23. Margaret D. Jacobs, "Entangled Histories: The Mormon Church and Indigenous Child Removal from 1850 to 2000," *Journal of Mormon History* 42, no. 2 (2016): 27–60.

24. See Fernetta Lerwick's post to "Reclaiming My Utah Tribe Ancestors," Facebook, March 22, 2023, https://www.facebook.com/groups/248040973888540/posts/6081708578755 48.

25. Angela Wilson, "Decolonizing the 1862 Death Marches," *American Indian Quarterly* 28, no. 1/2 (2004): 199.

26. Jeremiah Stettler, "Skeletons Found in Nephi May Reveal Details of 1853 Massacre," *Salt Lake Tribune*, September 15, 2006.

27. "The 24th in the Settlements," *DN*, July 31, 1878.

28. "Walker and Tintic Veterans," *Salt Lake Tribune*, February 2, 1902; "Pension Is Granted Walker War Veterans," *Inter-Mountain Republican*, June 17, 1909.

29. "Indian Who Fought on Side of White Men at Encampment"; "Ft. Green News," *Times-News*, March 24, 1938; "Death Claims Indian Who Aided Whites in Conflict," *Salt Lake Tribune*, September 12, 1938.

30. Peterson, *Utah's Black Hawk War*, 245–248; Turley, Martineau, and Rogers, "Circleville Massacre Memorial Dedication."

31. Turley, Martineau, and Rogers, "Circleville Massacre Memorial Dedication."

32. Mary Meyer, CEO of the Timpanogos Nation, which has no federal or state standing, has called for the creation of such a memorial.

33. As part of its series highlighting events from the city's history, the City of Provo has erected a small placard narrating the history of the Battle of Provo River near part of the battlefield. McKenna Park, "Native Americans Advocate Squaw Peak Name Change," *Daily Universe*, April 27, 2017; Abigail Gunderson, "Squaw Peak Name Change Highlights Sexual Violence Against Native American Women," *Daily Universe*, September 14, 2022.

34. Delores (Lola) Mondragón, "Rematriation and MMIWG2S Soldiers," *Harvard Divinity Bulletin*, Spring/Summer 2023, https://bulletin.hds.harvard .edu/rematriation-and-mmiwg2s-soldiers.

35. Newcomb, "Perspectives," 3.

36. The Talk," *DN*, June 14, 1865.

Index

Credit: Michael Stack

MAX PERRY MUELLER is an associate professor in the Department of Classics and Religious Studies at the University of Nebraska–Lincoln and is author of the award-winning *Race and the Making of the Mormon People*. His writing has appeared in *The Atlantic*, *The New Republic*, and *Slate*. He lives in Lincoln, Nebraska.

Thank you for reading this book and for being a reader of books in general. We ar so grateful to share being part of a community of readers with you, and we hope yo will join us in passing our love of books on to the next generation of readers.

Did you know that reading for enjoyment is the single biggest predictor of a child's future happiness and success?

More than family circumstances, parents' educational background, or income, reading impacts a child's future academic performance, emotional well-being, communication skills, economic security, ambition, and happiness.

Studies show that kids reading for enjoyment in the US is in rapid decline:

- In 2012, 53% of 9-year-olds read almost every day. Just 10 years later, in 2022, the number had fallen to 39%.
- In 2012, 27% of 13-year-olds read for fun daily. By 2023, that number was just 14%.

TOGETHER,
WE CAN COMMIT TO
RAISING READERS
AND CHANGE THIS TREND.
HOW?

- Read to children in your life daily.
- Model reading as a fun activity.
- Reduce screen time.
- Start a family, school, or community book club.
- Visit bookstores and libraries regularly.
- Listen to audiobooks.
- Read the book before you see the movie.
- Encourage your child to read aloud to a pet or stuffed anima
- Give books as gifts.
- Donate books to families and communities in need.

Books build bright futures, and **Raising Readers** is our shared responsibility.

For more information, visit JoinRaisingReaders.com

Sources: National Endowment for the Arts, National Assessment of Educational Progress, WorldBookDay.org, Nielsen BookData's 2023 "Understanding the Children's Book Consumer"